FROM TORAH TO APOCALYPSE

An Introduction to the Bible

Francis I. Fesperman

UNIVERSITY
PRESS OF
AMERICA

LANHAM • NEW YORK • LONDON

Copyright © 1983 by

University Press of America,™ Inc.

4720 Boston Way
Lanham, MD 20706

3 Henrietta Street
London WC2E 8LU England

Library of Congress Cataloging in Publication Data

Fesperman, Francis I.
   From Torah to Apocalypse.

   Bibliography: p.
   Includes index.
   1. Bible—Introductions. I. Title.
BS475.2.F47   1983   220.6'1   83-17057
ISBN 0-8191-3555-0 (pbk. : alk. paper)

Dedicated to my wife, Kathleen, and to the memory of my grandmother, Amelia Ann Kluttz Fesperman, who introduced me to the Holy Bible.

CONTENTS

MAPS

CHARTS

FOREWORD

It is the author's conviction that the Bible is an inheritance of unmatched value and excellence which we are privileged to explore and enjoy and by which we are nourished. This book was written to fill a need for a textbook for use in a college undergraduate one-semester course covering the entire Bible. It should also be useful for individuals who wish to understand and appreciate the books of the Bible more and who are serious enough in their desire to attempt it on their own. Certain church school classes, as well, may find it adaptable to their needs.

With a few exceptions, this book deals only with those books found in Protestant Bibles, that is, the "Old Testament" books which the Hebrews accepted as their scriptures, plus the New Testament literature which is the common heritage of Christendom.

The author assumes that the prospective reader has some acquaintance with the Scriptures, although not necessarily a detailed knowledge. He also assumes that the reader may not be aware of the gigantic strides which have been made in biblical research during the past century and a half. This book makes use of much of the knowledge gained by the literary, historical, and archaeological studies of hundreds of scholars. In this way, the contents of the Bible will become clearer and more meaningful. The more one knows about the circumstances which surrounded the writing of a book and the purpose the author had in mind, the more likely he is to understand the book's message. In like manner, the more one can learn about the land, the customs, the language, and the thought patterns of the world in which the book was written, the more accurate his perception of the book's contents will be.

The approach to the Bible taken in this book may be called reverently critical. Its reverence comes from the author's conviction that the Bible is God's medium of revelation. It is critical, not in the negative sense of that term, but in the sense that we need not hesitate to ask serious questions regarding the origin, purpose, transmission, translations, and literary types of the various books which compose the Scriptures. For those who wish to pursue their study of the Bible further there is a list of selected sources which may be useful for this purpose following the text.

1

I am grateful to the National Council of the Churches of Christ in the U.S.A. for its permission to use the Revised Standard Version in the scriptural quotations. I am grateful also to all those scholars whose research has made it possible for me to write this volume. Special thanks are due to Dr. Garth Kemerling, Professor Margaret Paysinger, and my wife for their invaluable encouragement and assistance in its writing.

Francis I. Fesperman
Newberry College

CHAPTER I

INTRODUCTION

Essential reading: Preface to the Revised Standard Version of the
Bible

It has often been noted that the Bible has outsold all
other books and continues to be the world's best-seller. This is
certainly good evidence of its broad influence and vast importance.
Three great religions depend upon it. Approximately four-fifths
of it (called by Christians "the Old Testament") are the Scriptures
of Judaism. The entire Bible constitutes the authoritative holy
book of Christianity and is an important secondary scripture for
Islam.

Further evidence of its influence is found in the widespread use of biblical characters, events, scenes, concepts, and
doctrines in the literature, art, music, and conversation of that
part of the world which we call the West. It is also true that
the laws, customs, and moral codes of the West which have developed over the past two thousand years are indebted in large measure to biblical teachings. This suggests that a knowledge of the
Bible is crucially important, not only for our religious guidance,
but also for our understanding of the world and the culture of
which we are a part.

What Is the Bible?

We call the Bible a book, and it certainly is that. But
it is more accurate to call it a collection of books, or even a
library, which is bound usually in one volume; for Protestant Bibles contain sixty-six individual writings, each having its own
author, setting, style, and purpose. Catholic and Orthodox Bibles
have even more (see below, pp. 10-11).

The Bible is a product of two major world faiths. The
Hebrew Scriptures (Old Testament) were created by Judaism over a
long period of time. If we include the earliest documents which
were used in the present books, we must say that they began at
least as far back as 1,000 B.C. and extend as far as c. 165 B.C.
The remainder of the Bible (New Testament) consists of twenty-
seven writings ranging over a century or less, having originated
between 50 A.D. and 150 A.D. Thus the writing activity which pro-

duced the biblical books extended over a period of approximately 1,150 years!

Thus the Bible is a collection of very ancient books. Yet it can not be claimed as the world's oldest book. Clay tablets which have been discovered at ancient Nineveh, capital of the Assyrian Empire, apparently included translations from Sumerian literature into the Akkadian language. The Sumerians, who lived in the area we now know as Iraq, had a flourishing civilization long before Israel began. The law code of Hammurabi, ruler of the Old Babylonian Empire, was in written form long before any of the biblical literature. Wisdom writings (literature somewhat like Job and Proverbs in the Old Testament) which have been discovered in Egypt and Mesopotamia originated much earlier than the Bible. Influences from some of these older works upon the concepts and literature of Israel may be discovered. We will have occasion to note some of these in later chapters.

Understanding the Bible Isn't Always Easy

Anyone who has read through the entire Bible knows that there are many parts which are difficult to comprehend. There are several reasons that this is so:

1. The vast difference between the world of the Bible and our world.

When the books of the Bible were written, there were not so many people around, their knowledge of the universe was severely limited, "science" was unknown, and communication was slow. It was assumed that the world was a three-storied affair, with earth situated between the heavens above and the waters below. A round earth spinning on an axis and at the same time revolving around the sun was a concept yet many centuries in the future. A book produced against such a backdrop will reflect assumptions which are strange to our world. This creates problems for the serious student of the Bible.

Perhaps the best way to handle such problems is to recognize that the Bible is not a book of science, or geography, or even history. To be sure, it contains a great many geographical names and a large amount of history. But it was written by persons of faith to give expression to that faith and not to present authoritative records of how everything began or accurate reports of military and diplomatic events.

2. The enormity and diversity of the biblical materials.

Books come in all sizes. Compared to most books one encounters in bookstores, the Bible is a large book. Twelve hundred full pages may be considered a rather common-sized edition. Big books discourage many would-be readers. But one fortunate thing about the Bible is that one can pick from sixty-six books, varying in length from one chapter to 150, and not have to worry about missing a vital part of the story. Each book is an independent unit.

The diversity of the materials is a bigger problem than the size. First, there are the two "testaments," one produced by one community of faith and the other produced by a different one. Second, literary classifications found in the Bible include legend, history, folklore, fiction, law codes, genealogies, poetry, prophetic oracles, proverbs, gospels, sermons, letters, and apocalyptic writings. Such a mixture makes for more interesting reading than would be the case if everything were of the same literary type, but it also requires care and discernment by the reader. It is very important to understand that what one is reading is (for example) from the Old Testament rather than the New, or is part of an apocalyptic work rather than an historical one.

3. The language problem.

Another serious difficulty results from the fact that the books of the Bible were originally written in languages which are no longer familiar to most persons. Most of the Old Testament writings were in ancient Hebrew, which had been replaced as the spoken language of Palestinian Jews in the time of Jesus by Aramaic, a related tongue. In fact, a few chapters in Ezra and Daniel were originally written in Aramaic, now a "dead" language. Hebrew has lately been revived as an official language of the modern state of Israel, but it is considerably different from biblical Hebrew and is not used much elsewhere.

All the books of the New Testament were written in koiné, the common Greek of the time, known and understood by most persons living in the Roman Empire. Greek is the language of modern Greece, but it is quite different from New Testament Greek and is not spoken widely outside of that country. All this means that, if we modern people are to get the Bible's message, we must either become proficient in the ancient languages or depend on the work of translators. For obvious reasons most of us choose the latter course.

The translator's work is by no means easy. His goal is to get the modern language translation to say to his generation what the original biblical writers were saying to theirs. The translator of an Old Testament book begins with the Hebrew text of that book. But which text shall he use? Ancient Hebrew manuscripts

5

vary greatly from one to the other. There are no originals in existence. The manuscripts available are the result of a long process of copying by hand, a process by which thousands of variations (mostly unintentional) have appeared in the manuscripts. The translator must depend upon competent textual critics to provide him with the best text, meaning the closest possible to the original writing, before he can even begin translating.

The textual scholar assumes that the older the manuscript the more accurate it is likely to be. He thinks that not so much copying has occurred as with younger manuscripts, hence the probability of fewer copying errors. Old Testament textual scholars were gratified and excited when copies of Old Testament books approximately one thousand years older than any previously known were discovered in 1947 and the following few years. Known as the Dead Sea Scrolls, they formed part of the library of an ancient Jewish sect which had built a community at Qumran, on the high and dry cliffs of the northern shore of the Dead Sea. They were not in perfect shape after their long storage in nearby caves, for the sect had lived there between c. 100 B.C. and c. 70 A.D., but they were extremely helpful in establishing a better Hebrew text for translators to use.

Textual criticism is a highly specialized skill and requires years of painstaking labor, consisting of careful comparing of manuscripts and deciding on the most probable reading. The same process has to be followed for the Greek texts of New Testament books, but the work is somewhat less tedious since the period of time involved is not so vast.

When the translator has a reasonably good text before him, he proceeds to use his expertise in the original language and his knowledge of the modern language in producing a readable, accurate unbiased translation, in which the reader can have sufficient confidence that, when he reads it, he is receiving the true biblical message. In doing this the translator is faced with many choices, such as which of two or more English (if that is the modern language with which he is working) words is more suitable to render the Hebrew or Greek word. The fact that we have so many different English translations indicates that translators have not always made the same choices.

The process of translating the Bible began long before the time of Jesus. Jews living in Alexandria, Egypt, were reared in the Greek language and could no longer read Hebrew. To make it possible for them to read their own Scriptures, a group of their leading scholars translated them into Greek between 200 and 100 B.C. This translation is known as the Septuagint (symbolized by

LXX). In 407 A.D., a very significant translation of the entire
Bible in Latin, then the official language of the Roman Empire,
was made by a priest named Jerome. Now known as the Vulgate, Jerome's translation became the official Bible of Roman Catholicism.

The Bible, or at least parts of it, has been translated
into well over one thousand languages and dialects. Obviously, we
have neither the need nor the ability to trace the whole process
of biblical translation, which is still taking place at an intense
rate. We shall not even attempt a complete history of English
translation but content ourselves with the more significant versions. The first attempt on record is attributed to a Benedictine
monk and historian known as the Venerable Bede, who translated
part of the Vulgate into Old English during the first half of the
eighth century. Other parts of the Bible appeared in English in
the tenth and eleventh centuries. Around 1384, an English priest
named John Wycliffe completed his work of translating the entire
Vulgate into his native language.

It should be noted that all the English translations mentioned above are actually translations of a translation (the Latin
Vulgate), which is not a very satisfactory way of ensuring accurate transmission of the original thought. Hence the work of Wil-
liam Tyndale who in 1525 translated the New Testament from the
original Greek and subsequently, parts of the Old Testament from
the Hebrew, is very significant. He was burned at the stake for
heresy and so was unable to finish the Bible, but his translation
of the New Testament and parts of the Old had considerable influence on later English versions.

During the time of Tyndale's labors in Germany, where he
had fled to try to escape persecution, another translation was coming into existence in that country. While in protective exile in
the Wartburg Castle, the reformer Martin Luther began translating
the Bible into German in 1522. Working, not from the Vulgate, but
from the original Hebrew and Greek, his Bible was completed in
1534. The impact of both Luther's and Tyndale's work was greatly
enhanced by the invention a century earlier by another German, a
printer named Johann Gutenberg, of movable type. This meant that
these new translations could be produced in quantity and distributed to a much larger reading public.

During the remainder of the sixteenth century several more
translations in English appeared, dependent in some measure upon
the work of Tyndale. In 1560 a group of English Puritans who had
fled to Switzerland to escape persecution by Mary Tudor, an ardent
Catholic, published the Geneva Bible. Two features of this pro-
duction were continued in later English versions: the use of ital-

ics to indicate words which the translator supplied for readability, and the division of the chapters into verses.

The most influential and popular English version of all time appeared in 1611, known as the Authorized or King James Version (KJV). King James I had appointed a group of able scholars to produce a Bible which would replace the several earlier English translations and serve as the official scripture for the English church. Although not well received at first, it eventually became acknowledged as a great masterpiece of English literature which served as a model in vocabulary, rhythm, and beauty of expression. It was influenced by the Geneva Bible and earlier translations which had appeared in England.

The KJV stood up much longer than the original translators expected but eventually changes in the language, more accurate knowledge of Hebrew and Greek, and the discovery of older, more accurate manuscripts indicated the need for a revision. A group of British scholars produced one, the English Revised Version (ERV) in 1885, which was followed by a similar effort from American scholars, the American Standard Revised Version, in 1901.

However, neither of these became popular, and a fresh attempt to obtain a more acceptable revision of the KJV began in the United States in the 1920's. The result is the Revised Standard Version (RSV), completed in 1952. The University of Chicago, in an attempt to provide a translation in the familiar language of the day, had published The Complete Bible in 1939, but it did not receive wide circulation. As its Preface states, the RSV seeks to preserve the beauty of the KJV while making it more understandable to modern readers. Of special value is the fact that it is based on much more accurate Hebrew and Greek texts than those which were available to the King James translators (see discussion of Dead Sea Scrolls above, p. 6). This originally Protestant effort has now been accepted by American Catholics. Of course, the Catholic edition, known as The Common Bible, includes the Apocrypha (see below, p. 10).

Despite the wide acceptance of the RSV, new English translations continue to appear. The English edition of The Jerusalem Bible, which includes the books of the Apocrypha, appeared in 1966. The New English Bible, which is not a revision but a fresh translation, was published in Great Britain in 1970. Two idiomatic translations in modern, readable English have enjoyed wide acceptance in the United States: The Living Bible (1971), a paraphrase by Kenneth Taylor, and The Good News Bible (1976), produced by the American Bible Society. Conservative American Protestants produced The New American Standard Bible in 1971, the New International Version in 1978, and The New King James Version in 1982.

The existence of so many versions, with more appearing from time to time, raises questions in the minds of persons who consider the Bible as authority for their beliefs and practices. Which of the translations is the correct one? Must absolute inerrancy be maintained in order to have an "inspired" Bible? Can God get his Word to the sincere reader despite the differences in the various versions? These questions are closely tied to the individual's faith and his own view of inspiration of Scripture. This is very personal and we do not intend to suggest any particular theory of inspiration here. We have merely tried to summarize the history of the efforts of hundreds of dedicated scholars to make sure the books of the Bible say to our day what the original writers were saying to their generations.

A few principles may be helpful to the person seeking a a reliable English translation:

1. It should be protected against changes by a copyright, something not in existence when the KJV appeared.

2. It should have used the oldest available copies of the Hebrew and Greek texts in making the translation.

3. A translation done by a group of competent scholars is more reliable and probably less biased than one done by an individual.

4. The language should be up-to-date and readily understood by the average reader.

5. Paraphrases and idiomatic translations have their value but the reader should be aware that they are not literal renditions.

Why These Books?

When it was stated above (p. 3) that the Catholic Bible includes more books than the Protestant, the matter of the canon was involved. Now we must investigate the question, How did it happen that in some Bibles the Old Testament contains thirty-nine books and in others it contains several more? The simplest answer is that the Protestant Old Testament follows the Hebrew canon, whereas the Catholic one adheres to the Greek canon. In this context canon refers to the official list of sacred books accepted as having authority for belief and practice.

The Greek canon consists of those books which were included in the translation which came out of Alexandria a century or so before Christ, known as the Septuagint (see above, p. 6). This was the Scripture inherited by the earliest Christians; hence it became their Bible. The Hebrew canon was settled upon by a council of Jewish rabbis who had survived the Jewish Revolt of 66-70 A.D. and who resented the Christian Church's taking over their Scriptures. Meeting at the Palestinian coastal town of Jamnia in 90 A.D., they gave formal approval to the books which the Jews had accepted as inspired, authoritative Scripture over the past several decades. This meant that not all the books in the Septuagint were included. The twenty-four agreed upon are actually the same material as the thirty-nine in the Protestant Old Testament; only the numbering is different (see Chart I below). The Protestant reformers of the sixteenth century, notably Martin Luther, determined that the rabbis at Jamnia had been right in excluding certain books found in the Septuagint. Ever since then, Protestant Bibles have excluded them or relegated them to a separate section under the heading "Apocrypha." The Roman church, however, retained them, not as a separate group, but distributed among the other Old Testament writings, with equal authority implied.

Chart I. The Books of the Old Testament

Hebrew Bible	Protestant	Roman Catholic
Torah	Pentateuch	Pentateuch
Genesis	Genesis	Genesis
Exodus	Exodus	Exodus
Leviticus	Leviticus	Leviticus
Numbers	Numbers	Numbers
Deuteronomy	Deuteronomy	Deuteronomy
Prophets:	Historical books	Historical books
Former	Joshua	Joshua
Joshua	Judges	Judges
Judges	Ruth	Ruth
Samuel	I & II Samuel	I & II Kings
Kings	I & II Kings	III & IV Kings
	I & II Chronicles	I & II Paralipomeno
	Ezra	I Esdras
	Nehemiah	II Esdras
		Tobias
		Judith
	Esther	Esther (+additions)
		I & II Maccabees
	Poetry and Wisdom	Poetry and Wisdom
	Job	Job
	Psalms	Psalms
	Proverbs	Proverbs

Chart I. (continued)

	Poetry and Wisdom	Poetry and Wisdom
	Ecclesiastes	Ecclesiastes
	Song of Solomon	Canticle of Canticles
		Wisdom of Solomon
		Ecclesiasticus

Prophets:
  Latter
    Isaiah
    Jeremiah

    Ezekiel

Prophets:	Prophetic books	Prophetic books
Latter	Isaiah	Isaiah
Isaiah	Jeremiah	Jeremiah
Jeremiah	Lamentations	Lamentations
		Baruch (incl. Epistle
		of Jeremiah)
Ezekiel	Ezekiel	Ezekiel
	Daniel	Daniel (+ additions:
		Prayer of Azariah
		Song of the Three
		Young Men
		Susanna
		Bel and the Dragon)
Book of the	Hosea	Hosea
Twelve	Joel	Joel
	Amos	Amos
	Obadiah	Obadiah
	Jonah	Jonah
	Micah	Micah
	Nahum	Nahum
	Habakkuk	Habakkuk
	Zephaniah	Zephaniah
	Haggai	Haggai
	Zechariah	Zechariah
	Malachi	Malachi

Writings
 Psalms
 Job
 Proverbs
 Ruth
 Song of Solomon
 Ecclesiastes
 Lamentations
 Esther
 Daniel
 Ezra-Nehemiah
 I & II Chronicles

The differences among the three columns in Chart I are important enough to require some comment:

1. Although the Hebrew Bible list (column one) contains only twenty-four books and the Protestant Old Testament (column two) has thirty-nine, the content is the same for both.

2. Besides having additional books the Roman Catholic Old Testament list (column three) differs in the names given some of the books it has in common with the Protestant list. When they appear on the same line, they are the same books even though the names may be different. The third column is also the correct list for the Eastern Orthodox Church.

3. The Hebrew order of books is different from the other two. Of the three divisions of Hebrew Scripture, the Torah was the first to be accorded the status of divine revelation. The Prophets were the next to be so regarded and, not until 90 A.D. were some of the books in the Writings category considered by all Jewish leaders as worthy of inclusion.

4. The Hebrew classification of books is not precisely followed by the other two. What it calls Former Prophets the Protestant and Roman Catholic columns label Historical books. The group called Writings in column one are scattered among all the categories except the Pentateuch in the other two columns.

The New Testament Canon

The story of the New Testament canon is not so complicated. There is no disagreement among Christians as to which books belong in it. However, that was not always the case. The epistles of Paul, the first three gospels, and the book of Acts were almost unanimously considered sacred scripture by the second century A.D. but it was not until Bishop Athanasius issued his list in 367 that a complete consensus was arrived at on the remainder of the twenty seven books.

The first attempt to establish an official list of Christian writings was made by a bishop named Marcion around 140 A.D. He chose the letters of Paul and the Gospel of Luke for his list, but he was not content to accept them as they were written. There were things in them with which he did not agree, so he simply removed them. Understandably, Marcion was branded a heretic and removed from office. But his attempt to form a canon of Christian scriptures forced the church to face this important question. Later in the same century the Muratorian Canon appeared, which included all four gospels, thirteen letters attributed to Paul, Jude,

12

Chart II.   The Books of the New Testament

Gospels

Matthew
Mark
Luke
John

Historical book

Acts

Epistles attributed to the Apostle Paul

Romans
I Corinthians
II Corinthians
Galatians
Ephesians
Philippians
Colossians
I Thessalonians
II Thessalonians
I Timothy
II Timothy
Titus
Philemon

General Epistles

Hebrews
James
I Peter
II Peter
I John
II John
III John
Jude

Apocalyptic book

Revelation

I and II John, Revelation, the Apocalypse of Peter, and the Wisdom of Solomon. Of course, the last two were excluded from the final list of New Testament books, but the Wisdom of Solomon had already become part of the Catholic edition of the Old Testament.

The inclusion of the Apocalypse of Peter in an early Christian list illustrates the fact that there were several pieces of Christian literature which many thought should be, but never became, part of the official canon. One collection of such literature, known today as the Apostolic Fathers, contains valuable writings, notably the Teaching of the Twelve Apostles, the First Letter of Clement, the Epistle of Barnabas, and the letters of Ignatius. A number of gospels also appeared, connected to names of apostles such as Thomas, James, Philip, and Peter, but most of them differed so radically from the canonical gospels that they were not taken seriously by the church. We may conveniently label all these, and several not mentioned, New Testament Apocrypha. Some are valuable for historical purposes, but others are fanciful and of little worth. The selection of the authoritative body of Christian writings to be added to the already existing Septuagint was a gradual process extending over three centuries. No ecumenical council made the decision; rather, the books chosen were those which stood the test of continued usage and acceptance by churches scattered throughout the Roman Empire.

Significant terms, names, and dates for this chapter

Hammurabi	Tyndale	Greek canon
Old Testament	Luther	Jamnia
New Testament	version	Apocrypha
Aramaic	edition	Torah
Koine	Geneva Bible	Former prophets
manuscript	KJV	Latter prophets
Dead Sea Scrolls	RSV	The Writings
textual criticism	Common Bible	90 A.D.
Septuagint	1611	Marcion
Vulgate	1952	Athanasius
Jerome	canon	Apostolic Fathers
Wycliffe	Hebrew canon	

CHAPTER II

BIBLE LANDS AND EVENTS

It is very important for us to realize that the Bible is not based on mythological accounts of fancied happenings in a never-never land. The Old Testament records the story of what happened to a very real people who lived at a definite period of time in actual locatable places on earth. The New Testament tells of one extraordinary descendant of the Old Testament people, the personalities he influenced, and the institution they began. He lived in a particular place at a specific time, and his followers traveled and preached at actual places and times. Geography and history are essential features of the biblical record.

The Lands of the Bible

It is helpful to distinguish between the terms, "the Holy Land" and "Lands of the Bible." This latter term refers to all the geographical areas in which any biblical action took place. The Old Testament action occurred in a large area, from the lands surrounding the Eastern end of the Mediterranean Sea eastward to the Persian Gulf. The New Testament events began at the same Near Eastern area but moved westward as far as Spain. In terms of modern countries the Bible lands included Spain, Italy, Yugoslavia, Albania, Greece, Turkey, Syria, Israel, Iraq, Iran, Lebanon, Jordan, and Egypt.

The Old Testament story has its main setting in that semicircular area we call the Fertile Crescent, which extends from the northern end of the Persian Gulf, through the somewhat parallel valleys of the Tigris and Euphrates Rivers, down the coast of the Mediterranean and on into the Nile River region of Egypt. "Fertile" should be understood in a relative sense: in contrast to the Arabian desert, which could support only a sparse population, such areas as Mesopotamia (the land between the rivers) would indeed appear fertile. Mesopotamia became the center of several great political powers during the Old Testament period, notably the Assyrian Empire, followed in turn by the Babylonian, the Persian, and the Greek empires. All of these ancient states had very direct impact upon the people of Israel.

15

Map 1

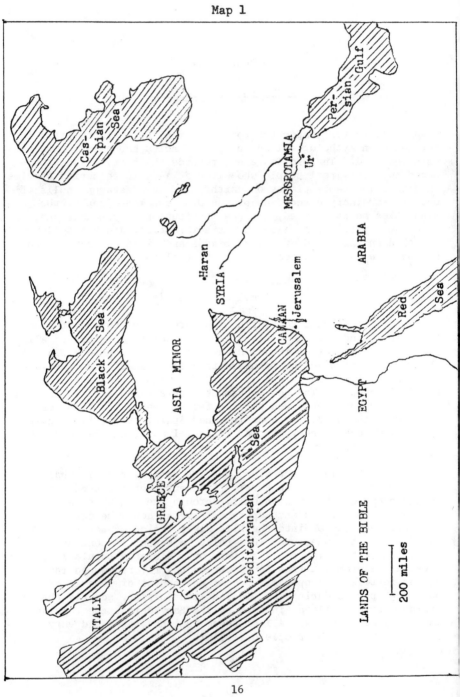

LANDS OF THE BIBLE

200 miles

The Holy Land

A very small region of the world, part of the area in which Old and New Testament spheres overlap, is that which we are accustomed to call the Holy Land. Jews consider it holy because it is the land promised them by God, conquered and ruled over by the great King David, and the locale of Solomon's Temple. It is holy to Christians because it was the scene of Jesus' dwelling, ministry, death, and resurrection. Moslems look upon it as holy because the Koran refers to it as "the blessed land" several times. All three of these faiths accord it a special place in their affection because within its borders lies its best known city, Jerusalem, which has sacred associations for each.

When this land is first mentioned in the Bible, it is called Canaan, probably meaning "Land of the Purple," so named because it produced from the murex shellfish an excellent purple dye which was used in the manufacture of expensive textiles. Later it was known as Palestine, a name which comes from the Philistines, a group of foreign invaders who conquered almost the entire land in the eleventh century B.C. That name has continued down through the centuries, but the Jews who live there today prefer the name of their state, Israel. Modern Israel, however, is somewhat smaller than the usual area called Palestine, since it has no land east of the Jordan River.

Although it has had a great influence upon world events and movements for so many centuries, it is actually a very small area. It contains only 10,000 square miles, which means it is scarcely larger than the State of Vermont. Its length from ancient Dan in the north to Beersheba in the south is less than 150 miles. Measuring from west to east, the distance from Acre in the north to the Sea of Galilee is only 28 miles, while the width from Gaza to the Dead Sea is but 54 miles. Ancient Palestine was somewhat wider in the north, for it extended several miles east of the Sea of Galilee and the Jordan River.

Each region has been given a local name by the inhabitants but, for our study, we shall simply call attention to four main sections, running from north to south:

1. The Coastal Plain. This runs the entire length of Palestine, interrupted only by Mt. Carmel, which juts out into the Mediterranean Sea and makes possible the modern port city of Haifa. The ancient Israelites were not known for seafaring, partly because this coast afforded such poor port facilities.

2. The Central Hill Country. This is an almost continuous range of hills broken only by the famous Valley of Jezreel.

Map 2

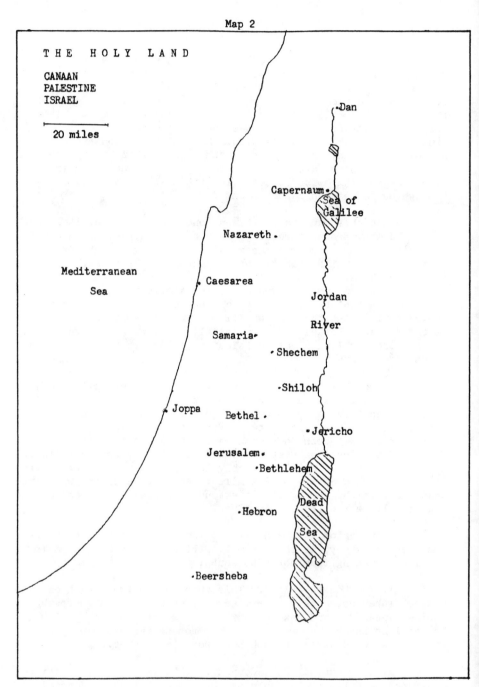

THE HOLY LAND

CANAAN
PALESTINE
ISRAEL

20 miles

•Dan

Capernaum•
Sea of
Galilee

Nazareth•

Mediterranean

Sea

•Caesarea

Jordan

River

Samaria•

•Shechem

•Shiloh

•Joppa

Bethel •

•Jericho

Jerusalem•

•Bethlehem

Dead

•Hebron

Sea

•Beersheba

The highest point is in the north, where the altitude is nearly 4,000 feet, but Jerusalem sits around 2,500 feet above sea level.

3. <u>The Jordan Valley</u>. This is part of a great rift which extends from Syria through the Red Sea into Africa. The Jordan River originates on the western side of Mt. Hermon, about 40 miles north of the Sea of Galilee. By the time it reaches that beautiful fresh-water lake, it has dropped to about 685 feet below sea level. From there it meanders in a very winding course southward to the Dead Sea, which is 1,275 feet below sea level, the lowest spot on the face of the earth. Waters emptying into that Sea have no outlet except by evaporation. Therefore it contains a heavy concentration of life-forbidding salt and mineral deposits; hence the "Dead" Sea.

4. <u>The Transjordan Plateau</u>. As the name implies, this is across the Jordan River from the major part of Palestine and is not a range of mountains, but a rather consistently high plateau well above the level of the Jordan Valley. The biblical regions known as Bashan, Gilead, and Moab are here. Today they belong to the nations of Syria and Jordan.

The remarkably varied types of terrain are accompanied by equally varied features of climate. The Coastal Plain boasts a mild climate, with an average annual temperature of about 67 degrees Fahrenheit at Joppa. Jerusalem, 34 miles away in the Hill country, enjoys a temperate 63 degrees average, while 15 miles farther east at 700 feet below sea level, Jericho has a tropical climate. In the winter, winds from the west or southeast bring clouds which release their moisture when they reach the Central Hill country. The rainy season extends from October through April. In summer there is virtually no rain, but northwest winds bring a comforting coolness.

A Thread of History

The Bible is not a history book but it does contain much history. As soon as one records events, stories of the adventures and migrations of peoples, one is writing history. Several "historical" works have found their way into the Bible, each written from its author's own point of view. That is to say, he wrote his record, not as an objective reporter, but as he interpreted the events he recorded from the standpoint of his faith. All the biblical writers believed firmly that God was active in human events. In other words, God works through history to accomplish his will.

Putting together the various histories in the Old Testament one finds a continuous thread of events. After the pre-historical material in Genesis 1-11, there are the stories of the earliest known Hebrews, Abraham, Isaac, and Jacob, usually referred to as Patriarchs. The story of the unusual character Joseph serves to explain how the Israelites came to be in Egypt. Exodus continues with the enslavement of the Israelites and the mighty act of God, known as the exodus, by which he gave them freedom and set them on their long journey to a land he promised them. This series of events covered roughly the period 1800-1300 B.C.

The establishment of the covenant relationship between God and these recent slaves was done through the outstanding leader Moses, who then led a complaining generation through a difficult wilderness trek to the edge of Canaan. Parts of Exodus, Numbers, and Deuteronomy tell this intriguing story, ending with the death of Moses. The task of leading the conquest of the promised land fell upon Joshua, whose exploits are told in the book which bears his name. Judges continues the narrative and tells of the dark two-century period following Joshua's death, which brings us to about 1025 B.C., the approximate time of the establishment of the monarchy.

The failure of the loose confederacy of tribes to deal with increasing aggression by the Philistines and others provoked the Israelite leaders to demand that a king be chosen to develop an adequate system of defense. Despite the opposition of the priest, prophet, and judge Samuel, a monarchy was set up. Israel's second king, the great David, succeeded brilliantly in doing what the people wanted done during his forty-year reign. Unfortunately, his son Solomon fulfilled his own ambitions by consuming the resources of the land by heavy taxation, so that by the time of his death the kingdom was in turmoil.

The united Kingdom lasted only a century, from around 1025 B.C. to 922 B.C., when Solomon's son foolishly rejected the pleas for redress of grievances and ten tribes seceded from the house of David to form their own kingdom. For the next two centuries there were two small kingdoms existing side-by-side, Israel in the north and Judah in the south. In 722 B.C. Israel was conquered by Assyria and was never re-established. Judah continued to exist until 587 B.C., when it fell to the mighty Babylonian Empire. Jerusalem was totally destroyed and the more skilled and educated people were forcibly relocated in Babylonia. All these events, from the work of Samuel to the fall of Jerusalem, are recorded in the books of I and II Samuel and I and II Kings, which, together with Joshua and Judges, make up what is known as the Deuteronomic History. The religion of the exiled Jews underwent considerable change in their new environment, but they used their Babylonian residency to consolidate their traditions, formulate their law codes, and write their history.

The exile officially ended in 538 B.C., when the Persian Cyrus, who had conquered Babylonia, issued a decree permitting all exiles to return to their homelands. Only a small percentage of the exiled Jews returned to Jerusalem to begin the long and difficult process of reconstruction. According to the books of Ezra and Nehemiah, the reconstruction of the Temple was completed in 515 B.C. and the city walls were rebuilt c. 444 B.C. The priest/scribe Ezra came from Babylonia to Jerusalem in 398 B.C. with a law-book which he read to the people and used as a basis for the reformation of their faith and practices. At this point the historical records of the Old Testament cease and we must depend on other sources, including the apocryphal book of I Maccabees, for our knowledge of the next four centuries.

Jerusalem remained a part of the Persian Empire until 333 B.C., when it fell to the armies of the Greek, Alexander the Great. After Alexander's death, Palestine was for a while under the Ptolemies, who ruled Egypt, but in 198 B.C. fell to the Seleucids, who ruled Syria. The oppressive policies of one of the Seleucids, Antiochus Epiphanes, provoked the Maccabean (Jewish) Revolt, which began in 167 B.C. and ended around 141 B.C. with the independence of the Jewish community in Palestine.

The period of Jewish national independence was brief, however, ending with the annexation of Palestine to the rapidly expanding Roman Empire in 63 B.C. This state of affairs continued into the New Testament period. Jesus was born in the last years of the half-Jewish puppet king known as Herod the Great. During the ministry of Jesus, his home province of Galilee was ruled by Herod's son, Antipas, while Judea and Samaria were governed by a procurator, Pontius Pilate, appointed by the Emperor. After the crucifixion and resurrection of Jesus, the Christian church began in the Jewish community in Jerusalem amid strong opposition from non-believing Jews. By the middle of the first century A.D., the church had spread through most of the Roman Empire. All of this we learn from the New Testament.

From the Jewish historian, Flavius Josephus, we learn of a bloody war, provoked by a Jewish revolt in 66 A.D., which resulted in the death of thousands of Jews and the destruction of Jerusalem again, in 70 A.D. The church also had difficulties with the Roman government in the last decade of the first century, as reflected in the book of Revelation. Another Jewish revolt occurred in 135 A.D., led by a supposed messiah named Bar Cochba. More loss of life and another destruction of Jerusalem resulted. Jews were excluded from the area when the city was rebuilt.

21

Chart III. Periods and Major Events in Biblical History

Approximate dates	Periods or Events
1800-1300 B.C.	Patriarchs (Abraham, Isaac, and Jacob) move from Mesopotamia to Canaan; their descendants move to Egypt and become enslaved
1300-1250 B.C.	Israelites released from bondage, are led by Moses through wilderness to edge of Canaan
1250-1025 B.C.	Israelites move to gain control of Canaan
1250-1225	Joshua leads campaign against Canaanites
1225-1025	Israel establishes tribal confederacy, with judges the only leaders
1025-922 B.C.	The united monarchy established under Kings Saul, David, and Solomon
922-722 B.C.	Kingdoms of Israel and Judah exist side-by-side, sometimes fighting, sometimes cooperati▌
722	Assyria conquers Israel, exiles some Israelit▌
722-587 B.C.	Judah continues under house of David, but as vassal state to Assyria, Egypt, or Babylonia
621	King Josiah orders reform of the religion in Judah, patterned on newly discovered lawbook
598	Babylonia invades Judah and exiles many Jews
587	Babylonia conquers Judah, destroys Jerusalem, and exiles more Jews to Babylonia
587-538 B.C.	Many Jews held in Babylonia against their wil▌ Jerusalem continues in ruins
538-333 B.C.	Under the Persian Empire the Jews gradually reconstruct Jerusalem
538	Cyrus of Persia conquers Babylonia, permits exiles to return home
515	Jews dedicate rebuilt Temple in Jerusalem
444	Jews, led by Nehemiah, rebuild city wall
398	Ezra brings lawbook from Babylonia to Jerusalem and institutes sweeping reforms
333-167 B.C.	Palestine brought into the Greek Empire; the Jews face Greek influences
167-63 B.C.	Jews in Palestine revolt against Seleucid oppression and regain their independence

22

Chart III. (continued)

63 B.C.-135 A.D.	Roman takeover of Palestine brings Jews under domination of yet another foreign power
6 B.C. ?	Jesus of Nazareth is born
30 A.D. ?	Jesus is executed
66-70 A.D.	Jews revolt against Rome, which quells the revolt and destroys Jerusalem
135 A.D.	Led by Bar Cochba, Jews again revolt against Rome

This brief overview of biblical history should be helpful in allowing us to see the thread of the continuing story of God's people from his covenant with Abraham to the early story of the movement (the Christian church) which stemmed from the conviction that Jesus of Nazareth was the Messiah longed for by many Palestinian Jews in the oppressive days of the Roman occupation. It should not be forgotten that Judaism continued as a parallel to the church and that at times church and synagogue were rivals, at times enemies, but rarely were they friends, although both came from the same roots.

Help from the Experts

Besides the textual critics and translators, about whom we learned in the previous chapter, hundreds of other scholars have given their lives to the goal of making the Bible's message more accessible and more understandable. Fortunately for those of us who can not, or who do not wish to spend our lives in such research, yet who yearn to understand the Bible better, these scholars have made available the results of their work in the form of books, pictures, maps, and journals. They are all designed to be "helps" for the serious student of the Bible.

The Introduction. Usually published as a single volume, such as the one you are now reading, this is a general resource which deals with such matters as geographical, historical, and cultural background and with the literary features involved in the individual books of the Bible. Questions such as Who wrote this book? Why did he write it? When was it written? Was it written by one person or several? What is its literary type, its nature, its theological stance? are dealt with.

The Bible Dictionary. This may be one volume or several.
It deals, in alphabetical order, with the names of persons, places
plants, animals, etc. which appear in the books of the Bible in a
more detailed way than the ordinary word dictionary is able to do.

The Concordance. This is a listing of all words (except
articles, pronouns, prepositions, etc.) which appear in the Bible,
in alphabetical order, with the places where they occur. The value of such a volume is especially great for finding references
when one knows only a word or two, or when one only suspects the
Bible may have something to say on a given subject. Each version
of the Scriptures needs its own concordance.

The Bible Atlas. This is simply a book of maps showing
the lands of the Bible and the Holy Land at various periods in
history. It is indexed to facilitate the quick finding of places
named in the Bible.

The Commentary. As the name suggests, the author of a
commentary is commenting upon the Bible. That is, he explains its
meaning, as he understands it. The commentary is a very valuable
instrument for helping one understand difficult passages. But it
should be selected and used with care. For, unlike the concordance and the dictionary, the commentary goes beyond the factual
and indulges in opinion. It is a good idea to consult more than
one commentary on passages whose meaning is unclear or controversial. Commentaries come in various sizes, from the one-volume
type to the multi-volumed sets. Some deal with the Bible in the
original languages and some only with the translation.

It is advisable, when one is shopping for "helps" such as
those described briefly above, to consult with an experienced
teacher or minister as to which particular ones may be suited to
one's purpose.

Significant names and terms for this chapter

The Holy Land	Dead Sea
Lands of the Bible	Coastal Plain
Fertile Crescent	Central Hill Country
Mesopotamia	Jordan Valley
Canaan	Transjordan Plateau
Palestine	Concordance
Israel	Bible Atlas
Sea of Galilee	Bible Commentary

CHAPTER III

THE BOOK OF BEGINNINGS

Biblical materials: Genesis

Essential reading: Genesis 1-4; 6-9; 11-15; 17-19; 22; 25:19-26:25
                     27-29; 35; 37; 41-43; 47; 50

The order in which we shall consider the books of the Old
Testament is the historical, insofar as that can be determined.
That does not mean the order in which they were written. It means,
rather, the order which will give us the best grasp of the progress
of the relationship between the God of Israel and his people.
Since the beginnings of that relationship are described in Genesis,
that is where we begin. We will follow the biblical order of
books (except for the fact that Ruth will be examined later) until
we get to the middle of II Kings. At that point we shall begin to
study the books associated with the prophets who were proclaiming
the oracles of God at their respective periods in the history.
This procedure will make understanding of their messages easier,
for we can hear what they are saying against the backdrop of the
problems and situations the kings and the people were facing at
the time.

When we have proceeded as far as the Old Testament record
carries us, that is, when we have looked at all the historical and
prophetic writings, we shall consider the books of poetry, of wisdom, and finally a group which the Hebrews placed in their third
division, the Writings.

The Pentateuch

The Hebrews call the first five books of the Bible the Torah, a term often translated simply as "law." However, it has a
much broader meaning and either "revelation" or "teaching" would
be a more accurate rendition. Although not the first to have been
written (in its entirety), it is the first division the Jews considered sacred scripture. It may be virtually the same book which
the scribe Ezra brought with him to Jerusalem as he left Babylonia
(see Nehemiah 8:1-3) and which he then read to the assembled citizens of Jerusalem. This body of writing is also known as the Pentateuch, a Greek term meaning five scrolls. This is an appropri-

25

ate name for, although it is a continuous work, it required five
standard-sized scrolls of prepared animal skins to contain it.

Another term often used for this same material is the Bo
of Moses. His name does not appear in Genesis, but Moses is cer
tainly the most prominent person in the other four books. For c
ries it was assumed that Moses was the author of the Pentateuch,
but many modern scholars have abandoned this notion for several
sons:
1. Moses is always referred to in the third person, not
the first, as would be natural were he the author.
2. The last chapter (Deuteronomy 34) could not be by him
cause it describes his death and burial.
3. Several names for the deity, for persons, and for pl
conflicting and duplicate accounts of the same event, and differ
ing theological viewpoints occur. These suggest several sources
rather than just one author.

The Documentary Hypothesis

The Pentateuch does appear to present a unified history
the Hebrews up to the point of their settling in Canaan. But a
ful study of its contents has led many scholars, Jewish and Chr
tian, to conclude that, in its final form, it is actually a comp
lation of several collections which were produced by several authors who lived at different times in the history of Israel. Th
pressive name given to this conclusion is the Documentary Hypoth
sis. What was it that led scholars to this theory?

1. Different parts of the Pentateuch use different names
for the deity. In some strains of tradition the distinctive nam
Yahweh was used from the beginning, whereas in others it is said
to be a later revelation. Exodus 6:2 says

> And God said to Moses, "I am Yahweh. I appeared to
> Abraham, to Isaac, and to Jacob, as El Shaddai, but
> by my name Yahweh I did not make myself known to
> them."

> [Note: Yahweh is translated in the RSV as "the LORD"
> and El Shaddai as "God Almighty."]

2. There are several instances in which the Pentateuch
gives two or more accounts of the same incident, sometimes conta
ing contradicting details.

3. Two widely differing accounts of creation occur back
back in Genesis, and the differences are significant.

4. The same persons and places are known by different names. Moses' father-in-law has three names; the holy mountain is called Sinai in some parts of the Pentateuch and Horeb in others.

5. Some laws appearing in the several law codes within the Pentateuch are in conflict with each other. Exodus 20:24 allows altars for worship to be built at many places but Deuteronomy 12:13-14 restricts it to one sanctuary.

To account for these facts the scholars theorized that, whoever the final editor (or editors) may have been, he used the older documents available to him and put them together without removing the overlapping material and inconsistencies in names and historical data. How many such documents he used and just what they were like have been subjects of much discussion among the Old Testament experts. Today, however, there is wide agreement among them that there were probably four such writings which can be identified and characterized with considerable confidence.

1. The Yahwistic source, usually designated with the letter J, because the German scholars working on the problem spell the characteristic name for God in this source Jahweh, and because the place in which it originated is thought to be Judah. Based on ancient memories and traditions, it was probably written in the tenth century B.C. It begins with a story of creation (Gen. 2) and ends with an account of the life and work of Moses. The J document is characterized by a rather primitive conception of God, who is represented as having human features and who converses directly with human beings. It represents mankind as capable of both noble obedience and sinful rebellion toward God. It appears to connect evil with the development of cities and to imply that the simpler rural life is closer to God's original intention for his creatures. The mountain of God is called Sinai and the inhabitants of Palestine are referred to as Canaanites. Most of J is found in Genesis and Exodus.

2. The Elohistic source, or E, so designated because it prefers the divine name Elohim and because it likely originated in the area occupied by the northern tribes, often called Ephraim. Composed a century or more later than J, it begins with Abraham and goes through the time of Moses. Thus it covers much of the same ground as J, emphasizing the role of Joseph in the patriarchal narratives. The E document speaks of God in a more sophisticated way and assumes that he contacts human beings through angels or dreams. It refers to the holy mountain as Horeb and calls the persons living in Palestine, Amorites. It, too, is mostly found in Genesis and Exodus.

27

3. The _Deuteronomic_ source, labeled <u>D</u>. Coming from the seventh century B.C., it is almost certainly the law-book accide tally discovered in the Temple (II Kings 22:8), which provided guidance for King Josiah's reform of the religion of Judah. It provides a second version of many older laws and is found only i the book of Deuteronomy. It manifests a more humanitarian conce than earlier law codes, stressing the demand of God for kindly treatment of the poor and impartial justice for all. It states clearly the doctrine of retribution, in which God promised rewar to the nation when it was obedient but threatened dire punishmen when it strayed from his law.

4. The _Priestly_ source, known as <u>P</u>. This contains very old material which was transmitted orally from one generation of priests to another and finally put into writing by the priests w were exiled to Babylonia after Jerusalem and the Temple were de- stroyed in 587 B.C. It contains a story of creation (Gen. 1), c siderable genealogical material, and a vast amount of law codes, priestly rules for worship, directions for building the Ark of t Covenant and the Tabernacle, selection of and dress for the prie and Levites, etc. Moses' role in the establishment of Isra el's cultic practices is emphasized, and theological bases for r ligious institutions are given. The P material is found in all the books of the Pentateuch except perhaps Deuteronomy.

According to the Documentary Hypothesis, these four sour were combined in various stages, probably attaining the final fe around 400 B.C. It is probable that J and E were combined into one narrative first, since they covered much the same ground. W can represent the long process by a simple formula: JE + D + P JEDP (the Pentateuch). It is important to recognize that the ma terials contained in the Pentateuch are much older than the date of its final composition. Some scholars believe that the priest and scribe Ezra, whose interest and expertise in the law is ex- pressly referred to in Ezra 7:6 and Neh. 8:1-2, may be the one p son most responsible for putting the Torah together in its prese form. Certainly from Ezra's time forward it is the book which p vides inspiration and guidance for the Jewish community.

In the Beginning

For most readers the most interesting book of the Penta- teuch is Genesis. Not only does it have stories of creation, fa and flood, but it also tells of the problems, successes, failure adventures, strengths, and weaknesses of some very human person: the Patriarchs. It ends with a long cycle of narratives of the legendary Joseph, who rose from imprisoned slave to prime minister of Egypt. The first eleven chapters stand apart from the rest of Genesis, both in nature and in content. They form a sort of prologue, or foreword, to the story of the Hebrews/Israelites, dealing with the beginnings of the human race from the standpoint of the faith of Israel that Yahweh is the God of nature as well as the God of history. In contrast to the remainder of the book, Genesis 1-11 is a sort of pre-history, in which theological truth is conveyed by stories telling of the interaction between God and human beings before the historical record starts. The reader who is familiar with Jesus' parables may see some similarity between them and the stories of creation and fall of the first human pair. Not necessarily "historical" truth, but a deeper truth about the reality of human nature and existence is presented in an appealing story. So with the creation stories there is a strong statement made of one of the central convictions of Israel's faith: the God who revealed himself to Moses is he who created the universe!

A Double Feature

Genesis begins with two separate and distinct accounts of creation. The first one, found in 1:1-2:4a, seems to have been derived from the P (Priestly) tradition. A very orderly account, it describes the creative activity of God on each of six days, with a concluding sentence for each day: "And there was evening and there was morning, (one) day." It is probable that this entire story was used in the congregational worship of the Israelites as a confession of their creation faith. The priest in charge may have read the account of each day's creative progress, the congregation responding with the concluding sentence as a refrain.

How and where God obtained the stuff of which he made the universe, or whether he simply commanded it into being, is not stated. It is best to take the ambiguous word of the writer, who pictures a dark, formless, watery mass from which God made a beautiful, illuminated, orderly, inhabitable world with appropriate amounts of sea and dry land. God's name in this story is Elohim, a plural form found frequently in the Old Testament. The Hebrew word yom, translated as "day," can mean a 24-hour day or an indefinite period of time, as when we speak of what happened in our forefathers' day. A significant fact of this first creation story is that humankind is left for the very last creative act. It is as though everything else in the world was all in existence and arranged as a preparation for the arrival of the highest of all creatures, man. This exalted status is underscored by the statement that man (male and female) was made in God's image. What that involved is not explained, but it should be noted that this is said of no other creature. Could it refer to man's having been given dominion over the other creatures? Or his superior intelligence? Or the ability to communicate with God? Whatever the content of being made "in the image of God," it is clearly the writer's way of saying that the human race is above and in control of the rest of the created order.

This contrasts sharply with the lowly status of man in an older Babylonian creation account, the Enuma Elish. Set against a polytheistic background this story tells of an enormous struggle among the gods, culminating in a fierce battle between Marduk, chief god of the Babylonian pantheon, and Tiamat, an enemy goddess Marduk eventually wins, kills Tiamat, and uses half her body to form the heavens and the other half to form the earth. Some of the blood of her henchman Kingu he uses to make a new creature whose task it will be to serve the gods by doing all the menial, distasteful chores which formerly the gods had to do themselves.

In the Priestly account of creation, God made provision for the reproduction of the various species, including man, and for the food which they would need. It should be noted that, at this point, food for all the creatures is limited to vegetation (1:29-30). An inspection tour of all creation indicated to God, as the sixth day came to a close, that everything was "very good." Such a statement reflects the basic Israelite view of the world; when God finished with it, it was good and to be enjoyed by its creatures.

The concluding paragraph (2:1-4a) states that God used the seventh day of this busy week to rest. Such resting by God became the basis for the Israelite concept of the sabbath day, which God "blessed . . . and hallowed." When the Ten Commandments were recorded they included one which orders the keeping of the sabbath holy, the rationale for which is the divine rest on the first sabbath (Exodus 20:8-11).

Immediately following the stately P story of creation comes another one (2:4b-25), which scholars agree is from the Yahwistic (J) source. The differences between the two are clearly seen. The deity is Yahweh Elohim ("the LORD God" in RSV), who created a male human being before anything else. Then he made plants ("planted a garden"), including a "tree of life" and a "tree of the knowledge of good and evil" (2:8-10). The man was placed in the garden of Eden and given responsibility for its care and cultivation, but strictly charged not to eat of the tree of the knowledge of good and evil. There was no restriction on any other of the fruits.

30

Only after the establishment of the garden, with the man in charge, and the subsequent creation of the birds and beasts, did the female enter the scene. The Lord decided to create her because the man was lonesome and could not really communicate with the other creatures. One of the man's ribs was used to begin the construction of the woman. When he saw the new creature, the man immediately recognized her as one sufficiently like himself to enable his loneliness to be relieved. There follows a brief statement of the institution of marriage as a one-flesh relationship and an allusion to the unabashed nudity of the pair, a point to be elaborated on in Genesis 3.

Besides the radically different order of creation and the names for the deity, other differences may be noted between the two creation stories. As the J story has no hint of a six-day progression, the P account makes no reference to the garden or the two special trees in it. The P story does not mention what material God used to make human beings, but the J version specifically states that man was made of "dust from the ground." This has the effect of tying the human race closely to the remainder of creation, so that man appears as an integral part of "nature." Instead of the command to "be fruitful and multiply" (P), the J account stresses the companionship of marriage.

Our brief summary of these two accounts of creation shows that they are two quite different writings of independent origin. The J account, which is less structured and reflects a more naive concept of the deity, is thought to be the older of the two. The P story, perhaps originating among the Jews exiled in Babylonia from 587 B.C. onward, may be their answer to the Babylonian story of how the world began. Not Marduk, as the Enuma Elish claims, but Elohim (later known as Yahweh) is the creator of the universe. The one point at which both biblical stories converge is the significant one: it is the God of Israel, by whatever name he may have been known, who did the creating. This is a faith statement, not an historical or a scientific report. We create unnecessary and inappropriate problems for ourselves when we set the biblical accounts over against modern scientific theories of the origin of the universe and insist that a choice must be made between them.

An Unfortunate Choice

The Priestly document has no follow-up story to tell what happened to the first pair of human beings, but the Yahwist does. Chapter 3 of Genesis continues the story in the previous chapter in the same style. God is alluded to in very anthropomorphic (human) terms, choosing the cool part of the day to walk noisily

through the garden looking for the man and his wife. This story
of "the Fall," as it is often called, introduces a new character,
the serpent, as a wily creature who is hostile to God but friendl
toward the woman. From very early times the snake has been looke
upon as possessing unusual powers, often demonic, always mysterious. Here he knows something the woman does not know: despite
what God had said, eating of the fruit of the forbidden tree will
not bring death. Instead, it will bring knowledge equal to God's
and God does not want that to happen. This is the real reason fc
the prohibition.

The point which causes the woman to try the attractive
fruit (it does not say "apple") is the promise that eating it wil
make her wise: "Your eyes will be opened, and you will be like
God, knowing good and evil." As we observed with respect to the
creation stories, this account of man's first disobedience is the
ological rather than historical. By the time the Yahwist did his
writing, it was clear that something very serious had happened tc
the innocence and goodness of creation. The idyllic existence of
Eden had been replaced by a life of hardship, pain, male domination, and fear. How and why did this reversal of conditions occu

Without attempting to solve the problem of the ultimate
origin of evil, the narrative which the Yahwist places here in
Gen. 3 does provide a way of accounting for the change without as
signing evil to God. Man was created good, with total freedom to
obey or not to obey God's rules. For an indefinite period he obe
ed and all was well. The temptation which kindled the creature's
desire to be like the creator was too great to be resisted. It
thus implied that the basic sin of humanity is man's desire to re
place God. God could not allow this rebellion, and so he punishe
all those involved, the result of which was a serious disruption
of the relationship which had existed between God and man. Anotl
er consequence of their sin is the awareness that they are naked
and the feeling of shame which they experienced (3:7,11). This
suggests that the relationship between themselves had also been
damaged.

In the account of the punishments God meted out to the
guilty parties, we may legitimately see several etiological fac-
tors at work. Man's curiosity over why snakes always crawl rathe
than walk and why they instill such fear in human beings that the
seek to obliterate them is satisfied by the statement that these
facts came about as punishment for the serpent's role in the fal
of man. Punishments to the woman and the man offer explanations
non-scientific to be sure, of other well-known facts of life in
those days, answering such questions as Why is child-bearing so
painful? Why are women subservient to their husbands? Why do w

32

have to work so hard for a living? Why must we die? The story
concludes with the expulsion of Adam and Eve from the garden of
Eden, with no possibility of return. The state of sinful, rebellious humanity is permanent. Man was created good and free, but
he abused his freedom, and everything changed. That is the theological message of Genesis 3.

The Great Catastrophe

In Genesis 4 the J writer continues his story of Adam and
Eve, telling of their three sons and a few of the interesting descendants of the eldest. It is implied that the sinfulness of the
race which they began was increasing. In a fit of jealous rage
Cain murdered his brother Abel and was punished by exile. Later
he married and became the founder of the first city, Enoch (4:17).
One of his descendants, Lamech, boasted of his violent act of vengeance (seventy-seven fold) after he had killed a man for striking
him. Chapter five likely comes from the P source of the Pentateuch and serves to tie together the time of Seth, the third son
of Adam and Eve, and the story of Noah and the flood. Genealogical in nature, this chapter features the renowned Enoch, who by-
passed death to be with God, and Methuselah, who holds the record
for longevity (5:27). Both these chapters depend on orally transmitted memories and folklore of the ancient Hebrews and fit well
into the pre-historical nature of this part of Genesis.

During the long, indefinite period of time between Adam
and Noah, the expanding human population and the developing civilization had grown progressively worse. Genesis 6-9 describes
this deteriorated situation and what God decided he must do about
it in what we call the story of the Great Flood. Actually there
are two stories, one each from J and P, but the Pentateuch's final
editor has combined them into one instead of placing them back-
to-back, as he did with the two creation stories. Not only are
there discrepancies in such details as the number of animals taken
into the boat and the length of time the waters covered the earth,
but there are two distinct introductions which explain why God
found it necessary to destroy the creation he had once declared
good (6:5-7 and 6:11-13).

These statements of human degradation leave the impression
that evil is in full control and the human race is totally corrupt.
Yahweh "was sorry that he had made man on the earth, and it griev-
ed him to his heart." The J writer is ascribing human emotions to
God, a practice known as "anthropopathism." The only exception to
the total corruption of the race is a family of eight persons, who

are selected to be survivors and progenitors of the second edition
of the human race, which God hopes will turn out better than the
first. Noah and his family are also charged with the preservation
of representatives of the animal kingdom in order that it, too,
may be reestablished after the deluge.

This terrible judgment upon the human race did not end in
unrelieved tragedy. As God protected Cain with the mysterious
mark (Gen. 4:15), he protected tokens of his creation and, by the
appearance of the rainbow, promised never to repeat such a watery
mass annihilation (9:13-15). The Yahwist relates that the first
act of Noah's family upon emergence from the ark was the offering
of animal sacrifices to Yahweh, which is the first instance in the
Bible of such worship. After God commanded Noah and his three
sons and their wives to begin repopulating the earth, he allowed
them to expand their diet to include meat (9:3), but the meat must
be free of blood. The sacredness of life is now protected with
the implication of capital punishment as the penalty for murder.
For "God made man in his own image" (9:6).

The Bible is not the only ancient literature which contains
a story of such a destructive flood. The story of Utnapishtim in
the Babylonian Epic of Gilgamesh has such close parallels to the
biblical account that it seems most probable that they both are
rooted in an actual widespread flood in the region of Mesopotamia
many centuries before the time of Abraham. The difference between
the Babylonian and Hebrew stories is chiefly noted in the vastly
different religious interpretations of the catastrophe. Unlike the
former, the biblical account depicts the deity in total charge
of the event, acting regretfully, but purposefully, and following
his justice with mercy and a new opportunity for mankind.

The genealogies of Noah's three sons, Ham, Shem, and Ja-
pheth, follow in chapter 10 and serve to connect the flood story
to the next incident, the tower of Babel. These represent the
three branches of the human race known to the ancient Hebrews and
leave the impression that a very long time elapsed between those
events. When the eleventh chapter begins, the earth was well on
its way to repopulation and God could get some idea as to how his
second edition of the race was going to turn out. The J writer
uses the first nine verses to report that Yahweh was displeased
with the prideful efforts of the men of Shinar (ancient Babylonia)
to build a city featuring a high tower to "make a name for ourselves." There may be a reflection in this story of the Yahwist's
feeling that cities encourage evil doings. In Gen. 4:17 he had
noted that the first city was built by the first murderer! The
condition of the human race had not deteriorated to the state
which brought on the flood, but men were putting trust in their

own accomplishments rather than in God. The punishment this time was a confusion of language and the scattering of the population. This is one way of explaining why the human race has so many languages, even if it differs drastically from current views on the subject.

The remainder of chapter 11 is more genealogical material and serves to connect the Babel incident with the patriarchal period. With the introduction of Abram (later called Abraham) in 11:26, what we have called the pre-historical section, or the foreword, comes to a close. Up to this point Genesis has dealt with mankind in general. But when Yahweh appeared to Abraham and proposed a covenant relationship, Hebrew history begins.

The Obedient Patriarch

Genesis 12-35 depicts the adventures of three ancestors of the Israelites whom they obviously thought to be of great significance. They are Abraham, Isaac, and Jacob, referred to by modern writers as "patriarchs" (father-rulers) because they were tribal chiefs or heads of large clans or families. The biblical narratives, mostly combined from the Yahwist and Elohist traditions, represent the three in a father-son-grandson relationship. Abraham excels in terms of strength of character, distance traveled, faithfulness to the Lord, and the number of people under his influence. Isaac is overshadowed by his eminent father and his illustrious but scheming son and does not get nearly so much space in the narratives as they. It is Jacob, despite his character flaw, who became known as Israel and whose twelve sons were the progenitors of the tribes who constituted the Israelites.

The Bible presents Abraham as the father of the Hebrews (Gen. 14:13), who include not only the Israelites but the Ishmaelites, the Midianites, the Edomites, and perhaps several other Semitic groups (Gen. 25:1-4). A descendant of Noah's son, Shem (from which comes "Semite"), Abraham first appears as a resident of a Chaldean (Babylonian) town named Ur, in the eastern tip of the Fertile Crescent. Terah, his father, took him and other members of the family along as he migrated northwestward, following the valley of the Euphrates to Haran, which today is located near the Turkey-Syria border. Gen. 12 begins with the first encounter between Yahweh and Abraham, after his father's death, in which Abraham was directed to pull up stakes and strike out for a strange land. If he would follow the Lord's directive, he was promised fame, a large progeny, and that he would both be blessed by Yahweh and become a channel of blessing to all others. This promise plays a big role in the subsequent narrative as it is repeated,

Map 3

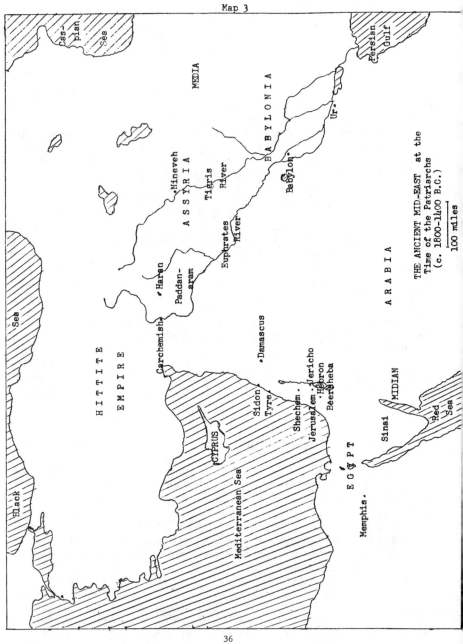

THE ANCIENT MID-EAST at the
Time of the Patriarchs
(c. 1800-1400 B.C.)

100 miles

placed in jeopardy, doubted, restated, and finally fulfilled. Abraham's steadfast belief that somehow, despite delays and disappointments, God would make good his promise, has earned for him the reputation of being a man of great faith.

Just when did Abraham live? The judgments of scholars differ on this matter, some placing him as early as the nineteenth century B.C. and others as late as the fifteenth. Since the Bible itself, at this point, does not deal in dates, we look to non-biblical records for some help. The term "Habiru" occurs in several documents in the Near East from the second millenium (2,000-1,000) B.C. It is probable that the word "Hebrew" is a form of this term; if so, we can learn a bit more than the Bible tells us about the origin of the Hebrew people. The Habiru were not a nationalistic or racial group, but a varied group of nomads wandering from place to place in search of water, grazing land, and temporary employment. The Amarna Letters, discovered at el-Amarna, Egypt, in 1887, tell of Habiru in Canaan, which at the time was under Egyptian domination. Letters from Canaanite kings to Egyptian pharaohs complain of the marauding Habiru, who were causing all sorts of trouble for the local rulers. Since these letters were written in the late fifteenth and early fourteenth centuries B.C., they provide some hint as to when the Hebrews were active in challenging the Canaanites for the use of the land.

Genesis 12:10-13:1 tells of Abraham and his wife Sarah, who, faced with famine in southern Canaan, moved into northern Egypt temporarily in search of food. And, of course, later in Genesis, Jacob and all his family moved into Egypt for the same reason. However, we do not know which generations of the biblical Hebrews the Amarna tablets are speaking of. It seems safe to assume, then, only that they are from the patriarchal period, which begins with Abraham, whose journey from Ur to Haran we shall suggest, in the absence of specific data, occurred around 1800 B.C.

After Abraham's Egyptian sojourn he returned to Canaan and settled in the Negeb, a general term for the South, and made his residence in Hebron. His nephew Lot, who had accompanied him in all his travels, moved to Sodom, situated near the Dead Sea. Later his family and fellow citizens of Sodom were captured and carried to an area north of Damascus. After Abraham, with his little army of menservants (318 of them!), had rescued the victims and their confiscated possessions and were heading homeward, they were served refreshments by Melchizedek, described as king of Salem (later Jerusalem) and "priest of God Most High" (El Shaddai) [Gen. 14:11-20]. Much is made of this otherwise obscure priest in the New Testament book of Hebrews.

A very significant part of the Abraham cycle of narratives is the establishment of the covenant between God and Abraham, an extremely important feature of which is God's promise that he would give to Abraham's descendants all the land of Canaan forever (15:17-20; 17:1-8). This promise is used by some in our time to support the claim of Israel to disputed parts of Palestine. Another feature of the covenant, God's promise to make of him "the father of a multitude of nations," became more and more difficult to believe as Abraham and Sarah grew older and older. In an act of desperation Sarah tried to assist God in fulfilling his promise by giving her personal servant Hagar to Abraham as wife. A son, Ishmael, was born but became a source of unreconcilable animosity between the two women after Sarah finally gave birth to the child of promise, Isaac. Under pressure from Sarah, her husband reluctantly discharged Hagar and Ishmael, who is considered the chief ancestor of the Arabs and instrumental in the founding of the Muslim faith.

Even after the birth of Isaac and it appeared that the promise was on the way to being realized, the strange incident related in Gen. 22 placed the whole thing in jeopardy. God commanded Abraham to sacrifice his son! Again Abraham's faith was exemplified in his readiness to do even that, and God reiterated the promise.

Isaac and Rebekah

On the basis of the biblical narrative, one must conclude that the most important thing about Isaac is that he was the child born in fulfillment of the promise God made to his parents. Nothing really distinguishes this rather ordinary person. Not possessed of the strong personality of Abraham, he meekly surrendered the watering place for his cattle to other claimants rather than challenge them for it. He showed no interest in marriage, which prompted Abraham to arrange for his marriage to Isaac's first cousin, Rebekah. It is interesting that Abraham decided to send, not Isaac, but a trusted servant to Haran to make the selection and arrange the terms of the deal. After a period of childlessness, Isaac and Rebekah did have fraternal twin sons, Esau and Jacob, who were entirely different in appearance, personality, and interests. They became victims of favoritism by the parents, for Isaac preferred the elder Esau while Rebekah favored Jacob (Gen. 24-25).

The Jacob Saga

Rivalry between Esau and Jacob began early. In their youth Jacob took advantage of his brother's famished state by trading him a bowl of pottage, ready for immediate consumption, for Esau's birthright as firstborn son (25:29-34). Some years later (ch. 27) Isaac, now blind and fearing that he may not live much longer, arranged for a ceremony in which the traditional patriarchal blessing would be pronounced upon the eldest son in the family. While Esau was hunting wild game to prepare his father's favorite dish, his mother and brother were conspiring to obtain this coveted blessing for Jacob. The deception was successful and set the stage for the deep disappointment and subsequent rage experienced by Esau when he learned the facts. Rebekah, fearing that Esau's anger would result in his killing Jacob, quickly convinced Isaac to send her favorite son to Haran, whence she had come, to select a wife from among her family. This, she argued, would be far preferable to having him marry one of the local women.

The brothers did not see each other again until perhaps twenty years later, by which time Esau had prospered and forgiven Jacob for his unethical behavior. The descendants of Esau, many of whom are listed in Gen. 36, became known as the Edomites, who became perennial enemies of the descendants of Jacob, the Israelites. Jacob's talent for chicanery did not cease, however, when he took up residence in Haran. There he became well-to-do, partly at the expense of his uncle Laban, who was also his employer and father-in-law, but largely by virtue of his skill and hard work as a husbandman of cattle and sheep.

But Jacob himself became the victim of deception when Laban gave him his older daughter Leah as wife instead of his beloved Rachel, for whom he had paid by seven years of labor. The two men reached a compromise whereby Jacob could also have Rachel but would be obligated to work for Laban another seven-year period. Later each wife gave her personal maid to Jacob as wife when they thought they could not have children. When Jacob finally left Haran to return to the land of promise he had four wives, at least one daughter, eleven sons, and numerous sheep and cattle. On the way home Rachel, who had earlier borne Joseph, died in giving birth to Benjamin, Jacob's twelfth son (Gen. 35:16-26).

The Bible does not shrink from relating the unattractive traits of the man who became the father of the Israelites. Not only the weak-willed Isaac, but the scheming, deceptive Jacob was selected by God to be a successor to Abraham in the covenant relationship. On the first night of his journey from Beersheba to Haran, Jacob had a dream in which Yahweh, identifying himself as the God of Abraham and Isaac, appeared with a restatement of the covenant with Abraham, but now it was renewed with Jacob (28:10-17). Understandably overwhelmed by the experience, Jacob set up a marker and named the place Bethel (house of God). Years later, when he was on his way southward from Haran, a strange thing happened to him near the Jabbok River (32:22-32). He wrestled with an unknown man during the night, but in the morning he learned that his opponent had been God! This is the occasion of Jacob's being renamed "Israel" (he who strives with God). In the later literature the name Israel is used both for the individual Jacob and for the entire group of his descendants, who are also referred to as Israelites. A second version of Jacob's name change and his naming of Bethel occurs in 35:1-15, which is indicative of the failure of the final editor of the Pentateuch to omit a story from one of his sources which duplicates one from another source which he had already used.

From Slave to Prime Minister

The central character of Gen. 37-50 stands out as a man of integrity, wisdom, talent, and high morality who frequently received messages from God through dreams. Joseph, like his father, was the recipient of parental favoritism. When this cycle of stories begins, he is the only adult son of Jacob's favorite wife, Rachel, for Benjamin is still a very young child. Most of the material in the Joseph cycle comes from the Elohist, who portrays God as delivering his message through dreams rather than direct speech, as is so often the case in the J document. Joseph's only fault, it seems, was his telling his brothers the dreams he had in which they were always depicted as inferior to himself, and that error in judgment may be attributed to his youthful naivete. This habit, coupled with blatant favoritism showered upon him by Jacob, provoked his brothers to get rid of him when the opportunity came. Some of them were willing to murder him, but the arrival of a caravan of Ishmaelite (or Midianite?) traders en route to Egypt suggested a better alternative. They sold him as a slave and reported to their father that he had been killed by a wild animal.

His Egyptian owner, Potiphar, was highly pleased with his responsible, talented slave and made him general overseer of his estate. When he repelled the advances of Potiphar's wife, she accused him of attempted seduction and he was imprisoned. His reputation as interpreter of dreams was recalled by a servant in the pharaoh's household who had been in jail with Joseph. When Joseph not only interpreted the pharaoh's troubling dreams but recalled them to the royal mind, he was released from prison and made prime minister of Egypt, second in power to the pharaoh himself. The dreams, reported Joseph to the pharaoh, meant that Egypt would be blessed during the next seven years with a superabundance of crops. But the bad news, he went on to say, was that there would follow

another seven-year period of famine. Then came the advice: set
up a system whereby the surplus from the first period could be
stored for use during the following famine years.

The pharaoh was so impressed with all this that he decided
Joseph would make the ideal person to be placed in charge of his
huge project. His willingness to elevate a foreigner to such a
position may be explained by the fact that the pharaoh himself was
not a native Egyptian, but a member of the Hyksos invaders who had
taken over the country shortly before 1700 B.C. Since we know
they were overthrown around 1550 B.C., Joseph's term of government
service falls in the period between these two dates.

After many years had passed, during which Jacob believed
Joseph to be dead and his brothers did not know what had happened
to him since they sold him into slavery, the famine which covered
both Egypt and Canaan provided an opportunity for Joseph and his
brothers to meet again. Gen. 42-45 is a lengthy narrative detail-
ing the encounters. News of food for sale in Egypt brought the
brothers to Joseph's presence, but his full brother Benjamin, now
enjoying the role of his father's favorite, was not with them.
Hiding his identity, Joseph insisted that their next trip must include Benjamin. When the brothers came the second time and he saw
they were solicitous for Benjamin's safety, Joseph revealed himself, to the amazement and fear of those who had wronged him so
harshly years earlier.

Joseph, in a display of forgiving generosity, sought to
allay their fears through a theological interpretation of what had
happened to him: "And now do not be distressed, or angry with
yourselves, because you sold me here; for God sent me before you
to preserve life" (45:5). Later, after Jacob died and their fear
returned, the brothers were again reassured that he bore them no
ill will and intended them no harm (50:18-21). God could take
men's evil deeds and turn them into beneficial accomplishments
which carried out his will, Joseph seems to be saying. His generosity included the insistent invitation for his father and all his
brothers and their families to move into Egypt and remain there,
where Joseph would make sure they had enough food until the famine
should end. He arranged that they should dwell in the area known
as Goshen, situated in northern Egypt, with the enthusiastic approval of the pharaoh. There they lived productively for the next
seventeen years (47:27-28), at the end of which Jacob died and was
carried back to Canaan for burial in the family cemetery.

The Joseph cycle of stories, interesting and edifying in
themselves, serves to explain how the descendants of Jacob happened
to be in Egypt, even though the land which God promised to Abraham,

Isaac, and Jacob as an everlasting possession, was Canaan. What is never explained, however, is why they remained in Egypt after the famine was over or why they did not move back home when Jacob died. The probable reason is that life was better for them there than they remembered it when they had lived in Canaan.

It should be noted that Joseph is said to have married the daughter of an Egyptian priest (41:45), who bore him two sons, Ephraim and Manasseh. When the tribal names of the Israelites are given later in the Pentateuch, there is no tribe bearing the name of Joseph. Instead, there are two tribes, named for his sons, who figured prominently in the later history of Israel. In fact, Ephraim is sometimes used as a synonym for Israel, the kingdom formed when the northern tribes seceded from the house of David in 922 B.

We should remember that the stories of the patriarchs were written from the vantage point of a later time, when the composers of the J, E, and P sources were drawing mostly upon oral traditions and looking back to the ancestry of the Israelite people. Literarily, the patriarchal narratives connect the pre-historical materials in Gen. 1-11 with the exodus event, which is unquestionably the most significant single happening in the formation of the people of Israel. Historically, they answer such important questions as Who are we, the people whom God rescued and offered a covenant relationship and whom he made into a great nation (as in the days of David and Solomon)? Theologically, they provide a foundation for the concept of chosenness, of being special, and of the faith proclaimed by Moses.

The narratives in Gen 12-50 say that already in centuries long past God had appeared to Abraham with the promise of continuing blessing, a significant mission to the world, and the assurance of a particular land as an inheritance. So when God appeared to Moses with the news that he was about to deliver Israel from slavery, he could direct Moses to say to them, "I am the God of Abraham, and the God of Isaac, and the God of Jacob." Morally, the stories provide a fund of appealing and relevant materials upon which leaders and parents could draw as they sought to instill in their followers and children virtues such as faithfulness, courage, perseverance, patience, trust in God, generosity, and forgiveness.

Significant terms and names for this chapter

Pentateuch	Abraham
Torah	Isaac
Documentary hypothesis	Jacob
Yahweh	Shem
Elohim	Hebrew
"J"	Amarna Letters
"E"	Sarah
"D"	Haran
"P"	Negeb
Patriarchs	Lot
Enuma Elish	Sodom
Marduk	El Shaddai
Garden of Eden	Melchizedek
The Fall	Hagar
etiology	Ishmael
Cain	Rebekah
Abel	Esau
Lamech	Laban
Noah	Rachel
anthropomorphism	Bethel
anthropopathism	Joseph
Epic of Gilgamesh	Potiphar
Tower of Babel	Hyksos

CHAPTER IV

THE BIG EVENT

Biblical materials: Exodus, Leviticus, Numbers

Essential reading: Exodus 1:1-6:9; 12; 14; 18-20; 32
Leviticus 16
Numbers 13

The event which, above all others, became the central
theme of the religion of Israel is the deliverance of the descend
ants of Jacob from Egyptian slavery. The most convenient
name for it is also the name of the book which describes it: the
Exodus, which means "the going out." It was looked upon by all
subsequent generations as the beginning point of the covenant relationship between Yahweh and Israel. In a real sense, the crea-
tion/fall/flood sequence and the wonderful patriarchal stories in
Genesis are the prelude to the exodus. When Genesis ends, the
families of Jacob's sons are well situated in the Goshen area of
Egypt. Exodus begins by listing the eleven sons who had joined
Joseph in that country during the famine and states that all thei
families totaled only seventy persons at that time. Verses 6-7 o
chapter one cover an indefinite period of time which saw phenomen
al growth in these families "so that the land was filled with
them."

A New King over Egypt

The remainder of Exodus 1 (vss. 8-22) explains how it happened that the people associated with the prime minister who had
literally saved the lives of thousands of Egyptians had become the
victims of oppression. When vs. 8 says "there arose a new king
over Egypt, who did not know Joseph," it is referring to the historical fact that the Hyksos rulers had been expelled and the current pharaoh (the title Egyptians used for their chief ruler) had
never heard of Joseph or his contribution to the country's well-
being. What concerned him was national security and the possibility that this fast-growing group of Hebrews would join an invading army coming in from the northeast. His solution was to slow

44

their birthrate by enslaving them. Two of their assigned projects were constructing the cities of Pithom and Raamses, to which Egyptian records refer as occurring during the reigns of Seti I and Ramses II, who were pharaohs of the XIXth dynasty. These same records mention Habiru people's hauling stone and working on the construction of royal cities.

When the Pharaoh saw that his enslavement policy did not produce the desired result, he tried other things without abolishing the slavery. He ordered the Hebrew midwives to dispose of all male babies at birth, an order which was simply ignored. His final decree was to have the Egyptians do away with all male infants born to the Hebrew families. How successful this new cruel policy was the Bible does not tell us, but it does tell of one resourceful mother's scheme to save her son from such a death. Exodus 2 tells how Jochebed, of the tribe of Levi, contrived to have her son discovered by the daughter of the pharaoh as he was afloat in the Nile near the princess' habitual bathing spot. In this way Moses' life was spared; he was cared for in his early years by his own mother and then reared in the royal palace, where he enjoyed all the privileges which go with such a life.

But Moses' privileged life style did not cause him to forget who he was. When he saw a fellow-Israelite being mistreated by an Egyptian, he defended the Israelite a bit too vigorously and killed the Egyptian. When he realized that the pharaoh had heard of the slaying, he did not depend upon his palace connections to protect him, but fled to Midian, which is separated from Egypt by the wilderness of the Sinai Peninsula. Here Moses, now forty years of age, began an entirely new phase of his life (Exodus 2:15-22). The account in Exodus is made up of materials from J, E, and P, woven together, but not so expertly as to prohibit our recognizing the varied sources from time to time. One such point is the name of Moses' Midianite employer, the priest introduced first as Reuel (2:18), but then called Jethro (3:1). Besides the job of shepherding his sheep Reuel also gave Moses one of his daughters, Zipporah, as wife. His upbringing among the elite surely had not prepared Moses for his new life in Midian, but he apparently adjusted to it during his forty-year stay there.

Moses' New Career

If the biblical writers have their statistics correct, Moses was eighty years old when God appeared to him in the burning bush incident at Mt. Horeb, "the mountain of God" (Ex. 3:1-6). He seemed content simply to continue in his job as shepherd in Midian, but the most exciting phase of his life lay ahead of him. What the religion of Moses was at this point we do not know, but he probably shared the faith of the family into which he had married. Jethro was a priest, but what god he represented is not stated. At any rate, when the deity spoke to Moses from the bush, he identified himself as "the God of your father, the God of Abraham, the God of Isaac, and the God of Jacob" (3:6). This suggests that Moses had no knowledge of the patriarchs' religion.

When he learned what God had in mind for him, becoming the instrument of deliverance of the enslaved Israelites from Egypt, Moses thought of several good reasons that he was not the man for the task. One such reason involved the identity of God. If he should take the job and announce to the Israelites that God had called him to this role, how would he answer their natural question, "What God?" The deity answered Moses by revealing his personal name YAHWEH, a form of the verb "to be" in Hebrew. This is the first time that that name appears in the Elohist's material, and it goes on to explain that Yahweh was the God of the patriarchs, even though they did not know him by that name (3:13-15; 6:3). By contrast, the Yahwist consistently used the same name for the creating God, the punishing God (the Fall and Flood stories), the God of the patriarchs, and the delivering God. God replied to all Moses' excuses for not taking the assignment in such a way that Moses simply could not refuse the call. The point that he was a very poor speaker (4:10) was taken seriously by the Lord, who reassured Moses that his brother Aaron would be appointed as his spokesman.

With all his excuses dismissed, Moses, at an age when modern American octogenarians are enjoying a leisurely retirement or withering away in an institution, embarked upon an uncertain and frightening, but challenging course. He, his wife, and sons set out for Egypt with Jethro's blessing. Directed by Yahweh, Aaron met Moses at "the mountain of God" (4:27), was briefed on the Lord's commissioning them for this new task, and accompanied Moses and his family to Egypt. Their first presentation to the elders of the people of Israel was well received and inspired hope in their hearts (4:29-31).

If Moses was encouraged with this initial success, it was to be the last good news he would receive for a long time. His and Aaron's first audience with the pharaoh not only was a failure, but actually resulted in a worsening of the lot of the Israelites (Ex. 5). This provoked Moses into a very frank conversation with Yahweh (5:22-6:1), in which he accused Yahweh of not keeping his promise to deliver the people, but Yahweh reassured him that the promise would be kept. The concept of the "Promised Land" is introduced in 6:8. After God had removed the people from oppression, he would bring them to the very land he had promised to Abraham, Isaac, and Jacob.

Chapters 7-12 of Exodus describe in considerable detail the struggles and disappointments experienced by Moses and Aaron in their attempt to persuade the pharaoh to release the Israelites. God sought to encourage the pharaoh to let them go by sending a series of calamities, some of which seem explainable by natural phenomena of the region. But the Egyptian ruler proved extraordinarily stubborn, so much so at times that the biblical writer can account for it only by the strange statement that God had hardened his heart (10:1). Known as the Ten Plagues of Egypt, they are related in rapid succession until chapter 12:1-28 intervenes to describe the origin of the Jewish festival of Passover before the story of the final and most terrifying of the plagues, the death of the Egyptian firstborn (12:29-32). Reaching even into the royal family, this catastrophe finally convinced the pharaoh that he must let these followers of such a powerful God go, lest more Egyptian lives be lost. However, a short time later, realizing that he was about to lose a large supply of cheap labor, the pharaoh changed his mind and tried to stop the Israelites' emigration.

Pharaoh's orders to the army to bring them back precipitated the most severe crisis Moses and his people had to face and set the stage for the great act of God which made all his promises credible. Poised between a body of water in front and the approaching army behind, many of them panicked and others besieged Moses with recrimination and complaint. The mighty act of deliverance dramatically described in 14:21-31 brought exoneration to Moses and belief in the God whom Moses had represented, Yahweh. The body of water which they had to cross in order to escape the pursuing Egyptians was, very likely, not the Red Sea, but the Reed Sea, a much narrower, more shallow body of water nearer to the land of Goshen. An examination of the map of the area will illustrate the improbability of the identification of the crossing site as the present Red Sea (see Map 4, p. 49).

The Wilderness Experience

The event of deliverance we call the exodus, which occurred approximately 1290 B.C., became the most significant happening for the faith of Israel as they recalled the origin of their covenant relationship with Yahweh. When in later years the prophets sought to call the people back into faithful commitment to him, they reminded them that it was he who had brought them up out of the land of Egypt and had given them the land of Canaan. The Passover, the origin of which is connected to the exodus, became

47

the annual ceremony of remembrance of God's deliverance, which set
the stage for the next significant divine act, the establishment
of the Sinai covenant.

The first phase of the actual operation of getting the Israelites out of Egypt was bringing them all together, alluded to
in Ex. 12:37. The number there mentioned causes some difficulty.
If there were 600,000 men, there would have had to be well over
two million persons involved in the great escape! When we recall
that the total given when Jacob and his descendants joined Joseph
in Egypt was only seventy (Ex. 1:5) and that only two midwives
were needed for the entire Hebrew population in the early years o
enslavement, we begin to see the problem. And when we remember
that this group (which also included some non-Israelites) lived
off the wilderness land for a whole generation, we realize that
the census figure is either inaccurate or out of place. Some sch
lars believe that the figure was taken from a much later census b
the writer, simply because it was the only figure available to hi
Others suggest that the word translated "thousand" may also be
translated "clan" or "family," in which case a definite number
would be unattainable.

After the crossing of the sea, Moses led the men in a vic
tory celebration while his sister Miriam stirred the women to
praise Yahweh for his powerful act of deliverance (Ex. 15:1-21).
The next several chapters (Ex. 15:22-19:25) describe something of
the progress made, the route taken, the difficulties encountered,
and the continuing assistance of God during the first months of
Israel's journey toward the "promised land." The places mentione
are Shur, Marah, Elim, the wilderness of Sin, Rephidim, and the
mountain of God (Sinai). The actual location of these sites, how
ever, is unknown to us today.

From the fourth century A.D., Christians have assumed tha
present Jebel Musa, located toward the lower end of the Sinai Peninsula, is the ancient Mt. Sinai. The Monastery of St. Catherin
was built on its northwestern slope in the sixth century. The
wide acceptance of this location for the holy mountain led to the
assigning of other locations between Egypt and Jebel Musa to the
places listed above (see Map 4, p. 49). This "traditional" route
of the exodus is at best uncertain and is regarded by scholars to
day as highly questionable for several reasons: (1) Jebel Musa i
much too far south to be part of a reasonably direct march from
Egypt to Canaan. (2) The area has no signs of volcanic activity,
almost certainly alluded to in Ex. 19. (3) The location does not
fit into the story of Moses' tending Jethro's sheep or Aaron's
meeting him at the mountain of God. (4) The reunion of Moses wit
his wife and children in Ex. 18, which took place at the mountain

Map 4

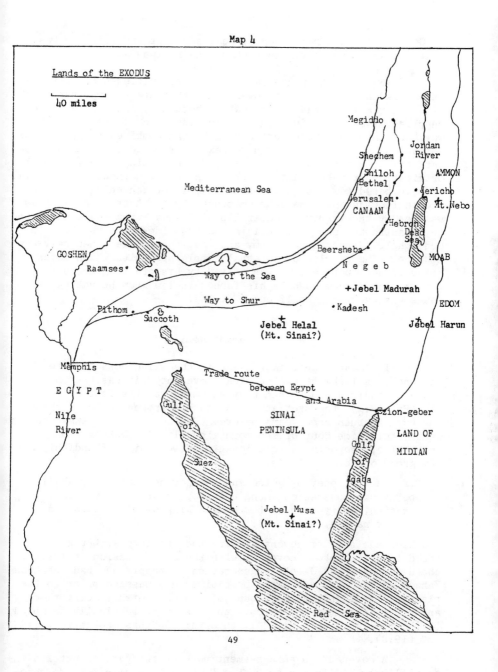

Lands of the EXODUS

40 miles

Megiddo

Jordan River

Shechem

Shiloh

AMMON

Bethel

Mediterranean Sea

Jerusalem · Jericho

CANAAN · Mt. Nebo

Hebron

Dead Sea

GOSHEN

Beersheba

Raamses ·

Way of the Sea

N e g e b

MOAB

Way to Shur

+Jebel Madurah

Pithom ·

· Kadesh

EDOM

Succoth

Jebel Helal
(Mt. Sinai?)

Jebel Harun

Memphis

Trade route

E G Y P T

between Egypt

Ezion-geber

and Arabia

Nile River

SINAI

LAND OF

Gulf

PENINSULA

MIDIAN

of

Gulf

Suez

of

Aqaba

Jebel Musa
(Mt. Sinai?)

Red   Sea

of God, makes much more geographical sense if its location was near Kadesh in the northern part of the Peninsula.

Whatever the route taken, the difficulties encountered and the assistance of Yahweh in overcoming them are an important part of the narrative. Bad water, water shortages, insufficient food supplies, lack of variety in the diet, hostile groups along the way, and internal discontent and bickering combined to provide Moses and Aaron problems enough to tax their patience. Yahweh took care of the water and food problems. His sending manna, probably originating from the tamarisk trees in the wilderness, is especially remembered (Ex. 16) as another example of Yahweh's saving the people from death. The problem caused by the hostile Amalekites was met by the inspired leadership of Joshua, whom Moses appointed to organize the men of Israel into a fighting force which, with God's help, defeated the enemy and gave the people a new self-confidence. The problem of internal complaints, with which Moses tried to deal personally, was solved by his creating a court system, a plan recommended by his father-in-law when he noticed that Moses was wearing himself out (Ex. 18).

The Covenant at Sinai

The most significant event in the wilderness experience was the establishment of the Sinai Covenant. It was the third month of their journey when they encamped at the foot of Mt. Sinai (Ex. 19:1), the spot at which God had spoken to Moses through the burning bush some years before. Now God (Yahweh) spoke to him again, this time "out of the mountain" (19:3). Yahweh took the initiative, proposing a relationship between himself and this motley group of former slaves:

> If you will obey my voice and keep my covenant, you shall
> be my own possession among all peoples; for all the earth
> is mine, and you shall be to me a kingdom of priests and
> a holy nation. (19:5-6)

God had made earlier covenants with the patriarchs, but now he offered to enter into a covenant with the entire nation of Israel, the descendants of Jacob, a generation of people who had not known Yahweh until Moses and Aaron proclaimed his message prior to the plagues. Against the background of Yahweh's mighty deliverance and providential care, the covenant was enthusiastically accepted by the people in unison: "All that the LORD has spoken we will do" (19:8).

A covenant is an agreement between two parties entered into willingly and freely by both. Each party promises to do something with respect to the other, and to abide by the promise until the covenant is dissolved. In the Sinai Covenant God promised to take Israel as his special people, make them a holy nation, and commission them to be his channel of blessing ("priests") to the other nations. Israel promised to obey God and keep his covenant. What that promise involved was revealed to them a short time later.

The Decalogue

After a series of frightful and impressive phenomena, Moses received a further revelation on top of Mount Sinai. Volcanic activity is strongly suggested by the details given: thunder, lightning, thick cloud, smoke, fire, the quaking earth. The revelation Moses received is known as the Ten Commandments (Greek: "Decalogue," meaning ten words), which state what Yahweh expected of Israel in terms of loyalty and conduct. The first one (20:1-3) is really the most fundamental requirement: absolute and exclusive loyalty to the God who had brought Israel out of Egyptian slavery. "You shall have no other gods besides me" ("besides" catches the intent better than "before" in RSV). In a world inhabited by many gods this demand for allegiance to one and exclusion of all others was something new and surprising to the Israelites. The commandment does not presuppose that Yahweh is the only God in existence, which would be a form of monotheism. Rather, it says that, of all the gods which may compete for Israel's devotion, Yahweh is the only one whom Israel shall serve. The term for this attitude is henotheism.

Closely related to the first commandment are those prohibiting idolatry (20:4-5), guarding the divine name (vs. 7), and protecting the sabbath (vss. 8-11). These all deal with the relationship between Yahweh and Israel. The remainder (20:12-17) are designed to protect the family, human life, personal property, and a system of justice. They are the type of laws any civilized society needs to maintain itself.

What is unusual about these commandments is their form. Known as absolute law, as distinguished from conditional law, they simply state what kind of behavior Yahweh will or will not accept, without spelling out the penalty for disobeying them. That is left for the later law codes, such as the "Covenant Code," which follows in Ex. 21-23. It may be that the original form of all ten of these rules was as brief as "You shall not kill," which in Hebrew is actually one word, and that those which are longer have been expanded somewhat for purposes of clarification. Certainly this Decalogue, revealed through Moses, became the heart of the Torah of Israel, and the basis of all the later law codes.

51

The Pentateuch describes no further movement by the migrating Israelites until Numbers 10. The reader naturally infers that all the law codes and cultic regulations recorded in great detail from Exodus 21 through Numbers 9 were part of the revelation to Moses at Sinai. It is likely, however, that most of that vast body of material originated at later times than Moses' and was inserted by the editor(s) at this point in the narrative. The result, probably intended, was the endowing of these codes and rules with the same Mosaic authority that the Decalogue possessed.

The nature and content of this material may be seen through a brief outline:

Exodus 21-23	The "Covenant Code," a body of law, possibly from Joshua's time, dealing with situations in an agricultural society
Exodus 24	Moses receives the Law Tablets on Mt. Sinai
Exodus 25-27	Directions for building the Tent of Meeting and its furnishings
Exodus 28-29	The priesthood is established
Exodus 30	Directions for constructing the Altar of Incense
Exodus 31-32	The Golden Calf incident
Exodus 33-34	The second edition of the Law Tablets
Exodus 35-40	The Tent of Meeting and Altar of Burnt Offering constructed
Leviticus 1-7	Rules of Sacrifice
Leviticus 8-10	Aaron and sons consecrated as priests; duties of the priests
Leviticus 11-15	Laws of cleanness and uncleanness
Leviticus 16	The Day of Atonement instituted
Leviticus 17-26	The Holiness Code, including appointed feasts
Leviticus 27	Laws concerning vows and tithes
Numbers 1-2	A census is taken and leaders appointed
Numbers 3-4	Duties of the Levites
Numbers 5-9	Laws concerning various subjects, including the Nazirite vow

It is clear that most of this section is concerned with matters having to do with the worship of the community. These rules and practices developed over a long period of time and were finally written down by a group of priests, who had a vital stake in such matters, during the Babylonian Exile (6th century B.C.).

The Tabernacle and Ark of the Covenant

One of the things which emerge from the last half of Exodus is the central place of the portable structure known as the Tabernacle, or Tent of Meeting, in the worship of Israel prior to Solomon's day. Made of animal skins attached to wooden poles, it could be rather easily taken down, transported to the next camp site, and set up again. The Levites (men of the tribe of Levi) were responsible for this task. The Tabernacle itself was quite small, measuring approximately 45' by 15', and surrounded by a court enclosed by a fence. The most sacred of its two rooms, the Holy of Holies, contained the Ark of the Covenant, the most sacred cultic object of the Israelites. Only the high priest was permitted entrance and he only on the Day of Atonement.

The other room, the Holy Place, into which only priests could enter, held three furnishings: the altar of incense, a seven-branched lampstand, and a table containing the Bread of the Presence. In the courtyard just outside the entrance to this room was the Altar of Burnt Offering, on which animal sacrifices were offered to God. Nearby was the laver, a basin containing water for the use of the priests before and after the sacrifice was made.

The Ark of the Covenant was a box-like object containing the Tablets of the Law and perhaps other items which were representative of the covenant relationship between Yahweh and Israel. On top of the Ark was a mercy seat made of gold, which was said to represent the presence of Yahweh. In time, the Ark was considered to have magical properties, and it played a significant role during the days of the Judges and the early years of the monarchy. When the Temple of Solomon was built, the Ark was given a permanent resting place, at least until the destruction of the Temple in 587 B.C. The record does not say what happened to it after that.

Sacrifice in Israel's Cult

The reader of the Pentateuch can not avoid the impression that animal and cereal sacrifice played a dominant role in the worship of ancient Israel. Just when and how this practice began among the Hebrews is uncertain. A verse in the book of Amos (5:25)

53

implies that it was not part of the wilderness experience. There
can be little doubt, however, that sacrificial worship was an important element in the religion of Israel from the early years of
their settlement in Canaan up to the time of the Fall of Jerusalem

Essential to the idea of sacrifice was the presentation of
the victim to God as a gift. The priests, who were the necessary
mediators between the deity and the worshipers and who did the actual offering of the victim, were the ones who benefited directly
from such gifts to the deity, for they depended upon them for
their food. The gift was presented to the deity for different
reasons. Sometimes it was to influence God to do something for
the worshiper. Sometimes it was in fulfillment of a vow made by
the worshiper to give God something in return for what God was expected to do for him. Other types of sacrifices were expiatory in
nature; that is, the animal's life was offered to God in lieu of
the life of the worshiper, which God could have required for a
grave offense against his laws. Other sacrificial acts were done
to preserve a communion between God and the worshiper.

To make a sacrifice, of course, cost the sacrificer something, whether the victim came from his own flock or field or whether he had to purchase it. The rules allowed a poor man to offer
a less expensive victim than the more affluent one. The prophets
were very critical of the attitude that a person could make up for
his lack of obedience by simply offering more sacrifices. Animal
sacrifice was suspended from the time Solomon's Temple was destroy
ed until the Second Temple was built (515 B.C.), and permanently
discontinued after Herod's Temple was demolished in 70 A.D.

The Holy Days

It is not known precisely when the full annual calendar of
fast and feast days became fixed, but the P and D portions of the
Pentateuch describe the more ancient ones in considerable detail.
These are:

The Passover. This commemorates the exodus event and is
designed to remind later generations of the bitter experience of
slavery from which Yahweh delivered the Israelites (who were in
Egypt) by his mighty acts of intervention. The name "Passover"
comes from the fact that, when the messenger of death visited the
Egyptian homes in the tenth plague, he passed over the homes of
the Israelites. Their doorposts had been marked with the blood of
the lamb slain in the afternoon for consumption at the evening
meal. The Day of Passover continues to be observed with a family
meal whose ingredients symbolize the experience of that last night

54

in Egypt. It falls on the 14th of the Jewish month Nisan, which is in March or April of the modern calendar.

The Day of Atonement. In Hebrew the name is Yom Kippur, a day of fasting on which the people confessed the sins of the past year and sought forgiveness. As described in Leviticus 16, it featured the "scapegoat" ceremony, ending with a goat's symbolically carrying away the people's sins. It was on this day alone that the high priest entered the Holy of Holies, bearing animals about to be offered as sacrifices. It is regarded as the most solemn day of the Jewish year.

The Feast of Weeks (later known as Pentecost). Falling in late spring, this began as a celebration of the grain harvest but later became the holiday commemorating the revelation of the Ten Commandments.

The Feast of Booths (or Tabernacles). A fall harvest festival similar in emphasis to our national Thanksgiving, this comes five days after the somber Day of Atonement, reminding the people that God is the true source of their blessings.

Two other festivals came into existence later in Israel's history. The book of Esther explains the origin of the Feast of Purim, which celebrates the triumph of the Jews over the scheming Haman. The apocryphal book known as I Maccabees describes how the festival of Hanukkah was instituted to celebrate the Jews' great victory over the oppressing Syrians and the rededication of the cleansed Temple. Purim falls in February or March, and Hanukkah comes in December.

The Sabbath, the last day of the week, is the only special day mentioned in the Decalogue and is considered by Jews the most important of all holy days. It is mentioned very frequently in both the Old and the New Testament and combines the ideas of rest, worship, and celebration of God as creator. The Jewish sabbath begins at sunset on Friday and ends at the same time on Saturday.

The priests, who have been mentioned frequently above, formed a significant class of professional religious leaders from the early history of Israel. The Pentateuch specifies that they shall be males descended from Aaron and carefully guards their purity by a host of strict qualifications and rules. They enjoyed a privileged position among their fellow Israelites, who regarded them as necessary mediators between themselves and God. There were occasional clashes between them and another group of leaders, the prophets, whose activites will be discussed later.

Following the mass of legal materials, Numbers 10 resumes the narrative of Israel's trek through the wilderness en route to the promised land of Canaan. There were still many problems to be faced by their aging leader, including criticism by his own brother and sister for marrying a woman of whom they did not approve (Num. 12:1-2). As they neared southern Canaan, the people's minds naturally turned to the actual taking over of the land of their dreams. Numbers 13 tells of Moses' decision, at Yahweh's direction, to send one man from each of the twelve tribes to gather information about the area in preparation for a possible invasion. The spies were unanimous in reporting the fertility of the land and the strength of the defenses. They disagreed, however, on the recommendations of the course the Israelites should follow. Ten of them recommended postponement of invasion, but Joshua and Caleb expressed confidence that they could win.

The majority opinion prevailed, which provoked a crisis in the morale of the group. Some of them actually wanted to return to Egypt, an attitude which Yahweh interpreted as a lack of faith in him as their God. The Joshua mentioned above is the same person who had successfully led the Israelites in battle against the Amalekites shortly after they had left Egypt, and the same Joshua who would head the conquest of Canaan after the death of Moses. He and Caleb would be the only exceptions to God's judgment that none of the Israelites who were adults when they left Egypt would be privileged to enter the promised land (Num. 14:20-24).

The problems of Moses were not yet ended. A group of the Israelites were not willing to postpone their entry into Canaan and, against Moses' advice, attempted to invade from the south, but without success. Some time later a sizeable revolt, usually called Korah's rebellion, against the leadership of Moses and Aaron occurred (Num. 16). It was put down and the rebels were severely punished. A water shortage at Kadesh and an encounter with "fiery serpents" in the vicinity of the Dead Sea added to the events which prevented boredom for Moses (Num. 21).

It seems likely that the greater part of the forty years (roughly, a generation) of wandering and waiting to get into the new land was spent in the area of Kadesh, where the death of Miriam occurred (Num. 20:1). Kadesh (Deuteronomy refers to it as Kadesh-barnea) was probably situated about sixty miles south of Beersheba, the southernmost town of Canaan. During their encampment there the younger generation was replacing the original freed slaves, and Moses abandoned the idea of invading Canaan from the south.

The decision seems to have been made to try to enter Canaan from the east, which meant the Israelites would have to come up the eastern side of the Dead Sea. They met some resistance, most of which they overcame by military action. But Numbers relates a rather long story about the attempt of the king of Moab to resist the advance of Israel by hiring a professional soothsayer, Balaam, to pronounce a curse on them. This did not work because Yahweh intervened and caused Balaam to bless them instead (Num. 22-24). A summary of the entire journey from Egypt to Mt. Hor, where Aaron died, is given in Numbers 33. The tribes of Reuben and Gad were permitted to settle down in Transjordan in return for their promise to assist the other tribes in conquering the land west of the Jordan River. The Numbers account ends with the Israelites encamped near Mt. Nebo, not far from the northern end of the Dead Sea and east of the Jordan.

Significant terms, names, and dates for this chapter
<u>Significant terms, names, and dates for this chapter</u>

Egypt	Decalogue
Goshen	henotheism
Exodus	monotheism
Moses	Covenant Code
Jochebed	Tent of Meeting
Reuel	Levites
Jethro	Day of Atonement
Zipporah	Ark of the Covenant
Midian	Holy of Holies
Mt. Horeb	Holy Place
Mt. Sinai	sacrifices
Aaron	Passover
Miriam	Feast of Weeks
1290 B.C.	Feast of Booths
Jebel Musa	Sabbath
Kadesh	Balaam
Joshua	Mt. Nebo
Caleb	

CHAPTER V

A CALL TO RENEWAL

Biblical materials: Deuteronomy

Essential reading: Deuteronomy 34; 6; 12; 16; 28:1-24

The final book in the Pentateuch is crucial to the understanding of the religion of Israel as well as of the Old Testament
history from Moses to the Fall of Jerusalem. Deuteronomy, meaning
"Second Law," was the name given it when it was translated into
the Greek Septuagint. Those responsible for this name considered
the book to be primarily a repetition of the laws contained in Exodus, Leviticus, and Numbers. However, as we shall see, it is far
more than a restatement of earlier law. From a literary point of
view, Deuteronomy consists mainly of three speeches delivered by
Moses to Israel during the final stages of its wilderness journey
toward Canaan.

The first speech (chs. 1-4) reviews the events from the
time Israel left Sinai (called Horeb in Deut.) until they reached
Mount Pisgah, possibly the highest peak of Mount Nebo. The second
speech (chs. 5-28) contains another version of the Decalogue found
in Exodus 20, an expansion of the Covenant Code in Exodus 21-23
and other ordinances in Leviticus and Numbers, in addition to
strong warnings against disobedience of God's law. The shorter
third speech (chs. 29-30) reiterates points made in the previous
one, especially the importance of keeping the Torah. After the
song and blessing of chapters 32-33 the book concludes with a
brief chapter (34) reporting the death of Moses.

In order to complete the narrative of Moses' career, we
shall examine chapter 34 before considering the other contents of
Deuteronomy. The description of the scene includes the names of
both Nebo and Pisgah, from which high point Moses got a partial
view of the destination toward which he had been leading this wavering group of people, through seemingly insuperable obstacles
and discouragement, for the past forty years. Moses himself did
not experience the elation of actually entering the promised land,
but he felt the satisfaction of having accomplished the task for
which he was commissioned at the site of the burning bush.

Significantly, the narrative points out that "no man knows

the place of his burial to this day," suggesting the passage of a long period of time between Moses' death and the time of writing. The age given for Moses was intended to indicate his significance; no person afterward, whose age is given, ever lived so long. The appraisal in vss. 10-12 includes the comment, "There has not arisen a prophet since in Israel like Moses."

The Mosaic Faith

Although the narrative does not mention it in this obituary of Moses, it is certainly true that there is another contribution he made which is equal in importance to the leadership of the exodus. That is his role as lawgiver, which led to the assumption in later years that Moses was the author of the entire Pentateuch. The fact that the vast majority of the words in the book of Deuteronomy are attributed directly to Moses reflects the traditional connection of Moses with Israelite law. Most, if not all, of the second speech (chs. 5-28) is very likely the "book of the law" accidentally discovered by workmen who were repairing the Temple in 621 B.C. (II Kings 22:8-20).

That book's origin is unknown, but it may have been produced in the northern kingdom of Israel prior to its fall, as a part of a "back-to-Moses" movement. If so, it was then carried southward to the only remaining center of the religion of Yahweh, Jerusalem. Its discovery came shortly after the reign of a faithless and idolatrous king in Judah, when the faith of that kingdom's people had sunk to a low ebb. The youthful and energetic new King Josiah, who had ordered the Temple's complete cleaning and restoration, used this document (the "D" or Deuteronomic code identified above as a source of the Pentateuch) as the basis for a reformation of Judah's religion. The beginning and ending chapters of Deuteronomy (1-4 and 29-34) appear to be later additions to the original work.

Although the structure of Deuteronomy as basically three speeches of Moses is surely a literary device used by a writer some time after 621 B.C., it is not inaccurate to say that the book is a sincere effort to present an interpretation of the covenant faith in the spirit of Moses. Thus there is some repetition of laws already recorded in other books of the Pentateuch, but there is also a great deal of reinterpretation, expansion, and humanizing of older law codes. It is quite possible that the teaching of the eighth century prophets (Amos, Hosea, Isaiah, and Micah) has influenced some of the attitudes reflected in Deuteronomy. A few of the distinctive themes in the book will now be considered.

1. The continuing relevance of the covenant relationship.
The introduction to the Decalogue includes the significant statement:

> The LORD our God made a covenant with us in Horeb. Not with our fathers did the LORD make this covenant, but with us, who are all of us alive this day. (5:2-3)

Each generation is called upon to realize the significance of the basic conviction that "The LORD your God has chosen you to be a people for his own possession, out of all the peoples that are on the face of the earth" (7:6) and the origin of that concept of chosenness (6:20-25).

2. The insistence of Yahweh upon total and exclusive devotion to himself. In what the Jews call the Shem'a,

> Hear, O Israel: The LORD our God is one LORD; and you shall love the LORD your God with all your heart, and with all your soul, and with all your might. (6:4-5)

this emphasis is stated, and followed by a command to the parents to saturate the children with knowledge of the Torah (6:6-9). The temptation for Israel to worship other gods was great throughout its history, requiring continual reminders from the prophets of this fundamental commandment.

3. Yahweh's concern for social justice. In prophetic-sounding terms Deuteronomy calls for humane provision for the welfare of orphans, widows, foreigners, slaves, and the poor (10:18-19; 15:7-18). An incorrupt system of justice is a must:

> You shall not pervert justice; you shall not show partiality; and you shall not take a bribe, for a bribe blinds the eyes of the wise and subverts the cause of the righteous.
> (16:19)

4. Israel's possession of the land of Canaan as a gift and a privilege. The people must never be allowed to forget that Yahweh brought them out of bondage, through the wilderness, and into this land. Just as he gave it to them, he can take it away from them. Keeping his commandments and retaining possession of the land are tied together:

> You shall therefore keep all the commandments which I command you this day, that you may be strong, and go in and take possession of the land which you are going over to possess, and that you may live long in the land which the LORD swore to your fathers to give to them and to their descendants.
> (11:8-9)

60

5. The two ways between which Israel must choose. Closely related to the preceding theme # 4, this pervasive concept is often called the Deuteronomic Theology. Most completely spelled out in ch. 28, it is succinctly put in 30:15-20:

> See, I have set before you this day life and good, death and evil. If you obey the commandments of the LORD . . . the LORD your God will bless you in the land which you are entering to take possession of it. But if your heart turns away, and you will not hear, but are drawn away to worship other gods and serve them, I declare to you this day, that you shall perish; you shall not live long in the land . . . therefore choose life, that you and your descendants may live.

In clear, stark simplicity Israel is told: Obey the Lord's commandments and he will bless you with protection, prosperity, and a good life; disobey them and you will experience invasion, poverty, and a hard life. You, as a people, must make the choice.

6. The importance of purity in worship. When the Israelites took possession of Canaan, they had to settle among the non-Israelites who were already there. They were commanded to maintain their separateness from the local people and their gods. Intermarriage was forbidden (7:3-4), idolatrous worship centers were to be destroyed (7:5; 12:1-3), and Israel's worship was to be centralized in one particular place (12:13-14). The place is not named in Deuteronomy but the people of Judah understood that Jerusalem was intended. The feast of Passover, the celebration which reminded Israel of who they were and the covenant relationship with Yahweh, was to be faithfully observed each year (16:1-8).

Several of the features mentioned above are the same as described in II Kings 23 as part of the reformation under King Josiah: destruction of Baal worship centers, concentration of all sacrificial worship at Jerusalem, and resumption of keeping the Passover. This is strong evidence for the probability that part of Deuteronomy came from the newly found law code Josiah was following.

The Deuteronomic History

Immediately following the Pentateuch in all Bibles is a large body of historical material, which the Hebrews term the Former Prophets but which Christians call the Historical Books. This material, Joshua through II Kings (omitting Ruth), tells the story of Israel from the conquest of Canaan through the fall of Jerusalem in 587 B.C. Composed in the early years of the Babylonian exile, it records the history of God's people from the viewpoint of the book of Deuteronomy, hence is often referred to as the Deuteronomic History. Especially themes five and six above can be seen at work throughout the document.

The ups and downs of the fortunes of Israel are explained on the basis of the Deuteronomic Theology, the belief that God blesses the nation when it obeys his commandments and punishes it when it disobeys. The sin of idolatry, worshiping gods other than Yahweh, was the cause of much of the suffering and defeat they experienced. The failure to destroy the altars scattered through the countryside and to confine the sacrificial worship to Jerusalem was another reason for their misfortune. These evidences of the people's disobedience to the terms of the covenant are closely related to the themes in Deuteronomy.

Significant terms and names for this chapter

Deuteronomy
Pisgah
Shem'a
Josiah
621 B.C.
Deuteronomic Theology
Deuteronomic History

CHAPTER VI

THE PROMISED LAND

Biblical materials: Joshua.   Judges

Essential reading: Joshua 4-6; 10; 24
                     Judges 1-2; 7; 11; 14

The Pentateuch closes with the Israelites poised on the edge of the land of their destiny. They had earlier learned that, even though it had been promised them by Yahweh, it was already occupied by other peoples who were not willing to share it with a large group of newcomers. This meant that they would have to fight for it, a course for which they had had some preparation in their struggles with Edom and Moab on the eastern side of the Dead Sea.

Those who had preceded them into the area are referred to variously as Canaanites, Amorites, and Hittites, as well as other names. Politically they existed as many independent city-states, each with its own king. An exception to this was a group of five of these cities in southern Canaan which formed a coalition to try to repel the Israelite invasion. There was no over-all Canaanite government at the time; nor was there an outside power in control of that region at this period. Egypt and the Hittite Empire had alternated in controlling Canaan in the decades preceding the Israelite conquest but a costly war between the two powers had left them both relatively weak in the thirteenth century B.C. This favored the Israelites' plans, for they arrived around the middle of that century. Although we can not be precise in dating the events of this period, we can suggest an approximate date for the escape from Egypt as 1290 B.C., and for the beginning of the conquest, c. 1250 B.C.

The Conquest according to Joshua

The Deuteronomic History contains two accounts of the conquest of Canaan, which differ from each other in quite important details. Joshua 1-12 describes it as a swift and destructive invasion, with all tribes participating under the leadership of Moses' successor, Joshua. Taking up the story at the point described in Deuteronomy 34, it presents Joshua making preparations for

63

the crossing of the Jordan River and the attack on Jericho, a well fortified city guarding the pass which leads into central Canaan. Since chapter four gives two versions of the crossing of the river the historian must have had more than one source at his disposal. The first campsite west of the Jordan was Gilgal, the exact location of which is unknown today. Joshua 6 tells the celebrated story of the capture of Jericho, whose walls "fell down flat" following the unconventional attack by marching, blowing trumpets, and shouting. The victory was seen as another example of Yahweh's powerful intervention on behalf of his covenant people. In fact, the battle of Jericho was part of a "holy war," fought on God's orders and in his name (6:2-7). In a holy war the rule of <u>cherem</u> was in effect, a fact brought out in the story of the next battle.

The <u>cherem</u> rule says that all life and goods in the enemy city belong to the deity of the attacking force; hence no spoil is to be taken and no life is to be spared. When the attack on Ai ended in embarrassing defeat of Joshua's forces, Joshua concluded that someone in his army had disobeyed the <u>cherem</u> rule in the previous battle and that this defeat was God's punishment for the violation. One can see the deuteronomic viewpoint in this story: disobedience is followed by punishment. When the guilty individual was identified and severely punished, the army resumed its winning ways (Joshua 7-8).

After the central hill country was taken, Joshua's forces moved into southern Canaan and defeated the city-states which had banded together in a vain attempt to resist them. The conquest is summarized in 10:40-42 and 11:16-23 as total and complete under Joshua's brilliant leadership:

> So Joshua defeated the whole land, the hill country and the
> Negeb and the lowland and the slopes, and all their kings;
> he left none remaining, but utterly destroyed all that
> breathed, as the LORD God of Israel commanded. (10:40)

Yet a few chapters later we encounter the surprising information that, in the waning years of Joshua's life, there was still a large portion of Canaan not under the control of the tribes of Israel (13:1-7).

In the remainder of chapter 13 and chapters 14-22, there is a detailed description of how the land was apportioned among the tribes (see Map 5), even though it would be quite some time before they could totally possess it. For the most part, the tribes bear the same names as the twelve sons of Jacob, listed in Genesis 35:23-26 and Exodus 1:1-5. However, instead of a tribe named Joseph there are two tribes bearing the names of Joseph's sons, Ephraim and Manasseh. The tribe of Simeon lost its identity

Map 5

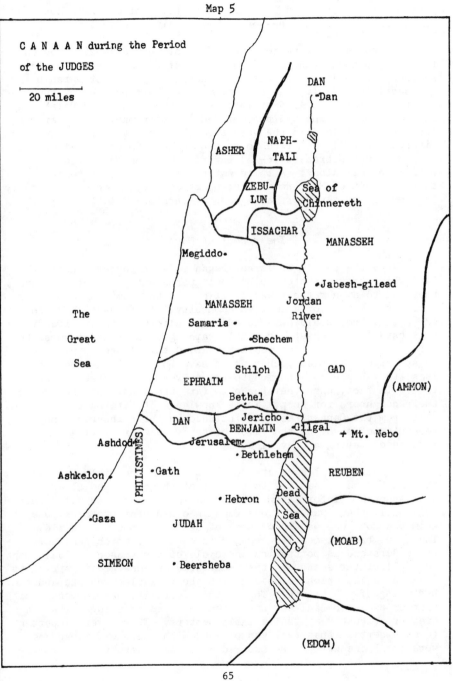

C A N A A N during the Period
of the JUDGES

20 miles

DAN
·Dan

NAPH-
TALI

ASHER

ZEBU-
LUN

Sea of
Chinnereth

ISSACHAR

MANASSEH

Megiddo·

·Jabesh-gilead

MANASSEH

Jordan
River

Samaria ·

·Shechem

The

Great

Sea

Shiloh

GAD

EPHRAIM

(AMMON)

Bethel

·

DAN

Jericho ·

Gilgal

(PHILISTINES)

BENJAMIN

+ Mt. Nebo

Ashdod·

Jerusalem·

·Bethlehem

Ashkelon ·

·Gath

REUBEN

·Gaza

· Hebron

Dead

Sea

J U D A H

(MOAB)

SIMEON

· Beersheba

(EDOM)

when it became absorbed into the large tribe of Judah. Thus the total number of the tribes of Israel remained twelve.

From all the tedious specifics of Joshua 14-22 a few interesting points stand out. The tribe of Levi was given no land. As those responsible for the maintenance of places of worship and the sacrificial cult, the Levites were to be supported by the other tribes (13:14). Also of interest is the request of Caleb, one of the two spies who had recommended invasion many years earlier, for a piece of land in the very area the other ten spies had considered too well fortified to be conquered. So he was given the region around Hebron (14:6-15) in order that he could prove he had been right all along! A third notable item is the statement (18:1) that the Tent of Meeting was set up at Shiloh, which was centrally located in the territory assigned to Ephraim.

The Appeal of Baalism

As the people of Israel began to gain possession of the land which they expected to be their permanent place of residence, they had to adjust their way of life from the semi-nomadic desert existence to that of a settled community. This meant that, for one thing, they would have to add agriculture to their already well-established sheep and cattle raising as a means of subsistence. As they faced the reality that, until a more complete conquest could take place, they would have to live among the Canaanites, they began to accommodate themselves to co-existence with them. In fact, when they began to farm the land, they turned to their neighbors for help. Their knowledge of farming the new land came from the Canaanites, who included in their instructions the necessity of securing the favor of the local fertility gods to be assured of having good yields.

These local gods are called Baals in the Bible, and were thought by the Canaanites to be sons of the chief god El and his wife Asherah. Information found by archaeologists suggests that originally there was only one Baal, who had many brothers, one of whom was Mot, who was in control of death and the underworld. These two brother-deities engaged in conflict, which Baal worshipers understood as portraying the cycle of the seasons. Baal spent the fall/winter season in the underworld and emerged in spring to live on earth, which coincided with the revival of nature and the beginning of new growth. The earth's fertility was connected with that of Baal, so Baal worship often included relations with "sacred prostitutes" at Baal worship centers. It was very important to make certain that Baal was pleased with one's offerings and worship if one were to be assured of a good harvest.

Baalism constituted a powerful threat to pure Yahwism, as taught by Moses and continued under Joshua. This threat underlay the big convocation described in Joshua 24, which says that "the elders, the heads, the judges, and the officers" of the Israelite tribes responded to Joshua's summons to a meeting to be held at Shechem, located in Manasseh's territory, about ten miles north of Shiloh. It is probable that Joshua chose Shechem because it was occupied by people related to or friendly to the Israelites. It is the only area which they did not have to fight to gain control of. The aging Joshua addressed the representatives of the people, reviewing the history of Israel from Abraham to the present. This may have been designed to bring Shechemites up-to-date on Yahweh's activity in offering a covenant and being God to Israel, in the hope that they would join with him and those who had shared the wilderness experience and the struggle to possess Canaan, in pledging allegiance to Yahweh.

Joshua's speech concluded with a ringing call for a decision:

"Choose this day whom you will serve, whether the gods your fathers served in the region beyond the River, or the gods of the Amorites in whose land you dwell; but as for me and my house, we will serve the LORD." (24:15)

Remembering the insistence of Moses and the Decalogue that Yahweh's people worship only Yahweh, and fully aware of the pull of Baalism upon a population seeking to make a living in a new land, Joshua reminded them that they could not be both Baal-worshipers and Yahweh-worshipers. His challenge met with a positive response (24:16-24) and a solemn promise: "We also will serve the LORD, for he is our God."

Like Moses, Joshua functioned as both leader of the people and lawgiver.

So Joshua made a covenant with the people that day, and made statutes and ordinances for them at Shechem. And Joshua wrote these words in the book of the law of God.
(24:25-26)

It may be that the law mediated by Joshua is found in Exodus 21-23, which we earlier labeled the Covenant Code. What Joshua wrote in that book became a sort of constitution to guide the loosely connected tribes in the difficult years that lay ahead. He was the last leader they would have for a long time who could in any sense be called a national leader. Each tribe was independent of the others. They were held together in a kind of tribal confederacy only by their common ancestry and history, their faith in Yahweh, and the responsibility of the other eleven tribes to provide for

67

the tribe of Levi. The statement that Joshua was 110 years old when he died is the historian's way of evaluating him and his contribution to Israel as only slightly less than Moses' (24:29).

Another View of the Conquest: Judges

The second account of the conquest of Canaan is told in the book of Judges. Purporting to tell the story of what happened after Joshua's death, the very first verse challenges the version of the conquest we saw in Joshua:

> After the death of Joshua the people of Israel inquired of the LORD, "Who shall go up first for us against the Canaanites, to fight against them?"

Judges 1:2-2:5 mentions instance after instance in which the Canaanites had not been displaced or destroyed, with the result that the members of the various tribes had to live among them. The swift, complete conquest reflected in the first part of Joshua is seriously qualified by the story in Judges, which is surely closer to the actual situation. The statement of 1:19 perhaps gives an accurate clue to the facts:

> And the LORD was with Judah, and he took possession of the hill country, but he could not drive out the inhabitants of the plain, because they had chariots of iron.

Archaeological evidence supports this explanation. Israelite objects found in remains of hill country settlements are older than those found in cities of the lowland.

The reader of Judges may be surprised when he gets to the report of the death and burial of Joshua (2:6-10), told in almost the same words found in Joshua 24:29-31. This suggests the use of multiple sources by the final editor of the Deuteronomic History, as we have noted before and will have occasion to point out again.

Judges 2:6-3:6 clearly reflects the Deuteronomic theology of history, which understands good times to be the result of faithfulness to Yahweh and hard times, defeat, and oppression as necessary consequences of the people's disobedience and lack of faith. It depicts a recurring pattern of apostasy--oppression--repentance --deliverance, which characterizes the period of the Judges (c. 1200-1025 B.C.). The apostasy (falling away) phase is described in 2:11-13, followed by the oppression phase in vss. 14-15. Repentance is not so clearly stated but is implied in 2:18b. Deliverance happened when God decided the people had suffered enough and had seen the error of their ways. He "raised up judges"(2:16) to save them. The judges, from whom the book gets its name, were

charismatic leaders who were able to inspire their fellow tribesmen to unite with them in a military-type operation in order to
drive out the oppressing enemy and restore order to the area.

Some of the enemies were invaders from outside Canaan,
such as the Mesopotamians, the Midianites, and the Ammonites. But
some were the local Canaanites whom Joshua had not succeeded in
displacing. An interesting interpretation is found in 2:23: "So
the LORD left those nations, not driving them out at once, and he
did not give them into the power of Joshua." The historian goes
on to say, in 3:1-6, that the LORD made use of these peoples in
the oppression phase of the cycle mentioned above to discipline
and punish the Israelites when they became disobedient. We should
also note that the relations between Israel and the Canaanites included not only competitive strife but intermarriage and mixing of
religions (3:6)!

Having explained the role and function of the judges in
general, the historian, in 3:7-12:15, recounts the activity of a
series of specific judges, some very briefly and others at considerable length. Careful reading of these stories will reveal the
fact that the judges were all local leaders; that is, their leadership usually extended over not more than three tribes, and not one
of them was a leader of all the tribes. This means that several
of them could have been acting to end the oppression of their respective tribes at the same time. It also means that the length
of the period of the judges can not be determined by totaling the
years given for the individual judges.

We shall include consideration only of those judges who
receive longer treatment in the book. The only one who is described as having actually functioned as a judge in the modern sense is
also the only female judge, Deborah (chs. 4-5). Also called a pro-
phetess, Deborah relied upon Barak (not called a judge) to be the
military leader of three Israelite tribes in defending themselves
against an army of Canaanites. Another woman, Jael, became a he-
roine when she single-handedly killed the exhausted Canaanite general Sisera. Her patriotic deed is celebrated in a song (ch. 5)
which scholars believe to be one of the oldest pieces of literature in the Bible.

The story of Gideon (also known as Jerubbaal) is the longest of all the tales of the judges, chapters 6-9. The fact that
he decided to wait until after dark to destroy the local Baal
shrine indicates the degree to which Baalism had been accepted by
some Israelites. Gideon is best remembered for his careful selection and training of 300 men and his using them in a strategy of

deception and surprise to rout a combined force of Midianites and Amalekites. His victory made him so popular that the people of Manasseh and neighboring tribes asked him to become their king. He refused on the ground that only Yahweh should be their king. However, one of his seventy-one sons, Abimelech, was not so squeamish and offered himself for the job. The name given him by his mother may have contributed to his ambition for its meaning is "my father is king!" Some of the citizens of Shechem responded by declaring him king. After three years of cruel, despotic rule over a small area, Abimelech was assassinated and the matter of having a king for Israel was laid to rest for a while.

An interesting and tragic figure who appears among the judges is Jephthah (chs. 11-12), an illegitimate son who was driven from his home by jealous relatives and took up a life of brigandage among non-Israelite peoples east of the Sea of Galilee. When the elders of Manasseh could not find a person to organize resistance against the invading Ammonites, they remembered Jephthah, sought him out, and begged him to come home and lead the fight. He agreed only on the condition that they make him their ruler after the enemy was defeated. With success and respectability riding on victory, Jephthah made what is often called a "foolish vow" to God to ensure his help in battle (11:30-31). His brilliant victory turned into personal tragedy when he understood his keeping of the vow to require the sacrifice of his daughter.

Mighty Enemy of the Philistines

Some time during the period of the judges a new group of immigrants had arrived in Canaan, the Philistines. Coming in boats from some islands in the Aegean Sea in search of a new homeland, they gained a foothold on the coast of southern Canaan and quickly began to expand inward. Eventually their influence was so great that men began to refer to the land by "Palestine" rather than Canaan. They are first mentioned in Judges 3:31, but it is not until chapter 13 that they are said to have caused problems for the small tribe of Dan.

A colorful member of that tribe, Samson, is the judge whose legendary exploits against them are described in Judges 13-16. Unlike the earlier judges, Samson did not lead an army against the enemy but chose to use his divinely-given personal strength to deal with them. According to the accounts in the book of Judges, he was quite successful in containing the Philistines until he was betrayed by Delilah. After Samson's death the Philistine expansion continued, causing the tribe of Dan to resettle in the far north, and eventually leading many Israelites to demand that a king be appointed to repel their inroads.

The lack of a king, says the historian, may have been responsible for other deplorable conditions of the period. Judges ends with the comment, "In those days there was no king in Israel; every man did what was right in his own eyes." A review of the stories of the judges, together with the sordid accounts of happenings in chs. 17-21, reveals that the moral and religious level was very low. Murder, torture, paganism, deception, inter-tribal war, stealing, kidnapping, and general lack of justice characterized this dark period in the history of Israel.

The religion of Moses was almost forgotten; the covenant with Yahweh established through him and renewed by Joshua was largely ignored. Pressure from invading enemies combined with temptations of Baal worship and lack of national leadership brought moral chaos and a religious crisis. The conquest of Canaan, which had begun so vigorously under Joshua, was still not completed. The aggression of the Philistines made the task much more difficult and, in fact, Israel did not gain total control of the land until the reign of David in the early part of the tenth century B.C.

Significant terms, names, and dates for this chapter

1290 B.C.	charismatic
1250 B.C.	Deborah
Joshua	Jael
Jericho	apostasy
Gilgal	Gideon
cherem	Abimelech
Baalism	Jephthah
Baal	Philistines
Asherah	Samson
Shechem	Delilah
Judge	Tribal Confederacy

CHAPTER VII

NATIONHOOD AND MONARCHY

Biblical materials: I Samuel

Essential reading: I Samuel 2:12-26; 3:19-4:18; 7-13
                                16:14-18:16; 31

The tribal confederacy inaugurated by Joshua was inade-
quate for the problems Israel had to face in the twelfth and elev
enth centuries B.C. The judges, gifted and dedicated as they wer
could not attain the unity and maintain the military strength nee
ed to withstand the advancing Philistines. Some of the influenti
elders among the Israelites began looking for a more effective sy
tem for defending the people and their possessions. I Samuel is
the story of how the transition was made from the loose league of
tribes to the beginnings of a monarchy. At the center of this
saga of change is a strong and unique man named Samuel. Trained
to be a priest, he functioned also as a judge and was known as a
prophet. He had the distinction of selecting, anointing, and
crowning Israel's first king, although probably not willingly. H
also anointed David, destined to become Israel's second and great
est monarch, but did not live to take part in his coronation.

The Priest, Judge, and Prophet

In continuation of the history from the book of Judges,
the Deuteronomic historian introduces Samuel as a child given to
Hannah, wife of an Ephraimite named Elkanah, in answer to prayer.
True to her vow, she turned him over to Eli for schooling in the
priesthood. The aging Eli, officiating priest at Shiloh, where
the Ark of the Covenant was located, was greatly distressed by th
immoral character and conduct of his two sons, who were also
priests. I Sam. 2:22-30 explains why Samuel, who was not of the
family of Aaron or from the tribe of Levi, was made Eli's successor instead of one of Eli's own sons.

Samuel's role as a prophet (one who speaks for God) is
stated in I Sam. 3:19-21, but it may be questioned that his reputation extended into all twelve tribes, which is what "from Dan t
Beersheba" implies. His judging activity is described in 7:15-17
from which it is clear that his concept of the judge's role was

72

not the same as that of Gideon or Jephthah. Never a military leader, Samuel held court on an annual circuit, which included his home town, Ramah, and three other towns, all of which were within the small tribe of Benjamin or not far from its borders.

The series of events narrated in I Sam. 4-6 indicates that the Philistine threat was an increasingly serious problem for the Israelites. Without Eli's knowledge the Ark of the Covenant was taken into battle against the Philistines, very likely on the assumption that it possessed magical powers. Its presence would guarantee the victory of Yahweh's forces. In an amazingly objective report (4:5-11) the Philistine viewpoint is presented. The presence of Israel's sacred object among its forces only motivated the Philistines to fight harder, with the result that the Israelites were defeated, the sons of Eli were slain, and the Ark was captured by the enemy. News of such a horrible combination of disasters was too much for the elderly, overweight priest. The report of his sudden death is followed by the information that he had also served as judge, probably in the manner of Samuel (4:15-18).

The Philistines kept the holy Ark for seven months, displaying it in several of their cities. But so many unhappy events occurred in those cities that the inhabitants concluded that they were caused by the presence of Israel's Ark. It was then returned to Israel and set up at Kiriathjearim (7:1-2), located on the border between the tribes of Judah and Benjamin. Shiloh had probably been destroyed by the Philistines, for it is no longer mentioned in the historical record.

Israel Gets a King

That Samuel was Israel's last judge and that he selected and anointed her first king are facts which are not in doubt. But the same can not be said of the attitude of Samuel toward the idea of having a king or the manner in which he went about selecting one. For in I Sam. 7-12 there are two very different versions of how the monarchy was established and of Samuel's role in the process. Scholars distinguish two different sources for the material in those chapters, sources which clearly reflect differing attitudes about Israel's having a king.

The Saul source is a convenient way of referring to the account in I Sam. 9:1-10:16 and ch. 11. Here Samuel, identified as a "seer" (9:9), took the initiative at God's direction and anointed the young, tall, handsome son of Kish, of the tribe of Benjamin, "prince" over Yahweh's people. But Saul was not public-

ly acclaimed king until after his victory over the Ammonites (ch
11). The Israelites who lived in Jabesh-gilead, on the east side
of the Jordan River, were faced with humiliating defeat but felt
that someone among the tribes of Israel would surely come to their
defense. How their messengers knew to contact the farmer Saul at
Gibeah is not explained. But he responded to their distress,
raised a volunteer army, and rescued them from the besieging Ammonites. This act removed all doubt as to Saul's qualifications for
leadership, and Samuel crowned him king at Gilgal, the first campsite Joshua had set up after he had crossed the Jordan.

The Samuel source, found in 7:3-8:22; 10:17-27; and ch.
presents a somewhat different picture of the transition from confederacy to monarchy. Samuel is depicted as a judge who called
for loyalty to Yahweh as the way to confront the Philistine threat
(7:3-4), as well as a respected dispenser of justice (7:15-17).
Apparently blind to the shortcomings of his two sons, Samuel appointed them judges in the expectation that they would replace him
when he died. He was offended when the elders came to him, asking
that he appoint a king for the nation, and did his best to talk
them out of it. He argued that to have a king would be to reject
God's reign, the very point which Gideon had made some decades previously. Further, in a long paragraph (8:10-18) which sounds as
though it is describing the reign of King Solomon, the aging judge
tried to show them how their ill-conceived plan of having a king
would completely change their lives for the worse and cause them
to regret it later.

The elders were not convinced by Samuel's fervent speech
and insisted upon having a king "that we also may be like all the
nations, and that our king may govern us and go out before us and
fight our battles" (8:20). When he saw their determination Samuel
faced reality, called the people together at Mizpah, by lot selected Saul, and presented him as the choice of the Lord (10:17-24).
But he made sure that Israel's king would not be just another ori-
ental despot by writing a constitution spelling out the duties,
powers, and limitations of the king (10:25). As a final gesture
in relinquishing his leadership role, Samuel addressed the assembled Israelites (ch. 12), reminding them of the covenant with Yahweh and reiterating the terms of the Deuteronomic Theology (vss.
14-15).

In which of the two sources described above do we find the
"real" Samuel? We have already observed that an anti-monarchy
viewpoint (Gideon) was being expressed, and we shall see that it
crops up years after the monarchy was established. It is quite

74

probable that Samuel shared that viewpoint. In the chapters which follow the stories of Saul's crowning, we observe Samuel, in the role of elder statesman and adviser to the king, severely condemning certain actions of Saul to the point of being unreasonable. When Saul acted as priest to prevent the further attrition of his army as they awaited the very tardy Samuel for a blessing-of-the-troops ceremony, he was told in clear terms that Yahweh disapproved of him and would punish him (I Sam. 13). When Saul spared the life of the king of the Amalekites and a few choice sheep for sacrificial purposes, at the end of a battle in which cherem was in force, Samuel announced Yahweh's rejection of Saul and refused to have anything more to do with him (ch. 15). This sounds as though his feelings against Israel's having a king were influencing his attitude toward the man whom he had grudgingly anointed. The probability is that the "Samuel source" most accurately reflects how Samuel actually felt about the demand for a king.

The reasons which the elders who approached Samuel gave for wanting a king included a desire to be like their neighbors, whose model of government was the only one they were familiar with, other than their own. But we may assume that the other reasons were more significant: we want someone who can govern us and fight our battles! It is probable that the conditions reflected in the book of Judges had not changed much. Samuel's moral and religious leadership, as far as it extended, was a positive force for improvement. But the problem presented by the Philistine ambition and aggression was still there and likely becoming more pressing. The cry of the Israelites, expressed by the group that came to ask Samuel for a king, was for a government which would have power to restore law and order to the cities and power to recruit and support a standing army for defense. They might have said to Samuel, "We've had two hundred years of the tribal confederacy and it doesn't meet our problems. It's time for a change!"

Chapters 13-31 are devoted to the account of the reign of Israel's first king, Saul of Benjamin. Although we can not be precise, we can say that the period of the judges extended roughly from 1200 B.C. to c. 1025. If the historian had filled in those blanks in I Sam. 13:1, we could be a bit more confident about the date Saul became king, for we know his successor came to power at c. 1000 B.C. Whatever the length of his reign, Saul discovered that his new job had many problems connected with it. As the first king, he had to deal with a group of tribes and individuals who were unaccustomed to being subjects of a monarch. They were not used to having their young men conscripted into the army or to paying taxes to support it. There were no trappings of kingship in existence, such as a royal palace or the machinery of administration. That is to say, Saul had to start from the beginning and that was not easy.

Other things, as well, made his reign difficult. As we noted above, Samuel, for whom Saul had enormous respect, was not as helpful and cooperative as he could have been. Saul had to fight the Philistines with inferior weapons (13:22) and with soldiers whose leaving for home he was powerless to prevent (13:8). A sense of having been deserted by Yahweh, coupled with a paranoid fear of the popular young David's ambitions, brought on long periods of depression, during which the country's needs were neglected. Despite these difficulties, Saul was very effective in the early years of his reign in dealing with the Philistine encroachment. This comes through the narrative even though it is clearly biased against Saul and in favor of the rising young officer whom Samuel anointed to become the next king, David.

The climax of Saul's frustration and sense of alienation from God is told in the strange story (I Sam. 28) of his contacting the dead Samuel through a medium, an act which violated Saul' own decree. His inability to get an answer from Yahweh in any other way (vs. 6) drove him to this desperate measure. According to the story, he did get a word from Yahweh, but it was a most disconcerting word, for it foretold not only the crushing defeat of his army by the Philistines but also the death of himself and his sons on the next day. The final chapter in I Samuel relates the fulfillment of Samuel's dire predictions. The extent to which the Philistines had penetrated Israelite territory is made plain by the fact that this fateful battle took place at Bethshan, in northern Israel. This suggests that Saul's campaign against the Philistine menace had not been very successful in his later years

Sheol

The story of Saul's contacting the dead Samuel calls for some consideration of the Hebrews' concept of life after death. Most of the Old Testament assumes that the dead go into an underground cavern of limitless size, called Sheol, or sometimes simply "the Pit." The mode of entrance was the grave; hence proper burial was extremely important. What occurred after entrance into Sheol can not accurately be termed "life," for it was merely existence or, at best, total rest. There was no joy for the righteous, as the later concept of heaven includes; neither was there punishment for the wicked. Basically, it was thought of as a depository for the departed, whose only advantage was to be at peace. This is reflected in the story when Samuel complained about being disturbed (28:15). Only in the very latest writings of the Old Testament does any change from the Sheol idea appear regarding the state of the dead.

76

Although we have said that I Sam. 13-31 tells the story of
the reign of Saul, it is also true that this material relates more
about David's activities than Saul's. Destined to become Israel's
greatest king, David is pictured as a man of dauntless courage,
strong character, reverence for God and the king, and brilliant
military leadership. There are two accounts of how Saul and David
met. Some time after Samuel anointed David to be the next king
(ch. 16), David was employed by the royal court to play soothing
music on the lyre in order to help the depressed Saul get through
his foul moods. Beloved by Saul, David served as his armor-bearer
when Saul was normal.

That story is followed by the well-known legend of David
and Goliath, the Philistine giant whose challenge to any Israelite
warrior to face him in a duel went unanswered until the youthful
David arrived in camp with food for his older brothers (ch. 17).
This son of Jesse, from the tribe of Judah, was incensed at the
offensive obscenities he was hearing from the "uncircumcised Philistine" (vs. 26) and proceeded to fight Goliath in a dramatic confrontation. After his amazing victory over the nine-foot warrior,
David was brought before King Saul and his commander-in-chief, Ab-
ner, and he introduced himself. Coming immediately after the
chapter which tells of David's serving Saul as personal musician
and armor-bearer, the Goliath incident poses a problem which could
be solved by simply transposing the two accounts of how Saul and
David first met.

An immediate and understandable consequence of the Goliath
slaying was the recruitment of David for Saul's army, in which he
distinguished himself as an effective leader in combat (ch. 18).
David's success made him a popular idol, but it was a mixed blessing for the king. It aroused Saul's jealousy at the same time
that it promoted his goal of defeating the Philistines. David's
close friendship with the king's son, Jonathan, and his marriage
to the king's daughter, Michal, did not prevent Saul's jealousy
and fear of David from developing into paranoid anger.

A series of attempts by Saul to kill him eventually forced
David to flee for his life. When the king pursued him through the
territory of southern Judah, where David had attracted a little
army of followers, David in desperation sought refuge in Philistine territory, where he was welcomed and given a town for him and
his men to live in (ch. 27). During their years as refugees in
southern Judah, David and his men lived off provisions from the
local farmers (not always voluntarily supplied), and David acquired two wives to replace Michal, who had been taken back by her

father (Saul) and married to another man, Palti (25:44; 27:3).

Israel's first experience with the monarchy was only partially successful. What had begun with great promise and early successes had degenerated, as a result of a combination of factor into an ineffective administration of a demented king. The historian felt it was necessary for him to explain why Saul did not found a dynasty but that his successor came from another family. True to his deuteronomic convictions, he provided such an explanation in the accounts of Samuel's denouncing Saul for disobeying God's (or Samuel's) orders:

> And Samuel said to Saul, "You have done foolishly; you have not kept the commandment of the LORD your God, which he commanded you; for now the LORD would have established your kingdom over Israel for ever. But now your kingdom shall not continue." (I Sam. 13:13-14)

> "Because you have rejected the word of the LORD,
> he has also rejected you from being king." (15:23b)

When we take into account the pro-David and anti-Saul tendencies in the literature, we can conclude that Saul's reign was not a total failure. At least it had gotten the people into the habit of looking to the king for leadership and thinking of themselves as subjects, and in that way laid the groundwork for the brilliant reign of the next monarch.

Significant terms and names for this chapter

Samuel	monarchy
Hannah	David
Eli	Sheol
Shiloh	Jonathan
Saul	Michal
Saul source	Goliath
Samuel source	Abner
Jabesh-gilead	Bethshan

CHAPTER VIII

THE HEYDAY OF ISRAEL

Biblical materials: II Samuel.   I Kings 1-11

Essential reading: II Samuel 3-7; 11-12; 15
                     I Kings 1; 3-5; 8:1-11; 10:1-11:10

We have already noted that David got a lot of space in
I Samuel. When we observe that the entire book of II Samuel is
devoted to David and his reign, we can begin to realize the important place David holds in the traditions of Israel. A truly charismatic figure, David succeeded finally in achieving what many
citizens had longed for: a strong, stable, independent nation
whose people were not living in constant fear of attack.

The Great King David

News of the death of Saul and three of his sons produced
genuine mourning in David, who lamented the passing of the king
whom God had chosen to lead his people and especially of his closest friend, Jonathan. David's first political move was to leave
his Philistine sanctuary and go to Hebron, a city located deep
within the territory of his own tribe, Judah. There he was proclaimed king by his fellow tribesmen, but his power was limited to
Judah.

For a while the northern tribes were under the nominal
control of Ishbosheth, a son of Saul, but the actual ruler was Ab-
ner, who had been commander of Saul's army. This state of affairs
continued for seven and a half years, ending in a deal David made
with the elders of the northern tribes by which he was acknowledged
to be king over all Israel. The thirty-three years he served in
this capacity, added to his stint as head of Judah alone, gave him
a forty-year reign, which began around 1000 B.C. (II Sam. 5:1-5).
One feature of the deal was the restoring of Michal, daughter of
the deceased Saul, to David as wife (3:13-16) without regard to
her wishes. It was not unrequited love, but the establishment of
royal prestige, which prompted David to insist upon her return,
even though it meant the break-up of her happy marriage to Paltiel.

As king of all the tribes, David quickly made plans to

79

solidify his power and use it to strengthen the Kingdom against its enemies. A good politician, he knew that Hebron was too far south and too closely tied to his own tribe to serve as his capital. On the other hand, if he selected Shechem, which had important associations with Israel's past, the people of Judah might be miffed, for that was well into the northern tribes. The obvious answer was to select a city close to the border between Judah and Benjamin, the next tribe to the north. He chose Jerusalem, at that time a small Jebusite fortress which was considered impregnable, and took it by force to serve as headquarters for the Kingdom Ever since, Jerusalem has been a place of controversy and significance out of all proportion to its size.

David entered into a contract with King Hiram of the city of Tyre (in present-day Lebanon) by which Hiram would supply cedar from Lebanon, together with skilled craftsmen, to build a palace for David in Jerusalem (5:11-12). Some time later, David decided that the Ark of the Covenant, which had been residing at Kiriath-jearim since the Philistines returned it, should be brought into Jerusalem. This was done with great pomp and ceremony (ch. 6) and added significantly to the growing importance of Jerusalem. Now it was the religious, as well as the political, capital of Israel.

After the merger of Judah and the tribes which had clung to the house of Saul for a short time, David wasted no time applying his expertise to the problem which had plagued Israel for so long: the Philistines. Having harbored David and his cadre of men in the latter years of Saul, they were not worried about any threat to them his kingship might pose as long as he reigned over Judah only. But when they heard he had been made monarch of all Israel, they decided they had better attack David's forces soon, before they became too strong (5:17). According to II Sam. 5, it was already too late. David defeated them in battle after battle and ultimately subjugated them, confining them to a narrow strip on the Mediterranean Sea in the area where they had originally landed. The major Philistine cities were Gaza, Ashkelon, Ashdod, Ekron, and Gath.

The Philistines were not the only group to feel the military might of David's Israel. The Moabites, the Edomites, the Ammonites, and the Syrians were subdued, and much of the territory they had controlled was added to Israel. The conquest of Canaan, begun two and a half centuries earlier under Joshua, was at last complete. David was without doubt a brilliant military leader, but he was fortunate to have come onto the scene at a time when there was no powerful nation seeking to expand its territory in the Fertile Crescent. Aided by his able commander, Joab, David was able to expand Israel northward beyond Damascus and southward to Ezion-geber at the height of his power.

Map 6

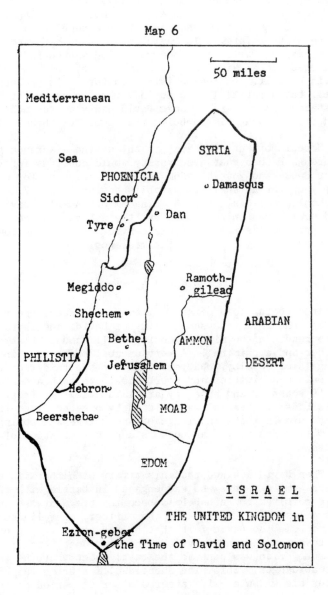

50 miles

Mediterranean

Sea

SYRIA

PHOENICIA

Damascus

Sidon

Dan

Tyre

Ramoth-
gilead

Megiddo

Shechem

ARABIAN

Bethel

AMMON

PHILISTIA

DESERT

Jerusalem

Hebron

Beersheba

MOAB

EDOM

I S R A E L

THE UNITED KINGDOM in

Ezion-geber

the Time of David and Solomon

When David had completed his conquests and had time for other things, it occurred to him that, while he was living in a luxurious palace, the Ark of God was being kept in a temporary structure, or tent (7:1-2). After discussing the situation with the court chaplain ("Nathan the prophet"), David decided he should build a permanent house for the Ark, one more befitting its importance. But the next day Nathan, who had received a word from Yahweh the night before, told David that Yahweh had vetoed the project as far as David was concerned. God wanted David's son who would succeed him as king to be the builder of the Temple rather than David himself. No reason is stated for God's preference in II Samuel, but a parallel account in I Chronicles, written much later, states that it was because David had shed so much blood that God did not want him to build the Temple (I Chron. 22:8).

More important, perhaps, is the divine assurance given to David through Nathan that his dynasty would continue forever: "And your house and your kingdom shall be made sure for ever before me; your throne shall be established for ever" (7:16). This is the theological basis for the Kingdom of Judah's conviction that God would indefinitely preserve the nation and the house of David to provide its rulers. This conviction figured prominently in the later history and prophetic messages.

The Court History

After being told of the military successes, the political genius, and the religious sensibility of David, one is rather surprised to read, in the middle section of II Samuel, that he was a poor father and a criminal! A very unusual phenomenon in the ancient annals of royalty, chapters 9-20 let the reader on the inside of palace activities and court gossip to such a degree that the king's weakness and humanity are laid bare. It is probable that this body of material was written by one who lived in the palace and had intimate knowledge of the goings and comings of the royal family. Its very frankness is a good indication of its basic accuracy.

When David learned that his affair with the wife of Uriah, one of his army officers who was engaged in battle with the Ammonites, had resulted in Bathsheba's becoming pregnant, he quickly arranged a leave for Uriah. But the officer, on religious grounds, did not go home, so David felt that he had to resort to other measures to cover up the adultery. He informed Joab, his army chief, to make sure Uriah was sent to the battlefront where he would be in greatest danger. This plan succeeded, for Uriah was killed and David took his widow as wife after a discreet period of mourning.

Thus the great king, who had yielded to the temptation to abuse his power for the sake of his own pleasure, thought that he had successfully covered up his adultery and had avoided scandal. But he had not counted on the condemnation of Yahweh, which would be pronounced by his prophet, Nathan.

The Prophets

Before we examine the encounter between Nathan and David, let us consider the role of the prophet in the faith of Israel. The word "prophet" has the primary meaning of "spokesman," one who speaks for another. A prophet of God, then, is someone who delivers God's message. Except for the cryptic reference to Abraham as a prophet in Abimelech's dream (Gen. 20:7), Moses is the first prophet the Bible mentions. But Moses himself, because of his faltering speech, had a prophet in the person of his brother Aaron, who delivered Moses' words to the pharaoh of Egypt. This relationship of Moses to Aaron is alluded to in that somewhat startling verse in Exodus (7:1): "And the LORD said to Moses, 'See, I make you as God to Pharaoh; and Aaron your brother shall be your prophet.'" The roles of prophet and priest were ordinarily kept separate in the Old Testament but, as in the case of Samuel, occasionally they were combined in the same person. Frequently there were clashes between priest and prophet, although ideally their functions were complementary.

The task of being God's spokesman often required the prophet to advise kings and, when the situation called for it, to pronounce judgment upon them. Nathan advised David about the building of a house for the Ark; he pronounced judgment when he learned of David's adultery and murder. Most of the prophets spoke also to groups of ordinary citizens, sometimes formally gathered for worship and sometimes in the street. The prophet's pronouncements were called oracles and often began with some such attention-getting assertion as "Thus says the LORD." The tone of the oracles could be that of condemnation, usually accompanied by threat of punishment, or that of promised blessing.

Often the oracles included prediction, but it was always short-term, conditional prediction. Today we use "prophecy" and "prediction" as though they were synonyms, but biblical prophets employed prediction only to threaten early punishment or promise early blessing. Prediction was always conditional: if you do not obey, this will happen; if you obey God's voice, he will bless you. Predicted punishment could be avoided and predicted blessing could be missed; it all depended upon the response of the people. But no Hebrew prophet engaged in trying to forecast events to come centuries into the future. The prophet's concern was to speak a relevant word to the situation at hand, calling for action on the part of the hearers either to avoid disaster or to retain God's favor.

What we have said about prophets applies to men such as Nathan, Elijah, and Elisha (whose exploits are recorded in the group of books the Hebrews call "Former Prophets"), who never wrote a word, as well as to the men whose oracles appear in books bearing their names (which the Hebrews call "Latter Prophets"). To be a prophet one did not have to be a member of any particular family or group. He had to be "called" in some manner which made him aware that he had been set apart for the task. Many of the prophets whose call experiences are recorded accepted their roles hesitantly. Often, later in their careers, they wished they had not become prophets, for the task of pronouncing judgment and predicting disaster was an unpleasant one. They met with hostility, apathy, doubt, and isolation, particularly when there were "false prophets" going around with opposite, more welcome messages.

Very commonly prophets, such as Nathan, were supported from the public treasury, but many of these fell prey to the temptation to say what their boss (usually the king) wanted to hear. The genuine prophet received the divine message through visions, sometimes ecstatic in nature. There are references to bands of prophets, or guilds, but most of the spokesmen for Yahweh in the Old Testament worked as individuals.

Nathan's Role

Nathan did not relish the assignment of declaring King David guilty and pronouncing judgment on him. If he would kill once to cover up a sin, perhaps he would do so again to keep the first one secret! II Sam. 12 records the careful way in which Nathan carried out his dreaded task. He got David to commit himself to the punishment of injustice by telling him a story of a rich man who took the pet lamb of a poor man to serve his guest instead of slaying one of his own. When David decreed capital punishment for the rich man, Nathan said pointedly, "You are the man" (vs. 7). When David confessed his guilt, Nathan pronounced God's forgiveness but also the punishment: the death of the child which Bathsheba would bear. In the course of time David and Bathsheba had a second child, whom they named Solomon, who would eventually succeed David to the throne of Israel.

Solomon was only one of many children of David and his

various wives. After one of them, Amnon, forced his attentions upon his half-sister, Tamar, her full brother Absalom avenged her by arranging the murder of Amnon. Absalom's running away before David could be told of the slaying caused his father much grief. After a three-year absence, Absalom was brought back home through the intervention of the commander, Joab, but he and his father were never really reconciled (14:28). Some time later, this same Absalom formed a conspiracy against David by secretly persuading some of the citizens of Hebron to help him gain control of the government (chs. 15-19). This revolt very nearly succeeded but was crushed when Absalom unwisely decided to pursue David and his army across the Jordan River. The capable and self-assured Joab, in defiance of his king's specific orders, personally killed Absalom when the opportunity arose. Again David was overcome with grief over a son to whom he was never really close.

Still very much the politician, David arranged for a large, ostentatious, "spontaneous" welcome as he and his army re-occupied Jerusalem. His later years were marred by still another rebellion, led by Sheba, of Saul's tribe, Benjamin. Sheba's revolt was forcefully put down under Joab's leadership, but his cry for independence will be heard again following the death of Solomon (II Sam. 20:1; I Kings 12:16). Surely these revolts were indicators of a growing discontent with some of David's policies or, perhaps, his lack of responsiveness to changing needs among the people.

A New King in Jerusalem

The Court History we have been examining in II Sam. 9-20 seems to pick up again in I Kings 1, where some in-palace conspiracies are described. Some scholars suggest that this block of material may be appropriately called the "Succession Narrative" because it explains how and why Solomon turned out to be David's successor as king instead of an older son of David, as would be expected. The groundwork for his selection had been laid in II Sam. 12:24-25, where it is pointedly said that Yahweh loved Solomon and conveyed that fact to Nathan. In I Kings 1:13, we learn that David had promised Bathsheba that her son should be the next king. Without doubt, Solomon's older brother, Adonijah, was aware of this promise but felt strongly that he, rather than Solomon, should occupy the throne (1:5-10). When David became seriously ill in his old age, Adonijah made plans to seize the royal power before the death of his father and the succession of Solomon could occur. The plan backfired, however, when Nathan learned of it and conspired with Bathsheba to convince the ailing King David to abdicate at once and declare Solomon king.

85

The new king moved quickly and decisively to consolidate his power and prevent more conspiracies by eliminating Adonijah and all those who had sided with him, including the crusty military leader, Joab. I Kings 3-11 describes the fabulous reign of Solomon, whose interests, upbringing, and talents were very different from those of his father. Coming to power at a time when Israel's enemies were totally subjugated, her government well established, and her economy in good shape, King Solomon was ambitious to make his country wealthy, the city of Jerusalem famous, and his own dwelling luxurious. He spared no expense in the fulfilling of his ambitions and was successful in doing so. The only problem, and it turned out to be a very big problem, was that the wealth was enjoyed by the privileged few but made possible by the work and sacrifice of the many.

From the standpoint of Israel's religious life, Solomon's most important achievement was the building of the Temple to house the Ark of the Covenant, the project which his father had wanted to undertake. Not a very large structure, it was beautiful and ornate, and added further to the central importance of the city of Jerusalem for Israel. Lacking the architects, skilled craftsmen, and fine materials in Israel, Solomon procured them from Phoenicia (David had already made a deal with King Hiram of Tyre.), which resulted in the Temple's having many non-Israelite features and designs. It probably followed the floor plan of the old Tabernacle for the two essential rooms, the Holy of Holies and the Holy Place, but around three sides were additional rooms for use of the priests. Of course, there was a permanent Altar of Burnt Offering in the large courtyard outside the entrance.

Since the beginning of Solomon's reign was c. 961 B.C., we may assume that the Temple, which was seven years in building, was completed around the middle of the tenth century. Repaired and refurbished from time to time, it served as the focal point of Yahwistic religion until its destruction in 587 B.C.

The only negative note sounded by the historian in recording the deeds of Solomon comes out of the strains of the variety of religions brought into Israel by his inordinate number of wives: "His wives turned away his heart" (11:3). Such a large family required large living quarters, so Solomon turned to King Hiram for help. The palace was thirteen years under construction but there were several other buildings, mentioned in chapter seven, including a special home for his most prestigious wife, the daughter of the pharaoh of Egypt. It should be mentioned that the reason for so many wives is probably that marriage to the king's daughter was part of his diplomatic initiative to keep the peace with all the neighboring city-states.

Solomon's name and fame have been connected prominently with wisdom. Tourists from all over the world, including the Queen of Sheba, visited Jerusalem in order to hear his wisdom, as well as to see his manifestations of wealth (ch. 10). An example is given (3:16-28) of how he used wisdom in the dispensing of justice. But the most informative passage about Solomon's wisdom is 4:29-34, in which it is claimed that "Solomon's wisdom surpassed the wisdom of all the people of the east, and all the wisdom of Egypt." It goes on to say that this wisdom included proverbs, songs, and plant and animal fables, all constituent parts of a wisdom movement which had flourished in Egypt and the Mesopotamian region more than a millenium before Solomon.

Samples of the literature of Babylonian and Egyptian wisdom have survived and are similar in form to the wisdom literature in the Old Testament (Proverbs, Ecclesiastes, and Job). Solomon's real connection with wisdom, apparently, is his use of the royal treasury to support the activities of professional wise men, or sages, who traveled to other countries, especially Egypt, to collect proverbs, fables, etc., then entertained the royal family and guests by reciting them and perhaps others of their own composition.

A man of wide interests, Solomon is credited with having the Phoenicians build a fleet of ships to facilitate his accumulation of exotic materials from the East, and then sail the ships for him (9:26-28). He bought and sold horses and chariots, keeping some for national defense at special cities built for the purpose (9:19; 10:26-29). Some of his projects brought income to the nation, but many of them cost more than they brought in. Eventually the expenditures surpassed the income, and Solomon could not pay all his debts to the Phoenicians. In an attempt to satisfy King Hiram, Solomon ceded to him twenty cities next to the border between the two countries.

Although the Deuteronomic historian is generally favorable in his reporting of Solomon's reign, he does include hints that not all was well in Israel. We may assume that the king's giving Israelite towns to Phoenicia was not a well-received decision. The high living described in 4:22-28 was very expensive and required high taxes in money, kind, and service from the people. To divide the burden equally, Solomon re-divided the Kingdom into twelve districts of similar size, ignoring the old tribal boundaries in the process. Each district was expected to provide one month's foodstuffs for the royal palace.

He used forced labor on many of his projects, a policy which caused much discontent. His official in charge of such labor, Jeroboam, took part in a revolt against Solomon and fled to Egypt to save his life. Toward the end of Solomon's reign he had to deal with attacks from the Edomites and others, which the historian explains as God's punishment for Solomon's letting his wives influence him toward idolatry (ch. 11).

The full extent of the discontent provoked by Solomon's policies was not evident until his death was reported (ch. 12) and his son had to confront the demands of the oppressed populace for redress of grievances. A realistic appraisal of his reign evokes serious questions: Just how wise was he? Was the Kingdom of Israel as well off at the end of his administration as at the beginning? Is greatness measured by magnificent splendor of the capital city or by genuine concern for the welfare of the masses? It is quite possible, as some have suggested, that the Yahwist (writer of J) did his story during Solomon's reign to remind the nation of where they had come from and of the kind of people God expected them to be.

Significant terms, names, and dates for this chapter

Judah	Joab
Hebron	prophet
Ishbosheth	oracle
1000 B.C.	Solomon
Jerusalem	Absalom
Tyre	Adonijah
Nathan	Temple
Court history	961 B.C.
Uriah	Phoenicia
Bathsheba	Hiram

CHAPTER IX

SECESSION AND RIVALRY

Biblical materials: I Kings 12-II Kings 17. Amos. Hosea

Essential reading: I Kings 12; 16-18; 21
II Kings 2; 5; 9-12; 15; 17
Amos 5; 7
Hosea 1-4; 6; 11

Division of the Kingdom

In accordance with custom in the ancient Near East, the pent-up discontent and resentment which had been building during the reign of Solomon was not released until the death of the king in 922 B.C. There was no question regarding the allegiance of the large tribe of Judah and the small neighboring Benjamin to the house of David, and Solomon's son, Rehoboam, was crowned king in Jerusalem. The northern ten tribes were also prepared to support Rehoboam and sent representatives to Shechem, where Rehoboam had arrived to accept their pledge of loyalty (I Kings 12). Their spokesman was Jeroboam, the ex-official in Solomon's administration who, after stirring up trouble for the king, had fled to Egypt for safety.

Upon learning of Solomon's death Jeroboam returned and led the group which met Rehoboam at Shechem. Their message was simple:

"Your father made our yoke heavy. Now therefore lighten the hard service of your father and his heavy yoke upon us, and we will serve you."

Their allegiance would be conditioned upon his answer to their demand to lower the taxes, which took the form not only of monetary payments, but also of manual labor and provisions for the royal palace. Three days later, after consultation with the advisers inherited from his father and then with advisers of his own generation, he gave them his answer. Siding totally with the younger advisers, Rehoboam said, in effect, the taxes would not be lowered; rather, they would be raised! (12:12-14)

This foolish decision resulted in the split of the United Kingdom of Israel, which had stood for approximately a century.

Map 7

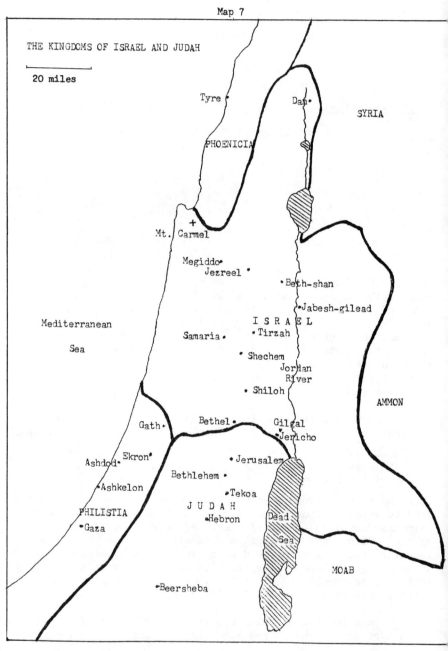

THE KINGDOMS OF ISRAEL AND JUDAH

20 miles

Tyre

Dan

SYRIA

PHOENICIA

Mt. Carmel

Megiddo
Jezreel

Beth-shan

Jabesh-gilead

ISRAEL

Mediterranean

Samaria

Tirzah

Sea

Shechem

Jordan
River

Shiloh

AMMON

Gath

Bethel

Gilgal
Jericho

Ashdod

Ekron

Jerusalem

Ashkelon

Bethlehem

Tekoa

PHILISTIA

JUDAH

Dead

Gaza

Hebron

Sea

MOAB

Beersheba

The northern tribes seceded and formed their own kingdom, with Jeroboam as king. Rehoboam's attempts to deal with the situation by force were ineffective. For the next two centuries there existed, side by side, two Israelite kingdoms which at times were at war with each other but at other times cooperated with each other. They were never reunited after this 922 B.C. division.

The Historian's Dilemma

The Deuteronomic historian clearly considers both kingdoms to be made up of God's people, to be under his law, and to have their fortunes controlled by their obedience or disobedience to that law. So he relates the histories of both, which is not an easy task, either for the writer or the reader. He could have told the story of one kingdom all the way to the end, then gone back to tell that of the other. But there was so much interaction of the two kingdoms that he chose to tell their stories by alternating back and forth, a method which requires careful attention to names on the part of the reader if he expects to make any sense of it. To simplify the history somewhat, we have provided an historical chart (Chart IV, p. 93), which includes all the rulers of both kingdoms, as the Bible gives them, together with the prophets, placed in connection with the kings ruling at the time they prophesied.

The new kingdom formed by the seceding northern tribes continued to use the name Israel, while the smaller southern kingdom, composed only of Judah and Benjamin, was known as Judah. All the accouterments of nationhood, except some military installations, remained with Judah. Jerusalem, with its magnificent palace and beautiful Temple, had served as the political and religious center of national life since the early years of David's reign. Therefore, when the new kingdom of Israel was formed, it had to arrange for its own government and place of worship. I Kings 12:25-33 tells how Jeroboam I went about this task.

His capital city was Shechem, a city with ancient associations for the Israelites. When Jeroboam noticed that his people were returning to the Temple in Jerusalem for the festivals, he feared this practice might one day lead to a re-unification of the tribes. To prevent this, he established two worship centers, one at Dan in the extreme north end of Israel, and the other at Bethel, close to the border of the kingdom of Judah. In place of the Ark of the Covenant, with its mercy seat symbolizing the presence of Yahweh, Jeroboam ordered the formation of a golden calf for each center.

To the historian this was a flagrant case of idolatry, hence roundly condemned. Yet, to Jeroboam it may have meant no more than providing his people a focus for worship which reminded them that Yahweh was present with them, too. At any rate, the hi torian judged each northern king on the simple criterion: Did he remove the golden calves from Dan and Bethel? If so, he was a good king, regardless of what else he did. If not, he was an evi king, irrespective of any accomplishments of his reign. Accordin to him, none ever removed them, so all the kings of Israel were evil! Besides the worship centers, Jeroboam instituted a non-Le vitical priesthood and appointed a series of feast days to replace the ones to which the people were accustomed. These measures, he hoped, would break all ties between the two kingdoms.

Judah's kings continued to be supplied by the house of Da vid, with but one exception, throughout its entire existence. The historian had to use a different criterion to evaluate Judah's kings. Influenced by his deuteronomic background, he rated them good if they concentrated all sacrificial worship in Jerusalem an evil if they allowed altars to remain throughout the countryside. The political stability of Judah was much greater than that of Is rael, for it was simply assumed that the next king of Judah would be the oldest surviving son of the current monarch, whereas in Is rael no one family provided the rulers. The strongest man became the king, which meant that the kings of Israel were more on the model of the charismatic leaders known as the Judges of an earlier era. There were several dynasties in Israel, but none longer than five generations.

Turmoil North and South

The Deuteronomic history hastens through the records of many of the kings of the two nations descended from Jacob but re lates in detail the reigns of others. We can not consider the do ings and shortcomings of all the rulers, but we shall mention those events and rulers which influenced the courses followed by Israel and Judah. The historian got much of his information from earlier writings which he mentions: the Book of the Chronicles of the Kings of Judah (I Kings 14:29) and the Book of the Chronicles of the Kings of Israel (15:31). In the early part of Rehoboam's reign, Judah was invaded by Egypt, which carried away much of the wealth which Solomon had accumulated in Jerusalem (14:25-28). Ac cording to I Kings 15:16, there was continual strife between Isra el and Judah during the first decades of the ninth century B.C. This was brought to an end when Judah made a pact with Syria, who agreed to invade Israel in return for an undisclosed amount of sil ver and gold. During the reign of Baasha, the capital of Israel was moved from Shechem to Tirzah.

Chart IV.   Chronology of the Kings of Israel and Judah
(all dates B.C.)

United Kingdom of Israel	Prophets
Saul 1025(?)-1000	Samuel
David 1000-961	Nathan
Solomon 961-922	

Israel   Judah

           Prophets

Israel	Prophets	Judah	Prophets
*Jeroboam I 922-901	Ahijah	Rehoboam 922-915	Shemaiah
		Abijam 915-913	
Nadab 901-900		Asa 913-873	
*Baasha 900-877			
Elah 877-876			
*Zimri 876			
*Omri 876-869		Jehoshaphat 873-849	Micaiah
Ahab 869-850	Elijah		
Ahaziah 850-849		Jehoram 849-842	
Jehoram 849-842	Elisha	Ahaziah 842	
*Jehu 842-815		#Athaliah 842-837	
Jehoahaz 815-801		Jehoash (Joash) 837-800	
Jehoash 801-786		Amaziah 800-783	
Jeroboam II 786-746	Amos	Uzziah (Azariah) 783-742	
Zechariah 746	Hosea		
*Shallum 745			
*Menahem 745-738		Jotham 742-735	Isaiah
Pekahiah 738			
*Pekah 737-732		Ahaz 735-715	Micah
Hoshea 732-722			
		Hezekiah 715-687	
		Manasseh 687-642	
		Amon 642-640	
		Josiah 640-609	Jeremiah
		Jehoahaz 609	Zephaniah
		Jehoiakim 609-598	Nahum
		Jehoiachin 598	Habakkuk
		Zedekiah 597-587	Ezekiel

*a new dynasty began

#interruption of Davidic line

93

Rapid changes in the leadership of Israel are reported in I Kings 16. Zimri, who had become king by assassinating his predecessor, was himself killed after a reign of seven days. The new king was Omri, who turned out to be one of the northern kingdom's most effective rulers. Although the historian can not bring himself to give Omri a positive evaluation because he did not remove the calves from Dan and Bethel, we learn from the Moabite Stone that he conquered and ruled Moab and was respected by the Moabites as a strong leader. The Bible does record the fact that he established a permanent, well fortified capital at Samaria for Israel.

Yahwism versus Baalism

Although a weaker and more evil king than Omri, his son Ahab gets more space devoted to a description of his reign than any other northern king. Most of I Kings 16:29-22:53 is concerned with events and personalities connected with Ahab. His colorful, strong-willed wife Jezebel, a princess from the Phoenician city of Sidon, was a devout Baal worshiper and persisted in promoting Baalism in her new homeland.

Equally colorful and determined was Elijah, prophet of Yahweh from east of the Jordan, who became the chief opponent of Jezebel and her retinue of Baal prophets. Elijah (whose name means "Yahweh is my God") appeared before King Ahab to announce a coming drought upon the land of indefinite duration, then disappeared for more than two years. When Elijah, whom Ahab called a "troubler of Israel" and "my enemy," returned to announce the end of the drought and resulting famine, he asked Ahab to arrange for a public contest, to be held on Mount Carmel, between himself, as Yahweh's prophet, and the prophets of Baal. The dramatic confrontation is described in I Kings 18:20-46. The very fact that Elijah thought such a challenge of Baalism's claim that Baal was the source of fertility was necessary indicates the success of Jezebel's evangelistic efforts on behalf of her religion.

The contest ended with a total victory for Elijah and his God and with the immediate end of the drought. There should have been no doubt in the minds of the onlookers that it was Yahweh, not Baal, who made good crops possible. But, for some reason, Elijah did not find himself elated over the victory. When Jezebel learned of it and of the violence done to her prophets by Elijah, she threatened to have his life within twenty-four hours. Prompted by the need of a reassuring word from Yahweh, Elijah traveled southward through Judah to Mt. Horeb, where Moses had received revelation centuries before. After experiencing the characteristic phenomena of volcanic activity, Elijah received his word from

Yahweh, who assured him that he was by no means the only faithful Yahweh worshiper left in Israel and told him to return home, where he had work to do (ch. 19).

Some time after his return to Israel, Elijah learned of Jezebel's illegal execution of Naboth in order to gain possession of his vineyard for her husband. Once again he confronted King Ahab, this time to pronounce a horrible judgment upon him and his wife. The historian's assessment of Ahab is predictably negative: "There was none who sold himself to do what was evil in the sight of the LORD like Ahab, whom Jezebel his wife incited" (21:25).

But the writer appears to be unaware of a rather significant event in which Ahab participated. The Assyrian Empire, located in Mesopotamia, nourished ambitions to control the entire Fertile Crescent, including Egypt. About the middle of the ninth century B.C., Assyria's army was moving in that direction and would doubtless have had little difficulty in conquering the small states which lay in its path, had they not taken decisive action to prevent that. The small countries, including Syria, Israel, and Judah, formed a coalition and used their combined armies to resist the Assyrians. They did not defeat Assyria, but they succeeded in stopping her advance at Qarqar, in northern Syria, in 853 B.C. We learn of this from a battle stele erected by the Assyrian emperor, in which it is said that Ahab provided the largest contingent in the coalition. This battle sent the Assyrians back home to rebuild their forces, and it was not until a century later that they were again threatening these same small nations.

Elijah's Succesor

Evidently the happenings in the northern kingdom supply the materials for a more interesting account, for as we move from I Kings into II Kings, the story of Israel continues with little mention of Judah until chapter eight. The account of Elijah's strange disappearance occurs in II Kings 2, where it is reported that he was last seen being swept up into the heavens by a tornado. This gave rise in later times to the expectation that one day Elijah would return, a tradition alluded to in the New Testament. A witness of Elijah's unusual departure was Elisha, who became his successor as prophet of Israel.

A group of stories about Elisha, attributing to him miraculous powers, appears in chapters 2-9. One of the most instructive of these stories concerns the healing of Naaman, the commander of the army of Syria, which at this time was an enemy of Israel. Stricken with leprosy and unable to find a cure in his native land,

Naaman acted upon a suggestion from an Israelite maid, captured on an earlier raid into Israel, and traveled to Elisha's residence (ch. 5). After Naaman reluctantly followed Elisha's prescription, his leprosy was gone and he wanted to reward the prophet, who refused any payment. Whereupon Naaman, fully convinced of the power of Elisha's God but believing Syria was out of Yahweh's territory, requested permission to transport to his home in Syria a quantity of Israelite soil sufficient to construct a small shrine. This, he reasoned, would enable him to worship Yahweh even though he would not be in his land. Interestingly, Elisha said nothing to contradict this notion that each land has its own deity but granted permission to Naaman to take the soil.

A King Zealous for Yahweh

Relations between Israel and Judah became quite close when Jehoram, king of Judah, married Athaliah, daughter of Ahab and Jezebel. When Ahaziah, the son of Jehoram and Athaliah, became king of Judah, he took his army to help Joram, the king of Israel, fight the Syrians. Wounded in the battle, Joram went to Jezreel, the summer palace of Israel, to recuperate. There he was visited by his ally, King Ahaziah of Judah. This set the stage for a story of violence, bloodshed, and fanatical religious zeal.

Having been anointed by a prophetic assistant of Elisha to become the next king of Israel, a young army officer named Jehu decided not to wait for the natural death of Joram but hastened to Jezreel, where he assassinated Joram and slew the fleeing king of Judah, Ahaziah. Jehu understood his commission from Yahweh to include more than being political head of the country. He saw himself as the divinely appointed leader of a crusade against Baalism a concept which was aided by the approval of a fundamentalist group of Israelites called Rechabites (II Kings 10:15-17,23). Using the only weapon that occurred to him, the sword, Jehu slaughtered thousands of Baal worshipers, not hesitating to lure them into a vulnerable position by deception. The slaughter included all the living members of the house of Ahab, including his widow Jezebel, who was still living in Jezreel.

In a real sense, Jehu was completing the task which Elijah had begun at Mount Carmel and fulfilling that prophet's prediction of a horrible demise for Jezebel (II Kings 9:30-37). Such zeal for Yahweh must surely have pleased him, the historian implies when he states simply, "Thus Jehu wiped out Ba'al from Israel" (10:28). But this is followed immediately by the negative state-

96

ment that Jehu failed to remove the golden calves from Dan and Bethel; so even Jehu, with all his single-minded devotion, did not receive a good rating from the Deuteronomic writer. Neither did he receive criticism for his violent methods!

Jehu's take-over of the kingdom of Israel had far-reaching repercussions in the kingdom of Judah also. His assassination of the visiting king of Judah at Jezreel created a vacant throne in Judah, which was seized by Athaliah, the deceased monarch's mother, the only woman and the only non-member of the house of David to rule in that country (II Kings 11). Athaliah's attempt to eliminate all possible claimants to the throne was thwarted by the action of the dead king's sister, who saved the infant boy Joash from the new queen's purge. After a reign of six years Athaliah was overthrown, and the seven-year-old Joash (also Jehoash) was declared king, with Jehoiada the priest advising him. Joash was one of the few kings of Judah to receive a good mark from the historian, doubtless because of his leadership in the repair of the Temple. But even this was qualified because some of the outlying altars ("high places") were left standing (12:2-3).

Jehu founded the longest of Israel's dynasties, which was in power for almost a century. The most illustrious member of the dynasty, other than Jehu himself, was Jeroboam, whom we refer to as Jeroboam II to distinguish him from Israel's first king after the secession. He is credited with strengthening the kingdom militarily and expanding its borders (14:25), but the historian had to rate him "evil" because he left the idolatrous objects which the first Jeroboam had made. But there were other things about Jeroboam II and his reign which did not please Yahweh, according to the prophet Amos.

A Shepherd Become Prophet: Amos

In the previous chapter we considered the role of the prophet in ancient Israel, and we have discussed the work of the earlier ones. With Amos we come now to the "writing prophets," men whose oracles have been preserved in part in books bearing their names. The book of Amos is one of twelve such collections of prophetic oracles short enough for one standard scroll to contain all of them. Because of their relative brevity, they are often referred to as the "Minor Prophets," but a few of them are of major importance. They are called the Book of the Twelve in the Hebrew canon, which places them among the Latter Prophets.

Amos is the first of four prophets who worked in the eighth century B.C., the others being Hosea, Isaiah, and Micah.

All we know about Amos the man is the little bit of information in the book itself, which tells us that he was a shepherd who lived at Tekoa in Judah at the time when Uzziah was king of that country and Jeroboam II was king of Israel (Amos 1:1). In the brief autobiographical statement in 7:14-15, Amos disclaims the title of prophet, but he obviously means he is not one of the professional prophets who received their salaries from the public treasury. He claims only to be a "herdsman, and a dresser of sycamore trees" whom Yahweh called to leave his sheep, cross the border into Israel, and proclaim his message to Yahweh's people there. He was not very far north of the border as he uttered these words, for 7:10 tells us he was at Bethel, one of the two worship centers established by Jeroboam I. It is probable that Amos had been to Bethel many times before, not as a prophet, but as a herdsman delivering sheep for sacrificial use at the sanctuary.

The context of his statement seems clear. His right to preach in the king's sanctuary (at Bethel) had been challenged by the priest in charge, Amaziah (7:10), who had sent a message to King Jeroboam II, probably at Samaria, asking him what to do with this radical preacher who had been predicting the exile of Israel and the death of the king. While awaiting the king's reply, Amaziah sought to persuade Amos to leave the country and go back to Judah, where he might receive some compensation for his prophetic activity (7:12). Amos' reply was that he was not a "regular" prophet, he did not expect payment, he was an ordinary man simply following Yahweh's orders, and he did not intend to leave town until he had delivered God's message: "'Now therefore hear the word of the LORD.'" (7:16)

One reason that Amos' message was unwelcome in Israel is that he was an outsider who had come into their country to point out the sins of Israel. He tried to overcome that in 1:3-2:5 by pronouncing Yahweh's judgment on the neighboring nations before zeroing in on Israel's shortcomings. A more significant reason, however, must have been the nature of the message itself. Injustice was rampant, he said; the rich oppressed the poor, the needy were neglected, men worshiped at the altars of Baal, bribery controlled court decisions, and the rich were living in luxury at the expense of the poor (2:6-7; 4:1; 5:10-12).

Even worse, their worship had been corrupted and abused by those who thought they could cover their multiplying sins by offering more sacrifices and performing more rituals. In what must have been the most shocking of his pronouncements, Amos represented Yahweh as expressing total disgust at what he saw and heard and smelled at the sanctuaries:

"I hate, I despise your feasts,
  and I take no delight in your solemn assemblies.
Even though you offer me your burnt offerings and cereal
    offerings
  I will not accept them,
and the peace offerings of your fatted beasts
  I will not look upon.
Take away from me the noise of your songs;
  to the melody of your harps I will not listen.
But let justice roll down like waters,
  and righteousness like an ever-flowing stream." (5:21-24)

Yahweh had stood firm in keeping his part of the Sinai Covenant,
said Amos, but the people had not kept theirs.

God had now determined to do something about their faithlessness and disobedience. Invasion, destruction, plunder, exile,
humiliation, and death of many awaited the nation (2:13-3:2;
3:11-15; 4:2-3; 5:1-3). It might be too late, even if they should
now repent (5:14-15), to avoid the punishment, which Amos seemed
to think would come from either the Egyptians or the Assyrians
(3:9-11). How much, if anything, Amos knew about international
politics we can not say. But it is a matter of historical record
that Assyria was building up her army and making plans for another
sweep through Syria and Canaan en route to Egypt around the middle
of the eighth century B.C. Like all the Israelite prophets, Amos
believed that Yahweh was in control of history, as well as of nature, and that he used kings and nations to accomplish his purpose.
Thus he might decide to punish his people Israel by using the ambition and might of Assyria to invade the land and oppress its inhabitants.

No wonder that the priest Amaziah wrote to Jeroboam II
that "the land is not able to bear all his words" (7:10)! He proclaimed certain punishment soon to descend upon a rebellious and
disobedient people with scant possibility that it could be avoided.
To follow justice and to pursue righteousness were their only hope.
Amos' prophetic activity took place around 760-750 B.C.

Hosea, the Unhappy Prophet

Despite the earnestness of his preaching and the determination to get Yahweh's message delivered, Amos apparently had little, if any, effect upon the religion and morals of the kingdom of
Israel. For a short time later another prophet, Hosea, a citizen
of Israel, appeared on the scene, making the same points and calling for the same kind of change among the people of his nation.

The only Israelite king mentioned in the opening verse of the book is the same Jeroboam II referred to in Amos, but there is mention of four kings of Judah, which would stretch Hosea's ministry at least as far as 715 B.C., which is seven years after the fall of his country. No mention is made, by name, of a succession of Israelite rulers covering the same period: Zechariah, Shallum, Menahem, Pekahiah, Pekah, and Hoshea. It is possible that he had them in mind when he said, "murder follows murder" (4:2), for four of the six came to power by assassinating the current king. Whatever the length of Hosea's ministry or however many monarchs sat upon Israel's uneasy throne, the utter faithlessness and rampant disobedience seem to have continued without interruption. The threat of invasion from Assyria, with the probability of total disaster for Israel, loomed ever larger.

Of all the biblical prophets, Hosea is unique in portraying the relationship of Yahweh to Israel in terms of his own family situation. Looking back upon his marriage from a time late in life, Hosea concluded that Yahweh had known that the woman he was about to marry, Gomer, would prove unfaithful (1:2) but wanted him to marry her anyway. Their three children are given meaningful names, which served as reminders of God's judgment upon the nation. In naming the first child Jezreel, he pronounced Yahweh's judgment upon the overzealous violence of Jehu, a judgment which is lacking in the Deuteronomic history. The names of the others, Not Pitied and Not My People, express God's total disgust with the people he had nurtured, forgiven, and protected through repeated manifestations of disobedience and rebelliousness.

The surprising and wonderful second chapter dares to compare faithless Israel to the adulterous Gomer and to suggest a parallel between Yahweh's treatment by his people and Hosea's being wronged by his wife:

"For their mother has played the harlot;
    she that conceived them has acted shamefully.
For she said, 'I will go after my lovers,
    who give me my bread and my water,
    my wool and my flax, my oil and my drink.'" (2:5)

"And she did not know
    that it was I who gave her
    the grain, the wine, and the oil,
and who lavished upon her silver
    and gold which they used for Ba'al." (2:8)

The words apply to both relationships. Gomer had been unfaithful to Hosea and she was either thrown out of his house or left of her own accord; Israel had been unfaithful to Yahweh and had committed idolatry with Baal, whom, despite Elijah's demonstration to the contrary, they acknowledged as god of fertility. In both cases a disruption of the covenant relationship resulted, and in both cases the faithless party was to be punished (2:13).

But Hosea's message does not conclude with punishment, as does Amos'. After Israel's faithlessness had been dealt with, and it would be a destructive time, there would be restoration (3:5). Again, Hosea saw in his own willingness to take Gomer back a reflection of God's unending love for his covenant people (ch. 3). They would be given another chance, but that would come after the severe chastisement:

> Woe to them, for they have strayed from me!
> Destruction to them, for they have rebelled against me!
> (7:13)

Hosea's list of sins committed by the people sounds as though they had deliberately taken the Ten Commandments and systematically gone about breaking each one in turn (4:1-2). Like Amos, Hosea found the worship practices to be only a cover-up for the people's disobedience:

> "For I desire steadfast love and not sacrifice,
> the knowledge of God, rather than burnt offerings." (6:6)

The Hebrew word here translated "steadfast love" is <u>chesed</u>, which really refers to loyalty to the covenant relationship between Israel and Yahweh. As evidence of Israel's lack of trust in Yahweh, Hosea cites the attempts of her kings to attain national security by forming alliances with the super powers of the time, Egypt and Assyria (7:11; 5:13). In chapter 11 the prophet depicts God's love for Israel in the form of the tender relationship between a father and his son. Despite the father's constant loving care, the son spurned his love. Despite the terrible hurt it would bring to the father, he must proceed with the punishment.

The Fall of Samaria

Heedless of the warnings and pleadings of her prophets, the northern kingdom of Israel continued her decline during the last half of the eighth century B.C. Menahem succeeded in holding off the Assyrian threat for a while by agreeing to pay Pul, king of Assyria, an annual tribute, which he collected through heavy taxation of the wealthy citizens (II Kings 15:19-20). During the reign of Pekah, Assyria returned and captured large sections of Israel, carrying the inhabitants away to Assyria (15:29). Pekah's attempt to persuade Judah to join Israel and Syria in forming a coalition to resist Assyria ended in failure. Assyria defeated

Syria in 732 B.C. (16:9), and little Israel was left to defend itself alone against the mighty Assyrians.

The dubious honor of being Israel's last king goes to Hoshea, who held on to his power for a while by making Israel a vassal state to Assyria (17:3). When Shalmaneser V, who had succeeded Pul (Tiglathpileser III) as king, learned that Hoshea had made a deal with Egypt, he brought his army to the capital, Samaria, and began the attack. It is a tribute to the effectiveness of the city's fortifications that it required three years for the Assyrian army to break through. Samaria fell in 722 B.C., after two centuries of stormy existence, and many more of the Israelites were forcibly resettled in various parts of the vast Assyrian Empire. This policy of scattering their captives was their way of preventing possible future revolts.

The fall of Israel can be adequately explained on the basis of international politics. The powerful, ambitious super power was simply eliminating a small, treacherous enemy state which stood in its way of controlling the Fertile Crescent. But for the historian, there is much more to be said about the reason for Israel's demise. In II Kings 17:7-18, he provides a theological reason: "And this was so, because the people of Israel had sinned against the LORD their God," followed by a long catalogue of their offenses. It mattered not at all that the Assyrian rulers had never heard of this God. He was using them to work his will, in this case, the punishment of his wayward people. Amos and Hosea had been right; Yahweh had finally given up on Israel!

After the exile of many of the Israelites to Assyria, other peoples whom Assyria had captured were resettled in the territory vacated by the Israelites. It should be noted that, before the Assyrian invasion, a considerable number of the citizens of Israel had voluntarily emigrated to Judah, where they continued to live as citizens of that kingdom. The new people who were brought into the area eventually intermarried with the neighboring Israelites, and their descendants came to be known as Samaritans. Their religion was an amalgamation of concepts from their native faiths, as suggested by 17:29-34. The people of Judah came to look upon the Samaritans as impure in their worship of Yahweh (17:34-41), an attitude which gave rise to increasing hostility between them in the years ahead.

Significant terms, names, and dates for this chapter

922 B.C.	Elijah
Rehoboam	Elisha
Jeroboam I	Samaria
Judah	Mt. Carmel
Israel	Naboth
Dan	Assyria
Bethel	Naaman
Omri	Jezreel
Ahab	Amos
Jehu	Hosea
Jeroboam II	Gomer
Menahem	chesed
Hoshea	Pul
Athaliah	Shalmaneser V
Jezebel	722 B.C.
Joash	Samaritans

CHAPTER X

THE HOUSE OF DAVID CONTINUES

Biblical materials: II Kings 16; 18-24.   Isaiah 1-39.   Micah.
                      Jeremiah.   Habakkuk.   Nahum.   Zephaniah

Essential reading: II Kings 16; 18; 21-24
                      Isaiah 6; 1; 5; 7-8
                      Jeremiah 1; 22:13-18; 26; 20; 36

During the final decades of the existence of the northern
kingdom, the kingdom of Judah was having its troubles too. While
Jeroboam II was ruling in the north, Uzziah (also called Azariah)
sat on the throne of Judah during a long and successful reign
(II Kings 15:1-2). Essentially he was a good king, the historian
says, but he failed to destroy the worship centers in the areas
outside Jerusalem and for that Yahweh smote him with leprosy in
the latter years of his reign (15:3-5). Since lepers were required to be isolated from non-lepers, the king had to live in a separate house and conducted the affairs of government through his so
Jotham, who became king in his own right at his father's death.
Jotham is said to have continued his father's policies, but all
that changed when his son Ahaz took over the kingdom. Behaving
more like a king of Israel than of Judah, he even practiced human
sacrifice (16:2-4).

Judah's Pact with Assyria

Ahaz suffered the misfortune of coming to power at the
height of the Assyrian crisis, which we considered in the previou
chapter. When Syria and Israel exerted heavy pressure upon Judah
to join their coalition against Assyria, Ahaz hesitated, even whe
those two nations sent soldiers to lay siege to Jerusalem. The
solution which Ahaz decided upon was to place Judah under the dom
ination of Assyria, in return for which Assyria was to attack Israel and Syria, thereby drawing their soldiers away from Jerusale
This plan did relieve the pressure on Judah's capital, for Syria
was defeated in 732 B.C. and Israel was so weakened that she caus
ed no more trouble for Judah. But Ahaz's diplomatic move also
meant that his nation lost most of its independence. To prove hi
good faith, Ahaz even went to the extreme of adopting Assyrian re
ligion, including the replacement of the altar of Yahweh with a

model of the Assyrian altar he had seen in Damascus (16:10-20).

Ahaz was succeeded by Hezekiah, whom the historian ranks as one of the few good kings of Judah. His rather thorough reform of Judah's religion included eliminating from the Temple all the foreign paraphernalia which Ahaz had introduced. This got Hezekiah into trouble with the Assyrian king, who interpreted this as evidence of Judah's rebellion. In 701 B.C. the Assyrian army invaded Judah, took many of its cities, and besieged Jerusalem. Hezekiah's foresight in having an underground aqueduct dug to connect a spring outside the city with a pool within it enabled Jerusalem to hold out against the Assyrian army until it was needed worse elsewhere and withdrew without harming the city. This event doubtless confirmed the inhabitants' belief that God would never allow Jerusalem to be destroyed. In the waning years of Hezekiah's reign he was flattered by a visit from representatives of a new power which was challenging Assyria for control of the Mesopotamian area. The new power was Babylonia, which was to be Judah's enemy and eventual conqueror.

Isaiah of Jerusalem

Before we pursue the story of Judah any further, we need to examine the oracles of one of the great prophets of Judah, who spoke for Yahweh during the reigns of Jotham, Ahaz, and Hezekiah. His messages are found in the book which bears his name, chapters 1-39, as well as in II Kings 19. Our present book of Isaiah contains the oracles of at least two other prophets, whose names are lost to us. Chapters 40-55 come from a prophet who lived two centuries after Isaiah of Jerusalem, and we refer to him as Second, or Deutero-Isaiah. The rest of the book (chs. 56-66) is from a still later time and is usually called Third Isaiah.

The reason for the presence of the work of at least three prophets on one scroll is probably an economic one. A full standard-length scroll, prepared from animal skins and measuring approximately forty feet in length, was only partially filled by the oracles of the first Isaiah. But parchment was too expensive to justify leaving the remainder blank, so the works of other prophets were copied onto the same scroll without the editor's bothering to make note of what he had done.

For a long time scholars tried to understand how the same prophet could be speaking to the people of Judah in the time of Ahaz and Hezekiah (eighth century) and to the Jews in exile in the time of the Persian Cyrus (sixth century). Recognition that the scroll contains materials from different prophets who lived in different centuries has been a great help to understanding the literature and fitting it into the proper background. There is some evidence to support the theory that chapters 40-66 came from disciples of the original Isaiah. We know that he had disciples (Is. 8:16), and we do find some of the same themes turning up in various parts of the book. For the time being, then, we shall confine our attention to Isaiah of Jerusalem, who was called to become a prophet in the year that King Uzziah died (742).

The remarkable call vision in chapter 6 is the best place to begin reading Isaiah. It is a visionary experience which he describes in the first person, reflecting a sense of total unworthiness by the prophet as he stood in the presence of the holy Lord of hosts. After he volunteered for an unknown assignment while under the spell of the ecstatic experience, he learned that he was now to be Yahweh's spokesman to an unreceptive people for an indefinite period. The oracles in this part of Isaiah are not in chronological order, and it is impossible to be sure under which king some of them were delivered.

When one reads the oracles in Isaiah 1-5, he is struck with the fact that the very same sins which Amos and Hosea had condemned in Israel are being identified also in Judah. It could be that Isaiah had both kingdoms in mind as he delivered some of his messages, for Israel was still in existence during the first two decades of his ministry. In the beautiful "Song of the Vineyard" (5:1-7), Yahweh's deep disappointment with both Israel and Judah is expressed. Instead of justice and righteousness which he expected from his covenant people, all he got was bloodshed and lip service (vs. 7). God's displeasure with the use of sacrificial worship and ritual observances to hide evil doings and oppression of the weak is stated in 1:11-17. The situation is not hopeless:

"If you are willing and obedient
you shall eat the good of the land." (1:19)

But neither should the people presume upon God's mercy:

"But if you refuse and rebel,
you shall be devoured by the sword." (1:20)

Here is the characteristic conditional prediction of the prophet. The nation's future depends upon its response to the prophetic word. If its choice turns out to be a continuation of its current disobedient course, terrible calamity is in store (3:13-4:1).

One portion of Isaiah which can be dated with accuracy is chapters seven and eight. The situation depicted in 7:1-2 is that described in II Kings 16:5: Syria and Israel were using force to persuade Judah to join them in a coalition which they hoped would stop the Assyrian advance. Ahaz, king of Judah, was hesitating and could not make up his mind as to what answer to give them. Yahweh directed Isaiah to go to the king with advice which sounded to Ahaz like merely doing nothing: "Take heed, be quiet, do not fear." (7:4) Ahaz was being asked to trust in Yahweh for deliverance from the crisis and not to become part of a military alliance.

When he demurred, the Lord invited him to ask for a sign which would indicate the validity of Isaiah's message. When Ahaz piously declined to ask for a sign, Isaiah announced that God would give him the sign anyway:

"Behold, a young woman shall conceive and bear a son, and shall call his name Immanuel. . . . For before the child knows how to refuse the evil and choose the good, the land before whose two kings you are in dread will be deserted."
(7:14-16)

The child to be born is most likely to be to the king and his wife (the young woman), who can monitor his development and know that the closer he comes to being able to decide what he likes and does not like, the closer Ahaz will be to the time when Syria and Israel will no longer exist.

In the King James version, the word which RSV correctly translates as "young woman" is rendered "virgin," although the Hebrew word really means a young woman of marriageable age, without regard to virginity. The Greek translation of the Old Testament (Septuagint) unfortunately chose to translate the term with a Greek word meaning "virgin." When Matthew wrote his Gospel, he found "virgin" in the Septuagint scriptures he was using, and it fit so beautifully the tradition he knew about the virgin birth of Jesus that he quoted Isaiah 7:14 as a prophecy fulfilled by Jesus' birth (Matt. 1:22-23). In fairness to Isaiah, though, we should remember that his concern was to speak a relevant, reassuring word to a worried monarch in a critical situation rather than to predict an event eight centuries into the future.

A second child is introduced in Isaiah 8 as a sign to reinforce the same message as that conveyed by the first. A son of the prophet and his wife, Mahershalalhashbaz would not be old enough to say "dada" or "mama" before Syria and Israel would be no more (8:1-4). As we noted above, Ahaz, disdaining the advice and reassurance of Isaiah, chose to conclude a pact with Assyria, which he realistically believed to be far more powerful than his two neighbors to the north. His decision apparently incensed the prophet, who ordered his disciples (8:16) to record his words and seal them up for future consultation. He was certain that events would prove his oracles to have been correct, and indeed they did. Syria fell in 732 B.C., and Israel followed suit a decade later.

107

Isaiah seems to have given up all hope of influencing Ahaz for he turns his attention to the future, in which he believes a far different and better ruler will arise. In 9:6-7 he envisions a mighty leader from the house of David who will bring stability, peace, justice, and righteousness to Judah. In 11:1-5 he predicts that a descendant of Jesse (David's father) will be guided by Yahweh's spirit to rule with enlightened power and benevolent concern for the poor and the meek. Likely he expected the successor to Ahaz to fulfill these predictions, and he may have withdrawn from public life until the death of Ahaz.

We know from II Kings 19 that Isaiah was active during the reign of Hezekiah, with whose reign he was very likely pleased. It appears that on two separate occasions the prophet advised the king to have nothing to do with a proposed coalition being formed in the area to resist Assyria. On the first, Hezekiah listened, but the second time he joined the revolt, only to have his country invaded and Jerusalem besieged. During the siege, as conditions in the city worsened, he sent for Isaiah, who advised him to trust in Yahweh and not surrender to the arrogant Assyrians, who dared to claim their might was superior to that of Judah's God (II Kings 19:20-28).

Isaiah may have accepted the view that Yahweh had so committed himself to the protection of Jerusalem and the house of David that he would never permit either to be destroyed. At any rate, we know that this conviction was held by the inhabitants of the capital city, and every time the city was spared what appeared to be certain doom, this conviction was strengthened. This belief made things difficult for a later prophet (Jeremiah) when he sought to warn the people of coming disaster. It is not known just when Isaiah died, but it is clear that his ministry extended at least into the early years of the seventh century B.C.

A Prophet from the Country: Micah

A contemporary of Isaiah, who likely was born and lived all his life in Jerusalem, was Micah of Moresheth, a small rural village. His preaching, preserved in the book of Micah, one of the Twelve, echoed some of the same concerns which Isaiah had, but he saw things from a different viewpoint. Living among poor farmers and observing how they were being squeezed by their city-dwelling landlords, he saw the evil of both Israel and Judah as being concentrated in their respective capital cities of Samaria and Jerusalem:

What is the transgression of Jacob?

Is it not Samaria?
And what is the sin of the house of Judah?
Is it not Jerusalem? (1:5)

Micah did not share the assumption we noted above that Yahweh would forever spare Jerusalem from defeat or destruction. Because of the gross sins of its people, "Jerusalem shall become a heap of ruins" (3:12), a prediction that provided a precedent which saved the life of another prophet a century later (Jeremiah 26:16-19).

But Micah did agree with the other eighth century prophets in identifying and condemning the disobedience and faithlessness of the people: bribery, injustice, greed, drunkenness, and the substitution of ritual and offerings for obedience.

He has showed you, O man, what is good;
and what does the LORD require of you
but to do justice, and to love kindness,
and to walk humbly with your God? (6:8)

A Record-breaking King

In contrast to the highly-rated Hezekiah, his son Manasseh, who succeeded him to the throne of Judah, promoted Baalism, built high places (altars) throughout the land, and practiced human sacrifice (II Kings 21:1-9). During his long reign and because of his evil influence, the historian says, the people of Judah performed more acts of disobedience than did the pagan nations who occupied Canaan before the Israelites. It is significant that, although "the prophets" are mentioned in connection with Manasseh's reign, none of them is mentioned by name. The probability is that the king did not permit any one of them to live long enough to establish a reputation and that some of the "very much innocent blood" (II Kings 21:16) he shed belonged to God's spokesmen. They were predicting that Yahweh would do to Jerusalem what he had already done to Samaria (21:13), and such a judgmental message Manasseh would not tolerate.

Repair, Reform, and Revival

Following the death of Manasseh, his son Amon had a brief reign, in which he continued his father's policies (21:19-22). He fell victim to a conspiracy, a rarity in the southern kingdom, and was succeeded by his eight-year-old son, Josiah. Coming to the throne at such an early age meant that Josiah could be influenced by persons more concerned about loyalty to Yahweh than had been Amon or Manasseh. Most likely the greatest influence upon his

109

faith and character came from the priests, for at the age of twen
ty-six he ordered the complete repair of the Temple, now more tha
three centuries old, the cost to be borne by the accumulated offerings in the Temple treasury (22:3-7).

In 621 B.C. the high priest, who was in charge of the repair project, reported the discovery of what he termed "the book
of the law," a discovery which created quite a stir in religious
and political circles because it contained laws which were being
totally ignored. After King Josiah had heard it read, he was ver
perturbed and asked that its authenticity be checked. The person
selected to render an opinion was a woman, Huldah "the prophet-
ess," who examined the scroll and pronounced her verdict. Not on
ly was the law book genuine, she declared, but Yahweh was ready t
vent his wrath upon Judah for her disobedience of the law. As fo
Josiah, because he had not been aware of the contents of the
scroll and because he had an appropriately repentant attitude whe
he heard it read, he would be spared God's judgment.

Greatly concerned over the spiritual condition of his peo
ple and over the possible future punishment of the nation, Josiah
called a meeting of priests, prophets, and ordinary citizens and
had this disturbing scroll read to them. Vowing himself to keep
all the ordinances it contained, the king issued orders for a
thorough reform of Judah's religion on the basis of the scroll.

All objects in the Temple which had any connection with
non-Yahwistic faiths must be destroyed. The worship center which
Jeroboam I had built at Bethel was demolished, as were all other
shrines outside Jerusalem. The Passover, which had been neglecte
for years, was to be immediately reinstated. The measures which
Josiah took on the basis of the lately discovered book parallel s
closely some of the laws in the book of Deuteronomy (chs. 5-28)
that scholars now believe that this scroll was the chief source o
that book (see chapter V above).

When the scroll originated, by whom it was written, and
how it happened to be in one of the rooms of the Temple are questions we can not answer with certainty. It may have had its origin in the kingdom of Israel before it fell and then have been
brought by some of the fleeing citizens to Judah. It could have
been used by someone during the reign of Manasseh to attempt to
counter the pagan practices which prevailed. If so, it was "put
on the shelf" for fear Manasseh or his officials would discover
it. Whatever the origin of this mysterious scroll, it was taken
seriously and became the guideline for a genuine attempt to reviv
the religion of Yahwism as promulgated by Moses. How effective i

was in producing genuine change in the hearts of the people is another matter. But Josiah's reforming activities earned for him the highest mark of the Deuteronomic historian:

> Before him there was no king like him, who turned to the LORD with all his heart and with all his soul and with all his might, according to all the law of Moses; nor did any like him arise after him. (II Kings 23:25)

The popular and pious King Josiah, however, met a tragic end at the relatively young age of thirty-nine. What motivated him to try to intercept the Egyptian army as it moved northward and what prompted Pharaoh Neco to order him killed are not explained (23:29). International politics lay behind the event. The former might of the Assyrians was rapidly waning as the seventh century B.C. was coming to a close, and a new power, Babylonia, was attempting to deal Assyria a death-blow. Taking note of this situation, Egypt decided that it was to her advantage to keep her perennial enemy, Assyria, strong enough to keep the Babylonians busy so that neither of them would be able to cause trouble for Egypt. When, in 609 B.C., Josiah went out to meet the pharaoh, the Egyptian army was on its way to assist the Assyrians in their struggle against the Babylonians. Egypt's help enabled Assyria to stay alive for a few more years, but in 605 Assyria fell to Babylonia, which had already, in 612, taken the Assyrian capital, Nineveh.

The Seventh-Century Prophets

Before we consider the events in Judah following Josiah's death, it will be well to notice the emergence of the prophetic voices again in Judah after the oppressive reign of Manasseh. Although his ministry extends well into the next century, we can classify Jeremiah as a seventh-century prophet along with Zephaniah, Nahum, and Habakkuk. The prophet about whom we know more than any other is Jeremiah, born around 640 B.C. into a priestly family at Anathoth, just north of Jerusalem. The book of Jeremiah consists of oracles recorded by his secretary, Baruch, together with the latter's memoirs, which explains how so much is known about Jeremiah. Unfortunately, the materials are not in chronological order, but careful attention to details enables us to obtain a fairly accurate sequence of events.

Jeremiah's ministry began in the middle of Josiah's reign and continued for an indefinite period beyond the fall of Jerusalem, which occurred in 587 B.C., a period of around forty years. It falls into three periods, corresponding to the reigns of the three kings, Josiah, Jehoiakim, and Zedekiah. At this point we shall deal with the first two and leave the third for consideration in the following chapter.

Jeremiah and Josiah

When the word of the Lord came to Jeremiah telling him that he had been appointed a prophet, he tried to get out of the assignment by pleading that he was too young, an excuse which was overcome by Yahweh's promise that he would tell him what to say and protect him (Jer. 1:1-8). His call vision included the symbolic touching of his mouth by Yahweh, who thereby put words in his mouth, and two visions: a rod of almond, which symbolized that God would perform what he said, and a pot boiling over toward the south, indicating that evil would come upon Judah from the nor Later, Jeremiah concluded that this foretold a threat to his count from Babylonia.

Jeremiah's prophetic activity began some five years prior to the beginning of Josiah's reform. He denounced the adulteries (religious faithlessness) of Judah, who should have learned a lesson from Israel's fate but did not (Jer. 3:6-10). He respected Josiah and seems at first to have enthusiastically supported his efforts at reformation. But when he saw that the royal decrees were not producing any real change in the hearts of the people, he became disillusioned with the movement.

One result of the order to demolish all rural shrines and limit sacrificial worship to Jerusalem was an overemphasis upon the Temple and its cult, which tied into the already strong conviction that Yahweh would never let Jerusalem or the Temple be destroyed. This development Jeremiah strongly opposed, probably because he saw that it fostered a superficial religion and allowed the people to think they were reforming without any deep change taking place in their hearts. He did not, however, lose any respect for the king, about whom he later was highly complimentary (22:15-16).

Jeremiah and Jehoiakim

After the death of Josiah, Pharaoh Neco made Judah a vassal of Egypt and put a member of the royal family of his own choosing on the throne (II Kings 23:34). Imprisoning Jehoahaz after a three-month reign, Neco chose another son of Josiah, Jehoiakim, as king of Judah. A cruel, greedy, unscrupulous ruler, he was denounced by Jeremiah (22:13-19) and soon became his enemy. Early

in his reign, Jeremiah stood on the court of the Temple and declared that, if genuine repentance and obedience were not forth-
coming, Yahweh would destroy both Jerusalem and the Temple (ch.
26). This so incensed the priests and other prophets that they
demanded Jeremiah's death. But someone remembered that, a century
before, the prophet Micah had made similar statements and he was
not put to death (26:16-19). This got Jeremiah out of danger temporarily, but his message was so repugnant to the majority of the
residents of Jerusalem that he found himself in constant peril.

He continued to predict the destruction of Jerusalem, directly challenging the cherished royal theology, which held that
God would never let that happen. Not only by word, but also by
demonstration he made his point. Once he threw down on the pave-
ment a ceramic vessel to demonstrate to some priests and city elders what was going to happen to their town (ch. 19). The chief
priest, Pashhur, had him put in the stocks for public mocking but
Jeremiah continued to preach even there, predicting that the priest
and his family would be exiled to Babylonia (20:1-6). Perhaps
Jeremiah's most reprehensible advice was that the king should surrender the country to Babylonia, advice which grew logically out
of his conviction that Yahweh had selected Babylonia as the instrument by which he would punish his people. This, understandably, earned for the prophet the charge of treason and increased
the hostility toward him from all sides.

Without family members from whom he might receive support,
this opposition from the king, the priests, other prophets, and
the general populace occasionally drove Jeremiah to despair. In
such times he would give vent to his feelings in occasionally bitter outbursts, usually referred to as his "confessions." A good
example is found in 20:7-18, where he expresses his impossible dilemma: when he preached the message Yahweh gave him, everybody
hated him; if he stopped preaching, he felt unbearable pressure
from within.

Just when Baruch became associated with Jeremiah as his
secretary and only real friend is not known, but Jer. 36 relates
an incident which happened in 605 B.C. in which they were working
together. At Yahweh's direction, Jeremiah dictated to Baruch all
the oracles he had pronounced, and Baruch wrote them on a scroll.
The secretary was then sent to the Temple area to read the scroll
aloud, since the prophet had been barred from there. Soon it came
to the attention of King Jehoiakim, who, having heard its contents,
destroyed it and ordered Jeremiah's arrest. Anticipating such a
result, Jeremiah and Baruch had gone into hiding, from where a
second scroll was produced, even longer than the first. It is
highly probable that this second edition of Jeremiah's oracles,

preserved by Baruch, is a major source of our present book of Jeremiah.

The Foe from the North

The Deuteronomic historian reports (II Kings 24) that, although he had been made king by Neco of Egypt, Jehoiakim was forced to switch his loyalty to Babylonia when its king, Nebuchadnezzar, brought his army into Judah. But in 598 B.C., probably encouraged by Egypt, Jehoiakim rebelled against Babylonia, which prompted the Babylonian king to send his army against Judah once again. It now appeared that the dire predictions of Jeremiah were about to be fulfilled. The historian provides a theological explanation for this invasion: Yahweh was punishing Judah for her sins, especially those committed under Manasseh (24:3-4).

By the time the Babylonians reached Jerusalem, Jehoiakim had died and his eighteen-year-old son Jehoiachin was sitting on the throne. He responded to the siege of Jerusalem by surrendering to Nebuchadnezzar, who took the young king and his family, together with political leaders, military leaders, and skilled craftsmen, to exile in Babylonia. Jerusalem was still standing, Judah was still nominally an independent state although in reality a vassal of Babylonia, the Temple was still intact, and a member of the house of David, Zedekiah, was on the throne. Jeremiah's opponents could still say Yahweh would never take away these sacred institutions!

Zephaniah

Jeremiah spoke of many "false" prophets who were preaching in his day and challenging his fearsome predictions. But there were a few "true" spokesmen for the Lord besides himself, one of whom was Zephaniah, a descendant of King Hezekiah (Zeph. 1:1). This "minor" prophet may have begun his preaching before his more famous contemporary, for Josiah is the only king this short book mentions. The severity of the judgment which he proclaimed suggests that his ministry occurred before the reform of Josiah had begun. Like Amos, he spoke of a coming Day of the Lord (1:7,14), which would be a time of terrible destruction brought on by the gross sins and utter faithlessness of Judah and her leaders. Officials, judges, prophets, and priests selfishly pursued their own interests without regard to God's law (3:3-4). Those who said that Yahweh neither blesses nor punishes would be surprised, for

"Their goods shall be plundered, and their houses laid waste.

Though they build houses, they shall not inhabit them;
though they plant vineyards, they shall not drink wine
from them." (1:13)

Jerusalem was depicted as hopelessly corrupt in an oracle which
certainly agreed with Jeremiah's view:

Woe to her that is rebellious and defiled, the oppressing
city!
She listens to no voice, she accepts no correction.
She does not trust in the Lord, she does not draw near to
her God. (3:1-2)

The tone of Zeph. 3:9-20 is vastly different from the condemnation
which prevails up to that point. This note of hope and promise of
a renewed people of God may stem from a disciple of Zephaniah who
was writing after the predicted calamities had taken place.

Nahum

Nineveh, capital city of the great Assyrian Empire, fell
to the Babylonian army in 612 B.C., seven years before the final
defeat of Assyria's forces. News of this event brought relief and
joy to the hearts of the people who had survived Assyria's cruel
dominance of the Fertile Crescent for more than two centuries. We
have noted in previous chapters that she was responsible for the
fall of Israel and the harassment of Judah, including the deportation of some of Judah's citizens in 701 B.C. Her reputation for
committing atrocities and mutilations upon captured populations
was well known, and she was universally feared and hated. Judah's
hatred of Assyria found eloquent expression in the little book of
Nahum, a minor prophet of whose life we know nothing.

Written near the time of Nineveh's fall, that is the sole
subject of the book. It is understood as the inevitable result of
Yahweh's judgment upon a haughty, wicked nation, whose capital city totally deserved its fate. Gloating over the destruction, this
super-patriotic prophet exclaimed:

Woe to the bloody city, all full of lies and booty--no end
to the plunder!
The crack of whip, and rumble of wheel, galloping horse and
bounding chariot!
Horsemen charging, flashing sword and glittering spear,
hosts of slain, heaps of corpses,
dead bodies without end--they stumble over the bodies! (3:1-3)

Nahum seems to delight in describing the slaughter and the gore,
results of Yahweh's vengeance upon the city whose demise was

mourned by nobody:

> All who hear the news of you clap their hands over you.
> For upon whom has not come your unceasing evil? (3:19)

In contrast to the other prophetic books, Nahum did not bring God's
word to bear upon current conditions except to suggest that God's
judgment upon the wicked is certain and universal.

Habakkuk

We know even less about Habakkuk the man than we do about
Nahum, whose home town at least was given. Chapters one and two
of this little book, one of those comprising the Twelve, are in
the form of a dialogue between Yahweh and the prophet. They reflect a concern, on Habakkuk's part, over the rise of a new power
in the Fertile Crescent which seemed to be following the same policies as the one God had so recently destroyed. Having wreaked
his judgment upon Assyria, why did Yahweh now permit the rise of
Babylonia (the Chaldeans, 1:6)? The prophet wants to know:

> Why dost thou look on faithless men,
>   and art silent when the wicked swallows up
>   the man more righteous than he? (1:13)

Eventually Habakkuk receives an answer which leads him to realize
that Yahweh planned to use Babylonia as an instrument of judgment
(1:12) upon his people, as he had used Assyria. And, just as he
had punished Assyria, so he would punish Babylonia after she had
served his purpose and when she used her might for bloody conquest
and inhuman cruelty (ch. 2).

The prophet comes close to questioning God's justice but
seems to have arrived at a position which stops short of saying
God is not always just. It may take some time to see it, but
surely it is still true that "the righteous shall live by his
faith (or faithfulness)" (2:4) because "the LORD is in his holy
temple" (2:20).

Chapter three identifies itself as a prayer of Habakkuk,
but it is more likely a liturgical psalm from another source. It
praises Yahweh for his power and majesty as manifested in his control over nature and his acts of salvation on behalf of his people.

Significant terms, names, and dates for this chapter

Uzziah	605 B.C.
Ahaz	Jeremiah
Damascus	Baruch
Hezekiah	Jehoiakim
Isaiah of Jerusalem	Babylonia
Immanuel	Nebuchadnezzar
Micah	Zephaniah
Manasseh	Nahum
Josiah	Nineveh
621 B.C.	Habakkuk

CHAPTER XI

DEFEAT AND EXILE

Biblical materials: II Kings 25. Lamentations. Jeremiah.
                     Ezekiel. Isaiah 40-55

Essential reading: II Kings 25
                     Jeremiah 29; 31:27-34; 38
                     Ezekiel 2-4; 18; 34; 37
                     Isaiah 40; 44-45; 52-53

        The king of Judah whom Babylonia put on the throne in Je-
rusalem after Jehoiachin was taken prisoner was his twenty-one-
year-old uncle Zedekiah (II Kings 24:18), whose eleven-year reign
was the final one for the kingdom. A man of some principle, he
was not strong-willed enough to control the princes who advised
and influenced him. Although Judah was in existence only by permission of the Babylonians, some of his advisers urged Zedekiah to
make an agreement with the Egyptians, who, they maintained, would
help Judah break free from its overlords. These advisers were ignoring the lessons of history, for the Egyptians had reneged on
similar agreements on several occasions.

                         Jeremiah and Zedekiah

        The new king seemed ready to listen to Jeremiah but could
not get the support of his officials to follow the prophet's advice and did not have the courage to try it without that support.
What Jeremiah proclaimed as the will of Yahweh in the situation in
which Judah found itself was too radical for either the political
or the religious leaders. Since the Lord had chosen the king of
Babylonia as his instrument, Judah should submit to him rather
than rebel against him. That, said Jeremiah, was the only way the
destruction of Jerusalem could be prevented (Jer. 27:8). His
credibility was damaged by the preaching of false prophets, such
as Hananiah, who was advising exactly the opposite course. When
Jeremiah demonstrated his point by wearing thongs and yoke-bars,
such as were placed on cattle to control them as they pulled carts
or plows, he was attacked by Hananiah, who broke the yoke and
claimed that this act proved that the yoke of Babylonia was also
broken (28:10-11). Convinced that his message was the correct one,
Jeremiah then had iron yoke-bars made, which Hananiah could not
break.

During the reign of Zedekiah (597-587 B.C.), there was considerable communication between the Jews in Jerusalem and those who had been exiled to Babylonia in 597. The exiles were concerned about getting back home, and some of the prophets were telling them not to get too settled over there for they would be returning within two years. Jeremiah did not see things that way and, in a letter addressed to them (ch. 29), said it would be more like seventy years. Therefore, he counseled them, they should build homes, plant gardens, raise families, get jobs, and live as normal lives as possible. He even told them to pray for the welfare of their new homeland because their own welfare depended upon that of the Babylonians.

News of the contents of this letter got back to Jerusalem and made Jeremiah the object of more bitter attacks. To the officials, Jeremiah's preaching and the letter added up to pro-Babylonianism and to them that meant the prophet was anti-Judah. When he started to visit his homeplace, north of Jerusalem, he was accused of trying to desert to the Babylonians and imprisoned (37:11-15). The king sought from him a word from the Lord and was told, "You shall be delivered into the hand of the king of Babylon" (37:17). Such treasonable statements deserved death, the princes decided, and they threw Jeremiah into an abandoned cistern and left him there to die (38:1-6). Rescued by the king's servant, Jeremiah was once again consulted by King Zedekiah. This time the prophet told him that the only way he could save Jerusalem and his own life was to surrender to the king of Babylonia (38:17-18).

Zedekiah knew he could not act on this advice, but he did allow Jeremiah to occupy a nicer prison for the remainder of his reign. Following the foolish counsel of his princes, the king did rebel against Nebuchadnezzar (II Kings 24:20). The result of this rebellion, recorded both in II Kings 25 and in Jer. 39, was the total demolition of Jerusalem, as Jeremiah had predicted, and the exile of many of the survivors to Babylonia. The sons of the fleeing Zedekiah were slain, the king's eyes were then put out, and he was carried to Babylon in fetters.

No mention is made of Jeremiah in the Deuteronomic history, but Jer. 39:11-14 tells us that, when he was found by the Babylonians in prison, they recognized him and treated him well because they knew of his advising that the city be surrendered to them. When he was allowed to choose whether he would go to Babylonia with the others or remain behind with the poorest people, he chose the latter, although he was sure that the future of Judah lay with the exiles.

Despite his many predictions of doom for Judah, Jeremiah had a firm belief that punishment was not to be the end of the story of God's people. His purchase of a field in Anathoth demonstrated his faith in the future (32:9-15). He believed that, after the exile, not only Judah but Israel also would be restored to the same land from which they had been removed (ch. 31). At that time the Lord would make a new covenant with both Israel and Judah

"I will put my law within them, and I will write it upon their hearts; and I will be their God, and they shall be my people. And no longer shall each man teach his neighbor and each his brother, saying, 'Know the LORD,' for they shall all know me, from the least of them to the greatest, says the LORD; for I will forgive their iniquity, and I will remember their sin no more." (31:33-34)

Baruch's memoirs record that he and Jeremiah were taken to Egypt by a group of Jews fleeing the wrath of Nebuchadnezzar, who they feared would annihilate them when he learned that his appointed governor had been murdered (Jer. 42-43). Jeremiah's preaching to his fellow Jews in Egypt was not appreciated, and his last word to them was one of severe judgment (Jer. 44). We do not know the story of his last days, but it is probable that they were no happier than his years in Jerusalem.

Prophet to the Exiles: Ezekiel

Among that group of Jews exiled to Babylonia in 597 was a priest named Ezekiel, who found that there was nothing for priests of Yahweh to do in that foreign land. Without a temple they could not offer sacrifices, and the only Temple was in Jerusalem. In the fifth year of his exile (593), Ezekiel received a vision, the weirdest in Scripture, which culminated in a divine call to become a prophet (Ezek. 1-3). His commission was to preach to those fellow Jews who were with him in Babylonia, particularly those who were living at Telabib, by the river Chebar. With considerable reluctance he began his new career, and his prophecies between 593 and 587 B.C. are found in chapters 4-24 of the book which bear his name. In tone and emphasis he agreed with Jeremiah, although no mention is made of their being acquainted with each other. Using drawings and acted-out messages, he too predicted the destruction of Jerusalem and a lengthy exile.

On a piece of tile he sketched the city of Jerusalem under siege as a sign for the people (Ezek. 4:1-3). Then he went out each day for a time and, in a place where he was sure to be noticed, lay on his left side for 390 days, each day representing a year of exile for Israel. After that he repeated the procedure on his right side for 40 days to indicate the length of Judah's exile. The total corruption of Judah's religion is depicted in a tremendous visionary experience described in chs. 8-11, in which Ezekiel pictures himself being transported back to Jerusalem to see for himself what was happening in the Temple and its precincts. Foreign deities were being worshiped, men were praying to the sun, and idolatrous figures had been painted on the walls. He saw the glory of Yahweh leaving the city.

In the lengthy sixteenth chapter the prophet portrays the history of Jerusalem as having begun when God discovered an abandoned child, the offspring of an Amorite father and a Hittite mother, unbathed and with the umbilical cord uncut. Yahweh saved the female child, reared her until she reached adulthood, then married her, a perfectly beautiful bride. But then she began playing the harlot with passers-by, a reference to the worship of other gods. She became so faithless that she surpassed her elder sister Samaria and her younger sister Sodom in her infidelities and abominations. Her punishment would be as severe as that of those two cities had been, but, like them, she would be restored in time and God would re-establish his covenant with her.

Some of the exiles complained that Yahweh was treating them unjustly, for they were being punished for the sins of earlier generations (ch. 18). The prophet chided them for quoting the proverb, "The fathers have eaten sour grapes, and the children's teeth are set on edge." This was no longer true, Ezekiel insisted, for the word of the Lord was "The soul that sins shall die. The son shall not suffer for the iniquity of the father, nor the father suffer for the iniquity of the son" (vs. 20). Ezekiel rejected their complaint, telling them that they were getting what they deserved. In true prophetic fashion he appealed to them to repent lest further punishment descend upon them (vss. 30-32).

It has often been pointed out that this eighteenth chapter marks a turning point in the Bible's teaching concerning individual responsibility. Heretofore the nation as a whole had been blessed or punished according to the corporate behavior of the people. But with Ezekiel and Jeremiah (see Jer. 31:29-30) came a new emphasis: each person will be held responsible for his conduct and not that of anyone else.

After a section (Ezek. 25-32) containing oracles against other nations, the book of Ezekiel takes on a radically different tone. Instead of condemnation and predictions of doom there are messages of comfort and forecasts of renewal. The shift in tone came about as a result of news from Jerusalem. The city had fall-

121

en! A new group of exiles was en route to Babylonia (33:21). Those already there had their hopes of an early return home crushed. The institutions in which they had placed their trust were all gone: the holy city, the Temple of Yahweh, and the house of David. Despite the preaching of Jeremiah and Ezekiel to the contrary, the masses had held on to their belief that these were inviolable. Now that they had found out otherwise, they wondered whether there were any future at all for them as the covenant people. Did this calamity mean that Yahweh had totally abandoned them?

The remainder of Ezekiel contains the prophet's answer to their despair. After the opening ten verses, in which the leadership of Israel is chastised, chapter 34 portrays the Lord as the loving, tender shepherd who promised personally to restore his people to their homeland:

"And I will bring them out from the peoples, and gather them from the countries, and will bring them into their own land; and I will feed them on the mountains of Israel, by the fountains, and in all the inhabited places of the country." (34:13)

The famous vision of the valley of dry bones (ch. 37) is another vehicle Ezekiel used to instill hope and confidence in the future. As the pile of dry, disconnected bones came together, were clothed with flesh, and became alive, so the "whole house of Israel" would be revived and brought home. Like Jeremiah, Ezekiel applied this promise to both Israel and Judah, predicting that they would be reunited under the leadership of the house of David. Chapters 40-48 picture a restored Jerusalem and a rebuilt Temple, more splendid than the original one, to which the glory of the Lord would return. This vision, the prophet tells us, came in 573 B.C., but we do not know how much longer his ministry among the exiles lasted.

The Jews in Babylonia

Undoubtedly the first part of the period of the exile was a time of bitter despair for the Jews in a foreign land. The book of Lamentations contains five poems which were composed during these years, all of them expressing the deep sense of loss and the overwhelming grief experienced by both the Jews left in the vicinity of Jerusalem and the exiles. The first one begins on a plaintive note: "How lonely sits the city that was full of people!" Even Yahweh's own house was not spared his wrath:

The LORD has brought to an end in Zion appointed feast and
  sabbath,
and in his fierce indignation has spurned king and priest.
The Lord has scorned his altar, disowned his sanctuary. (2:6-7)

This does not mean that all hope is lost:

For the Lord will not cast off for ever,
but, though he cause grief, he will have compassion
  according to the abundance of his steadfast love;
for he does not willingly afflict or grieve the sons of
  men. (3:31-33)

But the hope wavers a bit as the last poem closes:

Restore us to thyself, O LORD, that we may be restored!
  Renew our days as of old!
Or hast thou utterly rejected us?
Art thou exceedingly angry with us? (5:21-22)

That these poems were constructed with great care is suggested by
the fact that the first four are in the form of alphabetic acros-
tic. Each chapter has twenty-two verses (66 in ch. 3), each of
which begins with a succeeding letter of the Hebrew alphabet, beginning with aleph and continuing through all the twenty-two letters.

Obadiah

We can not fit the book of Obadiah precisely into the history of Judah but its strong condemnation of Edom suggests a time
shortly after the fall of Jerusalem in 587 B.C. This shortest of
Old Testament books pronounces Yahweh's severe judgment upon Edom,
a people descended from the brother of Jacob, Esau, for the Edomites' gloating over Judah's fall and participating in the looting
and pillaging of Jerusalem:

But you should not have gloated over the day of your brother
  in the day of his misfortune;
you should not have rejoiced over the people of Judah
  in the day of their ruin. (vs. 12)

you should not have looted his goods
  in the day of his calamity. (vs. 13c)

Their reprehensible behavior would surely be punished by a fate
similar to Judah's (vss. 15-18), while the Jewish exiles would return to repossess the land from which they had been taken (vss.
19-21).

The Experience of the Exile

The exile lasted officially approximately sixty years for the group captured in 598 B.C. and fifty for the 587 exiles. After the initial shock of defeat, deportation, and loss of their sacred institutions, the exiles began to adjust to their new environment. They began to take Jeremiah's advice about settling down, getting jobs, and raising families. They apparently were not used as slave labor by the Babylonians and so were free to shift for themselves. Many of them lived in the beautiful capital city of Babylon, where recently unearthed records indicate that some of them fared quite well financially. As to their religion, sharp alterations had to be made, for now they must worship without benefit of Temple or sacrificial cult.

The Deuteronomic historian ended his account of the Jews' fortunes and misfortunes with the story of the fall of Jerusalem and the final exile to Babylonia in 587 B.C. His last report is that of the murder of Gedaliah, the Jew whom Nebuchadnezzar had appointed as governor of the people who were left in the vicinity of Jerusalem (II Kings 25:22-26). As we noted in connection with Jeremiah, many of the people feared Babylonian reprisal and moved to Egypt.

The final paragraph in II Kings, generally considered a later addition to the historian's account, tells of an incident which occurred in 560 B.C. and which probably kindled the hopes of the exiles that they would soon be released. Jehoiachin, who had been taken captive in 597 after a three-month reign, was freed from prison and treated with respect after the death of Nebuchadnezzar. But this merciful act signaled no change in policy toward the exiles.

Since we do not have an historical record of other events and developments among the Jewish exiles, our knowledge of the period between 587 and 538 is somewhat limited. One thing of which we may be certain is that it produced a large part of what eventually became the Hebrew scriptures, including the historical account we have been following from Joshua through II Kings. The author, or authors, was thoroughly familiar with the law code discovered in the Temple in 621 B.C., which later became the major part of Deuteronomy. In fact, he was so saturated with the "Deuteronomic Theology" that he not only recorded the history of Israel and Judah, he interpreted it in terms of that theology. The high points in that history were understood to be the results of Yahweh's blessing the nation when it was obedient to the covenant, whereas calamities were seen as products of his punishment for its faithlessness and disobedience.

124

Most probably, the chief reason the Deuteronomic history was written was to explain why Israel and Judah had fallen, along with the city of Jerusalem, the temple cult, and the house of David. It was not just the working out of international politics but the inevitable consequence of a long history of unfaithfulness and disobedience which explained their demise. This explanation, taken along with the book of Deuteronomy and the oracles of the prophets, may have been the source of hope among the exiles that Judah would have a future.

Another important piece of literature which owes its origin to the period of the exile is the Priestly code, which, as we noted in Chapter III above, is found in the first four books of the Pentateuch. Using mostly oral traditions much older than the exile period, the Priestly writing is mainly concerned with cultic matters, such as sacrificial worship, regulations for the priests, rules governing special days and festivals, and directions for constructing the Tent of Meeting. Now that the Temple was no longer standing and most of the worship procedures connected with the Temple were no longer being followed, there was fear that knowledge of the significance and proper observance of these things would be lost. With time on their hands and with confidence that one day the Temple would be rebuilt, some of the exiled priests undertook the bringing together and writing down of all these traditional materials. One or more of their number may have been responsible for the ultimate blending of the Priestly writing with the JE and D documents to form the Pentateuch (see treatment of Ezra, below, pp. 136-138).

Just how the exiles of Judah worshiped in Babylonia is not known in detail. Observance of the sabbath, recitation of credal statements and songs of praise which had been preserved in the community memory, prayer, poems of lamentation recently composed (such as those in the book of Lamentations and Psalms 34 and 137), and liturgical materials (possibly including the creation account in Genesis 1) must have been important features of their worship. We do know that the exiles began to observe days of fasting as a way of mourning the fall of Jerusalem.

There is good reason to believe that a new institution, the synagogue, arose some time during the exile experience. Although the term is not used in the Old Testament, by the time of Jesus synagogues were found wherever a group of Jews lived and were taken for granted as old, established features of Judaism. Probably growing out of the practice of coming together on rest days for fellowship, worship, and instruction in their faith, they became so popular that, when the Temple was rebuilt, the synagogues remained.

A new professional group also seems to have arisen in this period: the <u>scribes</u>. It should be remembered that, even before the Pentateuch as we know it existed, there were written documents (JE and D) and collections of prophetic oracles (Amos, Hosea, Isaiah, Jeremiah, Micah, Ezekiel) which served to preserve and nurture the faith of the people. Scribes came into being to copy, read publicly, and interpret these written materials.

If we include in the Babylonian period not only the years of official exile (598/587-538 B.C.) but also the two centuries following, we can say that the religion of Judah was taking on new features as a result of the Jews' contacts with other religions, especially Zoroastrianism. Having originated in Persia, this faith came into Babylonia when that nation fell to the army of Cyrus in 538 B.C. From it Judaism apparently appropriated the concept of Satan as an opposing power to God in the universe, as well as the belief in unseen spirits, both good and evil, and the expectation of a meaningful life after death. Evidence may be seen in the later Old Testament literature of all of these ideas. Doubtless it was the ability of the Jewish leaders in Babylonia to adapt their traditions, beliefs, and institutions to the conditions which prevailed in this time of crisis that ensured the survival of the Mosaic faith. To be sure, the religion which emerged from this experience, called Judaism, was considerably different from the religion of Israel, but it grew directly out of the Israelite faith and held on to its basic convictions.

A Prophet of Hope: Second Isaiah

Our study of the prophets thus far may have produced the notion that, for the most part, the job of the prophet was to pronounce judgment and predict calamity. Toward the end of the exile, however, there arose from among the Jews in Babylonia a prophet who preached only words of comfort and hope, and predicted only a bright future for them. His name is not known but his oracles have survived as chapters 40-55 in the book of Isaiah; hence we refer to him as Second Isaiah. A keen observer of current events, this prophet was convinced that a Persian conqueror named Cyrus was Yahweh's chosen instrument for the deliverance of the Jews. Preaching sometime around 540 B.C., he knew that Cyrus had already conquered other nations in the Near East and predicted that Babylonia would be his next victim (Isaiah 45:1-13).

His written oracles begin with a resounding note:

Comfort, comfort my people, says your God.
Speak tenderly to Jerusalem, and cry to her

that her warfare is ended, that her iniquity is pardoned,
that she has received from the LORD's hand double for all
   her sins. (40:1-2)

Judah had suffered enough; the punishment was about over; Yahweh
was ready to act, he declared. But many of the Jews, who had
lived in the glorious city of Babylon for two generations, needed
convincing that Yahweh really could do something about their situation. The magnificent temple of Marduk, chief god of the Babylonian pantheon, stood as a reminder of the splendor and prosperity with which he blessed the Babylonians and which loomed in stark
contrast to the plight of the Jews. They must have been tempted
to ask, Can Yahweh, who could not prevent this humiliation we have
been enduring, really exert enough muscle to get us out of the
mighty Marduk's land?

   Second Isaiah dealt with that problem by asserting the in-
comparable majesty and power of Yahweh, who as creator of the universe can cause nations to rise and fall in accordance with his
will and purpose:

It is he who sits above the circle of the earth,
   and its inhabitants are like grasshoppers;
who stretches out the heavens like a curtain,
   and spreads them like a tent to dwell in;
who brings princes to nought,
   and makes the rulers of the earth as nothing. (40:22-23)

Not only the most accomplished poet, he is also the most skillful
theologian of the Hebrew prophets, as may be seen from his inter-
locking themes.

   1. Yahweh is the only God there is. From Moses onward
prophetic voices had maintained that Yahweh was to be the only deity for Israel, but none had stated unequivocally the monotheistic
(only god) position that there were no other gods. Its most suc-
cinct expression is in 44:6-8:

Thus says the LORD, the King of Israel
   and his Redeemer, the LORD of hosts:
"I am the first and I am the last;
   besides me there is no god.
Who is like me? Let him proclaim it,
   let him declare and set it forth before me.
               .   .   .
Is there a God besides me?
There is no Rock; I know not any."

This is indeed a bold assertion in the face of nearby evidences of
such deities as Marduk, Tammuz, and Astarte. If he is to be at

127

all convincing, the prophet will have to give some explanation of their presence, which is the next theme.

2. <u>All other so-called gods are only idols.</u> In one of the only two prose passages in this prophet's oracles (44:9-20), he tells a story about idol-making which is designed to destroy idolatry by ridiculing it. A carpenter cuts down a carefully selected tree, saws it into shorter pieces to use as fuel for heating and cooking, but saves one block to use to make a god for himself. Like all other idols, his newly-fashioned god has no eyes or ears and certainly no mind. Yet the woodsman falls down before it, worships it, and prays to it! If the prophet of the exile thinks to dispose of all deities except Yahweh by simply pronouncing them the products of human creativity, he will have to address a new problem: what about the thousands of persons who, totally ignorant of Yahweh, worship the false gods? Do they not have a god at all? He deals with that in his third theme.

3. <u>Yahweh is everybody's God.</u> This represents a genuine break-through for a Jew in the sixth century B.C., although it had been implied in God's original promise to Abraham: "by you all the families of the earth will bless themselves" (Gen. 12:3). But this universalism had long been forgotten, and the exiles must have been taken aback when they heard their prophet quoting Yahweh's message:

> "Turn to me and be saved, all the ends of the earth!
>   For I am God, and there is no other.
> By myself I have sworn,
>   from my mouth has gone forth in righteousness
>   a word that shall not return:
> 'To me every knee shall bow,
>   every tongue shall swear.'" (45:22-23)

This emphasis appears again in one of the Servant poems, in which Yahweh addresses the servant:

> He says:
> "It is too light a thing that you should be my servant
>   to raise up the tribes of Jacob
>   and to restore the preserved of Israel;
> I will give you as a light to the nations,
>   that my salvation may reach to the end of the earth." (49:6)

Of course, there are a great many people who have not heard of Yahweh, but that does not alter the fact that he is their God. That they have not heard is, by implication, a result of his chosen people's failure to spread the word. These three theological assertions have prepared (at least theoretically) the prophet's audience for the final theme, which is the main point of his message.

4. This all-powerful, universal, only God will shortly act to produce a new exodus for his people. Couched in terms which contrast with the first exodus, instructions for leaving Babylonia are followed by a reassuring promise:

> For you shall not go out in haste,
>   and you shall not go in flight,
> for the LORD will go before you,
>   and the God of Israel will be your rear guard. (52:12)

Yahweh has chosen to free his people by using a strong leader who probably knew nothing of the God of Judah. Likely a worshiper of Ahura Mazda, the Persian Cyrus is even referred to in 45:1 as Yahweh's _messiah_ (meaning "anointed"), a term which became laden with a variety of concepts of the future in later Jewish thought.

Second Isaiah's prediction of the nearness and the method of the exiles' deliverance was quite accurate. Cyrus' armies moved into Babylon unopposed in 538 B.C. and soon thereafter Cyrus issued a decree which permitted all persons being held in Babylonia against their wills to return to their homelands. The consequences of this proclamation will be considered in the next chapter.

The Servant Poems

A group of poems either by or about a special servant is scattered through Second Isaiah's prophecy: 42:1-4; 49:1-6; 50:4-9; and 52:13-53:12. If the servant is the same figure in all four poems, a problem arises regarding his identity, for at one point he is said to be Israel (49:3) while at others he appears as an individual addressing the people of Israel (50:4). The most discussed poem is the last one, often called the Song of the Suffering Servant, for in it the servant is depicted as having undergone horrible suffering and rejection, which was not deserved. Parts of the song seem to be Yahweh speaking, but other parts (e.g., 53:4-6) make sense only if they come from persons who feel that it was their sins for which the servant was suffering.

Interpretation of the passage has engendered a great deal of controversy. Jewish interpreters tend to identify the servant as the nation Israel, which had undergone a great deal of suffering, not all of which was justified by her own sins. Some have seen the servant as an individual prophet who was badly treated by his own people but who bore up magnificently and was eventually vindicated. Christian interpreters, on the other hand, have frequently found the correspondence between the servant's suffering and what happened to Jesus too great to overlook.

129

When the poem states

> Surely he has borne our griefs
> and carried our sorrows;
> . . .
> But he was wounded for our transgressions,
> he was bruised for our iniquities;

it seems to the followers of Jesus to be a perfect way of explaining why their sinless Lord was put to death: it was a vicarious atonement; that is, he died for the sins of others.

We, of course, can not know what or whom the original composer of the poem had in mind, but we have already observed that the prophets' concern was to speak a relevant word to their generation rather than to envision a distantly future figure whose appearance would have no present value.

Significant terms, names, and dates for this chapter

Zedekiah	Zoroastrianism
Anathoth	Judaism
Baruch's memoirs	Satan
Ezekiel	Second Isaiah
Babylon	Cyrus
Obadiah	Marduk
Lamentations	monotheism
Gedaliah	universalism
598 B.C.	538 B.C.
587 B.C.	messiah
synagogue	Suffering servant

CHAPTER XII

RESTORATION AND STRUGGLE

Biblical materials: I and II Chronicles. Ezra. Nehemiah.
Haggai. Zechariah. Malachi. Isaiah 56-66.
Jonah. Ruth

Essential reading: [Read in order listed] Ezra 1; 3-4; 6;
Nehemiah 1-2; 4; Ezra 7; 10:1-15; Nehemiah 8;
Haggai 1; Malachi 3; Jonah

The Work of the Chronicler

In addition to the J and E writings, which were sources of
most of the historical material in the Pentateuch, and the Deuteronomic history, there is another historical work in the Old Testament, which we shall simply call the Work of the Chronicler. It
consists of the books of I and II Chronicles, Ezra, and Nehemiah,
a continuous story beginning with (after eight chapters of genealogies) the united monarchy under Saul and ending with the work of
Ezra. Depending heavily upon the earlier books of Samuel and
Kings, it retells the story of the reigns of David and Solomon but
omits any details which would reflect upon their character. At
the same time, it adds to David's reputation a strong interest in
cultic matters, even to the point of crediting him with recruiting
and organizing artisans and musicians for service in the future
Temple. The Chronicler omits the story of the northern kingdom
after Jeroboam I led those tribes in rebellion against the house
of David, and stresses the importance of those kings of Judah who
fostered concern for the Temple and promoted religious reform:
Joash, Hezekiah, and Josiah.

Totally a product of Judah, it was written some time after
the reconstruction of Jerusalem, probably during the fourth century B.C., in an attempt to rekindle the Jews' fervor for the house
of God and the worship which centered in the Temple. It reflects
a time when some attitudes among the Jews were undergoing change.
For example, peace, rather than holy war, is emphasized. The theological problem implicit in the account (II Samuel 24) of Yahweh's punishing David for taking the census Yahweh had ordered him
to take is solved in I Chronicles 21, where it is Satan who ordered the census. The probability is that Zoroastrian dualism,
which accounts for evil by ascribing it to Ahriman, the foe of

131

Ahura Mazda, had influenced Jewish thinking.

Ezra and Nehemiah

The portion of the Chronicler's work which is far more valuable for our purposes, however, is that known to us as the books of Ezra and Nehemiah. It is almost our only source of knowledge of the reconstruction period and, although incomplete and not entirely accurate, helps us understand the problems and nature of post-exilic Judaism. The chronology of events is not correct, but we can overcome this by alternating between the two books (hence the sequence specified in the "essential reading" at the beginning of the chapter).

Conspicuously absent from the story of the return of the exiles and the re-establishment of a community of Yahweh's people in Jerusalem is any report of such a return of the citizens of Israel whom Assyria had carried away in 722 B.C. Despite the predictions of Jeremiah and Ezekiel that both Israel and Judah would be brought back to Canaan, and Ezekiel's optimistic vision of a reunited kingdom under the house of David, there is no record of any return of the northern exiles, hence often referred to as "the lost tribes of Israel." The Chronicler pointedly states, "So Israel has been in rebellion against the house of David to this day" (II Chron. 10:19).

By ending his story of the northern tribes at the point of their secession (922 B.C.), he leaves the reader with the impression that Yahweh's purposes, promises, and covenant are continued in the restored community of Judah. It should not be forgotten that an unrecorded number of Israelites from the ten northern tribes had emigrated to Judah during the Assyrian threat and had, in effect, become Judeans. Hence many "Jews" of a later time could trace their ancestry to a son of Jacob other than Judah or Benjamin or Levi (The Levites were scattered throughout the other tribes' territories.).

The Second Temple

As related in the books of Ezra and Nehemiah, the story of the reconstruction of Judah centers in the labors and leadership of three men: Zerubbabel, Nehemiah, and Ezra. Each made a specific and valuable contribution to the religious, political, and economic life of Jerusalem following the decree of Cyrus in 538 B.C. (Ezra 1:1-4), which authorized the Jews to return to their city, still in ruins, and rebuild the house of Yahweh. It is clear that there was no mad rush to pull up stakes and launch a massive cru-

132

sade to return to Judah. Instead, the migration was gradual, taking place over a period of more than a century. The majority of the Jews in Babylonia, where they had been for two generations, never did make the trek to Jerusalem, most likely because life in Mesopotamia was fairly good and because they were apprehensive about what it would be like in Judah. Their fears were justified, as we learn from the story of the problems faced by those who did return. Lack of housing, limited ways of earning a living, and hostility from the neighbors continued to plague them for decades.

Jewish hopes for release from exile were realized, as Second Isaiah had predicted, when the benevolent Persian Cyrus conquered Babylonia. Unlike the leadership of Judah when Jerusalem was threatened by Nebuchadnezzar, the leaders of Babylonia surrendered their magnificent capital, Babylon, to the invading Persians, who entered without killing anyone or destroying any buildings. Reversing the policy of his predecessors, Cyrus allowed all persons being held against their will to return to their native lands. To the Jews he gave permission to take with them the furnishings which Nebuchadnezzar's army had confiscated from the Temple.

The first group of returning Jews was led by Zerubbabel (also called Sheshbazzar), who was assisted by the priest Jeshua. Their first project upon reaching the site of Jerusalem was to build an altar of burnt offering (Ezra 3:1-7) and engage in sacrificial worship, something which had not happened for half a century. This was followed by the laying of the foundation for a new temple but, before the superstructure could be erected, the project was stopped. Some of the neighboring peoples, probably Samaritans, offered help in rebuilding the house of God but were rebuffed by the Jewish leaders, probably because they considered them religiously tainted (Ezra 4:3). Opposition to the Temple became so fierce that the Persian government (Cyrus was now dead.) withdrew its building permit until it could be satisfied that the Jews were not planning an independent state, as their enemies were charging. Understandably, the Jews turned their attention to providing homes and income for their families and, by the time the permit was renewed, had lost interest in rebuilding the Temple.

Haggai and Zechariah

About 520 B.C., two prophets arrived in Jerusalem from Babylonia with the express assignment of stirring up the Jews to resume work on the Temple. They are mentioned in Ezra 5:1, and their names identify two of the minor prophets, Haggai and Zechariah. The situation among the returned exiles in Jerusalem when

133

Haggai arrived was not good. In the prophet's words,

> "You have sown much, and harvested little; you eat, but you
> never have enough; you drink, but you never have your fill;
> you clothe yourselves, but no one is warm; and he who earns
> wages earns wages to put them into a bag with holes." (1:6)

The discouraged returnees, eighteen years after arriving in Jerusalem, were having a difficult time making a living. It was taking all their time and energy to stay alive. Even Zerubbabel had
lost his zeal for the reconstruction of the Temple. Haggai proclaimed to them that the cause of their pitiable economic situation was their selfish concern with building their own homes and
neglect of God's house (1:7-11).

Two months after Haggai's arrival in Jerusalem, another
prophet, Zechariah, came into town and reinforced his predecessor's call for resuming work on the Temple. In a series of eight
visions (Zechariah 1-6), he sought to inspire the Jews to enthusi-
asm for the task by picturing a glorious future for the area:
"Thus says the LORD of hosts: My cities shall again overflow with
prosperity, and the LORD will again comfort Zion and again choose
Jerusalem" (1:17). Zerubbabel and Joshua (the priest Jeshua in
Ezra), Zechariah announced, would be the two messiahs of the Lord
(4:14; 6:9-14). He pictured a future Jerusalem of peace, happiness, and prosperity (8:1-8), with Yahweh himself dwelling in her
midst.

Chapters 9-14 of Zechariah are quite different from 1-8
and are generally acknowledged to have originated at a later time.
"Second Zechariah" contains visions and predictions which have the
flavor of apocalyptic literature. (For an explanation of apocalyptic literature see the discussion of Daniel below, pp. 158-9.)
Perhaps the best known passage of this material is 9:9, which pictures Jerusalem's king entering the city victoriously on an ass, a
verse which the New Testament writer Matthew sees as being fulfilled by Jesus' entry into Jerusalem on Palm Sunday (Matthew
21:1-5; see also John 12:15).

The preaching of Haggai and Zechariah was effective, and
the Jews got busy again on the Temple project (Ezra 5:1-2; 6:14).
The work was completed in 515 B.C., and a joyous dedication ceremony was held (Ezra 6:16-18). The second Temple did not live up
to the optimistic vision in Ezekiel 40-48, for it was not so elab-
orate or splendid as Solomon's. But the Jews did have their Temple back, after having had to do without it for three quarters of
a century, and this was an extremely important fact for them. Now
all the cultic rules and directions for sacrificial worship which
the priests in exile had carefully preserved were put into effect,

the priesthood was again important, and temple choirs and musicians' guilds were organized to enhance the worship. This second Temple stood until rebuilt in the time of Jesus at the instigation of Herod the Great.

Malachi

What life in Jerusalem was like between 515 B.C. and the time of Nehemiah (c. 444 B.C.) we can not state with certainty, but the little book containing the oracles of the prophet Malachi probably stems from that period. It reflects conditions among a people for whom the hopes expressed by earlier prophets, especially Ezekiel and Zechariah, have not materialized. Like Haggai, the prophet Malachi saw the poverty and disillusionment as a result of the disobedience and self-centeredness of the population of Jerusalem.

He was distressed by their attitude toward sacrificial worship: they were offering less than perfect animals to God (Mal. 1:8). He was upset by the corruption he saw among the priests: they were incompetent teachers and unworthy examples for the people (2:7-9). He was shocked by the widespread practice of Jewish men's divorcing their wives in disregard of the marriage vows (2:13-16). He was unhappy over their withholding the tithes from the Temple, challenging the people to test God by bringing the full tithe; he assured them that if they did, God would bring prosperity to the land (3:8-10). Yahweh's messenger would be sent to cleanse his Temple and reform the cult (3:1-4), but, before "the great and terrible day of the LORD" came, Elijah the prophet would be sent to reconcile children and parents (4:5-6). This expectation of the return of Elijah to prepare the way for the messiah or the kingdom of God continued to play a role in Judaism, and is reflected in some of the New Testament gospels.

Third Isaiah

We have delayed consideration of Isaiah 56-66 until now because the material in that section seems to fit the time after the exile rather than that of either Isaiah of Jerusalem or Second Isaiah. Whether by one or several prophets we are unable to tell, but we can say that the oracles are primarily concerned with cultic matters. Proper observance of the sabbath, keeping the fasts, and avoiding idolatry are stressed, and it is probable that this prophet lived at a time close to that of Malachi. The book ends on a hopeful note, speaking of "new heavens and a new earth" and envisioning a Jerusalem in which joy, peace, long life, and prosperity will prevail (Is. 65:17-25).

135

The Wall Rebuilt

The situation in post-exilic Jerusalem as reflected in Malachi and Third Isaiah fits into the story of the next "hero" the reconstruction, Nehemiah. A Jew in a most responsible position in the Persian royal court, he received news from Jerusalem which disturbed him. Almost a century after the official end of the exile, the city wall was still in ruins and the Jews who had not been exiled were "in great trouble and shame" (Neh. 1:3). I what seems to be his memoirs, Nehemiah says he was granted a lea of absence by King Artaxerxes so that he could lead a group of Jews to Jerusalem and investigate the problems (Neh. 2).

His arrival in Jerusalem was not welcomed by the non-Jew and he encountered opposition all along the way in his attempt t rebuild the city wall. When ridicule of the project failed to stop it, Nehemiah's opponents attacked the workmen, for they did not want a restored state of Judah in the territory. By organizing his people into two platoons, one to stand guard while the other labored, Nehemiah succeeded in rebuilding the wall in the amazingly short time of fifty-two days (Neh. 6:15). The rebuilt wall was a great aid in protecting the Jewish inhabitants from o siders who ignored their religious institutions, but it did not cure all the city's problems.

About a decade later, Nehemiah made a second trip to Jer salem, at which time he instituted certain reforms. He cleansed the Temple of non-Jewish personnel, restored the Levites to control over it, and brought back the choirs. He tightened the rul governing the sabbath and persuaded the Jewish men to take an oa that they would not marry any more non-Jewish women. Nehemiah's first service in Jerusalem was c. 444 B.C., and his return occur red in 432 (the 32nd year of Artaxerxes I. Neh. 13:6).

The Book

The last, and in some respects the most important, leade of the reconstruction was Ezra, introduced in Ezra 7 as a descen ant of Aaron and a scribe "skilled in the law of Moses" (7:6). There is considerable confusion in the record as to the time of Ezra's work, probably stemming from the Chronicler's failure to recognize that the King Artaxerxes mentioned in Ezra 7:1 is most likely Artaxerxes II rather than the same one mentioned in connec tion with Nehemiah. Thus, rather than being contemporary with Ne hemiah (as presumed in Neh. 8-9), Ezra and his work are best unde stood if his arrival in Jerusalem is dated around 398 B.C.

When he got there, the Temple was standing, the city wall was intact, and no further building project was called for. Ezra's contribution lay in a different direction. When he left Babylonia en route to Jerusalem, he carried "the book of the law of Moses" (Neh. 8:1), possibly the Pentateuch (see above, p. 28). In his role as priest (Neh. 8:2), Ezra assembled the adults of the city in the square and read the book to them each morning for seven days. Assisted by others he then explained its meaning (Neh. 8:8).

On the basis of the book of the Law, Ezra instituted a number of sweeping reforms in Jerusalem which went farther than those of Nehemiah. Intermarriage with non-Jews was still being practiced, and in Ezra's opinion this posed a serious threat to the purity of Jewish religion. He persuaded the men not only to discontinue the practice but also to divorce the foreign wives they already had (Ezra 10:9-14)! This drastic measure was followed by the reinstitution of the feast and fast days specified in the book, the establishment of a Temple tax to support the priests and Levites, and resumption of the donation of the first fruits and the consecration of the first-born to the Lord. Taken together, Ezra's reforms resulted in the emphasizing of the people's Jewishness, which made them more aware of how they differed from their neighbors. Nehemiah 9:2 puts it succinctly: "And the Israelites separated themselves from all foreigners."

The work of Ezra, with his skill in the Torah and his deep appreciation of the Temple and its cult, brought two lasting emphases into Israelite religion, which have earned for him a reputation as the "father of Judaism." One of these features is the establishment of the book, the written law of God, as the source of authority for the faith and practice of the Jews. Later generations considered Ezra to be the last of the prophets. After him God revealed his word no longer through the oral proclamations of his spokesmen but through the words inscribed in a book. To help people find the answers they sought from the book, a whole new profession arose, the scribes, of whom Ezra may be properly called the first. A couple of centuries after Ezra, the prophetic oracles were added to the Torah as authoritative scripture, although some Jews never accepted them as such.

The second emphasis which grew out of the work of Ezra was the new stress upon the ethnic and religious purity of the restored Jewish community in Judah. A good Jew must worship Yahweh exclusively, participate in the Temple cult, and strictly obey the Torah, including the food laws and the strictures against intermarriage with foreigners. These are the very things which made the Jews aware of their specialness and encouraged them to limit contacts with Gentiles to the necessary commercial ones. Whether or

not it was Ezra's intention, one result of his reforms was a virtually isolated community which emphasized its differences from
the neighboring peoples and took pride in its religious purity.
But another result, one which he certainly intended, was that Judaism survived the powerful threat from the paganism of its environment.

A Different View: Ruth

The short book of Ruth, with its setting in the days of
the Judges, occupies a spot immediately following that book in ou
English Bibles, but it seems to belong to the period of Ezra or
thereafter. In itself it is an appealing story of loyalty and
love between Ruth, a Moabitess, and her mother-in-law Naomi, a wo
man of Judah. The book was likely included in the Hebrew scriptures because of the information it contains about the ancestry o
Israel's greatest king, David. But the relevance of the story to
the fourth century B.C. comes from the revelation that one of David's great-grandmothers was Ruth, a non-Jew. It is as though th
writer, by placing David's genealogy at the very end, were saying
"Maybe intermarriage with foreigners is not so bad; after all, ou
greatest king resulted from such a marriage!"

A Meaningful Protest: Jonah

The emphasis upon separateness from Gentiles and careful
observance of the laws which stressed the Jews' special relationship with Yahweh inevitably led to the assumption that Yahweh was
not really concerned with other peoples. On the other hand, if
the stress is placed upon the Jews' serving as Yahweh's priests t
the world, the resulting outlook must be universalism. God's
promise to Abraham reflects that, and the preaching of Second Isa
ah reinforces it. But post-Ezra Judaism had moved away from this
and assumed that, to be a holy nation, it must isolate itself as
much as possible from other nations.

The little book of Jonah, a delightful short story, was
designed to counteract that trend and to remind Yahweh's people
that he was the God of all people, not just the Jews. Choosing a
actual prophet as his "hero" (Jonah is mentioned briefly in II
Kings 14:25), the unknown writer depicts the narrow attitude of
his contemporaries by picturing him as stubbornly refusing to go
to the capital of Assyria, Nineveh, to deliver God's call to repentance. Only after he was convinced that there was no way to
escape the assignment did Jonah make the trip to the heart of ene
my territory. Later he was delighted at the prospect of witness-

138

ing Nineveh's destruction but became incensed when Yahweh changed his plan after the unexpected repentance of the entire city. The story ends with Yahweh's confronting Jonah, who was bemoaning a dead plant, with the pointed question,

"And should not I pity Nineveh, that great city, in which are more than a hundred and twenty thousand persons who do not know their right hand from their left, and also much cattle?" (Jonah 4:11)

The writer was saying, "Our God is everybody's God, and he is concerned with all peoples, even those we call our enemies."

But the messages of Ruth and Jonah represented only a small minority in Judah, and the attitude of narrowness and the practice of separateness continued until international events forced the Jews to re-examine their attitude toward other peoples and cultures. The Samaritans, descendants of those Israelites not exiled in 722 B.C. and the foreigners with whom they intermarried, had offered their assistance to Zerubbabel in rebuilding the Temple, but he had rather tartly refused it. Still claiming allegiance to Yahweh, they eventually built their own temple on Mt. Gerizim in central Palestine where, armed with their own version of the Pentateuch, they continued to practice their faith for centuries.

Hostility between the Samaritans and the Jews, who considered them half-breeds both ethnically and religiously, continued to grow during the latter centuries before Christ, and it had reached its peak by the time of Jesus. We know very little of the religious life of the Jews (the majority) who had not left Babylonia, but the likelihood is that it closely resembled that in Judah, where ninety percent of the Jews lived in the country outside Jerusalem (Neh. 11:1).

Significant terms, names, and dates for this chapter

The Chronicler	Malachi
Ezra	Third Isaiah
Lost tribes of Israel	Ruth
Zerubbabel	Naomi
Nehemiah	Jonah
Haggai	Nineveh
Zechariah	398 B.C.
515 B.C.	Judaism
444 B.C.	

CHAPTER XIII

ISRAEL'S POETRY AND WISDOM

Biblical materials: Psalms. Song of Solomon. Proverbs.
                      Ecclesiastes. Job

Essential reading: Psalms 8; 23; 44; 51; Song of Solomon 4
                      Proverbs 10; 1; 6; Ecclesiastes 1-3
                      Job 1-4; 42

Poetry in the Old Testament

The Hebrew Scriptures contain a great deal of poetry. Th
older English versions do not always put it into the familiar poetic format, but much of the prophetic material is poetic in nature. Even the Pentateuch (e.g., Exodus 15) and the so-called
historical books (e.g., Judges 5) contain poetry. Four books are
made up exclusively of poetry: Psalms, Proverbs, Song of Solomon
and Lamentations, the last of which was considered in chapter ele
ven. Most of Job and Ecclesiastes are also poetry.

Hebrew poetry has most of the characteristics of the poet
ry of other languages except the rhyming of words at the end of
lines. It does have rhythm, figurative expressions, play on word
and parallelism. Although found in English and other poetry as
well, the most significant characteristic of Hebrew poetry is
parallelism, which can be most readily identified in the two-line
verse. The idea or meaning of the first line is directly related
to the second in one of several ways.

The most common type of parallelism is the synonymous, in
which the thought of the first line is repeated, in different
words, in the second line. The following two verses illustrate
this type:

O LORD, who shall sojourn in thy tent?
Who shall dwell on thy holy hill? (Psalm 15:1)

What is man that thou art mindful of him,
    and the son of man that thou dost care for him? (Psalm 8:4)

It will be noted that some of the words in the two lines are the
same, but the key words have been changed, yet in such a way that
the idea expressed is almost exactly the same in both lines.

Awareness of this feature of biblical poetry sometimes guards against misinterpretation, as is the case in the second selection above. "Son of man" in the second line is synonymous with "man" in the first rather than some prefiguring of a term Jesus used of himself centuries later. One obvious effect of synonymous parallelism is that the point being made is more easily remembered, since it has been stated twice.

The next most frequent type is <u>antithetic</u> parallelism, in which the second line states the opposite of, or contrasts to, the first. Proverbs 10-21 abounds in this type. Two examples are:

A wise son makes a glad father,
    but a foolish son is a sorrow to his mother. (Prov. 10:1)

He who heeds instruction is on the path to life,
    but he who rejects reproof goes astray. (Prov. 10:17)

This type has the effect of clarifying a thought by stating its obverse, thereby aiding both the understanding and the memory.

Other types of parallelism, less profuse than the two above, have been identified by scholars, but the examples given will suffice to give the reader a greater appreciation of this pervading feature of Hebrew poetry. Sometimes the poet will complicate his structure by combining two types in one stanza of four or more lines, as in Psalm 30:5:

For his anger is but for a moment,
    and his favor is for a life time.
Weeping may tarry for the night,
    but joy comes with the morning.

Here the first two lines form an antithetical couplet. So do the second pair. But the second pair is in synonymous relation to the first.

Israel's Hymnbook: the Book of Psalms

The largest collection of Hebrew poetry, and the longest book in the Bible, is the book of Psalms. Unlike the other books, each chapter (psalm) of this book has its own author, time of writing, and purpose. Some of the individual psalms are quite old, surely reaching back to David's time, while others originated during or after the Babylonian exile. Since the book itself is clearly marked off into five shorter books (1-41; 42-72; 73-89; 90-106; 107-150), we may assume that it was made up of earlier collections which were used by the final editor in composing a hymnal for use in the second Temple. We do not know the date of its final editing, but the fact that Jesus and the New Testament writers quote from it frequently suggests that it already enjoyed popular acce ance as scripture by the time of Jesus.

The traditional association of the Psalms with David is both understandable and misleading. The great king's musiciansh and interest in Temple worship were emphasized by the Chronicler Yet we may be sure that David actually wrote only a very few of the Psalms, despite the titles containing his name which appear the beginning of many of them. These titles are not part of the original psalms and may indicate no more than some later editor' assumption that a particular psalm was composed on a specific occasion by a particular author.

All of the psalms are connected in some way with the religious or political life of Israel and Judah. But there are va differences in tone and attitude among them. It is helpful to classify the psalms according to their nature and purpose, and a very simple system of classification will include the vast major: ty of them. The reader does not have to be an expert to recogni that many of the psalms consist primarily of praise to God, whil many others are in a complaining or mourning mood. The primary classification, then, is into psalms of <u>praise</u> and psalms of <u>lament</u>. It is also clear from a simple reading that many of them are designed for the use of the whole community as it assembles for worship while others are more suited for individual use. Hence a second classification is into <u>community</u> and <u>individual</u> psalms. This provides us with our four basic classes:

1. <u>Community praise</u>, or thanksgiving, characterizes a large number of the psalms, which are also known as <u>hymns</u>. Yahwe is praised for his majesty, power, goodness, mercy, creation, et as may be seen in Pss. 8, 24, 48, 67, 113, and many others.

2. <u>Individual praise</u>. This type is a vehicle useful for the person who has his own reason for praising God. He may have recovered from a serious illness, have been delivered from an ene my, or enjoyed a particular stroke of good fortune. Psalms 18, 23, 27, and 30 are examples of this type.

3. <u>Community lament</u>. In times of national disgrace, defeat in battle, subjugation by invaders, exile to a foreign land, and so forth, the psalmists did not hesitate to let their complaints be known to Yahweh, who was called upon to get busy and something about their situation. Psalms 44, 60, 74, and 137 fit into this category.

4. <u>Individual lament</u>. Someone who had been wronged by a

neighbor, or taunted by an enemy, or overcome with illness or despair must have found this group of psalms a satisfying way of venting his feelings and urging the Lord to take away the cause of his complaint. Psalms 6, 13, 17, and 51 exemplify this class of psalms.

The hymns (class # 1 above) are sometimes sub-classified into enthronement psalms (e.g., Ps. 97), which praise God for his reigning over the earth, and songs of ascent (Pss. 120-134), composed for the use of pilgrims on their way to Jerusalem to observe one of the festival or fast days. There are also a few royal psalms, which relate in some way to the human king of Israel or Judah (e.g., Ps. 45). Such a variety of compositions must have been a most useful treasury of worship materials for the Jews of the latter centuries of the Old Testament period. They have continued in the centuries since to provide suitable channels for expressing the deepest feelings and thoughts of Jews and Christians and to provide a source of comfort, hope, and reassurance in life's trying crises.

The community hymns and laments were doubtless sung to musical accompaniment, as is indicated in I Chronicles 16 and II Chronicles 5. The mysterious word "selah," which appears in the margins of many of the psalms (e.g., Ps. 3), is probably some direction to the accompanists.

Biblical Erotica: the Song of Solomon

The Song of Solomon, understood literally, is so obviously erotic in its description of love between a man and a woman that many readers have wondered why it is in the Bible. This beautiful collection of love songs was carefully examined by the rabbinical council at Jamnia in 90 A.D., which made the final determination of the contents of the Writings, the third division of the Hebrew canon. Only after it was decided that the book should be interpreted allegorically as describing love between God and his people was it admitted. Christian interpreters, faced with the same problem of what to do with so passionate a writing, decided that it is an allegory of the love between Christ and his bride, the church! The fact that the book makes no mention of God or Christ and contains no religious or ethical ideas, however, has led modern scholars to question the propriety of the allegorical interpretation.

Although the name of Solomon appears in a few passages, it is widely agreed that he is not the author of the book. It is best to take the work just as it is for what it appears to be: an anthology of love lyrics united only by the common theme of love

143

between the sexes. It would have been, and probably was, a good
source of songs to be sung at the week-long wedding festivities
which were customary in the Near East. It would seem appropriate
that the goodness of this mutual physical attraction of man and
woman, implied in the stories of creation (Gen. 1 and 2), be celebrated in the Scriptures without apology or embarrassment. It is
not necessary to devise some hidden meaning to avoid the literal
interpretation of this book. We do not know enough about the time
of writing to suggest a precise date for it, although modern scholars tend to assign it to the late Persian or Greek period (fourth
or third century B.C.). Individual songs within the collection
may be considerably older.

The Wisdom Literature

Already in the third millenium B.C., there was an active
wisdom movement in Egypt and Mesopotamia, as is known from writings which have survived. Wisdom, as used here, is not a virtue
but a mode of acquiring and transmitting knowledge. In one sense,
the wisdom of the ancient Near East can be called the forerunner
of philosophy. Relying upon human observation rather than divine
revelation, the wise men distilled their insights into short proverbs, slightly longer essays, fables, and riddles which were
first used in royal courts to instruct princes or entertain royal
families and their guests. Later they composed extended dia-
logues, in which some weighty problem was examined and discussed.
Israelite wisdom should be understood as proceeding from this ancient wisdom tradition.

According to the Bible, Solomon was the first Israelite to
manifest an interest in wisdom. He employed sages (wise men and
women) to gather wisdom materials from any available source, and
Egypt appears to have been the most fruitful source of supply for
them. The name of King Hezekiah is also connected with wisdom.
Sages are mentioned several times in the Old Testament, although
much less frequently than priests and prophets. An instructive
reference to the roles of these religious leaders occurs in Jeremiah 18:18:

> Then they said, "Come, let us make plots against Jeremiah,
> for the law shall not perish from the priest, nor counsel
> from the wise, nor the word from the prophet."

Counsel, which would include instruction and advice, is associated
with the sage ("wise") in this passage.

Because of the international origin of the wisdom materials, and because the sage depended more upon his own observation and reflection than upon a heavenly vision or written ordinance, Israelite wisdom is less distinctive and more universal in character than the historical and prophetic materials. This is especially true of the practical wisdom (Proverbs) as distinguished from the speculative wisdom (Job and Ecclesiastes), which may deal with a specific problem from the standpoint of Israel's faith. But most of the observations about human nature and the advice on how to live a successful, well-adjusted life found in Proverbs are just as applicable to Arabs, Chinese, and Americans as they are to Jews. Allusions to the sacrificial cult, the Temple, the covenant relationship with Yahweh, and the peculiar history of Israel are rare in the wisdom literature.

The Book of Proverbs

An excellent collection of practical wisdom materials, Proverbs is more an anthology than a monograph. That is, like the book of Psalms, it is obviously composed of a number of smaller collections which come from different sources and a variety of time periods. Scholars generally assume that the collection entitled "the proverbs of Solomon" found in 10:1-22:16 is the earliest part of the book, because it contains exclusively the short, pithy, one-verse sayings to which we commonly give the name "proverbs." Being a perfect vehicle for contrasting wise and foolish behavior, antithetic parallelism (see above, p. 141) predominates in this section. Typical sayings of this section are

> The simple believes everything,
> but the prudent looks where he is going. (14:15)

> A man of quick temper acts foolishly,
> but a man of discretion is patient. (14:17)

> He who oppresses a poor man insults his Maker,
> but he who is kind to the needy honors him. (14:31)

The first nine chapters of the book consist of longer essays on a variety of subjects, probably an advance in style from the two-line proverb. The purpose of the book is clearly given in the opening stanza (1:2-6):

> That men may know wisdom and instruction,
> understand words of insight,
> receive instruction in wise dealing,
> righteousness, justice, and equity;

and so on in the same vein. The standpoint from which all the sections of Proverbs are written is that of the mature wise man

145

imparting the benefit of his accumulated wisdom to young men who
are about to launch out into the world on their own, in the hope
that the younger generation will profit from the experience of
their elders and thus be spared unnecessary pain. Occasionally
(as in 1:7 and 3:11-12) the distinctive name of Israel's God appears in Proverbs, but most of the advice it contains is equally
useful to young men of any country or any religion. Each man (the
book is unapologetically male-oriented) must choose between two
alternatives for his life: the way of a fool, to which "Dame Folly" beckons, or the way of the wise, to which he is urged by "Lady
Wisdom." In a lengthy speech (8:4-36) attributed to this personi-
fication of wisdom, she claims to have been present at creation,
to be the source of royal wisdom, and to reward her followers with
a happy life:

> "To you, O men, I call,
> and my cry is to the sons of men.
> O simple ones, learn prudence;
> O foolish men, pay attention." (8:4-5)

> "The LORD created me at the beginning of his work,
> the first of his acts of old." (8:22)

> "And now, my sons, listen to me:
> happy are those who keep my ways." (8:32)

The simple division of all men into fools and the wise is
closely akin to the doctrine of retribution which characterizes
the Deuteronomic Theology, in which there are also only two ways:
obedience or disobedience. The foolish man is the one who disobeys Yahweh's laws; the wise man is he who follows them diligently

> The fear of the LORD is the beginning of knowledge;
> fools despise wisdom and instruction. (1:7)

Other essays in this section warn against getting involved with
the "loose woman" (5:1-14), signing other people's notes (6:1-5),
laziness (6:6-11), and adultery (ch. 7).

Section Three (22:17-24:34) is patterned after an ancient
Egyptian wisdom writing, with its thirty chapters suggesting the
"thirty sayings" of Proverbs 22:20. Especially applicable to
young men with political ambitions, it warns against over-indul-
gence in strong drink (23:29-35), mistreatment of the poor, lack
of etiquette, failure to discipline children, and partiality in
meting out justice. More "proverbs of Solomon" follow in chapters
25-29, but then come two short sections (30:1-33 and 31:1-9), attributed to otherwise unknown sages, Agur and Lemuel, most likely
non-Israelites. The book of Proverbs closes with the remarkable
description of a good wife (31:10-31), conclusive evidence that
this book is by males and for males!

The various sections which make up the book of Proverbs agree in advocating wisdom over folly and in the assumption that every man has the power and responsibility of choosing which course he will follow. They agree also in their descriptions of the rewards of wisdom and the punishments of folly. The wise, obedient man may expect to be rewarded with long life, prosperity, and abundant offspring, while the foolish man will be deprived of these. A glorious life after death as part of the reward is missing from Proverbs, so avoidance of Sheol as long as possible is a desirable goal. But the wise can look forward to a kind of immortality, for he will live on in the memory of his family and neighbors:

> The memory of the righteous is a blessing,
> but the name of the wicked will rot. (10:7)

Ecclesiastes

A good example of the speculative type of wisdom literature is the somewhat irreverent, sometimes cynical book of Ecclesiastes. It is impossible to know precisely when it was written, but it surely came after Proverbs, for it directly challenges some of that book's primary assumptions. That it was quite late in the Old Testament period is suggested by the fact that it refutes the belief in an afterlife, an idea which was quite late in gaining acceptance among the Jews. The name of the writer is Koheleth, improperly translated "Preacher" in many English versions, a professional wisdom teacher, or sage. The book may, in fact, be a lecture he was delivering to his class, which could be engaging in dialogue with their teacher. This could account for its rambling, somewhat disjointed nature.

The theme of the book seems clear enough: Is there any meaning to life and, if so, where may it be found? Chapters one and two describe the life-long search which Koheleth pursued for meaning, and the remainder contains his rather pessimistic answer. Assuming, for literary purposes only, the stance of King Solomon (1:1,12), whose connection with wisdom we have already considered, the sage begins with the cynical observation "All is vanity" (1:2). After twelve chapters of discussion, he ends with the same words (12:8). The remaining verses (12:9-14) are later attempts to tone down the sharpness of the book and are probably what made it admissible into the canon.

Koheleth reports that he had tried every conceivable avenue to discover meaning in life: the way of wisdom (1:16-17), the pleasure route (2:1), losing himself in great projects (2:4), accumulating wealth (2:7), entertainment (2:8), and fame. But in none of these, nor in any combination thereof, did he find meaning

> Then I considered all that my hands had done and the toil
> I had spent in doing it, and behold, all was vanity and a
> striving after wind, and there was nothing to be gained
> under the sun. (2:11)

"Vanity," as Koheleth used the term, refers to the temporary, futile nature of things, which, he is saying, have no real meaning and no lasting value. A little farther on (2:24), he expresses the ultimate conclusion of his search: "There is nothing better for a man than that he should eat and drink, and find enjoyment in his toil."

Like Proverbs, Koheleth does not accept a doctrine of an after-life, but he feels called upon to defend his position. He admits that God has made it possible for man to conceive of such a thing (3:11-12) but insists that death ends existence for man just as it does for the beasts (3:19-22). The way the subject is raised in Ecclesiastes indicates that the idea of a life after death, a new concept for the Jews, was being advocated by some persons in Koheleth's day.

Unlike Proverbs, Koheleth does not insist that the righteous always get rewarded (in this life) and the wicked always get punished. The fact that the opposite often happens is an example of the vanity of life (8:14-15). Life is not always fair, and a person has no basis on which he can assume that life's unfairness in this world will be corrected in the next, the sage implies.

Although Koheleth repeatedly recommends that one enjoy life as much as he can, he does not advocate immorality. And, despite the fact that the God whom he occasionally mentions is a transcendent deity who really is not much concerned with what happens on earth, he does recognize that God is he who created the world and ordered it in such a way that man can find enjoyment in it. Without doubt, Ecclesiastes is the most pessimistic book in the Bible and so out of harmony with the other writings that only a postscript (12:9-14) by a later hand made it acceptable.

Job

One of the most remarkable writings in the Bible is the other canonical example of speculative wisdom, the book of Job. Using an old folktale about a near-perfect man who suddenly was overwhelmed by a series of undeserved calamities as a way of introducing his characters and the situation which formed the back-

ground, the unknown author (whom we shall call "the Poet") constructed a daring, beautiful, and skillful theological discussion
of a crucial issue: the proper relationship of a man to his God.
The structure of the book is clear:

Chs. 1-2   Prose prologue: Job's goodness, the heavenly wager,
            Job's calamities, arrival of his friends

3-27   Three cycles of speeches: discussion among Job and
            friends of why he is so miserable

28   A poem about wisdom, probably a later addition to
            the Poet's work

29-31   Job's final statement, in which he maintains his
            innocence

32-37   The Elihu speeches, added after original book was
            completed

38:1-42:6   Yahweh's speeches and Job's repentance

42:7-17   Prose epilogue: Job vindicated and his fortunes
            restored.

The modern reader should not be too concerned about the
heavenly cabinet meeting or the wager between Yahweh and the Satan
in chs. 1-2, for the Poet is simply taking the well-known folktale
to set the stage for what he wants to do. It should be noted that
the Satan is one of Yahweh's officials and not the evil tempter of
late Jewish and Christian writings.

In the second part of the book each of Job's friends, Eliphaz, Bildad, and Zophar, makes three speeches, in which the old
doctrine of retribution is stoutly upheld despite Job's stubborn
insistence that, in his case, it does not hold true. The only rationale they can suggest for Job's miserable condition is that he,
or perhaps his deceased children, has sinned. Job, who begins the
speechmaking and replies to each of the friends' speeches, insists
that he is innocent, that he has done nothing to justify his continual suffering, and that he is getting what wicked people deserve. He complains that God will not explain why this has happened to him, will not give him a hearing, and is therefore either
cruel or does not care about him. As for the friends, Job acknowledges that they mean well but have proven to be totally ineffective as comforters.

The challenge to the honored doctrine of retribution,
which plays a small part in Ecclesiastes, has grown into a major
theme in Job. In his many speeches, Job has accused God of not
running things fairly and justly. The Poet brings the discussion

149

to a climax when he has Yahweh, after complete silence to that point, address to Job a series of questions which he can not answer. Taking note of Job's charge that he is unjust, Yahweh even offers to change places with Job and let him run things (40:6-14)! In the Poet's structure of the book, this is too much for Job to handle. He responds by meekly repenting of all his charges (42:1-6) against God without ever having received an explanation of his misfortunes and suffering. The question with which the Poet deals is not, Why must the righteous suffer? as is often stated, but What is the appropriate stance of a man before God?

The answer which is proffered makes it clear that it is not appropriate for the creature to question the creator or to assume that he knows better how the universe should be governed. Implied in the answer is the admission that there are many things which do not seem fair, but that does not give man the right to question Yahweh. What man must do is to remember who he is, a creature of the Lord, and to trust him completely.

Wisdom in the Apocrypha

Two wisdom books included in the Greek canon (Septuagint), but not in the Hebrew canon, of the Old Testament are of such high quality that they deserve at least brief comment. Ecclesiasticus (also known as Wisdom of Jesus ben Sirach) was written around 180 B.C., too late to be inspired Scripture in the opinion of the Jamnia Council. Resembling the biblical book of Proverbs, it contains practical advice for happy, successful living, moral essays, proverbs, and observations about human nature. On most subjects it agrees with Proverbs, rejecting life after death and advising obedience to the Torah, but it qualifies the desirability of having a large number of children. If they turn out to be useless or ungodly, it is better to die childless (16:1-3)! Perhaps the most notable passage is chapter 24, in which wisdom personified is depicted as having sought a resting place on earth, and to have found it among the people of Israel, where it became the Torah of Moses.

The Wisdom of Solomon was likely composed in the latter part of the first century B.C. by an unknown learned Jew who wanted to encourage other Jews to remain faithful to Judaism and perhaps bring about the conversion of some Gentiles. Literarily, it appears to be King Solomon's address to the rulers of the world (1:1) and exhorts its readers to seek wisdom. Unlike the other wisdom literature we have considered, the Wisdom of Solomon promises a reward and immortality to the righteous and punishment in the hereafter to the wicked (chs. 3 and 5). Long life is still considered a blessing, as in Proverbs, but old age is determined by the quality, not the quantity, of a person's years (4:7-9).

Wisdom is characterized as "a breath of the power of God, and a pure emanation of the glory of the Almighty" (7:25) who "orders all things well" (8:1) and "teaches self-control and prudence, justice and courage" (8:7), which happen to be the four cardinal virtues of the philosopher Plato. The last half of the book (chs. 10-19) uses the history of Israel to demonstrate how wisdom brought blessings to the Israelites and calamities to the heathen. The Wisdom of Solomon reflects a Judaism which had come under the influence of Greek learning and philosophy.

Significant terms and names for this chapter

parallelism	Proverbs
synonymous parallelism	"Dame Folly"
antithetic parallelism	"Lady Wisdom"
hymns	Koheleth
community lament	Ecclesiastes
individual lament	Job
individual praise	The Satan
Song of Solomon	Ecclesiasticus
wisdom literature	Wisdom of Solomon
doctrine of retribution	

CHAPTER XIV

TWO WRITINGS AND A PROPHET

Biblical materials: Joel. Esther. Daniel

Essential reading: Joel 2; Esther 9; Daniel 1-7; 11-12

After the work of the Chronicler, no biblical writing continues the history of Judah in the centuries following Ezra, which means that we are very limited in our knowledge of events in and around Jerusalem from 400 to 200 B.C. Fortunately, the story of Judah in the second century B.C. is told in I Maccabees, a reliable source even though it is not included in the Hebrew canon. It is very helpful in our understanding the book of Daniel and its place in Jewish history. But we are still uncertain as to where the other two books not considered thus far, Joel and Esther, fit into the history of Israel.

Joel

This clearly prophetic book begins with a vivid description of the damage done by a plague of locusts (1:4), which the prophet saw as a sign of the nearness of the day of Yahweh (1:15). This would be

> a day of darkness and gloom
> a day of clouds and thick darkness! (2:2)

The locusts reminded him of a great invading army (2:4-5), which might be the Lord's judgment upon the land (2:11), a judgment which could be avoided by a thoroughgoing, sincere repentance of the whole population (2:12-17). If they should respond to his oracles and repent, Joel assured them of a prosperous future in which Yahweh's spirit would be active in their midst (2:24-29) and they would gain victory over the nations which had been troubling them (2:30-3:21).

The prophecy of Joel seems to fit best in the period after Ezra and in the struggling community in Judah. Things obviously still were not going well for the restored Jewish community. The Temple was standing, but the Jews were still scattered, food was not plentiful, and neighboring nations were raiding their land and abusing many of its inhabitants. For the first time the Greeks were mentioned (3:6), as a distant people who had bought Jews as slaves. In the latter half of the fourth century B.C., the Greeks changed the entire history of the Near East, and mention of them here may reflect their nation's growing strength.

Esther

Several mysteries surround this controversial writing, which poses as an historical account of persecution of the Jewish minority living in Persia in the reign of King Ahasuerus. When was it written? For what purpose? By whom? How is its presence in holy scripture justified when it lacks any mention of God or any religious ideas? Modern scholars typically characterize the book as a novella, by which they mean a very short historical novel which makes a point. Persian court life seems to be accurately reflected in Esther, but there are several inaccuracies in the order of events and personages involved.

The author, about whom we know nothing except that he was a Jew and a master story-teller, skillfully uses four main characters to carry out the plot: Ahasuerus, the king; Haman, his prime minister; Mordecai, the faithful Jew; and Esther, his beautiful cousin. Haman, the villain, planned the execution of Mordecai because he would not bow to him and persuaded Ahasuerus to order the extinction of all Jews in the land. But Esther, now married to the king, risked her life to plead for her people and persuaded her husband to stop the planned execution of Mordecai and the genocide of the Jews. Haman was hanged on the very gallows he had prepared for Mordecai, and the Jews successfully defended themselves against their prejudiced enemies.

For several days the Jews celebrated their victory, which they named <u>Purim</u>, after the Persian word for the lot which Haman had cast for their destruction. In fact, the only discernible reason for including the book of Esther in the Hebrew scriptures is that it provides an explanation of the origin of the annual Feast of Purim, which falls around March 1. When the book is read at the observance of this Feast, it serves as a reminder to Jews of the heroic resistance which is often necessary to ensure their survival in the face of continuing anti-Semitism.

Not a religious book, its vindictive spirit caused hot debates among first century A.D. rabbis over its presence in the scriptures, but its popularity among the masses won its inclusion. Martin Luther, too, had serious doubts about its value, but at least it may be said that it shows the horrible consequences of prejudice and hatred and provides an example of good's triumphing over evil. It may have been written as early as the last half of the fourth century B.C. or as late as the Maccabean period (2nd century B.C.).

The Greek-Seleucid Empire

Judah, with its main city Jerusalem, remained a part of the Persian Empire from the time of Cyrus (538 B.C.) until the conquests of Alexander the Great brought Palestine into the Greek Empire in 333 B.C. The son of King Philip II of Macedon and a pupil of the great philosopher Aristotle, Alexander combined the political ambition inherited from his father with the love of Greek learning and culture imparted by Aristotle and his extraordinary talent for leadership to become one of the most influential personalities of history. When he was only nineteen years old, the murder of his father in 336 B.C. placed Alexander at the head of Greek city-states. He lost no time in training his army to begin the job of wresting from the Persian Empire those Greek cities in Asia Minor which were under Persian control. From there he marched his army into Palestine, which he added to his conquests in 333 B.C., and continued on to Egypt, which he also conquered. Then he headed eastward, conquering everything in his path, which included the entire Middle East.

Mesopotamia, which had been the territory of the Assyrians, the Babylonians, and the Persians, in turn, now became part of the great Greek Empire, which stretched from Greece in the west to the border of India in the east. What Alexander's empire might have achieved, had he lived to carry out his plan, we can never know, for he died at the age of thirty-two. Yet, although his reign lasted only twelve years, he began a movement which affected the lives of millions for centuries afterward.

Alexander was not interested in conquest for conquest's sake or in becoming personally famous. His education in things Greek had convinced him that the Greek language, culture, and learning constituted the high point of civilization, and he sincerely felt that they ought to be shared with the rest of mankind. Hence he ordered Greek teachers to follow Greek armies into the newly acquired territories in order that they might enlighten the poor souls who had been denied the glory of being Greeks. One important result of this policy was the spread of the Greek language as a means of communication among all parts of the vast Empire. This had far-reaching effects upon Judaism, as well as upon the spread of Christianity when it appeared over three centuries after Alexander.

Since he had no heirs, Alexander's death brought about a division of his empire among some of his powerful generals, one of whom, Seleucus, got Syria, Asia Minor, and Mesopotamia. The rulers who succeeded him came to be known as Seleucids, some of whom played a critical role in Jewish history. Egypt was allotted to another general, Ptolemy, who was followed in power by the Ptolemies. For the century or so following Alexander's death Palestine was under their control, which meant that the Jews in Jerusalem and environs suffered no great restriction in the practice of their faith.

Hellenism, the process of educating non-Greeks in the ways and language of Greece, begun by Alexander, continued after his death. This affected not only those Jews who were living in Judah and Egypt, but also those who had never left Mesopotamia (around Babylon) following the exile. Many of the Jews in Judah found Hellenism, as promoted by the Ptolemies, quite attractive, especially since it did not seem to interfere with their faith and traditions. A rather large number of them migrated to Egypt, resulting in the formation of a large Jewish quarter in Alexandria (named for Alexander the Great). This set the stage for the translation of their scriptures into the Greek language, known as the Septuagint (see above, p. 6).

The fortunes of Palestinian Jews changed radically in the second century B.C., when their land was taken over by the Seleucids. As already mentioned, we have no Jewish account of events between 400 and 200 B.C., but there is a very reliable history of the tragic period, 175-134 B.C., in the apocryphal book of I Maccabees. The Seleucid king Antiochus III had gained control over Palestine in 198 B.C., proclaiming the right of the Jews to live according to their law and customs. But after he had lost much of his empire, and thereby a great source of revenue, he began to change his attitude toward the Jewish community. He raised their taxes sharply and demanded payment from those who sought the office of high priest, which amounted to interference in religious practice.

A tremendous crisis arose for Jews in Palestine when Antiochus IV came to power. Thwarted by the Roman Empire in his ambition to expand his territory, he decided to strengthen control of the empire by vigorously promoting Hellenism among the entire population. Departing from the policy of his predecessors, Antiochus IV demanded that even religion be hellenized. This brought him into direct confrontation with many of the Jews, who had not strongly opposed the hellenizing process as long as it did not extend into religious matters.

155

The more the Jews resisted, the more determined the emperor became. Nicknamed "Epiphanes" ("He thinks he's a god") by the Jews, he outlawed Jewish religion, abolished sabbath observance, made possession of a copy of the Torah a capital offense, and forbade circumcision. In their stead, he commanded that his subjects adopt Greek religion, and forcibly erected an altar to its chief deity Zeus in the Temple. Prohibiting sacrifices according to Jewish rules, he ordered that a pig be sacrificed on the altar of burnt offering and forced some priests to eat of its flesh. His total desecration of the Temple produced outrage among the Jews, and many of them lost their lives in a futile attempt to resist his decrees.

Before Antiochus Epiphanes had come to power, a great many Jews had accommodated themselves to the new Greek ways, especially in dress and athletic games. Even when he had defiled their Temple, some of them gave in to his demands. But there was a group of Jews, the Hasidim, who had stoutly opposed efforts at hellenization from the start. They were now joined by many other Jews who had found nothing offensive about Greek culture until religion was included.

The new Seleucid policies greatly increased the zeal of the Jews, and their rage was rapidly growing to the exploding point as the Syrian (Seleucid) officers were dispatched throughout the rural areas to enforce them. An elderly priest, Mattathias, was so enraged when his altar in Modein was about to be desecrated that he impulsively killed the Jew and the Syrian officer who rejected his protest. This heroic act, recorded in I Maccabees 2, sparked the revolt which led to great suffering and loss of life for the Jews over the next quarter century. Mattathias quickly gathered his family and any of his neighbors who shared his zeal and fled to the hills, where they were soon joined by many others, including a group of the Hasidim. His eldest son, Judas Maccabeus became the leader of an effective army of guerilla fighters who carried the battle to the Syrians with amazing success against superior numbers.

This resistance movement has come to be known as the Maccabean Revolt, so-called because of the leadership of Judas Maccabeus. The revolt began in 167 B.C. Three years later Judas and his forces gained control of Jerusalem and, in 164 B.C., cleaned the Temple of all the offensive things Antiochus Epiphanes had introduced. It was rededicated to Yahweh in a great celebration, which gave rise to a new annual festival in Judaism, the Feast of Hanukkah, which falls in December.

But the war was not over. Eventually Judas was killed in

battle and his brother Jonathan succeeded him as commander. At Jonathan's death, another brother, Simon, took charge and finally led the Jews to the gaining of their independence in 142 B.C. The period 167-142 B.C. had been a critical one for the Jews in Palestine. The Seleucids' heartless attempts to force Greek religion upon the Jews, who had struggled for centuries to maintain their identity as Yahweh's people and the purity of their faith, produced a variety of responses.

Many Jews resisted vigorously, risking their lives rather than surrender to Antiochus' blasphemous demands; thousands actually lost their lives in heroic efforts to stop the enemy. Many others chose to go along with the hellenizing of their religion, probably on the quite understandable basis that it is better to stay alive than risk death in a lost cause. As the fighting between the Maccabean forces and the Syrians continued, some Jews felt torn between the staunch idealism of the Hasidim and the pragmatic accommodation of the "realists." Doubtless there were many attempts by the faithful to persuade the wavering Jews to join them in resistance to the death. One such attempt has survived and to it we now turn our attention.

The Book of Daniel

Although the book of Daniel is grouped with the prophetic literature in our English Bibles, it really does not belong there. The Hebrew canon placed it in its third division, the Writings. It is quite different from all the other Old Testament books, and it is important for the reader to recognize that as he seeks to grasp its message. The most likely setting for Daniel is the situation described in the previous paragraph. The writer, very likely a member of the zealous Hasidim, was trying to convince the wavering Jews to remain faithful to Yahweh, no matter the consequences, and to encourage the faithful to persevere in their conviction.

The method he chose to accomplish this purpose is indeed ingenious. In the first half of the book (chs. 1-6), he recounted stories of Daniel, Shadrach, Meshach, and Abednego, Jews who lived in the Babylonian and/or Persian periods (his history is confused). These faithful men encountered strong opposition from persons who tried to force them to worship gods other than the God of Israel, but they kept the faith. As a result, God protected them from the fury of their enemies, even when they were thrown into a fiery furnace or a den filled with hungry lions (Daniel 3; 6). The point of such stories' being retold in the Maccabean period is clear: We, too, must remain faithful, as did Daniel and his companions, and God will protect us as he did them.

157

The latter half (chs. 7-12) of the book attempts to encourage the embattled Jews in a vastly different way. In this section we encounter a new type of literature, known as apocalyptic. Influenced by the prophetic writings, this kind of writing always appears in a crisis and attempts to deal with the crisis. More of it turns up in later Jewish and Christian literature, the best known example of which is the book of Revelation in the New Testament.

In most such books, the writer's name is not given, and in all of them, he uses a sort of code language consisting of numbers, figures, animals, symbols, etc. The code is used to convey a message which will be understood by the intended readers but not by the "wrong" people, the enemy. Apocalypses (or "revelations") predict a series of calamities which indicate that the present age is about over and that a day of judgment, or renewal, is about to appear, at which time God will vindicate the righteous and overthrow the wicked. In this way they become messages of hope, assuring the faithful that God has not forgotten or forsaken them in their time of desperation and suffering but will act in their behalf at a time he has set.

All of these characteristics apply to Daniel 7-12. But there is an additional one: in his zeal to predict a brighter future for the Jews, the author assumed the role of the historical Daniel, who was predicting centuries earlier than the writer's day the events which would culminate in the overthrow of the evil Antiochus Epiphanes and the deliverance of God's faithful people. Apparently the reason for this device is to establish the credibility of the predictions. By having Daniel, in his visions, predict events which have already happened, an amazing record of accuracy is attained. But when the writer gets to his own time, of course, he has to predict without benefit of history.

Actual prediction begins at 11:40, and in the paragraph ending with vs. 45, he foretells a battle between Egypt ("the south") and Syria ("the north") resulting in victory by the king of the north (Antiochus Epiphanes), who will lose his life while he is encamped somewhere between Jerusalem ("the glorious holy mountain") and the Mediterranean Sea. The time of Antiochus' death is to be within three and a half years (12:7), after which event the Jews' troubles will be over. This proved to be quite accurate, for Antiochus did die in 163 B.C., although the site of his death was not in Palestine but in Babylonia.

In the typical apocalyptic "code," nations are represented by beasts and rulers by horns on the beasts. We see this symbolism used in Daniel 7, where the Greek-Seleucid Empire is represented by "a fourth beast, terrible, and dreadful and exceedingly strong" (vs. 7). Among the horns on the fourth beast is a little horn (vs. 8), which represents Antiochus Epiphanes, who "made war with the saints, and prevailed over them, until the Ancient of Days came, and judgment was given for the saints of the Most High, and the time came when the saints received the kingdom" (vss. 21-22). Antiochus is referred to also as "a contemptible person" (11:21) who "shall exalt himself and magnify himself above every god, and shall speak astonishing things against the God of gods" (11:36).

The writer of Daniel felt called upon to deal with a very real problem faced by his contemporaries. The stories of how God had delivered Daniel and his friends may have been inspiring, but the fact remained that many Jews in the Maccabean period were not being protected; they were being killed by the thousands. In chapter 12 the writer deals with this serious problem by announcing a resurrection of the dead, at which time some will be rewarded with everlasting life but others will receive "shame and everlasting contempt" (vs. 2). Except for a late passage in Isaiah 26, this is the only affirmation of a meaningful life after death in the Hebrew canon of the Old Testament. The idea seems to have caught on rather quickly, however, for by the time of Jesus most Jews were apparently taking a resurrection of the dead for granted.

Daniel is clearly a tract for the times. The writer's purpose was to shore up the faith and encourage the persistence of his fellow Jews in a crisis which threatened once again to exterminate Judaism. God is in control of history, he implies, and will not allow the forces of evil to prevail indefinitely. The day of reckoning will be soon, he insists, and those who hang on to their faith in God will be gloriously rewarded. Probably the latest book in the Old Testament, Daniel should not be misused as a blueprint of future history or as a formula for predicting the end of the world.

The Hasmonean Period

The book of Daniel may well have produced the intended effect, for the Jewish resistance stiffened and its guerilla army continued to win battle after battle, even though usually outnumbered. The death of the hated Antiochus did not bring an immediate end to the struggle, but it encouraged the faithful and convinced them that total victory was inevitable. The sons of Mattathias continued to provide the courageous leadership required by the situation, even after independence was won in 142 B.C. Later

159

generations of the family came to be known as Hasmoneans, after the name of an ancestor, Hasmoneus. Unfortunately, the latter members of the family were not as proficient in governing an independent nation in peacetime as were Judas and his brothers in fighting a war.

Simon, the surviving son of Mattathias and the leader when victory over the Syrians was achieved, was elected as permanent high priest, military commander, and governor (I Maccabees 14:41-49) of Judah, now a nation free of foreign control for the first time in over four centuries. At Simon's death his son, John Hyrcanus, took charge and began to expand the territory of his little state. Samaria to the north, Idumea (formerly Edom) to the south, and some land east of the Jordan Valley were added to Judah. The Idumeans were forcibly converted to Judaism and made to abide by Jewish law. John Hyrcanus' rule also saw the beginning of a trend, continued under the later Hasmoneans, of introducing Hellenistic ways into the Jewish life-style without giving up the essentials of Judaism. Not the purist attitudes of the Hasidim, but the more tolerant views of the upper class families in Jerusalem were increasing in influence.

For our knowledge of the Hasmonean period following the death of Simon, we must depend upon the work of a Jewish historian of the first century A.D., Josephus. In telling of Hyrcanus' rule, Josephus describes a party within Judaism which we frequently meet in the New Testament gospels, the Pharisees. Apparently the successors to the Hasidim and scribes who devoted themselves to studying and interpreting the Torah, some of the Pharisees were critical of Hyrcanus' policies. This led to his break with them and his dependence upon the Sadducees for support. This group, also mentioned frequently in the gospels, was made up of the priestly families, many of whom had supported earlier tendencies toward hellenization. It is important to note that some of the influential religious movements which characterized Judaism in the time of Jesus had their roots in this period. It was becoming less and less a unified faith as the Jews reacted to new influences and ideas coming into their community.

Hyrcanus' successor, Aristobulus I, was the first Hasmonean to claim the title "King of the Jews." A cruel and ambitious man, he added Galilee to his kingdom and forced its residents to convert to Judaism. After his early death, his widow, Alexandra, married his brother Janneus, and arranged his elevation to both the top positions in Judah, king and high priest. He added still more territory to the kingdom, but not all his subjects were happy with their leader. The Pharisees, Josephus reports, challenged

160

his fitness to be high priest, to which Janneus responded with
cruel actions which set off a six-year revolt.

At his death (76 B.C.), his wife Alexandra became queen
and bestowed the office of high priest upon her son Hyrcanus II.
Her short reign was relatively calm and saw a resurgence of Pharisaic influence. At her death (67 B.C.), another son, Aristobulus II, seized the throne with the aid of the Sadducees and the
military. The next four years were chaotic ones for Judah, for
the two brothers were engaged in a bitter struggle for power with
little concern for the well-being of the populace. Meanwhile a
new power was making itself felt in the region; Rome had taken
Syria away from the Seleucids, and when the Roman general Pompey
arrived in Damascus in 63 B.C., he was seen by the beleaguered
Jews as the one possible "savior" from the anarchic, chaotic situation in which they found themselves less than a century after
they had won independence. This brings us to the New Testament
period, the consideration of which will be reserved for the next
chapter.

Significant terms, names, and dates for this chapter

I Maccabees	Judas Maccabeus
Joel	167 B.C.
Esther	164 B.C.
Mordecai	Hanukkah
Purim	Jonathan
Alexander the Great	Simon
333 B.C.	Hasidim
Hellenism	Daniel
hellenization	apocalyptic
Seleucus	Hasmoneans
Seleucids	142 B.C.
Ptolemy	Josephus
Ptolemies	Alexandra
Antiochus Epiphanes	Janneus
little horn	Hyrcanus II
Zeus	Aristobulus II
Mattathias	63 B.C.

CHAPTER XV

PALESTINE UNDER THE ROMANS

The year 63 B.C. serves as a convenient dividing point between the Old and New Testaments. That year saw a decisive turning point in the fortunes of the Jews in Palestine, for it marked
the end of their short-lived independence, which had been won at
great cost. The anarchy produced by the fierce struggle between
the forces of Hyrcanus II and those of his brother Aristobulus II
for control of the country resulted in the annexation of Palestine
to the Roman Empire by General Pompey, who would later become the
emperor.

What the Jews had in mind when they urged Pompey to restore law and order in their land was that, once peace and normal-
cy were achieved, the Romans would withdraw and leave Judah an independent state. But things did not happen that way, and Judah
found itself under the domination of yet another foreign power
which proved as oppressive as previous overlords. Throughout the
New Testament period, which extended from 63 B.C. to approximately
150 A.D., Rome kept firm control of Palestine as part of the province of Syria, and the Jewish people did not regain independence
until the modern state of Israel came into being in 1948.

When Rome moved eastward into what we call the Near East,
it encountered a population made up of a variety of ethnic and religious groups, all of whom had been influenced by the Greek culture which had been operating in the region since the time of Alex
ander the Great. The civilization which grew out of this conflu-
ence of Greek culture and Roman political and military organizatio
is known as the Graeco-Roman world, and provided the milieu in
which Christianity began, expanded, and flourished in its early
centuries of existence. The Greek language provided a useful vehicle for the spread of ideas, while Roman political control, aided by an excellent system of roads, facilitated communication
among the various parts of the great Roman Empire.

Occupation by Pompey

Pompey had to use considerable force in taking control of
Palestine, especially the Temple area. Josephus related that
twelve thousand Jews were killed by the Romans and that Pompey

himself desecrated the Temple by entering the Holy of Holies.
Other Jews, including Aristobulus II and his family, were taken to
Rome as exiles. Judea (as Judah was now called) was now part of
the Roman Empire and had to suffer the humiliation of having an
army of occupation in the city of Jerusalem and the hardship of
paying a large indemnity to the Roman government. Several cities,
mostly east of the Jordan River, which were occupied by non-Jews
were separated from Judea and formed their own league, called the
Decapolis.

Hyrcanus II was appointed high priest, but an Idumean, Antipater, was designated by Pompey to "assist" Hyrcanus. Indeed,
it was Antipater, whose wife was Jewish, who had the actual power
and, according to Josephus, he was a man of great ability and justice. He had to call on Roman troops for help in quelling several
revolts by Aristobulus II (who had escaped from Rome) and his sons,
who were still hoping to regain control of Judea. When Julius
Caesar came to power in Rome, Antipater switched his loyalty from
Pompey to the new leader and was rewarded by being appointed governor of Judea. He then appointed his son Phasael governor of Jerusalem and another son, Herod, governor of Galilee.

Herod the Great

It was this second son of Antipater, Herod, who made a
name for himself and who provides the link between the Hasmonean
period and the time of Jesus. After the murder of Julius Caesar
in 44 B.C., the Parthians invaded Syria and Palestine in an attempt to take advantage of the situation and gain control of that
area. They seized Jerusalem and declared Aristobulus' son, Antigonus, the king and high priest, for he had joined the Parthians
in their fight against Rome. Herod managed to escape to Rome,
where, in 40 B.C., he was confirmed as "king of Judea." With Roman help, Herod captured Jerusalem from Antigonus in 37 B.C. and
gradually expanded his kingdom to include Idumea, Judea, Samaria,
Galilee, Perea, and an unnamed area north and east of the Sea of
Galilee.

Always aware of the fact that he held power only because
of Roman approval, the able and ambitious Herod rebuilt and beau-
tified many cities in Hellenistic style, and constructed fortress-
es at various places, including the famed one at Masada. He built
a beautiful seaport on the Mediterranean and named it Caesarea.
It served as his main place of residence. He orderd the reconstruction of much of Jerusalem, hoping to gain the approval of the
Jews by having the Temple rebuilt, a project which continued many
years after his death.

Herod held on to his power by ruthless and often cruel measures, which extended to members of his own family. He did not hesitate to execute anyone, including his Hasmonean wife, Mariamne, whom he suspected of disloyalty, or any persons, including three of his sons, who he feared were plotting to seize power. During much of his reign (37-4 B.C.), he maintained a secret police organization to keep down possible revolt and used brutal force to suppress any opposition. The New Testament account (Matthew 2:16) of his ordering the slaughter of male infants in Bethlehem to eliminate any possible claimant to his throne is perfectly in keeping with his character.

The Division of Herod's Kingdom

A half-Jew, Herod wanted his fellow Jews to accept him as Jewish, but on this point he never succeeded, for he ignored or suppressed his religion whenever it was expedient and practiced it whenever it suited his purposes. His last will specified how his kingdom was to be governed, and the Roman emperor Augustus followed it after his death. It was split among three sons (see Map 8, page 165). Archelaus was designated ethnarch of Judea and Samaria, but his ten-year administration (4 B.C. to 6 A.D.) was so corrupt and inept that the Romans replaced him with their own non-Jewish appointee with the title of procurator. Another son, Philip, was appointed tetrarch of the area north and east of the Sea of Galilee.

The territories of Galilee and Perea, which are not adjacent to each other, were given to a third son of Herod, Antipas, who reigned as tetrarch until his banishment in 39 A.D for suspected conspiracy against Rome. He is the Herod most frequently mentioned in the gospels, for it was in his territory that Jesus spent most of his life and ministry. Jesus once referred to him as "that fox," but John the Baptist was more severe in his assessment of Antipas, openly condemning his marriage to Herodias, the wife of his half-brother (Mark 6:14-29). This led to John's imprisonment and eventual execution by order of Antipas, who was later haunted by the possibility that Jesus was actually the resurrected John!

Judea and Samaria continued to be governed by a series of procurators from 6 to 66 A.D., the most notorious of whom was Pontius Pilate, during whose ten-year administration Jesus was executed. Most of the procurators, being outsiders, were not sincerely interested in the welfare of the Jewish people and looked upon their position as temporary, always hoping for a more desir-

Map 8

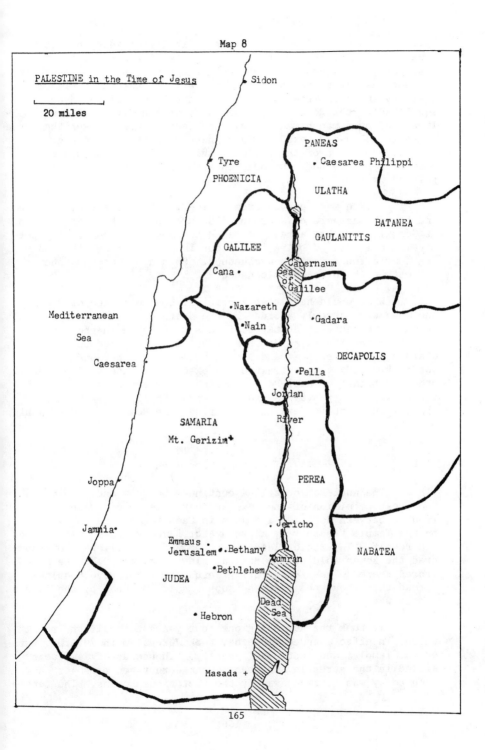

PALESTINE in the Time of Jesus

20 miles

Sidon

PANEAS

• Caesarea Philippi

Tyre

PHOENICIA

ULATHA

BATANEA

GALILEE

GAULANITIS

Cana •

•Capernaum

Sea
of
Galilee

•Nazareth

Mediterranean

•Gadara

Sea

•Nain

Caesarea •

DECAPOLIS

•Pella

Jordan

River

SAMARIA

Mt. Gerizim

PEREA

Joppa

•Jericho

Jamnia•

Emmaus •

NABATEA

Jerusalem •• Bethany

•Qumran

•Bethlehem

JUDEA

Dead
Sea

• Hebron

Masada +

able appointment. Their chief responsibilities were collecting taxes for the Roman government and maintaining order. For the most part, they were hated by their subjects, and the procurators did not take great pains to change that. Occasional anti-Roman activity surfaced from time to time, but it was always decisively squelched by the Roman army. As early as 6 A.D., a serious rebellion, led by a man named Judas, occurred in Galilee over the issue of being ruled and taxed by foreigners. Judas founded a group, probably the sect of the Zealots, which continued to oppose payment of taxes to Rome and obedience to any ruler except one appointed by Yahweh.

Pilate was removed from office in 36 A.D. for his unwise and brutal massacre of a group of Samaritans who had gathered on Mt. Gerizim. He had already enraged the Jews in Jerusalem by permitting soldiers to bring idolatrous images into the city and using Temple funds for a new aqueduct. He had to put down their protests with force and bloodshed.

What would have been a critical confrontation of Romans and Jews was narrowly avoided by the death of the Emperor Caligula, who had ordered that a statue of Zeus be erected in the Temple in Jerusalem in 39 A.D. A Jew named Theudas, mentioned in Acts 5:36, claimed to be a prophet and led several hundred persons to the Jordan River, but was arrested and executed around 45 A.D. Still other outbreaks of anti-Roman feeling occurred in the middle of the first century A.D. A group known as the Sicarii began to assassinate certain Jews known to side with Rome, including a high priest.

The Great Rebellion

The anti-Roman feeling continued to grow and culminated in the Great Rebellion of the Jews against Rome which began in 66 A.D. Trouble between Gentiles and Jews in Caesarea, added to the raid on the Temple treasury by a procurator named Florus, precipitated the revolt. The Zealot leader Menahem and his followers overpowered the Roman soldiers at Masada, slew them, and took the arms stored there to use in capturing Jerusalem. The revolt quickly spread throughout the land and soon was looked upon by the Jews as a holy war.

It took the Roman legions four years to quell the revolt, which, in effect, ended when they took Jerusalem in 70 A.D., burned the Temple, and destroyed the city. Thousands of Jews were killed in the struggle, thousands more were taken prisoner, and much booty was carried away by the victorious Romans. The fortress in southern Judea, Masada, now a famous site and tourist attraction, was occupied by zealous Jews (probably consisting of both Zealots and Essenes) who held out until 73 A.D., when they committed mass suicide rather than fall into the hands of the Romans.

The Great Rebellion must be ranked with the greatest of the crises which Judaism faced in its history. The Temple was never rebuilt after this, and the sacrificial worship, so closely tied to the Temple, came to an end. Most of the priests were killed, and the few who survived had no real function to perform. Those surviving Jews, who had fervently expected Yahweh to intervene in this holy war and bring them victory over the hated Romans, were forced to re-examine their beliefs and search their scriptures for his word to the covenant people. Since the Sadducees, as a group, did not survive the Revolt, it was left to the Pharisees to preserve Judaism from extinction.

By this time the Christian Church had been in existence for approximately three decades, and the congregation in Jerusalem, according to Acts, was composed of Jews who had accepted Jesus as messiah and Lord. Some time between 66 and 70 A.D. that congregation had left Jerusalem and established itself at Pella, east of the Jordan River and outside Jewish territory. This act of "desertion" was resented by other Jews and caused relations between church and synagogue to worsen in the decades following the Rebellion.

When the Pharisaic rabbis gathered at Jamnia in 90 A.D. and formed the "Great Synagogue" they took action which made it impossible for Jews to accept Jesus as messiah and remain members of a synagogue. This is the occasion on which they also decided on the content of their scriptures, choosing the Hebrew canon (see above, pp. 9-11) rather than the Greek, which the church was using as its scriptures. These developments drove a deeper wedge between church and synagogue, and the growing animosity between them is reflected in many passages in the gospels. As the first century A.D. came to a close, the church was on the way to becoming a Gentile movement. Christianity was no longer seen as another branch of Judaism; now it was a separate religion.

Despite the horrendous defeat by the Romans in 70 A.D., Jewish nationalism and apocalyptic hope found expression in still another revolt in the second century. When the emperor Hadrian announced that he would rebuild Jerusalem as a Roman city with pagan temples, Jewish zeal and patriotism were rekindled. When the claim of Simeon bar Cochba to be the messiah was substantiated by

167

the respected Rabbi Akiba, he had little trouble in organizing a revolt which began in 131 A.D. and took the Roman army four years to put down. Then, as Hadrian had originally planned, a Roman city was erected where Jerusalem had stood, and it was named Aelia Capitolina. This brings us to the end of the New Testament period but the student should be aware of the fact that Jewish history does not end at this point. The Jewish people and Judaism did survive this revolt and have remained viable ethnic and religious entities into modern times, sometimes prospering, sometimes suffering incredible abuse.

The Graeco-Roman World

It is clear from the previous section that the political situation in Palestine in the time of Jesus was tumultuous and volatile. Shortly after Jesus was born, the kingdom of Herod the Great had been divided among three of his sons, all of whom ruled in subservience to Rome and only so long as they pleased the emperor. Many of the Jews, especially the priestly families, accommodated themselves to the Roman occupation, but many others seethed with the desire for vengeance and a land free from foreign domination. Taxation was the focal point of much discontent, for taxes were heavy and the method used in collecting them was considered unfair and subject to abuse. The vast majority of Palestinian Jews were poor, some extremely so, with the result that the cities had large numbers of beggars whose very survival depended upon the generosity of others.

Of course, Palestine was only a very small part of a vast area which was to become the field for planting the Christian Church. We customarily refer to it as the Graeco-Roman world, for it was the result of the melding of Greek culture, language, and ideas with Roman political control and military domination. This does not mean that there was only one way of life throughout the entire region. Local customs, traditions, language, and religion continued to be followed, alongside the new influences being introduced by increased traffic among various segments of the vast Roman Empire. For instance, even though Greek was the universal medium of communication, many continued to speak their native languages as well, learning only enough Greek to make commerce possible, or perhaps learning none at all. Others, such as the Jews in Alexandria, completely forsook their native tongue and used Greek alone.

The great amount of commercial activity which followed military expansion and political control brought the various parts

of the empire even closer together. Such contacts opened the door
to the exchange of ideas and religions. The ideas of the great
Greek philosophers of the fifth and fourth centuries B.C. continued to influence the thinkers of the first century A.D. but had
been considerably modified and somewhat perverted in the attempt
to transplant them from one culture to another. One significant
result of the philosophies, all of which are based on human reason,
was the virtual annihilation of belief in the gods of the Greek
and Roman pantheons.

The Greek notion that man is composed of two distinctly
different parts, body and soul, the latter of which is immortal,
continued to enjoy popular acceptance. Then there were the eclec-
tics, who tried to combine the elements they liked from several
philosophical systems into one. One such eclectic was the Jewish
philosopher Philo, who lived in Alexandria in the first century
A.D.. He was convinced that the knowledge which the Greek philosophers had attained through reason was the same truth as that
which the Jewish scriptures taught from revelation.

As for the religious life of the Graeco-Roman world, variety is the basic word. Into the vacuum created by the passing of
the ancient gods came a stream of faiths known as "mystery religions." Many had their roots in the old fertility religions of
the Near East, such as Baalism. Seeking to meet the need for salvation from the evils of existence and for assurance of a life in
the hereafter, the "mysteries" centered around a myth which portrayed the male deity's death in the fall and his rising again to
life in the spring. The female deity, usually thought of as wife
or mother to the male, mourned the death of the male and rejoiced
at his resurrection.

Meals which the devotees shared enabled them to participate in the life of the deity and to be assured of immortality.
Their rites were kept secret, hence the name "mystery" religions.
Most of them were fully democratic in the sense that men and women,
high and low, were given equal status. They did not, as did Judaism and Christianity, demand exclusive allegiance of their members,
and many persons belonged to more than one such religion. There
were some persons, usually the more educated and those of higher
economic status, to whom the mysteries did not appeal. Many such
persons found skepticism or agnosticism more to their liking.

Politically, the Romans had devised an efficient and successful system for governing a large area with a diverse population. Where possible, they allowed the subject peoples to be governed by their own leaders, as we noted in our description of the
period of the Herods, above. But the power was centered in Rome,

with the emperor sharing authority with the senate. Some territories were called provinces, with the leader designated as proconsul, legate, or procurator, depending upon the type and size of the province. Others were called kingdoms, with the governors bearing the title of king, ethnarch, or tetrarch. This flexibility of organizational patterns was largely responsible for the success and efficiency of the Roman system. But sharing the credit for it must certainly be the fact that, when a province or kingdom stepped out of line, the Roman army was immediately dispatched to restore order and Roman authority.

Significant terms, names, and dates for this chapter

63 B.C.	Antipas
Aristobulus II	Herodias
Hyrcanus II	Pontius Pilate
Pompey	Sicarii
Judea	Great Rebellion
Decapolis	66 A.D.
Antipater	Pella
Herod the Great	70 A.D.
Antigonus	Jamnia
Masada	Hadrian
Caesarea	Simeon bar Cochba
Mariamne	131 A.D.
4 B.C.	Aelia Capitolina
Archelaus	mystery religions
procurator	Philo
Philip	

CHAPTER XVI

JUDAISM AFTER THE MACCABEES

Ezra, the priest and scribe who brought the Torah from Babylonia to Jerusalem and made it the "constitution" of the Jewish community, is often called "the father of Judaism." Whether that honor is deserved or not, it is certainly true that the religion of the Jews, while growing directly out of the religion of Israel, took a new turn from Ezra's time (c. 400 B.C.) onward. Later generations spoke of Ezra as the last of the prophets, and any writing known to have originated after him was not considered holy scripture. Henceforth, the will of God for his people would be discovered by reading and studying the written Torah rather than by listening to men claiming to have a fresh vision from God.

Jewish Institutions and Leaders

The Synagogue. The Hebrew scriptures do not mention the Synagogue, and there is no known account of its origin. But by New Testament times it was a well-established institution, taken for granted as though it had been a part of Judaism from the beginning. The most likely theory of its origin is that which assumes it arose during the exile in Babylonia, where the Jews were without their accustomed Temple. According to Deuteronomic tradition, Yahweh forbade the erection of a house for himself at any place other than Jerusalem. Doubtless, the Jews in exile assembled in various localities for fellowship, worship, and study of the Torah. From this very practical way of meeting their spiritual needs, it is probable that a new institution came into being. The name "synagogue" itself, which comes from the Greek, supports this theory, for it means "bringing together."

The synagogue, however, should not be thought of as a substitute for the Temple. In fact, when the Temple was rebuilt, the synagogue was not abandoned for the simple reason that it performed a valuable function which the Temple did not. Apparently it never was used as a place for sacrificial worship but served well as a gathering place for instruction, fellowship, and worship of a non-sacrificial kind. Synagogue worship consisted of the singing of psalms, the offering of prayers, the reading of scripture, and the interpretation of scripture.

Since a priest was not needed for this kind of worship, the task of expounding the scripture was usually done by the local rabbi ("teacher") or a learned person who happened to be visiting. Regular worship occurred on the sabbath, which had become, in addition to a day of rest, the day for worship. Instruction of the boys took place during the week, as well. The gospels mention a "ruler" of the synagogue, but just what his responsibility was is not clear. By the time of Jesus each city or settlement where a group of Jewish families lived had its own synagogue. Even Jerusalem, with the glorious Temple, also had its synagogues.

As mentioned above (ch. XI), Judaism in exile had taken on other new features and ideas, including a concept of life after death, a belief in invisible beings such as angels and demons, and a revised notion of Satan. No longer a member of the heavenly cabinet, as in Job 1-2, Satan was now thought of as a mighty personality in opposition to God, and chief of the demons, who cause all kinds of evil things to happen to people. Not all the Jews of the first century A.D., however, accepted these new ideas, as we shall have occasion to point out below.

The Temple. The Jews in the first century A.D. were scattered throughout the Roman Empire, with large concentrations in Alexandria, Asia Minor, and Rome. But, wherever they lived, the Jews were aware that the symbolic center of their faith was the Temple in Jerusalem. Since Jerusalem was the only acceptable place for offering sacrifices, it was the goal of all Jews to make a pilgrimage there at least once in their lives, but the majority of the Diaspora (a term used of all Jews living outside Palestine) for financial reasons, never got there. Still, it was a unifying force among the scattered Jewish population as long as it stood.

The Temple, as rebuilt by decree of Herod the Great, contained several courts, the outermost of which was known as the "court of the Gentiles" and could be visited by non-Jews. Beyond this was "the women's court," which could be entered by Jewish women. But they were not allowed to go into the next area, "the court of Israel," or into the innermost "court of the priests," forbidden to all non-clergy. The Temple proper, or "the house," as it was called, was patterned after the specifications for the Tent of Meeting in Exodus. It was off limits for all except those priests who were officiating at the time, and only the High Priest was permitted in the Holy of Holies. Other priests took turns in their service at the Temple, serving two weeks out of each year.

The High Priest was the chief officer of the Temple, which had become an important political and economic, as well as religious, institution. Under the Roman occupation, he was the most powerful Jew in Palestine, for the Roman officials chose to com-

172

municate with the Jews through their own high priest. This coveted post often went to the highest bidder, or the one with the most powerful political support.

The Sanhedrin. Another duty of the high priest was to preside over the Jews' highest court, the Sanhedrin. This added further to his prestige and authority. It was a sort of combination of legislature and court, dealing mostly with interpretation and infractions of the Torah. Composed of seventy-one members, all male, it was theoretically governed by strict rules of justice. Most of its members came from the priests, the scribes, and prominent men of wealth and influence. The supreme Sanhedrin convened in Jerusalem, but there were probably lower bodies of similar structure and purpose in other cities. Many authorities believe that the Sanhedrin was not authorized by the Romans to hand down the death penalty.

The Scribes. Since the Torah had come to occupy such a significant place in Judaism after Ezra, it should not be surprising to learn that a new professional group, the scribes, had emerged as specialists in the Torah. At first, they were primarily copyists of the Torah, a task requiring infinite skill and patience. But by the time of Jesus, they had become authorities on the interpretation of the Torah. If the priests were the "clergy" of the time, then the scribes must be looked upon as laymen. Unlike the priests, they received no payment for their services. Sometimes called "rabbi" out of respect, they made their living by other means, but devoted themselves to hours of study. For the most part, they operated in the synagogues, but some of them invited disciples (learners) to follow them from place to place as they taught the Torah. Many of them belonged to the party known as the Pharisees.

The Major Parties

The Pharisees. The Jews in first century Palestine were not in total agreement on either religious or political matters. They differed on such things as the content and the interpretation of their scriptures, recently promulgated doctrines, and the proper attitude of a Jew toward the Roman government. The gospels frequently mention the Pharisees, often as criticizing Jesus' actions and sometimes as the objects of Jesus' disapproval. Most likely originating in the Hasidim of the Maccabean period, the Pharisees stressed strict obedience to the Scriptures, which for them included both the Torah and the Prophets. Besides the written Torah, they also accepted the idea of an oral Torah, by which they meant teachings revealed to Moses but never written down.

This was their way of making the old Torah and its laws relevant to changing times. Disagreement even among the Pharisees resulte in at least two schools: that of Shammai, which emphasized a stri interpretation of the Torah, and that of Hillel, which was consid erably more liberal.

Composed entirely of laymen, the Pharisees had embraced belief in a life after death, to which persons were resurrected t receive rewards or punishments; the existence of invisible angels and demons which affected men's lives for good or evil; and (by some) that the glorious age of messiah, led by a descendant of Da vid, would soon arrive. The righteous lives of the Pharisees wer admired by the common people, who had neither the time nor the ability to follow the demands of the law very carefully. They were influential among the scribes and in the synagogues and, after the tragic Revolt of 66-70 A.D., were the ones responsible fo the survival of Judaism.

The Sadducees. Priests and men from priestly families made up the Sadducees, who are also referred to in the gospels. very conservative group, they disagreed with the Pharisees on sev eral points. They acknowledged only the Torah (Pentateuch) as th Jewish scriptures, which meant that a teaching not based therein was not accepted. Hence they did not believe in a resurrection o the dead or in the existence of angels and demons. Nor did they look for a messianic age, for they were satisfied with things as they were.

Occupying a rather privileged position under the Roman oc cupation of Palestine, they were eager to prevent any disruption of the system lest it cause a lowering of their status. After th destruction of the Temple in 70 A.D., no more is heard of the Sad ducees. Apparently they found Jesus too much akin to the Pharisees and too revolutionary for their tastes.

The Essenes. Although they are not mentioned in the New Testament, the Essenes were in existence during the time of Jesus and we learn a great deal about them from the writings of the his torian Josephus. They found the doctrines of the Pharisees more compatible than those of the Sadducees, and considered the priest hood in Jerusalem to be illegitimate. Eventually they moved from Jerusalem into the wilderness, where they established self-contained communities which operated on a communal pattern and followed a simple lifestyle.

Their arduous study of the scriptures convinced them that they alone were the true people of God and that his judgment woul

174

one day fall on all others. They lived by a strict moral code and required a probationary period for those who wished to join the community. It is highly probable that the Qumran community, which produced the Dead Sea Scrolls (see above, p. 6) was made up of members of this sect. It appears that the Essenes did not survive the Jewish Revolt.

The Zealots. A group with a more political orientation was the super patriotic organization known as the Zealots. They fervently believed that Roman dominion over the land of Palestine was against God's will and dedicated themselves to its overthrow. The membership was secret and pledged to respond immediately to the call from the leader to begin the revolution. The identity of the leader, of course, was also unknown to any but the Zealots themselves. Their presence, along with the secrecy, created a fear among the general population that a revolt would break out at any time. It finally did, in 66 A.D., and the Zealots fought valiantly until overcome by the superior might of Rome. At least one of Jesus' disciples, Simon the Zealot, belonged to this group.

The Herodians. Another politically oriented group, the Herodians, is mentioned a few times in the gospels, but we know nothing of their religious beliefs. Their name suggests that they favored local rule by a descendant of Herod the Great but under the control of the Roman Empire. When they are mentioned in the New Testament they are pictured as joining with the Pharisees in opposing Jesus.

The People of the Land

The vast majority of Palestinian Jews did not belong to any of the parties or sects just described. What we would today call the "common people" were referred to as the "People of the Land." They were not schooled in the fine points of the Torah, as were the scribes and Pharisees. Their long hours of hard labor did not permit extended study of the scriptures, and their social and economic status did not allow them full participation in the religious or social life of the country. The Pharisees and Sadducees looked upon them as inferior and avoided associating with them insofar as possible.

Judean versus Galilean

In the first century A.D., the bulk of Palestinian Jews lived in Galilee and Judea, separated by the land where the hated Samaritans lived. Traffic between these two sections usually took the route east of the Jordan, although it was somewhat longer, rather than have contact with the inhabitants of Samaria. The Jews in Judea were more isolated from Gentile contact and influence than their brethren in Galilee and were consequently more concerned about ritual purity and Jewish distinctiveness. They were proud of the fact that the Temple and the holy city of Jerusalem were in their territory. The Galilean Jews were more open to non-Jewish influences, spoke Aramaic with a noticeable accent, and were not as careful about keeping the Torah as their Judean relatives. Pharisees and Zealots were found in both areas, but the Sadducees kept close to Jerusalem.

The Diaspora

At the time of Jesus, there were more Jews living outside Palestine than within it. Although we do not have accurate statistics, it is estimated that about one million Jews still were living in Babylonia. Within the Roman Empire, Palestine had about two and a half million, and another approximately four million were scattered throughout the rest of the empire. Those living outside Palestine were often referred to as the Diaspora ("the scattered ones") and were generally more tolerant of Gentile ways and customs than were their relatives in Galilee and Judea. The language of a great many of them was Greek, at that time the official language of the empire, and hence they may be termed Hellenistic Jews, or simply "Hellenists" (Acts 6:1). When they visited Jerusalem, they were immediately recognized as such by the Aramaic-speaking residents.

Just how strictly the Diaspora Jews observed the laws and customs which distinguished them from their Gentile neighbors is not known, but we may be sure that the degree of adherence varied greatly from place to place and from family to family. Synagogues were located in almost every town where there were Jews, and enjoyed special privileges from the government as expressions of a legal religion. They were exempted from the requirement that images of the emperor be located in their places of worship and that prayers and sacrifices be made to him. Jews were allowed to keep the sabbath and to send the half-shekel Temple tax (required of all male Jews) to Jerusalem.

The Messianic Hope

It should by now be clear that Judaism of the first century A.D. was marked by great diversity. Geographic, cultural, political, linguistic, and religious differences contributed to the

176

rich variety of that faith. There was still another area of disagreement: the hope for the future. Prophetic and apocalyptic literature (some non-canonical) provided a number of models of a better future for God's people. One such envisioned an era in which the righteousness of God would prevail, evil would be put down, and a time of plenty, peace, and justice would begin. Another model pictured an ideal king to come from David's line to establish Israel as a dominant, glorious kingdom which would be independent of all foreign control. The term <u>messiah</u> was applied to such a leader, and the despised Roman Empire's presence in the Jewish homeland quickened the hopes of many that his appearance would be soon. Some of the Jews, notably the Sadducees, had no vision at all of a future which would differ from the present, and were suspicious of those who encouraged such hopes.

Such was the confused, uncertain, divided Judaism in existence when Jesus of Nazareth arrived. We may be sure that his own thought and faith and life were in part shaped by these various influences and ideas. It is important to remember that he was a Palestinian Jew from Galilee in the first century A.D., who originated, not from either of the parties or sects then in existence, but from the People of the Land.

<u>Significant terms and names for this chapter</u>

synagogue	Sadducees
rabbi	Essenes
Temple	Zealots
High Priest	Herodians
Sanhedrin	People of the Land
scribe	Diaspora
Pharisees	Messiah
Judea	Galilee

CHAPTER XVII

PORTRAITS OF JESUS

The New Testament consists of twenty-seven books which, with the exception of Revelation, are of totally different literary types from those we call the Old Testament. All of them were produced by followers of a Galilean Jew whom his parents named Jesus and who was called Jesus Christ, Christ Jesus, or the Lord Jesus Christ in many New Testament writings. "Christ" is the Greek translation of the Hebrew "messiah." When it was first applied to Jesus, it amounted to a confession of faith that he was the messiah of some Jewish expectation. Later it simply became a second name, as "John Smith." From "Christ" came the term "Christians," first applied to his followers in Antioch of Syria several years after his resurrection (Acts 11:26), probably to cast ridicule upon them. The New Testament, then, is a Christian book, the individual writings of which were produced between 50 and 150 A.D.

Sources of Our Knowledge of Jesus

As is the case with the Old Testament, the first books in the present order of the New Testament were not the first to be written. Nevertheless, it makes sense to have them first because they tell of the person who is the central character of the entire New Testament. Called "gospels," they were a new literary type at the time the earliest one, Mark, was written. The first Christian books to be written or, at least, to survive, were the letters written by the church's greatest missionary, Paul, to churches he had begun, directly or indirectly. Of course, they would never have been written if the person to whom the gospels bear witness had not lived, died, and been raised from the dead.

Since Jesus himself apparently wrote nothing, for our knowledge about him we must depend upon what others wrote. Of those "others," the vast majority were Christians, hence may be expected to reflect a heavy bias toward presenting him in a most favorable light. We shall begin with a brief description of the non-Christian sources, which are either impartial or prejudiced against Jesus.

So far as is known, the only two Roman authors, of the period in which the New Testament books were written, who made reference to Jesus were Suetonius and Tacitus. In his <u>Lives of the Twelve Caesars,</u> Suetonius somewhat incidentally alludes to a Jewish disturbance in Rome, during the reign of Claudius, which was stirred up by someone named Chrestus, probably a variant of Christus. This likely refers to a disturbance in the Jewish community caused by Christian evangelists' preaching about Jesus. Elsewhere in the same volume, Suetonius mentions Nero's persecution of Christians in Rome in 64 A.D.

Tacitus, who lived around 60-120 A.D., in his account of the history of Rome from 14 to 68 A.D., reported that Nero had persecuted Christians to divert attention from his own rumored involvement in the burning of the city. He stated that the Christians had derived their name from Christus, who had been executed by Pontius Pilate during the reign of the Emperor Tiberius. In addition to these two Latin authors, there is a letter from Pliny the Younger, as governor of Bithynia, to the Emperor Trajan, in which he mentions that Christians in his province sang to Christ as God. This was written around 110 A.D.

Jesus is alluded to in two Jewish sources. Flavius Josephus, an historian who lived in Palestine just after Jesus, refers to Jesus only twice in his <u>Antiquities of the Jews.</u> In one place, he alludes to him as a miracle-worker and teacher, stating that Pilate crucified him. Statements to the effect that he was the Christ and that he arose from the dead are most likely Christian alterations of Josephus' original writing. In the other place, Josephus simply reports the death of James, whom he identifies as the brother of Jesus who, he notes, was called the Christ.

The second Jewish source is the <u>Talmud,</u> written in the fifth century A.D. but containing traditions which are much older. As would be expected, it does not speak flatteringly of Jesus but does record that a Yeshua of Nazareth performed miracles, led Israel astray, used a Pharisaic method to interpret scripture, had five disciples, and was executed for being a false teacher on the day before the Passover.

These non-Christian sources tell us very little about Jesus but have value in the fact that they provide evidence for the reality of Jesus' earthly life from persons who had nothing to gain from such reports. It is perhaps surprising to learn that Jesus made such a faint impression on the Roman world outside Palestine. What is not surprising is that the allusions to Jesus in literature produced by Jews who did not accept him as the messiah are somewhat negative, some even polemical. This reflects the widening gap between Church and Synagogue in the period following the Jewish Revolt.

Christian Sources outside the Bible

There were several early Christian writings which did not become part of the New Testament and which are known as the New Testament Apocrypha. Some of them purport to be accounts of events in the life of Jesus, and some claim to convey sayings of Jesus not found in the canonical gospels. Among the documents discovered in 1946 at Nag Hammadi, Egypt, was one written in the Coptic language and now called the Gospel of Thomas. It contains 114 sayings attributed to Jesus, some very much like the ones in the gospels. It is possible that some of the others are also authentic.

Other "gospels" have been known for a long time, but their historical value is highly questionable. In general, they attempt to provide information about Jesus which is not found in the canonical gospels. For example, the Infancy Story of Thomas presents Jesus as a child who performed miracles in the presence of his playmates and caused the death of a boy who ran into him on the street. Others purport to give details of Jesus' trial or of his descent into hell. The products of devout Christians who wanted to meet the demand for more information about Jesus than the canonical gospels provide, these writings are so fanciful and unreliable that they can not be of any historical value for our knowledge of Jesus.

The New Testament Gospels

Our brief survey of Roman, Jewish, and non-canonical Christian sources clearly indicates that we must turn to the New Testament to find reliable information about Jesus of Nazareth. Even there not much is told about him in the writings outside the four gospels. In his letters, Paul included early accounts from the tradition he had received about Jesus' last meal with his disciples and his appearances after he arose from the dead (I Corinthians 11:23-26; 15:3-8), but very little else about the earthly Jesus.

The gospels, then, must be our primary sources for knowledge of Jesus. It is important to recognize that, written by Christians largely for Christians, they are in no sense objective accounts by impartial observers. The word "gospel" itself gives a good clue to the nature of these writings; it means the good news of salvation. The basic purpose of all four gospels is to proclaim Jesus as Son of God and Savior of the world. They are not biographies of Jesus. Rather, they are theological documents written to promote the Christian faith. They were produced by the Church, but without the Christ which they proclaim there would have been no Church.

Why Four Gospels?

If a gospel were simply a biography, then perhaps one gospel would be adequate to portray the life of Jesus. But, as we noted above, a gospel is not a biography, although it contains material of a biographical nature. The gospels are woefully incomplete as "lives" of Jesus. Only two of them report his birth. Only one records an event in Jesus' life between infancy and the age of thirty. The earliest gospel begins with Jesus as an adult and shows no concern to provide any information regarding his background, parentage, or education. No gospel provides a sequential account of his travels or appearances after his public ministry began. One-third of each gospel is occupied with the final week of Jesus' life.

It is far more satisfactory to speak of the gospels as portraits of Jesus. If we view them as four different expressions of the way four different first-century Christians understood Jesus and his significance for their faith, the fact that there are more than one such writing becomes understandable. As early as the second Christian century there was concern about the fact that the church was using four gospels. The heretical bishop Marcion, mentioned earlier in connection with the formation of the New Testament canon, proposed that Luke be the accepted gospel. Tatian, a Syrian Christian, combined the four into one, called the Diatessaron, but it was never accepted beyond the bounds of his own country.

The most likely explanation for the fact that the New Testament has four gospels is as follows: The authors did their work in scattered geographical areas, possibly in populous Christian centers such as Rome, Corinth, Antioch in Syria, Ephesus, and Alexandria. Each gospel became accepted in the region which produced it, and the local Christians were unwilling to surrender their "favorite" when the knowledge of other gospels became widespread. Even though each gospel reflects a different understanding of Jesus, all four of them were considered "orthodox" (doctrinally correct) and consequently accepted by the universal Church.

181

Each gospel supplemented the others and contributed its own distinctive shading to the rich portrait of the church's Lord.

The Synoptic Gospels

The careful reader of all four gospels becomes aware of a striking similarity among Matthew, Mark, and Luke, and an equally striking difference between these three and the Gospel of John. Not only does the style in which Jesus speaks in the Fourth Gospel (John) differ from that in the others, but the content of his message in John is distinct from the other three. John has none of the frequently used parables of Matthew, Mark, and Luke but, instead, presents Jesus speaking in long, philosophical-sounding discourses. John depicts Jesus' ministry as alternating between Galilee and Judea, whereas the others mention only Galilee as the scene of his activity until he went to Jerusalem a few days before his death. In the Fourth Gospel Jesus' ministry lasted about three years, but in the others it could have been as short as one year, or even less. Only a few narratives recorded in the first three gospels appear in John, and he records several which they do not. These and other differences indicate that Matthew, Mark, and Luke arise out of a different viewpoint and set of concerns than those which produced John.

The similarity among Matthew, Mark, and Luke led to their being called "Synoptic" (seeing together) gospels, which also sets them apart from the Fourth Gospel. But to stress their similarity is not to say they are identical. In fact, they are quite different from one another in content, order of events, wording, and even theological point of view. Scholars have gotten into the habit of calling this interesting combination of similarities and differences the Synoptic Problem, which consists of two questions: (1) How may we account for the similarities among Matthew, Mark, and Luke? (2) How shall we explain the differences among them?

Several decades of painstaking study by many scholars have produced a widely held consensus as to the solution of the Synoptic Problem. The main points of the solution are the following:

(1) Mark was the first gospel to be written and was used as a major source by both Matthew and Luke.

(2) Matthew and Luke had a second common source, which scholars have labeled "Q" (from German word for "source," Quelle), unavailable to Mark.

(3) Matthew and Luke each had other sources, unknown to the other and to Mark, called "M" and "L", respectively.

182

(4) Materials which they had in common were not always placed in the same order or in the same frame of reference.

(5) Each author composed his own introductory and transitional sentences, and sometimes altered or condensed materials from a common source.

Points 1, 2, and 3 may be illustrated by the following diagram:

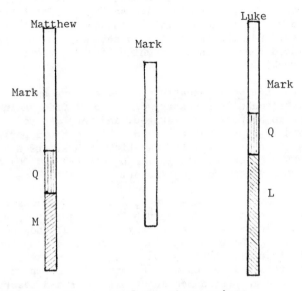

Let us examine each of the above points.

(1) <u>The priority of Mark.</u> Several observations led scholars to the conclusion that the shortest gospel, Mark, was also the first: Except for six short passages, all of Mark is contained in either Matthew or Luke. The outline of materials used by Mark is, in general, followed by the other two. In word choice, Matthew and Luke sometimes "improve" upon Mark's rougher, more vivid style.

(2) <u>The hypothetical "Q".</u> Approximately 200 verses appear, often word-for-word, in both Matthew and Luke but not in Mark. They are not, however, in the same order in both. This material consists almost entirely of Jesus' sayings and may have existed as a written collection of teachings of Jesus which Christian preachers found useful in their work.

(3) <u>Exclusive materials.</u> After materials from Mark and Q have been identified, there remain in Matthew and Luke large

amounts of material unique to each gospel. Many of the well-known parables of Jesus, such as the Prodigal Son (Luke) and the Wise and Foolish Maidens (Matthew), are found in these sections. Scholars have assumed that each author had access to traditions, perhaps some written and some oral, not available to the other, or to Mark, which they incorporated into their respective gospels.

(4) Ordering of materials. The evangelists (gospel authors) were not simply collectors of materials or copyists stringing together their narratives and sayings of Jesus haphazardly. They selected from the available sources the parables, sayings, narratives, and miracle stories which would further their purpose and arranged them in an order which fit into their view of Jesus and his work.

(5) Editorial creativity. As authors and theologians, the evangelists found it necessary often to provide an introductory statement to a story or a parable, and they did so [as noted in (4) above] in such a way as to advance their own portrait of Jesus and to serve their own interpretation of his person and work. Of course, this practice, along with points (3) and (4) above, gave their work a distinctive character.

These widely-acknowledged results of dedicated literary study of the gospels have contributed enormously to our understanding of the nature of these writings. We shall now consider each of the Synoptic Gospels individually before attempting to use the materials from all three to construct a composite picture of what Jesus was really like, what he taught his contemporaries, and what the early church proclaimed about his death and resurrection. The Fourth Gospel will be considered later.

The Gospel of Mark

The name "Mark" was given this first gospel by early Christian tradition, but it should be noted that the gospel itself does not give the author's name. Indeed, this is true of all four gospels. The only person named Mark in the New Testament was a resident of Jerusalem (Acts 12:12) who accompanied his cousin Barnabas (Col. 4:10) and Saul part way (Acts 12:25; 13:13) on a missionary trip and whom Paul (Saul) later lists as a "fellow-worker" (Philemon 24). It is possible that the tradition connecting him with the gospel is correct, but the one which says he received his information from Peter is certainly not. More reliable is the tradition which says the gospel was written in Rome or its vicinity. Most New Testament scholars today believe it was written between 64 and 70 A.D., which would place it shortly before the fall of Jerusalem in the year 70.

We do not know whether there were any written documents available to Mark when he wrote his Gospel. We do know there was a great deal of material in oral circulation, some of which Paul had already made use of in his letters. A connected narrative depicting events in the last week of Jesus' life, featuring his death and resurrection, formed the heart of the early Christian preaching. Shorter units of tradition, useful in the evangelizing, teaching, and preaching of the church, were in circulation. Such easily-remembered units as parables, miracle stories, short sayings, stories about Jesus (e.g., his baptism by John), and pronouncement stories (a pronouncement story is one which creates the setting for an important statement by Jesus, such as Mark 12:13-17) formed a fund of materials from which Mark selected what he needed for his purpose.

The shortest of the gospels, Mark has nothing about Jesus' birth, childhood, or adolescent years but begins with a description of John the baptizer, to whom Jesus came to be baptized. It contains fewer parables than do the other Synoptics and very little of the kind of teachings found in the "sermon on the mount" (Matthew 5-7; Luke 6:17-49). It reports that Jesus arose from the dead but says nothing about any post-resurrection appearances. Its organization is simple:

chs. 1-9   Jesus' ministry in Galilee and vicinity
ch. 10   Jesus on the way to Jerusalem
chs. 11-16   Jesus in Jerusalem.

From this brief outline, it appears that Mark is organized on a geographical basis, with Galilee as the home territory of Jesus, the locale of most of his ministry, the area from which his first disciples came, the place where he announced his coming suffering and death, and the place to which he will return after his resurrection. Jerusalem, on the other hand, is the place where resistance to his message is greatest and climaxes in his execution. Mark, who appears to be writing primarily for Gentile readers, may be using this device to explain the transition from unbelieving Jews to believing Gentiles as the major component of the church.

Another interesting feature of Mark is the concept of the "messianic secret." Although the writer himself has no doubt about who Jesus really is (Mark 1:11), time after time he records that Jesus commanded silence from any who seemed to be recognizing his true identity. Even when his disciples, somewhat belatedly, confessed that they knew who he was (8:27-30), they were commanded not to make it public. Not until the hearing before the Sanhedrin was the "secret" revealed (14:61-62). This is likely used by Mark to assist the reader in understanding why the Jews, Jesus' own people, rejected him. Jesus' true identity has been such a well-kept secret that it should come as no great surprise that the Jewish leaders do not accept his claim to be messiah!

Somewhat related to the messianic secret motif in Mark is the continual misunderstanding of Jesus, even by his own disciples. They do not understand some of his teaching (4:10), they fail to grasp the significance of some of his miracles (4:41; 6:52), they can not accept Jesus' prediction that he will suffer (8:31-33), they can not believe that he would be interested in talking with children (10:13), and they have the wrong idea of what it will mean to share in his "glory" (10:37-45). His old friends think Jesus is "beside himself" (3:21), his family does not understand his mission (3:31-35), and his disciples desert him at a critical time (14:50). Whereas Peter, the most outspoken of his disciples, denies three times any acquaintance with Jesus, a Roman soldier, presumably a stranger, acknowledges him as "a son of God" (15:39)!

We can not be certain why Mark stresses this misunderstanding so strongly, but it has the effect of emphasizing the role of the Gentiles to the disparagement of the Jews in the spread of Christianity. It also depicts a Jesus who refrains from making grandiose claims, from demanding special treatment, and from overwhelming friends, family, and disciples with the aura of divinity, despite Mark's opening line, which states matter-of-factly that Jesus Christ is the Son of God (1:1).

The Gospel of Matthew

Several years after Mark was written and had had time to become widely circulated among the various Christian centers, two other gospels, both using Mark as a primary source, were produced. Known to us by the names of Matthew and Luke, their authors most probably knew nothing of one another's efforts until much later. Tradition connects Matthew with the predominantly Gentile church in Antioch of Syria, which played a very important part in the missionary efforts of Paul and his companions, according to the book of Acts.

Assuredly not the Matthew (also known as Levi) listed among Jesus' disciples, the unknown author probably did his writing between 75 and 90 A.D. His book quickly became the preferred gospel because it contained most of the material in Mark and a great deal more. After the story of Jesus' birth and infancy in chapters 1-2, Matthew follows closely the narrative he found in Mark, inserting sections of teaching by Jesus at five points.

186

Much of this teaching is found also in Luke, hence we conclude
Matthew got it from the hypothetical source Q, mentioned above.
Still more is found only in Matthew, who must have had access to
traditions unknown to the other evangelists. For convenience we
label this group of sources "M." The blocks of teaching occur as
follows:

Chs. 5-7	"Sermon on the Mount"
10:5-42	Mission instructions to the disciples
Ch. 13	A group of parables
Ch. 18	Teachings on childlikeness, discipleship, church discipline, and forgiveness
24:37-25:45	Parables of watchfulness and judgment

After this fifth block Matthew follows Mark, with a few additions,
through the Passion Narrative (26:1-28:10), then closes with a
story of the risen Jesus' appearing to the disciples in Galilee.

It has been suggested that the Gospel of Matthew was intended to be a church manual for use in guiding and instructing
its members. It is the only gospel in which the word "church" appears (16:18; 18:17) and in which Jesus is said to have made provision for the establishment of the church. It provides a specific procedure for disciplining church members who did not live up
to their profession (18:15-17).

Compared to Mark, Matthew presents a stronger image of Jesus' power and divine nature. Jesus is presented as the fulfiller
of Israel's messianic expectations, a new Moses who interprets
perfectly the Law and the Prophets, and a healer for whom no dis-
ease is incurable. The Kingdom of Heaven is a dominant theme in
this Gospel, and the Sermon on the Mount (5-7) is a compilation of
Jesus' sayings which describe the style of life which is appropriate for a member of the Kingdom, which is understood as the realm
in which God's will prevails.

In the time since Mark was written the animosity between
the Church and the Synagogue had increased. This widening rift is
reflected in Matthew, especially seen in the strong condemnation
by Jesus of the scribes and Pharisees in chapter 23, and the statement (27:25) that the crowd (Jewish) assumed responsibility for
Jesus' death. Matthew treats the disciples more kindly than does
Mark and downplays their slowness to understand who Jesus was as
well as some of his teachings. Mark's story stating that the brothers James and John requested positions of privilege in Jesus'
future kingdom (Mark 10:35-37) is altered by Matthew to place the
onus of that request upon their mother (20:20-21)! Matthew includes several parables which encourage preparedness for the last
days which are not in either Mark or Luke (22:11-14;25:1-13,31-46).

187

He presents Jesus as a defender of the Jewish Torah (5:17-19) in contrast to the radical reviser of the Law of Mark 7:19b.

The Gospel of Luke

About the same time in which Matthew was being written, another Christian leader living in another part of the Roman Empire felt it necessary to produce "an orderly account" which would improve upon earlier efforts to narrate the beginnings of Christianity (Luke 1:1-4). Tradition has connected this Gospel with the Luke to whom Paul refers as "the beloved physician" (Colossians 4:14), but his name does not appear in the Gospel itself and there is no hard evidence to support this tradition. It is better to assume that, as is the case with Matthew, we do not know who wrote it and to concentrate on its contents. What we can be certain of is that the author of the Gospel of Luke also wrote the book of Acts, as can be seen by his dedicating both volumes to Theophilus in the hope that he would underwrite the cost of publication. He also tells us that he belonged to the second generation of the Christian tradition (1:2).

Like Matthew, Luke used both Q and Mark as primary sources but was able to draw upon a wider fund of oral tradition, which scholars for convenience have labeled "L," probably unknown to Mark and Matthew. More than one-third of his Gospel is composed of this material. He used seven-tenths of Mark, which he concentrated in three large blocks. After the infancy narratives (chs. 1-2; 3:23-38), he followed for the most part Mark's order and simply inserted two large non-Markan sections (6:17-8:3 and 9:51-18:14) into it. He also added several paragraphs to Mark's Passion Narrative. By his additions, rearrangements, connecting links, and improvements of Mark's rhetoric, Luke managed to give his Gospel a distinctive flavor and to emphasize certain themes which he considered important.

More than the other gospels, Luke pictures Jesus as exemplifying God's love for persons often despised or overlooked: sinners, the Samaritans, women, and the poor. At the same time, Jesus strongly warns against the temptations of riches and pronounces "woes" upon the affluent and the "full" (6:24-25). By grouping three parables centering in something which was lost and later found (ch. 15), he creates a strong witness to God's love for sinners, which contrasts sharply with the attitudes of many of his critics. By placing the story of Jesus' being rejected by his hometown people at the beginning of his ministry (4:16-30) instead of the middle (Mark 6:1-6) and expanding it, Luke established the idea that from the outset Jesus was rejected by his own people.

Luke, perhaps a Gentile himself, certainly was writing for Gentile consumption, hence stressed at various places the universal nature and appeal of Jesus' mission. He went out of his way in the Passion Narrative to insist that Jesus was not condemned by a Roman official (23:4,13-16,22). When we notice that, in his second volume (Acts), no Roman official ever condemned a Christian missionary or preacher, we conclude that Luke was consciously building a case that the Roman Empire had nothing to fear from the new Christian movement, which deserved to be granted the status of a legal religion, a privilege already enjoyed by Judaism.

Luke appears to be the first "historian" in the Christian movement. That is to say, he is the first to fix the earthly ministry of Jesus firmly into the events going on in the world and to see that ministry as a feature of on-going history. Both the birth of Jesus and the beginning of John's ministry are set within the context of the current political and religious leadership (2:1-4; 3:1-2). Taken together, Luke and Acts present the history of salvation as occurring in three distinct periods:
(1) The time of the Law and the Prophets, which ends with John the Baptist (16:16).
(2) The ministry of Jesus (told in the Gospel of Luke).
(3) The time of the Church (told in the book of Acts), in which the writer was living.

This third period Luke sees as continuing indefinitely; hence, the problem caused by the delay of the Second Coming of Christ (which many expected shortly after Jesus' ascension) is dealt with without denying the truth of the expectation. The Spirit of God which descended upon Jesus at his baptism (3:22) controlled his ministry (4:1,14,18), established and empowered the Church (Acts 1:8; 2:4; 7:55), and guided its preachers and missionaries in spreading the good news (Acts 13:2,4,9; 15:28; 16:6; 19:21). The Spirit is pictured as having been active in all three periods of salvation history (Acts 28:25; 2:15-18).

Luke, the longest of the gospels, contains exclusively some of the best-known of Jesus' parables: the Good Samaritan, the Rich Fool, the Great Banquet, the Prodigal Son, the Rich Man and Lazarus, and the Pharisee and the Tax Collector. It has been pointed out that Luke emphasizes prayer more than the other Synoptics. Two parables which encourage persistence in praying are the Friend at Midnight and the Importunate Widow. All these parables add to the richness of the third Gospel, which portrays Jesus as a compassionate, understanding champion of the cause of the despised, the neglected, and the outcasts of society.

Christ

gospel

Suetonius

Tacitus

Josephus

Talmud

Gospel of Thomas

Synoptic Gospels

Synoptic Problem

"Q"

"M"

"L"

Mark

Matthew

Luke

messianic secret

50-150 A.D.

64-70 A.D.

75-90 A.D.

CHAPTER XVIII

PREPARATION FOR MINISTRY

Biblical materials: Matthew 1:1-4:11. Mark 1:1-13. Luke 1:1-4:13

Essential reading: Mark 1:1-13
                    Matthew 1:18-4:11
                    Luke 1:5-2:52

The fact that Mark began his gospel with Jesus as a grown man suggests that for him and the church of which he was a member, Jesus' parentage and childhood were of little or no concern. But by the time Matthew and Luke were written, there was a great deal of interest in such matters. Doubtless, one reason for this was a natural curiosity about the origin and background of a person whose followers were making him the focal point of their preaching and teaching throughout the Roman Empire. Credal statements, such as those in Philippians 2:5-11 and I Corinthians 12:3, in which Jesus is confessed as Lord, Messiah, Savior, being in the form of God, etc., produced an understandable yearning for information about the beginnings of such a remarkable personage.

The Infancy Narratives

Matthew and Luke attempted to satisfy this curiosity by providing stories from the traditions available to them about Jesus' birth and parentage. But by this time, three quarters of a century removed from his birthdate, reliable information was difficult to obtain. When the infancy stories of these two evangelists are compared, it is apparent that they came from quite different traditions. Matthew begins his Gospel with a genealogy of forty-two generations, which traces Joseph's ancestry through his father Jacob to Abraham. He follows this with an explanation (1:18-25) of the embarrassing pregnancy of Mary, a virgin betrothed to Joseph, who was reassured in a dream that everything was all right, for Mary was the instrument for the fulfillment of a prophecy.

After the birth of the child (1:25) in Bethlehem, the story of a visit of some "wise men," probably Zoroastrian priest/astrologers from Persia, is told. This rumor of a king's being born excited the interest of Herod the Great, who ordered the massacre

191

of all male infants in Bethlehem who were no older than two years. But Joseph, following instructions delivered via a dream, had already taken his little family to Egypt, where he remained until Herod's death. Apparently he intended to settle at Bethlehem, but when he learned that Herod's son, Archelaus, was in charge of Judea, he found another place to live, outside Archelaus' territory: Nazareth of Galilee.

Luke's narrative is much longer. He gives a detailed account of the announcement of the coming birth of John to Elizabeth and Zechariah, the announcement of the coming birth of Jesus to a virgin named Mary who was living in Nazareth, a prolonged visit between Mary and Elizabeth, and the birth of John. Included in this long chapter one are three early Christian hymns related to the events described. Chapter two relates the birth of Jesus in Bethlehem, to which Joseph and Mary had traveled from their Nazareth home in compliance with an imperial decree regarding a new census. Shepherds just outside the town were notified by an angel of the birth of the "Savior" in a cattle-stall of the local inn. After a quick visit to the scene they returned to their sheep, praising God.

Luke then says the little family visited Jerusalem, performing appropriate rites at the Temple before returning to Nazareth. Jesus' childhood is covered by one short sentence (2:40), which is followed by an account of his attending a Passover celebration in Jerusalem with his parents when he was twelve years old. Luke has a genealogy in 3:23-38, which says Heli was Joseph's father, and traces his ancestry on beyond Abraham to Adam.

Although the differences between these two sets of infancy narratives are numerous and the reliability of the details is questionable, they do converge at several points: the names of Jesus' parents, the place of birth, and the town in which he grew up. They may be considered historically accurate. Matthew and Luke also agree on the virgin birth tradition, but it is worth noting that they are the only New Testament books that mention it. This suggests that the authors of the other books either knew nothing of it or did not consider it significant.

As for the date of Jesus' birth, we can not be certain. The Roman monk in the sixth century who fixed the year as 1 A.D. was, unfortunately, mistaken. Of course, his intent was to place Jesus' birth at the dividing point of history so that even the calendar would become a confession of faith. If Matthew's infancy narrative is accurate, we must place Jesus' year of birth prior to 4 B.C., the year of the death of Herod the Great. Herod's order for the annihilation of the male infants in Bethlehem included those up to two years old, which was based upon information given him by the visiting Magi on the basis of the appearance of the special star. Some experts think the "star" was a close conjunction of the planets Jupiter and Saturn, which occurred in 7 B.C. Luke's reference to a census (2:1-2) does not help since our information about such a census is very scanty. It is probably best to say that Jesus was born between 8 and 4 B.C. The day of the birth is even less certain. It was not until the fourth century that December 25 was agreed upon in Rome, and the Eastern Orthodox churches still observe January 6 as the proper day.

Later statements in the gospels allow us to add to our knowledge of Jesus' family. Joseph was a carpenter, and Jesus, as was customary, also learned and practiced carpentry. Jesus had four younger brothers and at least two sisters. We may assume that he was reared in a lower-income family, that he had a normal childhood and adolescence, and that he was educated in the local synagogue, where the study of the Torah prepared him to become a "Son of the Law" at age twelve.

His native language was Aramaic, although most of his recorded sayings are in Greek. Actual Aramaic sayings are recorded in Mark 5:41 and 15:34 (parallel in Matthew 27:46). It is not certain whether Jesus could speak Greek, which was the official language of the Roman Empire. Despite fictional accounts (some apocryphal gospels) that indicate otherwise, it is probable that Jesus, prior to his baptism, did not impress the neighbors as being especially holy or precocious. This explains why the hometown folks were so shocked when he visited Nazareth as an itinerant rabbi in the middle part of his ministry (Mark 6:1-6).

Jesus and John

We have earlier observed that the gospels are not biographies of Jesus. This fact is underscored by the enormous gap between the infancy narratives and the beginning of Jesus' ministry, which, according to Luke 3:23, occurred when he was thirty years of age. Absolutely nothing is told about the previous eighteen years. When Mark begins his story, Jesus is an adult coming to John the baptizer, who is depicted as a popular rural preacher who stresses repentance and performs baptisms as a token of forgiveness. According to Luke 1, Jesus and John were related, John being six months older than Jesus.

John's preparation for ministry is not told. He somewhat suddenly appeared in the Judean wilderness, near the Jordan River,

193

as an intense, ascetic, fiery preacher with such an appealing message that crowds came from Jerusalem and elsewhere to hear, see, and in some cases, respond to this austere figure. His unheralded appearance in the desert, together with his ascetic life-style, has led to the suggestion that he had been a member of an Essene community (see above, pp. 174-5), which he had left, possibly because of a disagreement over that sect's mission. At any rate, the gospels present him as the forerunner of Jesus who acknowledged and proclaimed Jesus' superiority to himself. It occurred to some Jews that John might be the expected messiah, but Luke says that he discouraged such speculation (Luke 3:15-18). The Fourth Gospel (John 1:19-36) has John stating emphatically that he is not the messiah, which reflects the fact that a group of the followers of John the Baptist persisted in their belief that he was the messiah for several decades. Luke (3:10-14) adds that, in addition to his announcing a day of wrath and judgment, John called for ethical and social behavior which reflected justice, compassion, and restraint.

The Baptism

The Synoptic Gospels report that Jesus came to where John was preaching and presented himself for baptism. We, of course, can not know what prompted Jesus to ask for John's baptism, but he apparently saw it as a kind of commissioning for his ministry. Matthew (3:13-17) felt that he must explain to his readers that it was not out of a sense of sinfulness that Jesus came to the Jordan he insisted on being baptized because to do so would "fulfil all righteousness," certainly an ambiguous statement. At least, it would help Christians preserve the concept of Jesus' sinlessness and enable them to rebut the charges of non-believers that Jesus' coming to be baptized amounted to a confession of sin.

Mark states that when Jesus emerged from the river following his baptism, he saw "the heavens opened and the Spirit descending upon him like a dove," following which he heard a voice from heaven, "Thou art my beloved Son; with thee I am well pleased" (1:10-11). Although Mark and Luke understood this as a completely private experience for Jesus, Matthew makes it into a general announcement which all bystanders could hear (3:17). It is impossible to say just what significance these phenomena had for Jesus. Many have suggested that here is the point at which he realized he was the messiah. In any case, it was an important turning-point for him. After this, there was no going back to the carpenter's shop; his real life's work lay in another direction.

After his baptizing Jesus, John faded from the scene, hav-

194

ing been imprisoned by Herod Antipas (Luke 3:19-20), who later executed him to keep an ill-considered promise he had made to his step-daughter (Matt. 14:3-12; Mark 6:17-29). Matthew and Luke record that, sometime during his imprisonment, John sent disciples to Jesus to inquire of him directly whether he were "he who is to come" (Matt. 11:2-6; Luke 7:18-23). After they had gone, Jesus had highly complimentary things to say about John, describing him as "more than a prophet" and saying that there had been no human being greater than he. Clearly, the Synoptics represent the ministry of John the baptizer coming to an end at about the same time that Jesus' ministry began.

The Wilderness Experience

Immediately following his baptism, Jesus felt compelled to retreat into the wilderness for a period of dealing with agonizing questions about his future. The Synoptics say that he was tempted by Satan during this forty-day stint, during which he ate nothing. Matthew and Luke, probably drawing upon their common source Q, provide a more detailed account of the temptations which Jesus faced. The three which they describe appear to be related to common conceptions of the appearance of the messiah.

By turning stones into bread Jesus could not only satisfy his own immediate hunger, he could usher in a period of plentiful food for all, one of the popular ideas of what the messianic age would bring. By jumping from the pinnacle of the Temple he would fulfil another messianic expectation: that, when the messiah came, he would appear there first. By submitting to Satan, who in the thought of many was in control of the world, Jesus could gain political dominance and rid the land of Roman domination. All of these would be much easier ways to "be the messiah" than the road which Jesus actually followed. (Matt. 4:1-11; Luke 4:1-13)

If the temptations recorded in Matthew and Luke faithfully represent the nature of Jesus' struggle in that deserted area, the wilderness experience was a further preparation for his coming ministry. Having been given the Spirit at baptism, he had now confronted the powers of evil, personified as Satan, and had won the battle by steadfastly clinging to the words of the Torah. This would be one of many confrontations with Satan which Jesus would experience. Jesus is seen in the gospels as the leader of the Kingdom of God who is engaged in a continuous encounter with the kingdom of Beelzebul. Every time he exorcizes a demon, he has achieved one more victory over Satan.

<u>Significant names, terms, and dates for this chapter</u>

messiah

infancy narrative

Magi

Herod the Great

Archelaus

Joseph

Mary

Zechariah

Elizabeth

John the baptizer

Nazareth

Bethlehem

Egypt

8-4 B.C.

Aramaic

Herod Antipas

Satan

CHAPTER XIX

JESUS' MINISTRY IN GALILEE

Biblical materials: Matthew 4:12-18:35. Mark 1:14-9:50
                     Luke 4:14-18:14

Essential reading: Mark 1:14-3:35; 4:35-7:37; 8:27-38; 9:2-8
                    Matthew 5-7; 13; 16:13-23
                    Luke 4:16-30; 10:25-42; 15; 18:1-14

All three Synoptic Gospels depict Jesus as conducting most of his ministry in Galilee, one of the regions governed by Herod Antipas, where Jesus had spent most of his life. Matthew (4:13) reports that Jesus moved his residence from Nazareth to Capernaum, the largest city in Galilee, situated on the Sea of Galilee. Unlike John the baptizer, who stayed in wilderness areas and had the people come to him, Jesus went where the people were. He spent a lot of time on the road, carrying his message that "the kingdom of God is at hand" (Mark 1:15). The kingdom of God ("kingdom of heaven" in Matthew) was the central theme of Jesus' preaching.

The Kingdom of God

Instead of a time of judgment and calamity, of which John warned, Jesus spoke of the kingdom of God as a new age which was about to appear. This is good news ("the gospel," Mark 1:15), and his own appearance in the world was the beginning of the kingdom's manifestation. Some of Jesus' statements assume that it is already here, while others imply that it is still in the future. This apparent confusion is removed if we look upon Jesus as the herald of the kingdom, which is already in process of being established but whose full realization lies ahead.

The term "kingdom" is, of course, subject to more than one interpretation. For many Jews the word meant a political entity with observable boundaries and customary organs of government and defense. The Old Testament furnished plenty of precedent for such a concept. The kingdom of David was a source of historical pride for the Jews, even if his successors had proved to be less effective. Even earlier than David the Israelites thought of God himself as their king. This was such a strong tradition that some of them could not bring themselves to agree with the proposal that they also have a human king. Some of the prophets had spoken of the appearance of an ideal king in the future (Isaiah 9:6-7; 11:1-5). In light of the political situation in Palestine when Jesus was preaching, it is not surprising that talk about the kingdom of God should arouse patriotic feelings and dreams of independence among the Jews. Even Jesus' own disciples thought Jesus was going to set up an earthly kingdom (Mark 10:35-37).

Jesus' own concept of his kingdom was a purely spiritual one. Translating "reign" of God rather than "kingdom" might make it easier to understand his teaching on the subject. Like the Israelites' acknowledging the kingship of Yahweh (see Psalms 93, 95, 97 and 99), Jesus called upon his hearers to become God's subjects allowing him to reign over their lives. So Jesus can speak of the kingdom as coming upon a person, as being among men, and as belonging to men but more often he talks about their entering the kingdom.

There are qualifications for admittance. One must "repent and believe" (Mark 1:15); one must have childlike trust and receptivity (Mark 10:14-15); one must be willing to surrender whatever stands in the way of total allegiance (Mark 10:21-27). Many of Jesus' parables illustrate some characteristic of the kingdom: it is of supreme value, it has power within itself to grow and expand it is not built by human endeavor, it is a gift from God which demands a decision from each person it confronts, and to enter it is to enter "life." (See below, pages 203-204.)

The Rabbi Gathers Disciples

Jesus' first activity after his initial preaching, according to Matthew and Mark, was the inviting of four Galilean fishermen to follow him. This indicates that Jesus was thinking of himself in the role of the traditional Jewish rabbi, who would travel from place to place accompanied by a retinue of followers, whom he would teach as they walked along the roads. It was also traditional for the rabbi to have a trade by which he could support himself and for him to be married. Apparently Jesus followed only the first of these traditions.

Although the gospels say that Jesus had twelve disciples, the Synoptics report only the calling of five of them: Simon Peter and his brother Andrew; James and John, sons of Zebedee; and a tax collector named Levi (according to Mark and Luke), also known as Matthew (Matthew 9:9; Mark 3:18). Mark records a total of twelve but tells us nothing about the other seven, except for Judas Iscariot. It is interesting that the Talmud's references to Jesus say he had five disciples.

Three of the original group of fishermen, Simon Peter, James, and John, formed an inner circle of disciples who accompanied him to places the others did not go. Except for Judas, the other nine are referred to only as a group, the disciples (which means "learners"). The selection of the number twelve was probably symbolic, reflecting the well-known twelve tribes of Israel. According to Luke, one of them, Simon the Canaanean, was a member of the superpatriotic party, the Zealots, and it is possible that Judas Iscariot also belonged to that group or one with similar goals. It is likely that most, if not all, of Jesus' disciples were Galileans. Apparently none of them was from the elite, highly educated, or influential segments of Palestinian society.

Mark reports that, after the twelve had been with Jesus for a while, he sent them out in pairs on a preaching/healing mission. Following his instructions, they took no luggage, food, or money with them but depended on generosity of the villagers to whom they ministered for their needs (Mark 6:7-13). The mission, which included the exorcizing of demons, was successful. Luke records a second mission (10:1-20), in which seventy additional persons were involved. Just how or when this larger group received the necessary training and experience is not explained, and the absence of any reference to this mission in Matthew or Mark has led some scholars to question its accuracy. At any rate, it is clear that Jesus consciously selected a group of men to become a core who would carry on his work when he would no longer be around. Except for Judas, they all became witnesses to Jesus' resurrection and, according to Acts, were active in the establishment of the first congregation of believers (Acts 1-2).

Exorcist and Miracle Worker

Immediately following the account of the calling of the first group of disciples, Mark tells of the teaching and healing activity of Jesus. His first teaching platform was provided by the synagogue in Capernaum. Fully aware of his Jewishness, Jesus readily followed the traditions of his people and frequented their institutions. On the occasion Mark describes (1:21-28), Jesus, as a visiting rabbi, amazed the congregation with the manner and power of his teaching. Presumably his directness and authoritative style in proclaiming the will of God contrasted with the way their local rabbis taught.

At the same service, Jesus performed his first-mentioned exorcism. Demon possession was a widely accepted phenomenon in first-century Palestine, and exorcism was practiced before Jesus came along. In Jesus' exorcisms, the gospel writers see a confrontation between the kingdom of God and the kingdom of Satan, who was thought to be the chief of the demons, invisible powers who often inhabited persons and made them behave in abnormal, irrational ways. The demons had superhuman knowledge, as is illustrated by the identification of Jesus as "the Holy One of God." Jesus commanded the demon to be silent, which is characteristic of Mark's account both of exorcisms and healings (see discussion of messianic secret, above, pp. 185-6). The word about this extraordinary exorcist/teacher quickly spread through Galilee, says Mark.

Later the same day, Jesus and his four disciples went to Simon Peter's home, where his mother-in-law was ill. The nature of the illness is not described but Jesus healed her of whatever was causing the "fever." This was the first of many healings he performed that day, which Mark may have wanted his readers to see as a typical day in the early weeks of his ministry. When the sabbath was over ("at sundown"), the sick and demon-possessed citizens of Capernaum were brought to Jesus (Mark 1:32-34), and Mark says he healed and exorcised "many." In their report of this incident, Matthew and Luke, not wanting their readers to think there were some persons whom Jesus could not help, say that he healed all who came (Matt. 8:16; Luke 4:40).

This heavy demand on Jesus' time, energy, and power for healing and exorcizing demons forced him to re-examine the purpose of his ministry. His compassion for the masses of people who were suffering from a variety of physical and mental illnesses and handicaps could easily lead to a career of healing alone. But was this why the Spirit had descended upon him and God had designated him as his beloved Son? After several hours of private meditation and prayer, he arrived at a clear understanding of what God wanted him to do. He would not abandon the healing and exorcizing, but his priority must be preaching (Mark 1:35-38).

Before we examine the content of Jesus' preaching, we shall review Mark's narratives of Jesus' continuing miracle-working activity. His "mighty works" (The gospels do not use the term "miracles.") can, for convenience, be classified into four types: healing, exorcism, nature miracle, and raising the dead. The healings include Jesus' curing persons of leprosy (1:40-45), a withered hand (3:1-6), blindness (8:22-25; 10:46-52), and deafness/speech defect (7:32-37). His exorcizing activity, besides that in the Capernaum synagogue, includes a highly dramatic encounter with a multi-possessed man in non-Jewish territory (5:1-20) and cleansing a boy of a "dumb spirit" (9:14-29).

To the type we call nature miracles belong the stilling of

the storm (4:35-41), walking on the water (6:45-52), and two cases of Jesus' feeding a large group of people with a small amount of food (6:34-44; 8:1-9). It is probable that there was only one multitude feeding which came to Mark's attention in slightly different accounts. Matthew follows Mark and relates both (Matt. 14:13-21; 15:32-39) while Luke is satisfied with reporting only the feeding of the five thousand (Luke 9:11-17).

Only one case of raising the dead is reported by Mark (5:22-24,35-43), but Luke tells of the raising of a widow's son at Nain (7:11-17). Certainly the miracle-working activity of Jesus was understood by the gospel writers to be a significant part of his ministry. Not only did it demonstrate his special relationship with God, but it depicted him as a person of great compassion for those who were unable to find help from their fellows. On no occasion did he do a mighty work in order to convince a person to believe on him; he always did it to help persons in great need.

Amazing Teacher

The gospels report that Jesus had no trouble getting a hearing for his preaching and teaching. Members of the synagogues were amazed, common people skipped lunch to hear him, sinners found new hope in his messages, and the experts on the Torah were often incensed by his pronouncements. We have already considered some of his teachings about the kingdom of God. Matthew collected from his "Q" and "M" sources a variety of Jesus' sayings having to do with the kind of life appropriate for those in the kingdom. He put them together as though they constituted a "sermon" Jesus delivered on one occasion and inserted the collection into the outline he got from Mark just after the summary statement about a preaching and healing campaign throughout Galilee (Mark 1:39; Matt. 4:23-25). We know it as the "Sermon on the Mount," so named because of the way Matthew introduces it (5:1-2), and it occupies chapters 5-7 of his gospel. Much of it also appears, but not in the same order, in Luke (6:17-49; 11:9-13; 12:22-31).

The Sermon on the Mount, Matthew says, was directed not to the crowds but to Jesus' disciples. It constitutes an excellent summary of Jesus' ethical teachings, or the manner of life God wants his people to follow. The Beatitudes, perhaps the best known of Jesus' sayings, introduce the sermon and state in poetic form the attitudes and behavior God desires, together with the blessings which follow from them (5:3-12).

The picture of Jesus which emerges is that of a new Moses, who does not deliver additional laws but who correctly interprets

the law (Torah) already revealed. He says that an absolute entrance requirement to the kingdom is righteousness which is superior to that of "the scribes and Pharisees" (5:20), then demon-
strates that such superior righteousness proceeds from a deeper
understanding of God's commandments (5:21-48). It is the intent
of the heart that matters to God more than the outward deed. For
example, the commandment "You shall not kill" means not only that
you are forbidden to commit murder but also that you are not to be
angry at another or to assault him verbally (5:21-22).

This section includes the so-called "hard sayings" of Jesus pertaining to non-resistance to evil (5:38-42) and love of enemies (5:43-48). Such difficult prescriptions for conduct have
led some to wonder whether Jesus ever intended them to be taken
literally. It is probably best to understand Jesus' teachings as
statements of what God really desires as human conduct without any
consideration of human ability or inability to achieve it.

Also included in the Sermon are the Lord's Prayer, used by
Jesus as a model for praying appropriately (6:7-13), a warning
against over-anxiety about material things (6:25-34), the caution
about judging others (7:1-5), and the famous Golden Rule (7:12).

Although Mark contains much less of Jesus' teaching than
do Matthew and Luke, it attributes some rather radical sayings to
him. After some Pharisees and scribes had asked him why his disciples did not observe the "tradition of the elders" (7:5), Jesus
heatedly charged them with putting the tradition above the divine
commandment. He was, in effect, upholding the written Torah over
the so-called "oral" Torah when he accused his questioners of having devised a way of avoiding the commandment which says, "Honor
your father and your mother" (7:9-13).

But in what follows, Mark represents Jesus as actually
calling for a change in the written Torah! When Jesus said,
"There is nothing outside a man which by going into him can defile
him," Mark explains that he was declaring all foods clean (7:14-23)
Luke does not use this section of Mark at all, and when Matthew
reproduces it (15:1-20), he omits Mark's explanation. In fact,
Matthew presents Jesus as more inclined to defend the Torah (Matt.
5:17-19) at the same time that he illustrates his authority to re-
interpret it (5:21-48).

Another radical saying attributed to Jesus in Mark is the
statement regarding divorce (10:2-12). Pharisees had differing
opinions on the acceptable grounds for divorce and attempted to
draw Jesus into the controversy. Citing the creation story in
Genesis (1:27; 2:24), Jesus stated forthrightly that, despite
Moses' rule permitting divorce, it was God's intention that there

be no divorce. This means that Jesus was pitting one section of the Torah against another and acknowledging that one takes precedence over the other.

By the time Matthew wrote his Gospel, this saying of Jesus had been found too severe and one ground of divorce, adultery, had been inserted (Matt. 19:9; see also 5:32). Jesus' teaching on divorce as presented in Matthew is in agreement with the position of the Pharisaic school of Shammai. Mark's version of Jesus' statement about divorce can be classed with the "hard sayings" we noted above in the Sermon on the Mount. Jesus was expressing the will of God for his people without making allowance for human frailty. He was not establishing ecclesiastical law.

The Parables

Although the Fourth Gospel does not mention that Jesus taught in parables, the Synoptics give the impression that this was perhaps his favorite and most effective method of teaching. The word "parable" is used in the gospels to refer to a variety of forms of his sayings. Mark calls the saying, noted above, about foods' not causing defilement a parable (7:14-17). Matthew labels the analogy in 13:33 a parable: "The kingdom of heaven is like leaven which a woman took and hid in three measures of meal, till it was all leavened." But most of the materials called parables are stories about things with which Jesus' hearers would be familiar, stories which Jesus used to establish or clarify a spiritual truth. They served much the same purpose as illustrations which speakers use to shed light on a point. So it is somewhat perplexing to read a statement such as Mark 4:11-12, which seems to say that Jesus used parables to prevent understanding rather than to further it. This may be connected to Mark's "messianic secret" theme, but surely it misrepresents Jesus' purpose in using parables. He came to enlighten, not to confuse or to conceal.

Many of Jesus' parables pointed to some feature of the kingdom of God. The parables of the Sower (Mark 4:1-8), the Seed Growing Secretly (4:26-29), the Mustard Seed (4:30-32), and the Leaven (Matt. 13:33) emphasized the kingdom's innate power to grow and were told to encourage the disciples in times of poor response to their preaching. The parables of the Hidden Treasure (Matt. 13:44) and the Precious Pearl (13:45-46) stressed the supreme value of the kingdom. The nearness of the kingdom is the theme of the parables of the Talents (Matt. 25:14-30), the Pounds (Luke 19:11-27), and the Wise and Foolish Maidens (Matt. 25:1-13).

He used others to illustrate attitudes and virtues which

203

members of the kingdom ought to manifest. God's concern for sinners is powerfully stated in the parables of the Lost Sheep, the Lost Coin, and the Lost Son in Luke 15. That he told them in reply to those who criticized him for associating with sinners indicates that God expects his people to show the same concern for such persons that Jesus did. Akin to this theme are the parables of the Pharisee and the Tax Collector (Luke 18:9-14) and the Laborers in the Vineyard (Matt. 20:1-16).

What it means to love the neighbor is beautifully illustrated in the parable of the Good Samaritan (Luke 10:25-37), and stressed in the parable of the Sheep and the Goats (Matt. 25:31-46 which Matthew uses to warn of the coming judgment day. By telling the parables of the Friend at Midnight (Luke 11:5-8) and the Unjust Judge (18:2-5), Jesus encouraged his followers to pray, even to be persistent when they did not get an immediate answer. He urged responsible stewardship of one's possessions in the parables of the Rich Fool (Luke 12:13-21) and the Rich Man and Lazarus (16:19-31). We have not alluded to all of Jesus' parables, but this quick overview may serve to indicate something of the scope and significance of the parabolic materials in the Synoptics.

Clashes and Conflicts

The gospels contain many indications that Jesus' teaching, as well as his mighty works, attracted crowds of people and made him a popular figure among the common people of Galilee. However there were persons, mostly other teachers of the Torah and religious leaders, who were not so pleased with Jesus' activities and his interpretations of the Torah. Much of this opposition doubtless stemmed from sincerely held differences, but some may be attributed to a feeling of jealousy over the fact that this non-traditionalist was drawing bigger crowds than they were. The gospels identify several points at which Jesus was challenged by scribes, Pharisees, and others.

The Sabbath. Early in his ministry Jesus clashed with the authorities over sabbath observance. He agreed with them that worship in the synagogue was a proper activity for that day, but when he healed on the sabbath or defended his disciples when they plucked, cleaned, and ate grain on the sabbath, his critics saw those acts as defying the prohibition against work. It is clear that Jesus simply disagreed with them on this subject, for he reminded them that the sabbath had been established for man's benefit (Mark 2:27) and that it was perfectly legal to minister to human need on that day (Mark 3:1-6).

As noted above, Jesus did not agree with some of the scribes of his day on other facets of the Torah, especially when he perceived they were emphasizing "their traditions" to the downgrading of the written law. Although he is depicted by Matthew as approving of <u>fasting</u> (6:16-18), neither Jesus nor his disciples seems to have participated in that customary expression of Jewish piety. He defended their lifestyle by pointing to the newly-arriving kingdom, whose character and message were so new and fresh that the old forms and customs seemed inappropriate (Mark 2:18-22). On another occasion he acknowledged the difference between his and John's way of life. There were those who said John the Baptist was demon-possessed because of his extremely ascetic lifestyle. Now, Jesus said, they were calling him "a glutton and a drunkard" because he lived a fuller life (Luke 7:33-34).

<u>His associating with tax collectors and sinners</u> was another point on which Jesus and his critics were miles apart. The scribes and Pharisees apparently thought that a genuine rabbi would associate only with the righteous, pious keepers of the Torah. It is clear that Jesus not only taught and healed among the lower classes of society but also sought them out and even ate with them. Luke records that he invited himself to the home of a chief tax collector named Zaccheus (19:1-10). When his friendliness toward the riff-raff was challenged, he replied by telling parables illustrating God's joy over a repentant sinner (Luke 15) and by pointing out that his mission was to sinners, not the righteous (Mark 2:15-17). It was noted that one of his disciples was a tax collector. Doubtless it had also occurred to his critics that none of his disciples had come from the ranks of the learned, well-to-do, respectable citizenry.

Jesus simply did not fit the accepted pattern of a rabbi. The fact that he had grown up in Galilee, rather than in Judea, caused the Jerusalem leadership to consider him of little importance. When they could no longer ignore him, they charged that "He is possessed by Beelzebul," the chief of demons (Mark 3:22). The best his friends could do by way of explaining his actions was to say, "He is beside himself" (Mark 3:21). It is likely that his family tried to persuade him to forsake his mission and come home with them (Mark 3:31-35). His popularity with the common people, together with the criticism from the influential leaders of society, must have caused them considerable embarrassment.

When word reached Herod Antipas of the work of Jesus and his disciples, the reports reminded him of John the Baptist. He even pondered the possibility that John had been raised from the dead, according to Mark 6:14-16. Luke reports a rumor that Herod wanted to kill Jesus (13:31). Jesus' reaction to the rumor reflects a considerable disdain for Antipas, whom he referred to a "that fox." It is doubtful that the two men ever met, at least prior to the hearing which Luke describes on the day of Jesus' crucifixion (23:6-12). There Luke says that Herod had wanted to meet Jesus for a long time and was glad for the opportunity afforded him by Pilate.

The Big Question

At some point toward the close of his Galilean ministry, the Synoptics say that Jesus confronted his disciples with a significant question regarding his identity. Mark and Matthew say that it came as he and his disciples were in the vicinity of Caes area Philippi, which was located well within the territory govern ed by Herod Philip. Possibly they were on a "vacation," or retreat from the busy routine in Galilee.

The subject of who Jesus was had come up on previous occa sions. Demons had referred to him as "the Holy One of God" and "Son of the Most High God" (Mark 1:24; 5:7). After he had calmed the storm on the Sea of Galilee, his disciples had discussed with one another, "Who then is this, that even wind and sea obey him?" (Mark 4:41) The home town folks recognized him as the carpenter they used to know (Mark 6:3). As noted above, Herod Antipas wondered whether he could be a reincarnated John the Baptist.

That the matter had been discussed by others is made clea by the answers Jesus received to his first question, "Who do men say that I am?" (Mark 8:27-29) All the possibilities mentioned were reincarnations of some previous, outstanding prophetic figur Like Herod, some had thought of John; others posed the name of Elijah, the idiosyncratic prophet of the ninth century B.C. whose unique method of leaving the world had given rise to speculation that he would return one day. Jesus himself, in the Gospel of Mark, had claimed no title for himself to this point, with the possible exceptions of 1:11 and 2:28.

The second question Jesus addressed to his disciples on this occasion required a collective judgment from them and may have been used by him as a sort of test of their ability to perceive the significance of what they had experienced in the preced ing months. They had been called to be his followers, they had been taught by him almost daily, they had carried out a successfu mission without him, and they had seen many exorcisms and other mighty works done by him. It was time for the big question: "Wh do you say that I am?"

206

The only answer Jesus received came from the lips of Peter: "You are the Christ." Whether this reply truly represented the collective opinion of the twelve or whether it was an intuitive flash of insight by one man is not indicated in Mark. Matthew's version, however, favors the latter alternative (16:17). "Christ" is the Greek translation of the Hebrew "messiah," a term which carried important connotations for Jews of first-century Palestine. Their messianic expectations and hopes were quite varied, but one very popular concept looked for a human ruler from the line of David who would rule over an independent Jewish nation with right-eousness and justice. His reign would be marked by peace and abundance of life's necessities for all. This is very likely the picture of the messiah which Peter had in mind when he made his famous "confession."

It should be noted that in Mark's account of this event, Jesus neither commended nor condemned Peter for his answer. Mark simply reports that "he charged them to tell no one about him" (8:30) and then proceeded to predict his coming suffering and death. This earned a rebuke from Peter, who found it impossible to fit his identification of Jesus as messiah into the idea that he should suffer defeat, indignities, rejection, and ultimately execution. His messiah would be a conquering, ruling, majestic figure. But Peter got rebuked in turn by Jesus, who vehemently connected Peter's objection to satanic reasoning. Taking all the details of Mark's narrative (8:27-33) into accouint, we must conclude that either (1) Jesus did not accept the designation "messiah" for himself or (2) he thought of himself as messiah, but not the type of messiah of which Peter was thinking.

When we read Matthew's account of the "confession," which is later than Mark's, we can see how it has been significantly expanded (Matt. 16:13-23). To Peter's simple statement, "You are the Christ," has been added "the Son of the living God." Jesus' response is enthusiastically approving of Peter's identification of Jesus as messiah. Verses 18 and 19 are totally new. By interpreting the "rock" on which Jesus says he will build his church as referring to Peter, the Roman Catholic Church used these verses as the foundation of the office of pope. Protestants, on the other hand, understand the "rock" as the faith expressed in Peter's confessional statement. Jesus was obviously using a play on words here, for the Greek word for rock is petra and the Greek form of Peter's name is Petros.

Did Jesus think of himself as messiah in the Synoptics? Only once, other than his approval of Peter's statement in Matthew, did Jesus accept that title for himself (Mark 14:62), and even this occasion was reported differently by Matthew (26:64) and Luke

(22:67-68). Yet it must be said that some of his actions, such as cleansing the Temple and riding into Jerusalem on an ass, seem to have been done in conscious fulfilment of messianic statements in Scripture. Perhaps we would be safe in concluding that, if Jesus did think messianically of his mission, he was not thinking in terms of the kind of messiah which was in Peter's mind, or in the minds of James and John (Mark 10:35-37) when they asked for the second and third highest positions in Jesus' kingdom.

A term which Jesus did use of himself in the Synoptics was son of man. What his concept of that title was is difficult to know. It is found in the Old Testament, but not as a title. As a term, it is used to mean mankind (Ps. 8:4), and, in Ezekiel, as substitute for a name or a pronoun: God addresses the prophet as "son of man." In Daniel 7:13 a heavenly figure is described as one "like a son of man," meaning like a human being. It is clear that Jesus used the term both to mean "mankind" (Mark 2:28) and as a substitute for the pronouns "I" and "me" (Mark 8:31).

Why Jesus chose the term to refer to himself is not clear. Perhaps he considered it a term which was fairly neutral and which would not lead to false hopes regarding his mission. But there are a few times when he seems to have used "son of man" as though he were speaking of a person other than himself, a heavenly figure (Mark 8:38; 13:26; 14:62). This person apparently was one whom Jesus expected to descend from heaven to inaugurate the new age. We conclude that the term son of man is not one which will help us understand Jesus' concept of his own person and mission.

It seems appropriate to mention at this point another event reported by the Synoptics (Mark 9:2-8; Matt. 17:1-8; Luke 9:28-36) which relates to the general subject of who Jesus was. Known as the Transfiguration, it describes an experience by the inner circle of disciples in which they saw Jesus bathed in a glorious brilliance and carrying on a conversation with two Old Testament heroes, Moses and Elijah. Like earlier manifestations of divine presence or revelation, this dazzling scene took place on a "high mountain," which is not identified but which is thought by some to be Mt. Hermon, by others, Mt. Tabor. The gospels intend to show Jesus as the fulfiller of the Torah (represented by Moses) and the prophets (represented by Elijah). The voice coming out of the cloud placed the divine stamp of approval on Jesus' ministry by using essentially the same words that came from heaven at his baptism: "This is my beloved Son; listen to him" (Mark 9:7).

This story focuses our attention on another title often used of Jesus: Son of God. Mark used it in the title of his Gospel and tells us that, in addition to the heavenly voice at the

208

Baptism and the Transfiguration, it was applied to Jesus by the demons and the centurion at the cross (Mark 15:39). Although there is no account of his bluntly having stated, "I am the Son of God," it is surely the case that Jesus thought of himself as related to God in an intimate way. At the age of twelve, Luke reports, he referred to the Temple as "my Father's house" (2:49). In Mark 13:32 he implies that he is the Son, who is not privileged to know everything his Father does. He addressed God as Father in his own prayer (Mark 14:36), as well as in the model prayer he taught his disciples (Luke 11:2; Matt. 6:9).

Another title applied to Jesus in the Synoptics is prophet (Luke 7:16; 24:18-19; Matt. 21:11,46; Mark 6:14-15; 8:28). Occasionally Jesus referred to himself as a prophet (Mark 6:4; Luke 13:33), and he certainly fit the Old Testament role of prophet as one who speaks God's message. Some scholars believe that Jesus thought of his mission in terms of the suffering Servant of Isaiah 53. He never used the term of himself, but he made several references to his coming suffering and death (Mark 8:31; 10:45; 14:24) in such a way as to remind one of the Isaiah passage. Jesus was sometimes addressed as Lord in the Synoptics, but it probably meant no more than a respectful term, such as "sir" in modern English. After Jesus' death and resurrection, of course, it did mean more than that; it became a title of worship and a confession of faith.

We have not included the Fourth Gospel or the other New Testament writings in this brief survey of titles and terms applied to Jesus. We shall consider that material in later chapters. The sum of the evidence in the Synoptics indicates a great variety in the opinions of Jesus' contemporaries on the subject of who he was. The evangelists themselves, writing out of their own faith and several decades removed from the ministry of Jesus, had no doubt that Jesus was messiah, Son of God, a rabbi, a prophet, and the Lord. No one title that they knew of could adequately identify him.

As for Jesus' view of himself, we are forced to admit that there is very little about which we can be certain. The character of the Jesus depicted in the Synoptics was such that he did not go around making claims about his identity. He was far more interested in speaking about God than about himself. He did speak of God and his will for his people with an unique authority. He did perform mighty works out of compassion for the ill, the infirm, and the disturbed. He did summon persons to follow him and to become members of the kingdom. He was aware that he had been selected and commissioned for a special task. Whether he conceived

of that task in terms of any of the titles which have been applied
to him we simply do not know.

Significant names and terms for this chapter

Kingdom of God	Sermon on the Mount
Rabbi	Beatitudes
Capernaum	sabbath
Simon Peter	parable
Andrew	Antipas
James	Caesarea Philippi
John, son of Zebedee	Peter's confession
Levi	messiah
Simon the Canaanean	petra
disciple	Son of man
exorcism	Transfiguration
demon	Suffering servant
Beelzebul	Lord
nature miracle	prophet

CHAPTER XX

JESUS' MINISTRY IN JUDEA

Biblical materials: Matthew 19-25.   Mark 10-13.   Luke 18:15-21:38

Essential reading: Mark 10-13
                     Matthew 25
                     Luke 19:1-10

It was not until the final weeks of his life that Jesus
left Galilee and headed south toward Jerusalem, according to the
Synoptic Gospels. Except for the trip at age twelve, reported by
Luke (2:41-51), there is no indication that Jesus had ever been to
Jerusalem prior to his Palm Sunday entrance. By contrast, the
Fourth Gospel depicts Jesus as frequently shuttling between Judea
and Galilee, not hesitating to take the most direct route, which
was through Samaritan territory.

We can suggest several points which would favor John's understanding of the locale of Jesus' ministry: (1) Jesus had close
friends at Bethany, just two miles east of Jerusalem. (2) Matthew
and Luke report that, as Jesus approached Jerusalem, he lamented
the fact that, although he had tried on several occasions to minister to its people, they had rejected him (Matt. 23:37; Luke
13:34). (3) It is difficult to imagine that so dedicated a Jew
and religious teacher as Jesus was would not have visited the center of Judaism at least occasionally. However, since we are following the Synoptic narrative, we shall consider its report of Jesus' coming to Jerusalem as though it were his only visit since
reaching adulthood.

The Decision to Leave Galilee

Jesus did not go quickly or directly to Jerusalem when he
left Galilee. As noted earlier, Luke includes a large amount of
material between his statement that Jesus "set his face to go to
Jerusalem" (9:51) and his noting that "he was near Jerusalem"
(19:11). Matthew agrees with Mark in reporting that Jesus spent
some time in "the region of Judea beyond the Jordan," surely a
reference to Perea, the trans-Jordanian area administered by Herod
Antipas (Mark 10:1; Matt. 19:1). Luke suggests that Jesus consciously and deliberately decided that it was time for him to head

211

for Jerusalem. Likely he was timing his journey so that he would arrive there just before the Passover.

His mission to his people could not be accomplished without his preaching to those living in the holy city of Jerusalem. It may be, as some scholars have suggested, that Jesus expected the kingdom of God to arrive (see Luke 19:11) very soon. Whatever was in his mind as he approached the city, he seemed to be aware of an impending climax of some sort. En route to Jerusalem, Jesus warned his disciples for the third time that opposition, rejection, and death awaited him there (Mark 10:32-34).

The ministry of Jesus in Perea and Judea, although much briefer than that in Galilee, appears to have been much like it. He debated Pharisees on points of the Torah, continued to instruct his disciples, and healed a blind man at Jericho (Mark 10). Matthew and Luke remind us that Jesus was still teaching in parables (Matt. 20:1-16; Luke 19:11-27) as he approached Jerusalem.

The last week in the earthly life of Jesus, which Christians refer to as Holy Week, is described in considerable detail by all four gospels. On the basis of Mark's chronology of the week, the sequence of events appears to be:

Sunday	Entry into Jerusalem
Monday	Cleansing of the Temple
Tuesday	Controversies with Jewish leaders
Wednesday	Anointing at Bethany and betrayal by Judas
Thursday	Preparation for the Passover, the Last Supper, prayer in the garden, and arrest
Friday	Hearing, Trial(s), Crucifixion, Burial
Saturday	The Sabbath
Sunday	The empty tomb discovered, Jesus' Resurrection announced.

Entry into Jerusalem

All four gospels tell of a special entrance, carefully planned in advance, by Jesus and his disciples into the city of Jerusalem. Jesus is depicted as riding from Bethany into the holy city on an ass, while his disciples and some others, probably Jews coming in for the Passover observance, accompanied him on foot, waving green branches, or spreading their garments on the roadway, and shouting patriotic slogans (Mark 11:1-10; Matt. 21:1-9; Luke 19:28-38; John 12:12-16). John reports that some persons who had arrived in Jerusalem ahead of Jesus heard of his approach and went out to meet him, waving palm branches as they shouted their acclaim

It is from this account that the event gets its label "Palm Sunday." Matthew saw the event as the fulfilling of Zechariah 9:9. He was so intent upon having the event and the scripture match that he actually changed the story he found in Mark to have Jesus ride into the city on an ass and a colt! Apparently he did not understand the way synonymous parallelism works in Hebrew poetry (see above, ch. XIII) and thought the Old Testament passage was speaking of two different animals.

This ride into Jerusalem has often been termed "triumphal" but the appropriateness of that adjective is questionable. The size of the "crowd" accompanying Jesus varies from gospel to gospel. Mark mentions only "many" and "others," but Luke refers to the "whole multitude" while Matthew talks of "crowds," and the Fourth Gospel says "a great crowd." However, since it is well known that the Roman officials maintained close surveillance of the Jews on such occasions and moved quickly to break up gatherings which could become riots or even rebellion, it is safe to assume that the procession of disciples and pilgrims with the man on the donkey approaching the Eastern gate was not very large.

Of more importance than the size of the procession is the question: What did Jesus have in mind by this act? Since all the gospel accounts include references to a coming king or kingdom in the shouts of the marchers, it seems certain that the evangelists understood this to be a deliberate messianic act by Jesus. True to his emphasis upon the kingdom of God in his preaching, Jesus may well have been announcing that the kingdom was arriving. It is quite understandable if the disciples and pilgrims, chafing under Roman occupation, had a different kind of kingdom in mind as they shouted "Hosanna!" to the rabbi from Galilee.

The Clearing of the Temple

Matthew and Luke say that Jesus, having made his entrance into Jerusalem, proceeded at once to drive out the merchants and money-changers from the Temple. Mark, however, reports that Jesus went into the Temple, looked around, and then left, returning with his disciples to Bethany to spend the night. The following day, according to Mark, is when the "cleansing" of the Temple occurred. The Fourth Gospel, having placed this event at the beginning of Jesus' ministry (John 2:13-22), omits it from the events of the final week. Yet this clearing of the Temple plays a very important role in the Synoptics' structure of the climactic week in Jerusalem. Jesus was so incensed by what he saw and heard in that part of the Temple complex known as the Court of the Gentiles that he vigorously and dramatically cleared it of what he considered inappropriate activity.

213

This outermost court of the Temple had been built to provide Gentiles a place to worship the God of Israel. When Jesus went into the area, he saw that it was being used as a place of business by the merchants who were selling sacrificial animals to worshipers and changing their Roman money into the Temple coin which was required for the annual Temple offering. The resulting noise and confusion made worship impossible. In an outburst of righteous indignation, Jesus "began to drive out" the merchants and money-changers, who had paid a fee for the privilege of doing business in the area. This bold act by Jesus was considered by the "chief priests" (Mark 11:18) a direct attack upon their domain and an infringement upon their authority. Mark makes it clear that it was this attack on the Temple, more than anything else, that provoked the Jerusalem establishment into deciding that something must be done about this brash troublemaker from Galilee.

Again the question arises: What did Jesus have in mind? Was he so filled with zeal for the purity of the Temple that he simply could not tolerate the desecration? Or was he consciously performing some symbolic act which fit his own understanding of his mission? There existed in Jewish tradition the expectation that one day the Temple would be a center of prayer for all peoples and the God of Israel would be acknowledged as the only God. Jesus may have seen himself, as herald of the kingdom of God, to be the one through whom God would bring this to pass. The evangelists understood this act, as they did the entry into the city, as a deliberate messianic move on the part of Jesus.

Days of Controversy

If we follow Mark's account, we may assume that Tuesday and Wednesday of Jesus' final week were taken up with discussions with Jewish authorities and legal experts in Jerusalem. After spending the night in the somewhat more serene surroundings in the village of Bethany, Jesus and his disciples would return to the bustling holy city the following morning. On the day following the cleansing of the Temple, a group described as "the chief priests and the scribes and the elders" challenged Jesus regarding the nature of his authority to take charge of an area which only the high priest legally controlled. His reply was to ask them an embarrassing question about John the Baptist, whom they had for the most part not taken seriously (Mark 11:27-33).

There follows a parable (Mark 12:1-12) about some wicked tenants who mistreated the servants whom the landlord sent to collect the rent, who murdered his son and thereby earned eviction and punishment. Whatever the intention of Jesus in telling the parable, Mark says it was interpreted by the religious authorities as being directed against themselves. Only Jesus' popularity prevented his being arrested at this point.

The second question aimed at Jesus was voiced by some Pharisees in cooperation with the Herodians, and delved into the political situation: "Is it lawful to pay taxes to Caesar, or not?" (Mark 12:13-17) The Jews themselves were divided on the question, and it appears to have been put to Jesus in order to force him into making enemies, no matter what his answer. If he sided with the Zealots and gave a negative answer, he could be accused of sedition. If he took the Herodian position and replied affirmatively, he would lose his popularity with a large number of Jews. His answer both amazed and disappointed his critics. They could not disagree with "Render to Caesar the things that are Caesar's, and to God the things that are God's." Yet the statement was somewhat ambiguous, for it left up to each person to determine just what "Caesar's things" were.

The next group to try its hand at embarrassing Jesus was the priest-dominated party of the Sadducees. Their question was about the resurrection and was designed to make belief in life after death appear totally absurd, as well as to test Jesus' knowledge and wisdom (Mark 12:18-27). Jesus' reply turned the tables on the questioners. He explained that earthly institutions are irrelevant in heaven; hence the question about whose wife the oft-married woman would be there was inappropriate. Using typically rabbinic reasoning, he found a basis for belief in a resurrection even in the Torah, the very body of scripture which the Sadducees accepted.

The fourth question directed to Jesus was one which the rabbis had been discussing for a long time: "Which commandment is the first of all?" (Mark 12:28-34) Of the 613 laws identified by the Pharisees, which one took priority? Jesus answered with the familiar Shem'a from Deuteronomy 6, which states the oneness of God, followed by the commandment to love God, which continues in the same chapter. To this he connected, as on a par with the first, the commandment from Leviticus 19:18, "You shall love your neighbor as yourself." Jesus was not the first teacher of Israel to choose these two commandments as the greatest or to connect them so closely that they appear to be two parts of the same law. Perhaps this is why Jesus' questioner agreed with his answer so enthusiastically.

Mark concludes his account of Jesus in debate with the various leaders of Judaism with a brief warning by Jesus against the insincerity and self-serving attitudes of the scribes (Mark

12:38-40). Matthew chose to insert at this point in Mark's narrative a lengthy tirade, attributed to Jesus, against the scribes and Pharisees (23:1-36). Uncharacteristically harsh, this section labels them "hypocrites" (six times) and "blind guides" who are unworthy of being followed and emulated by the people. They are charged with not practicing what they preach, burdening their followers with trivial regulations, seeking praise by acts of external piety while inwardly corrupt, and emphasizing minor points but neglecting the "weightier matters of the law" (vs. 23). Since this section is absent from the other gospels, it may be that it reflects more of the animosity between Christians and Jews at the time and place Matthew was writing than the actual attitude of Jesus. As we have already noted, Jesus was occasionally critical of the religious leaders and teachers of his people, but this section represents him as being inordinately hostile.

An Apocalyptic Interruption

The story of the events in Jesus' final week is interrupted by the somewhat mysterious thirteenth chapter of Mark, which is for the most part picked up by Matthew (ch. 24) and Luke (ch. 21). The first two verses record Jesus' prediction of the destruction of the Temple, a statement cited by one of the witnesses at Jesus' hearing before the Sanhedrin (Mark 14:58). It is a fact that the Temple actually was destroyed in 70 A.D., but it appears to have been still standing when Mark wrote his Gospel. The wording of Matthew's and Luke's versions suggests that the Temple and city had already been destroyed by the time they were writing.

Several other subjects are dealt with in the chapter. There is a warning against false messiahs (vss. 5-6,21-23), prediction of violent happenings (vss. 7-8,24-25), encouragement in the face of threats and persecution (vss. 9-13), and a cryptic saying about a "desolating sacrilege" (vss. 14-20). It closes with a statement that no one knows when the described events will occur and with the advice to maintain an attitude of watchfulness (vss. 30-37).

The chapter appears to be composed of some genuine sayings of Jesus, some attributed to him on the basis of later events, materials from the Old Testament or other apocalyptic Jewish writings, and some editorial comments. Evidently it was designed to give reassurance and encouragement to Christians, probably during the fearful days of the Jewish Revolt (66-70 A.D.). Verse 14 may refer to the Roman standards which were brought into Jerusalem in the latter days of the Revolt and to the subsequent removal of the Christian congregation to neutral ground. The Christians had left

216

Jerusalem before the fall of the city and had established residence at Pella, located east of the Jordan River in non-Jewish territory.

Matthew once again inserts extra material into Mark's outline. From the Q source he adds the story of the faithful and wise servant (24:45-51) and from his own special sources (M) he adds the parables of the Ten Maidens, the Talents, and the Last Judgment (ch. 25). All of these pertain to the coming end of the age, as Matthew understands them, although Jesus may have originally told them in order to encourage preparedness for the kingdom of heaven.

Significant names, terms, and dates for this chapter

Bethany

Judea

Perea

Jericho

Holy Week

Palm Sunday

Court of the Gentiles

Caesar

Pella

70 A.D.

Jewish Revolt

CHAPTER XXI

THE CRUCIAL THREE DAYS

Biblical materials: Mark 14-16. Matthew 26-28. Luke 22-24. John 18-21

Essential reading: Mark 14-16
Matthew 27:3-10; 28
Luke 23-24
John 20-21

The last three chapters of each of the Synoptic Gospels constitute what is often called the "Passion Narrative." It presents a connected narrative of events from the conspiracy against Jesus (Mark 14:1-2) to his resurrection. It was the heart of the earliest Christian preaching, hence probably the first connected story of any part of Jesus' life. The Synoptics are in agreement on the essential details of the narrative but do have their own distinctive additions and interpretations.

Mark pinpoints the time of the event he is about to describe as "two days before the Passover," which is the fifteenth of the Jewish month Nisan. The Synoptics understood that this date fell on Friday that year, so Mark is referring to what happened on the previous Wednesday. At this time the chief priests and scribes were conspiring to have Jesus killed, but their plans were hindered by Jesus' rising popularity. They decided they would have to make their move "by stealth," that is, when few people would be with Jesus. Before Mark reports how a solution presented itself, he relates an incident which occurred at Bethany, where an unidentified woman anointed Jesus with an expensive ointment. Jesus dismissed the criticism that the money she had spent for the ointment could have been better used to relieve the misery of some poor people with the observation, "She has anointed my body beforehand for burying" (Mark 14:8).

Judas Iscariot

The dilemma of the chief priests was solved when one of Jesus' twelve disciples came to them with the offer "to betray" Jesus (Mark 14:10-11). The betrayal by Judas Iscariot, whose name seems destined to live in infamy, consisted simply of telling the

218

priests when and where they could find Jesus without a large crowd of his followers around, and then identifying him to the arresting officers.

More difficult is the matter of Judas' motivation. Why would he be willing to cooperate with Jesus' enemies? The Synoptics do not provide an adequate answer, although Matthew suggests he was doing it for money (26:14-16). The characterization of Judas as a chronic thief in the Fourth Gospel (John 12:6) would fit the greed motive, but three facts argue strongly against it: (1) The amount of money involved was quite small. Thirty pieces of silver was worth about twenty dollars, the price of a slave. (2) Mark and Luke say that the money was the priests' idea, not Judas'; they probably did it to make the deal binding. (3) When Judas saw what the result of his betrayal was going to be, he refused to keep the money (Matt. 27:3-10).

What other possible motive could there have been? One suggested motive which seems to be supported by the scant evidence found in the gospels involves the likelihood that Judas misunderstood the mission of Jesus. According to this theory, Judas shared the hopes of the Zealots that Rome would be driven out of the land and expected Jesus to be the leader of the revolt against the Empire. After Jesus had failed to take advantage of several opportunities to get the revolt started, the disappointed Judas decided to put Jesus into a position which would force him to resist and to send out the call for armed revolution. Thus, his arrangement with the priests was, for Judas, only to bring about the confrontation, not to result in Jesus' execution.

Of course, the plan backfired when Jesus refused to resist the arresting officers. Judas was so shocked at the unexpected turn of events that he returned the money and committed suicide. Some scholars offer in support of this theory that the name Iscariot may be related to a group of super-patriots similar in nature to the Zealots. This theory of motivation for Judas' betrayal of Jesus is not proven but seems to fit the facts better than any other which has been suggested.

The Last Supper

The Synoptics state clearly that the last meal which Jesus had with his disciples was the traditional Passover meal, and that it took place after sunset on Thursday. Since the Jewish day begins at sunset, the meal, the trials, the crucifixion, and the burial of Jesus took place within the span of a single day! On Thursday afternoon, the Day of Preparation, arrangements were made for the evening meal, to be held in the now famous "upper room" in Jerusalem (Mark 14:12-16).

There is a significant difference between the Synoptics and the Fourth Gospel as to the nature of the Thursday evening meal. John states that the Passover that year did not begin until Friday at sunset (hence it fell on the sabbath), by which time Jesus was dead and entombed. In the Fourth Gospel, then, the meal with the disciples was not the traditional Passover and no other special name is given it. Which view of the nature of this last supper is correct has been the subject of much debate among scholars. Perhaps it is wise to admit uncertainty on the issue and to inquire separately into the meaning of the supper in the two traditions.

Whether a Passover meal or not, it is clear that it held great significance for Jesus. He seemed convinced that it would be the last meal with his disciples until some indefinite future time "in the kingdom of God" (Mark 14:25). He was aware that he would be "betrayed" by one of his own but probably did not know, or at least did not indicate, which of the twelve it was. After Jesus' death and resurrection, the disciples looked back upon the event with renewed interest and a deeper sense of its significance. Not the full-course meal but the extra passing around of the bread and wine now seemed especially important. The earliest account, that in I Corinthians 11:23-26, speaks only of the latter. By the time Paul was writing that letter (the mid-fifties), the sacrament of the Eucharist was being regularly celebrated throughout the church as a significant way of <u>remembering</u> Christ's death and the "new covenant" which it had inaugurated.

Although Mark's account stresses the covenant's being ratified by Jesus' blood, represented by the wine, it says nothing about the memorial aspect of the supper. Matthew adds that the blood of the covenant was being "poured out for many for the forgiveness of sins" (26:28). It is helpful to distinguish the Last Supper (the full meal, whether Passover or not) from the Lord's Supper, the blessing and distribution of the bread and wine as symbolic of his own body and blood. It is the latter which is repeatedly observed by Christians under a variety of names, such as the Mass, the Eucharist, the Holy Communion, and the Sacrament of the Altar.

John's version of the supper, which he clearly says was <u>before</u> the Passover, is found in chapters 13-17 of his Gospel. It says nothing about the bread and wine episode but includes a rather lengthy story about Jesus' washing the disciples' feet as an example for them to follow (13:2-15). Following the prediction of

220

his coming betrayal is a long monologue by Jesus (chs. 14-16), in which he sought to prepare the disciples for life without his presence, assuring them of the arrival of the Counselor (Holy Spirit) to empower and assist them. A lengthy prayer (ch. 17) of intercession for the disciples concludes the Fourth Gospel's account of the Last Supper. Most of the material in this account does not appear in the Synoptics.

Gethsemane

Mark reports that the Last Supper event ended with the singing of a hymn, which could be the traditional Hallel used to end the Passover. Then Jesus and his disciples, minus Judas Iscariot, left the upper room and headed for the Mount of Olives, east of Jerusalem and just across the Kidron Valley. On the way Jesus predicted that all his followers would desert him in the coming crisis. After Peter sought to reassure Jesus that he could be counted on despite the defection of the others, Jesus forecast that Peter would deny him three times before daybreak.

After they had entered the Garden of Gethsemane, located on the Mount of Olives, Jesus took his inner circle of Peter, James, and John with him as he went deeper into the garden. The genuine humanness of Jesus emerges in the description of what followed. Admitting to his profound sorrow, Jesus prayed twice that, if it were possible, the "hour" or the "cup" be removed as a necessary step to be taken (Mark 14:34-36). Both those terms are euphemistic ways of referring to the terrible suffering and death which seemed so inexorable to Jesus. But this petition is followed immediately by "yet not what I will, but what thou wilt."

The Synoptics depict Jesus as the fully human, yet totally obedient son, who addresses God as "Father." In Mark not only the Greek word for father but also the Aramaic word, "Abba," is attributed to Jesus. The Fourth Gospel omits entirely the account of Jesus' pressure-packed prayer in the garden. For John, the garden is merely the place where Jesus was arrested (John 18:1-3). Perhaps the image of Jesus agonizing over, or even seeming hesitant about, his imminent death did not fit his conception of Jesus as the strong son of God.

After three periods of prayer, Jesus was confronted by Judas and "a crowd" sent by the chief priests, scribes, and elders. Presumably they had expected resistance by Jesus and his disciples. From this point onward through the account of the crucifixion, the Fourth Gospel corresponds fairly closely to the Markan outline. After Judas identified Jesus in the dark garden by the infamous kiss of betrayal, there was a brief act of protection by one of the disciples, who drew his sword and cut off an ear of one of the arresting officers. John says the brave disciple was Simon Peter, the wounded man was Malchus, and it was his right ear that was severed. Luke adds that Jesus restored the ear! (John 18:10; Luke 22:51) When it became clear that Jesus was not going to resist arrest, the feeble display of courage ceased, the disciples scattered, and Jesus was led to the high priest in Jerusalem. All of this must have been very late, perhaps after midnight.

Judicial Proceedings

There is some confusion among the four gospels over the nature and number of hearings and/or trials to which Jesus was subjected in that brief period between his arrest in the Garden of Gethsemane and nine o'clock Friday morning. What seems most probably correct is that there was a trial (or, more likely, a hearing to determine charges) before the Jewish court, the Sanhedrin, in the pre-dawn hours, followed by the Roman trial before Pontius Pilate shortly after daybreak.

The first hearing (Mark 14:55-65) was presided over by the high priest Caiaphas, who found a great deal of discrepancy in the testimony of the witnesses. Perhaps it was out of exasperation that he turned directly to Jesus with the question, "Are you the Christ (messiah)?" When Jesus answered in the affirmative, Caiaphas was satisfied that they had heard enough, and the members of the Sanhedrin unanimously (according to Mark) pronounced him guilty of blasphemy and deserving of the death penalty. Questions have been raised about the legality of this procedure, such as the fact that it was held at night, but, since the Jewish court was not permitted by the Roman government to carry out a death sentence, the legality questions are of little significance.

At this point, Mark tells the story of Peter's denial of Jesus (14:66-72), an act Peter had vehemently declared a few hours earlier that he would never commit. At least Peter seems to have been closer to the scene of the hearing than were the other disciples, whether out of bravery or curiosity. The fact that he spoke with a definite Galilean accent led one of the high priest's maidservants to assume Peter was an associate of the accused. The crowing of the cock (probably near dawn) jolted Peter's memory to recall Jesus' prediction, and he was overwhelmed with grief and guilt: "And he broke down and wept." One disciple had betrayed him; another had denied him. Where were the other ten?

The next event in the Passion Narrative is the trial before Pilate, the Roman procurator of Judea and Samaria (Mark 15:1-15; Matt. 27:1-2,11-26; Luke 23:1-5,13-25; John 18:28-19:16).

222

Although Pilate's headquarters was in Caesarea, he had come to Jerusalem because he knew there would be a large number of Jews from other places crowding into the city for the Passover activities, and he wanted to be in a position to deal forthrightly with any threat of disorder or revolt. It may be that he was anticipating trouble, for he knew there were a great many Jews, such as the Zealots, who hated the Romans and wanted them out of Palestine. Pilate's decision as to what he should do with Jesus should be analyzed against this background.

The trial stories in all the gospels seem to go out of their way to place major blame for Jesus' execution on the Jewish leadership. The chief priests and scribes (the Pharisees are not mentioned) do not mention blasphemy as the crime of which they accuse Jesus, for that is purely a religious matter and would mean nothing to Pilate. Instead, they accused him of "many things" (Mark 15:3), which include, according to Luke 23:2, "perverting our nation, and forbidding us to give tribute to Caesar, and saying that he himself is Christ a king." Such charges Pilate could not ignore. The Synoptics report that Jesus did not make a vigorous defense against such charges but the Fourth Gospel records an extended discussion by Jesus and Pilate on the nature of kingship and truth (John 18:33-38).

Luke breaks into the narrative of the trial before Pilate to inform the reader that Pilate, having learned that Herod Antipas was also in Jerusalem, decided to send Jesus, who was from Antipas' territory, to him for trial (23:6-12). This attempt by Pilate to shift responsibility for deciding Jesus' case to Herod failed miserably when Jesus refused to utter a word in Herod's presence. This incident is used by Luke to add to the impression that Pilate was convinced of Jesus' innocence (23:13-16). He had already stated his finding that Jesus was not guilty (Luke 23:4) and would assert it a third time (23:22). Even the centurion who was in charge of the execution declared Jesus' innocence, in Luke's version (23:47).

Yet Pilate gave the order for the crucifixion. The only explanation offered for this Roman official's acting against his conviction is the tremendous pressure brought to bear on him by the influential Jewish leaders, who even managed to have the heinous criminal Barabbas released instead of Jesus when Pilate sought a way out of his dilemma (Mark 15:6-11). Matthew adds to the impression of Jewish responsibility for Jesus' death by relating Pilate's symbolic handwashing with the people's response, "His blood be on us and on our children!" (27:24-25) The Fourth Gospel joins the Synoptics in stressing the innocent verdict (18:38; 19:4,6).

223

Despite the heroic efforts by the evangelists to shift responsibility for Jesus' death away from Rome and onto the Jews, the gospels contain plenty of evidence to suggest that the Romans were at least partly to blame. It was a Roman official who gave the order for the execution, it was a contingent of Roman soldiers who carried it out, and it was a crime against Roman law which brought on the capital punishment. In order that execution might serve as a deterrent to other would-be criminals, it was done in public, with the crime written on a placard attached to the cross. The one on Jesus' cross read "The King of the Jews" (Mark 15:26). Without absolving the priests and scribes of guilt in the matter, we may conclude that there was sufficient reason for the Romans to want this potential trouble-maker who could attract a large following out of the way. He never denied that he was a king or that he had announced the coming of a kingdom. He was punished for the crime of high treason according to the method prescribed by Roman law.

The Crucifixion

According to Mark, Jesus was crucified around nine o'clock ("the third hour") on Friday morning, the event commemorated by Christians as Good Friday, the most solemn day in the Christian calendar. Just before that, he had been severely beaten and subjected to all sorts of indignities, for a condemned man had no rights. Crucifixion was an exceedingly cruel and painful method of execution, so horrible that it was not used on Roman citizens. The evangelists have spared us the excruciating details, stating simply "they crucified him" (Mark 15:24; Matt. 27:35; Luke 23:33; John 19:18).

The place of crucifixion was called Golgotha, probably located just outside the city wall but no longer identifiable with certainty. Crucified at the same time and place were two other criminals, one of whom, Luke says, acknowledged the innocence of Jesus and asked for a place in his kingdom (23:39-43). Since we can not be precise about the year of Jesus' execution, we place it between 30 and 33 A.D.

Victims of crucifixion had been known to linger as long as several days before death came, but Jesus' death occurred after six hours, a cause of surprise to Pilate (Mark 15:44). By combining the testimony of all the gospels, we can identify seven statements Jesus made while on the cross. Known as the Seven Last Words, they are:

224

(1) "Father, forgive them, for they know not what they do."
                                          Luke 23:34

(2) To the repentant convict, "Truly, I say to you, today you
    will be with me in Paradise." Luke 23:43

(3) To his mother, "Woman, behold your son!" and to the be-
    loved disciple, "Behold your mother!" John 19:26-27

(4) "My God, my God, why hast thou forsaken me?"
                                  Mark 15:34; Matt. 27:46

(5) "I thirst." John 19:28

(6) "It is finished." John 19:30

(7) "Father, into thy hands I commit my spirit!" Luke 23:46

Among those present at the scene of crucifixion, according
to the Synoptics, were an unspecified number of women who had been
followers of Jesus in Galilee, including Mary Magdalene. Only
John states that Mary, mother of Jesus, was there. No mention is
made of the presence of any of the twelve disciples at the scene,
unless the "disciple whom he loved" in John 19:26 was one of them.
Matthew describes the tragic end of Judas immediately following
his statement that Jesus had been taken to Pilate for trial
(27:3-10).

Since Jesus died in mid-afternoon, there was not sufficient time before the sabbath began (at sunset) for the customary
embalming process. A member of the Sanhedrin, Joseph of Arimathea,
secretly a disciple of Jesus, secured permission to bury Jesus in
the tomb he had chosen for himself. John says the tomb was in a
garden not far from the place of crucifixion (19:41). According
to Luke, the Galilean women took note of where Jesus was entombed,
planning to return when the sabbath was over to complete the embalming process (23:54-56). Matthew alone reports that the stone
door to the tomb was sealed with the official insignia of the Roman government and that a contingent of soldiers was assigned to
guard the tomb. This story has the effect of discrediting any
charge which may be made later that Jesus' body had been removed
by his disciples.

The Resurrection

The Synoptic Gospels agree that early Sunday morning some
women went to the tomb in which Jesus had been placed for the purpose of completing the task of anointing the body and that, when
they arrived, the tomb was open and Jesus' body was gone. They
also agree that the women were informed that Jesus had risen from

225

the dead. On the details, which are of lesser importance, they vary considerably. The Gospel of Mark ends with this empty tomb story, without mentioning any appearance of Jesus after he arose from the dead. The last thing which he reports is the fear of the women as they fled from the tomb (16:1-8).

The other gospels contain accounts of post-resurrection appearances of Jesus which have little, if anything, in common. Matthew reports that Jesus met the women after they had left the tomb (28:9-10), and sometime later met the disciples (without Judas, of course) on a mountain in Galilee (28:16-20). The Gospel of Matthew ends with Jesus' commanding them to evangelize, teach, and baptize all nations and promising them his perpetual presence.

Luke relates a lengthy story of how Jesus walked and talked, unrecognized, with two disciples, one named Cleopas, the other unnamed, from Jerusalem to Emmaus, a village seven miles west. After they had recognized him, they returned immediately to Jerusalem, where they were told that Jesus had already appeared to Simon (24:13-35). Momentarily Jesus appeared to the whole group of disciples in Jerusalem, ate a piece of fish, and appointed them to be witnesses of his passion and resurrection "to all nations" (24:36-49). The Gospel of Luke closes with a brief account of Jesus' ascension into heaven from Bethany.

The Fourth Gospel states that Jesus' first appearance after his resurrection was to Mary Magdalene, who had come alone to the tomb on Sunday morning (20:1-18). That same day Jesus appeared to the disciples, who were assembled in a secret place in Jerusalem, and bestowed on them the Holy Spirit (20:19-23). Thomas, who had not been present on "Easter Sunday," got his chance to see and touch Jesus a week later (20:24-29), when Jesus again appeared to the whole group. Finally, in what appears to be an appendix to the original Gospel of John, Jesus appeared to the disciples by the Sea of Galilee (or Tiberias) and had breakfast with them (21:1-14). A scene which may be described as the reinstatement of Peter follows, during which Jesus asked him to pledge his love to him three times, probably understood as an antidote to the three-fold denial (21:15-17).

Besides the nine post-resurrection appearances recorded in the gospels, there is an even earlier account in I Corinthians 15:3-8, where Paul, passing on the tradition he had received from the early church, lists six appearances, including one to himself. Some of those in Paul's list can be correlated with some described in the gospels, but the appearance to a group of more than five hundred and the one to James (Jesus' brother) are not found elsewhere. As Paul makes clear in that passage, the resurrection faith was a vital element in the earliest Christian preaching. Without it, we may be sure, there would have been no knowledge of the Galilean named Jesus, no church, and no New Testament.

Significant names, terms, and dates for this chapter

The Passion Narrative	Pontius Pilate
Bethany	Barabbas
Judas Iscariot	crucifixion
The Last Supper	Mary Magdalene
The Lord's Supper	Golgotha
Passover	Joseph of Arimathea
Gethsemane	Cleopas
Mount of Olives	Emmaus
Caiaphas	Thomas
Sanhedrin	30-33 A.D.
Herod Antipas	

CHAPTER XXII

CHRISTIANITY IS BORN

Biblical materials: Acts 1-12

Essential reading: Acts 1-2; 5-6; 7:51-8:8; 9-10; 11:19-26

The Book of Acts

The author of the Gospel of Luke followed up his story of the earthly ministry of Jesus with a second volume, in which he related the events which followed the resurrection of Jesus for approximately three decades, according to the information available to him. That second volume is the book of Acts, which begins with a dedication to the same Theophilus mentioned in the opening verses of his Gospel, which is referred to as "the first book" (Acts 1:1).

The title of this book which appears in our Bibles is "The Acts of the Apostles," but it is somewhat misleading. The book does not attempt to trace the activities of each of the twelve disciples, who are now called "apostles." Only Peter and, to a much less degree, John have their ministries chronicled in Acts. It is logical to assume that all of them, empowered by the Holy Spirit, preached, taught, perhaps healed (as did Peter and John in Acts 3), and traveled as missionaries after they left Jerusalem. Information about their several ministries was simply not available to Luke. He knew a lot more about the life and work of one who was not one of the original twelve, a zealous Jew named Saul, better known by the Roman form of his name: Paul. The last half of Acts is focused on his work and travels.

Luke's main purpose in writing Acts appears to be to relate how the Holy Spirit brought the Christian Church into existence and then led and empowered its leaders to carry the message of salvation throughout the Roman Empire. When Acts begins, there are 120 "brethren" (1:15) who can be called believers. When it closes, the Christian Church has permeated the empire and is firmly established in the city of Rome. In order to accomplish this expansion, the apostles had to have their vision broadened, their horizon expanded, and their understanding of God's universal concern deepened.

The Holy Spirit is the force that kept the first group of believers from remaining simply another sect within Judaism and inspired them to be faithful to the commission given them by Jesus during the forty-day period following his resurrection (Acts 1:8). That commission served Luke as an outline for the book:

1-7	Witness in Jerusalem
8:1-11:18	Witness in all Judea and Samaria
11:19-28:31	Witness to the end of the earth

Another purpose Luke may have had in mind as he wrote Acts was to secure for Christianity the same status as a legal religion that Judaism had enjoyed for many decades. This, he presumed, would ensure freedom from persecution. This purpose is developed in two ways: (1) Luke maintains that the true Israel is no longer "the Jews," for they have forfeited that privilege by refusing to accept Jesus. He had already begun to make this point in his first volume (Luke 4:16-30). The true Israel is now the body of believers, regardless of Jewish or Gentile background (see Acts 13:44-50; 18:5-6; 28:23-28).

(2) Christianity is presented as being in no way a threat to the security of the empire. This emphasis, too, Luke had begun in his Gospel, especially by stressing that Jesus was innocent of any crime against the state. In Acts the case is strengthened by his depicting Christian preachers and missionaries as never being in trouble with Roman authorities and, in fact, as often being rescued by them from the Jews and others.

In modern times the accuracy and reliability of Luke's report of early Christian history has been questioned. The time of composition, which had to have been after the first volume and probably 80-90 A.D., was considerably removed in time from the events he describes. Although there may have been some written sources available to him, Luke probably had to depend largely on oral traditions. Nothing like Mark and Q, sources he used for his Gospel, seems to have been at his disposal, although Acts does contain some diary-like material written in the first person (16:10-18; 20:5-21:18; 27:1-28:16).

As far as we know, Luke was the first church historian, and he used the same techniques other historians of the time employed, such as composing speeches for various historical figures which would seem appropriate for the situation. Most of the speeches in Acts are attributed to Peter and Paul, but the longest one is by Stephen. The essentials of Luke's own understanding of the early Christian message may be found in the speeches, regardless of who the speaker is.

229

The Kerygma

The fundamental elements of the <u>kerygma</u> (message proclaimed by the early church), as Luke reports them, are: (1) The Hebrew scriptures have been fulfilled by the coming of Jesus, who was the promised messiah. God's revelation to his people during their long history has culminated in the establishment of the church. (2) The suffering and death of Jesus are the redeeming activity of God on behalf of sinful men. His resurrection indicates God's approval of his ministry and self-sacrifice. (3) Jesus, now designated both "Lord and Christ," has returned to the heavenly realm, where he lives in majesty and exaltation. In the near future he will return in glory and judgment, bringing the present age to a close.

We do not have other church histories with which Acts can be compared, as we have other gospels, but the letters of Paul contain frequent historical references which parallel events in parts of Acts. Sometimes there is agreement between Paul and Acts but often there is not. Scholars agree that, when they do differ, preference should be given to Paul's account since he was writing about events with which he was closely associated, whereas Luke was not. It is curious that Acts makes no mention of the letter-writing activity of Paul.

As a historian, Luke appears to view all history as falling into three epochs: (1) From the beginning until John the Baptist, that is, the time of Israel, the law and the prophets (Luke 16:16); (2) The time of Jesus, the mid-point of history, which Luke covers in his Gospel; (3) The time of the Church and the activity of the Holy Spirit, dealt with in Acts. This third epoch could extend indefinitely into the future and apparently was Luke's way of dealing with the problem of the delay of the return of Christ, which was expected by the early Christians to happen soon.

We conclude that the book of Acts, although not purely objective history and although dependent on sources which are not always reliable and although incomplete, is a very valuable source of information about the church from about 30 to 60 A.D. It is the only such work we have.

The Ascension and Pentecost

In chapter one of Acts, Luke provides a somewhat fuller version (1:6-11) of the Ascension of Jesus than that in his Gospel (24:50-53). During the forty days which preceded it, the risen Jesus had appeared an unspecified number of times, the last of

230

which is described in 1:6-11. Jesus' being lifted up and disappearing from sight was understood by the disciples as his way of telling them that he would no longer be with them in person. He had earlier charged them to remain in Jerusalem for their baptism with the Holy Spirit (1:5). But they were already looking past that event to Jesus' physical return. As at the empty tomb (Luke 24:4), two men in white robes made an announcement: "This Jesus, who was taken up from you into heaven, will come in the same way as you saw him go into heaven" (1:10-11). This proved to be a very important statement for it became the basis for the universal expectation of Christ's second coming. Although there is no time mentioned for the return, the disciples apparently assumed that it would be soon. Paul and all other first-generation Christians we know of expected the early return of Christ and, with it, the end of the age.

The waiting apostles were joined by Jesus' mother and brothers, who had apparently experienced a change in their attitude toward Jesus as a result of the crucifixion and resurrection, and some unnamed women (1:14), probably those from Galilee mentioned in the gospels. The vacancy created by the demise of Judas, which is briefly described (1:18-19), was filled by the election of Matthias, about whom we are told nothing except that he had been a follower of Jesus from the beginning of his ministry and a witness to the resurrection (1:15-26).

The period of waiting ended with the spectacular outpouring of the promised Holy Spirit on the day of Pentecost, a Jewish festival which celebrated the giving of the Torah on Mt. Sinai. The only phenomenon which was observed by other Jews was that of speaking in tongues, which Luke understood as being able to use actual languages with which the apostles had not before been familiar. Dismissing the explanation by some wag that the apostles had overindulged in new wine, Peter, now finding a courage that had been eluding him for some time, stood up and addressed the gathered Jews (2:14-36). Accusing them of partial responsibility for the death of Jesus, Peter proclaimed that God raised him from the dead and made him "both Lord and Christ" (2:36). When some asked what they should do, Peter replied, "Repent and be baptized." The response was unexpected and overwhelming. Luke reports that approximately three thousand were baptized that day and became affiliated in some way with the apostles in this new movement.

It should be noted that, according to Acts, all of these persons were Jews and they were not giving up their Judaism by submitting to baptism. They continued to practice their faith as before, "attending the temple together" (2:46), although we customarily speak of this event as the birthday of the Christian Church.

231

Two features distinguished them from the other Jews: (1) their belief in Jesus as messiah and Lord and (2) their sharing of possessions in order to make sure everyone was provided for (2:44-45 How long this practice of the "common treasury" endured is not told, but it is described in greater detail in 4:32-37. The result was "There was not a needy person among them" (4:34). Eventually problems arose with the system, as we see in Acts 5 and 6.

The Jerusalem Congregation

The new fellowship of baptized believers continued to grc and to cause considerable commotion among the inhabitants of Jeru salem. Reaction to the healing, by Peter and John, of a congenitally lame man presented Peter with the opportunity to make anotl er speech (ch. 3) to the amazed bystanders. But the Temple authorities reacted differently. They arrested Peter and John and brought them before the Sanhedrin, who warned them to stop preacl ing in the name of Jesus (ch. 4). This warning was ignored by tl apostles, for "they were all filled with the Holy Spirit and spol the word of God with boldness" (4:31).

The unity and unselfishness of the first congregation of believers found expression in the common ownership of property, c scribed a second time in 4:32-37. Here we are introduced to Barnabas, a native of Cyprus, who brought money he received from the sale of a field to the common treasury. Barnabas figures prominently in the later story of Paul. But in chapter five the apostles have to deal with a problem which arose when a couple tried to deceive the group by claiming that they were donating the entire proceeds of the sale of a piece of property to the congregation's treasury when, in fact, they were keeping a part of it for themselves. There must have been other cases of this sort as tir went on.

Another problem is described in 6:1-6. The Hellenists complained that their widows were receiving less than were the He brew widows when the food was distributed each day. All members of the congregation, according to the Acts accounts, were Jews. The Hellenists were Greek-speaking Jews who were not native to Ju dea and who tended to have a more open attitude toward Gentiles than did the Hebrews, Aramaic-speaking Jews who had been born and continued to live in and around Jerusalem. Taking the Hellenists complaint seriously, the apostles decided to appoint another grou of men to take care of this important part of the congregation's activity, while they concentrated on the spiritual needs. The seven men chosen (6:5) included two persons about whose activitie Acts tells us more in the material which follows.

232

This is the last mention in Acts of the common treasury, so we do not know how long it continued. It is likely that one reason the group had been willing to pool their resources and abandon the private property concept was their expectation of the early end of the age. As time passed and the hope of Christ's early return began to dim, it may well be that private ownership of property was again seen as a more feasible way of living. We are told several times in later chapters that the problem of taking care of the poor remained, and offerings from Christians in other places were received and sent to Jerusalem to help relieve the situation.

The Christian community in Jerusalem continued to grow (Acts 5:14) and to attract attention from surrounding villages. Acts even mentions mass healings effected through the apostles (5:15-16). Once again the apostles were arrested and haled before the Sanhedrin for disobeying the order previously given. Peter boldly replied, "We must obey God rather than men"(5:29). The rage of the members of the court was so great that it required the most persuasive powers of the respected teacher Gamaliel to prevent a decision to have the apostles put to death (5:33-42).

Persecution and Growth

Stephen, one of the seven Hellenists appointed to oversee the charity work, proved to have other talents as well. His skill as a debater brought him victories over all his opponents and earned him their resentment and jealousy. As a result, he found himself in the presence of the Sanhedrin, charged with speaking against the Temple and the Torah (6:8-15). When offered an opportunity to defend himself, Stephen responded with a long speech, in which he reviewed the history of the Jews from Abraham to Solomon (7:2-50). After he had made the point that God did not confine himself to man-made temples, he turned to his accusers with a vitriolic attack (7:51-53) which totally enraged them. In a paragraph which is reminiscent of Luke's description of the execution of Jesus, the stoning to death of Stephen is described. This probably illegal act produced the first Christian martyr, which means "witness" in Greek. Luke notes the presence and consent of "a young man named Saul" at the scene (7:54-8:1a).

The death of Stephen incited a general persecution of the church in Jerusalem, in which this same Saul (later known as Paul) played a leading role (8:1b-3). At this point begins the second phase of the church's witness. It was this persecution that forced the Christians (likely only the Hellenist Christians) to leave Jerusalem and scatter throughout Judea and Samaria. They, of course,

233

took their faith with them and, as a result, the church was sprea
rather than stamped out. Philip, another of the Hellenist leader
is credited with a very successful mission among the Samaritans
(8:4-8). He was also responsible for the baptism of an Ethiopia
official (8:26-40), who may have been instrumental in the planti
of the church in his country.

The Call of Saul

At this point (9:1-31) Luke inserts the story of how Sau
a vigorous persecutor of those belonging to "the Way" (vs. 2), wa
changed into a preacher and missionary for Christ. Saul's conve
sion (as it has been called) was an important event in Luke's st
ry of the expansion of the church, as is evidenced by the fact
that it is recounted twice more in the book of Acts (22:3-16 and
26:9-18). According to this account, there were a number of Chr
tians in Damascus, an important and ancient city in Syria more
than one hundred miles north of Jerusalem.

How and when Christianity reached Damascus is not told.
Did that also result from the persecution in Jerusalem? A belie
er in the city, named Ananias, was directed to attend Saul, whose
reputation as a persecutor had preceded him. His ministry to Sa
included the restoring of his sight, baptism, and the bestowal o
the Holy Spirit. His testimony to the Jesus whom Saul had come
Damascus to oppose aroused hostility among the Jews. Only caref
planning by his new-found Christian friends allowed him to leave
the city alive.

According to Acts, when Saul left Damascus, he returned
directly to Jerusalem, where he attempted to become associated
with the church (9:26-31). When the apostles were skeptical of
the genuineness of his profession of faith, Barnabas (mentioned
4:36-37) showed confidence in Saul and vouched for his sincerity
Then he was allowed to preach and debate with "the Hellenists,"
doubtless non-believing Hellenist Jews. When his life was again
imperiled, he left Jerusalem for Tarsus, his home town, accordin
to Acts. No more is said about Saul until 11:25, where it is re
ported that, still at Tarsus, he was sought out by Barnabas and
brought to Antioch.

In his letter to the Galatians, Paul (Saul) alludes to
these events in his earlier life (Gal. 1:13-24). He mentions hi
violent persecution of the church, done out of his zeal for Juda
ism. His "conversion" included a vision of Jesus and a commissi
to "preach him among the Gentiles." Differing rather sharply fr
the Acts account, Paul then says he did not go immediately to Je

rusalem but went to Arabia for an unspecified period, after which he returned to Damascus. It was three years later when he got to Jerusalem, where he saw only Cephas (Peter) and James, brother of Jesus. After a stay of only fifteen days, he went to Syria and Cilicia, which could include Tarsus.

Paul is no more helpful than Acts in telling us what he did while in Syria and Cilicia. What we know about his nature and personality suggests that he was not idle, but probably was engaged in preaching the gospel, along with practicing his tent-making trade (see Acts 18:3). Paul's account of these events leaves the impression that he had not lived in Jerusalem before the Damascus road experience. He even states, "I was still not known by sight to the churches of Christ in Judea" (Gal. 1:22), which is indeed strange if he had been such a vigorous persecutor of the church in that area (Acts 8:1-3).

Witness to Gentiles

Following the summarizing statement about the church in Judea and Galilee (9:31), which is typical of Acts, some missionary activity by Peter in the Judean towns of Lydda and Joppa is reported (9:32-43). At Joppa, located on the Mediterranean Sea, Peter is said to have raised from the dead a dedicated follower of the Way, a woman named Tabitha. Before he left Joppa (modern Jaffa), Peter had another experience which was to initiate a revolutionary change in his religious outlook.

He had a significant vision, in which the Lord was commanding him to eat both clean and unclean foods (10:9-16). While he was trying to figure out what this meant, three men arrived from Caesarea, some thirty miles north of Joppa, with an invitation from a Roman centurion named Cornelius to visit him and present his message (10:17-23). The previous day Cornelius had had a vision (10:1-8), in which God had directed him to contact Peter. Connecting his own vision with the invitation from the Gentile Cornelius, Peter concluded that God was directing him to accept the invitation to enter the home of a Gentile. Such an action went against his Jewish upbringing.

When he arrived in Caesarea, Peter learned that Cornelius expected to have a message delivered to him (10:33) and proceeded to preach the crucified, risen Christ to his entire household. Peter and those traveling with him were not prepared for what happened next. The whole family believed, the Holy Spirit came upon them, and they were baptized (10:44-48). This experience forced Peter to open his mind to the fact that God loved Gentiles as well as Jews and that the gospel of salvation was intended for all per sons. The implications of Jesus' commission to the disciples (Mat 28:18-20) were only beginning to be understood.

This is the very first instance which Acts reports of the gospel's being proclaimed to non-Jews. When Peter was criticized by some of his Jerusalem colleagues for what he had done in Caes area, he simply related the entire story. His critics could only admit, "Then to the Gentiles also God has granted repentance unto life" (11:18). This broadened vision of the church leaders in Je rusalem would seem to be paving the way for a vigorous mission to the Gentiles. However, the only other instance of evangelization among non-Jews reported in Acts prior to Paul's missionary jour neys is that described in 11:19-26. Recalling the persecution of Christians mentioned in 8:1-3, Luke says that some of the Hellen ist Jewish believers who had fled Jerusalem had gone to Phoenicia Cyprus, and Antioch, a large city in Syria approximately 350 mile north of Jerusalem.

It was at Antioch that Cypriot and north African Chris tians preached to Gentiles, who responded in large numbers. This resulted in a rapidly growing, integrated (Jews and Gentiles to gether) congregation which attracted the attention of the church in Jerusalem, apparently considered the "mother church" at this time. The apostles, who were still in Jerusalem, sent Barnabas, himself a native of Cyprus, to Antioch to take charge of the work He soon realized that he needed help, remembered the zealous Saul of Tarsus, whom he had befriended in Jerusalem years earlier, and made him his associate pastor (11:25). The year during which this arrangement was in effect is apparently the time in which the in cident Paul describes in Gal. 2:11-14 took place. Luke notes that Antioch was the place where "Christians" got their name, but he neglects to tell us how it came about. It is probable that it was an epithet applied to them by someone who sought to oppose or rid icule their doctrines.

Apostolic Martyrdom

Most of Acts 12 has its setting in Jerusalem. Without stating any reason, Luke reports that Herod (Agrippa I), grandson of Herod the Great and ruler of virtually all the territory once governed by that famous ancestor, ordered the execution of James, the brother of John. With the exception of Judas, this is the first of the original twelve disciples whose death is mentioned. But the public reaction to James' death was so favorable that Agrippa planned a repeat performance, with Peter as the victim. Through divine intervention Peter was able to avoid the tragedy

236

and soon thereafter left Jerusalem permanently (12:17).

Despite such harassment, Acts says, "the word of God grew and multiplied" (12:24). Since the time of Agrippa's reign as king was 41-44 A.D., we can place the death of James within this time span. Mention is made in this chapter of John Mark, a resident of Jerusalem, who later became a missionary (12:12). He accompanied Barnabas, his uncle, and Saul on their return trip from Jerusalem to Antioch (12:25) after they had delivered "relief" sent by the Christians in Antioch to those in Judea (11:29-30). The stage is thus set for the missionary journeys of Saul and his associates.

Significant names, terms, and dates for this chapter

Theophilus	martyr
kerygma	Philip
Saul	Damascus
80-90 A.D.	Ananias
30-60 A.D.	Cephas
Ascension	Tarsus
Matthias	Joppa
Pentecost	Tabitha
Peter	Caesarea
John, son of Zebedee	Cornelius
common treasury	Antioch in Syria
Gamaliel	Herod Agrippa I
Barnabas	41-44 A.D.
Hellenists	James, son of Zebedee
Hebrews	John Mark
Stephen	

237

CHAPTER XXIII

CHRISTIANITY MOVES WESTWARD

Biblical materials: Acts 13:1-18:22. I and II Thessalonians
                      Galatians 1-2

Essential reading: Acts 13; 15:1-21; 15:36-18:22
                      I Thessalonians 3:1-5:11
                      Galatians 1-2

        Except for part of chapter 15, the last part of Acts (chs
13-28) is concerned with the activities of the missionary Paul an
his fellow-workers. When it is realized that this is well over
one-half of the book and that the story of his conversion occupie
almost an entire chapter in the first part of Acts, it becomes
clear just how much importance Luke attaches to Paul and his work
Although not one of the "apostles," Paul is viewed in Acts as the
central figure in the story of the church's mission to Gentiles.

        Paul was not the first nor the only missionary to non-Jew
but he certainly was the most prolific. Luke presents Paul's mis
sionary work as consisting of three distinct journeys, parts of
which can be fitted into what Paul tells us in his letters.
The structure of Acts 13-28 may be seen in a brief outline:

    13:1-14:28   First missionary journey
       15:1-35   The Jerusalem Conference
    15:36-18:22   Second missionary journey
    18:23-21:16   Third missionary journey
    21:17-26:32   Paul in Jerusalem and Caesarea as prisoner
     27:1-28:16   Voyage to Rome as prisoner
      28:17-31   Paul in Rome as prisoner

Paul's First Missionary Journey

        Neither Acts nor Paul tells the reader much about the way
the early Christian congregations were organized. The Jerusalem
congregation, of course, was led by the apostles until they left
the city, probably during the reign of Herod Agrippa I. Then a
group simply called "elders" was in charge, with James the brothe
of Jesus as their chief, or presiding elder. In the Antioch congregation, according to Acts 13:1, there were prophets and teach-

ers, of which Barnabas and Saul were two of the five named. Thus, when the Holy Spirit directed the church to send Barnabas and Saul on a special assignment, the congregation was not left without leadership.

It is worthy of note that it was not the mother church in Jerusalem, but the integrated, rapidly growing church in Antioch which sponsored all of Paul's missions. This suggested that very early in the church's life, certainly by the late 40's, there were at least two large, influential centers of Christianity. The size of the original congregation in Jerusalem had been sharply reduced when the Hellenists fled the persecution, the remaining membership consisting of the more conservative Hebrews. But the Antioch church continued to grow and, with a membership comprised mostly of Gentiles and Hellenistic Jews, was much more open to the need for evangelizing activity among the mixed population of the Empire.

After an extended and doubtless impressive commissioning service (13:3), the team of three missionaries—Barnabas, Saul, and John Mark—were sent out "by the Holy Spirit" (13:4). Their first destination was the island of Cyprus, the native land of Barnabas and a Roman province lying about 150 miles off the Syrian coast. Luke did not have enough information to enable him to provide a complete narrative of events on the journeys. We are not surprised, therefore, to notice that only two items are included in the Cyprus report (13:4-12): (1) The missionary team, all Jewish Christians, began their work in the local synagogues. This was true, not only in Cyprus, but in every place they visited which had a synagogue. What Acts does not tell us is whether this strategy was included in their original commission or was simply a practical way of gaining an entree in a town where they were total strangers. Acts does not say what sort of reception they were given at the Cypriot synagogue. (2) Despite strong opposition from a court magician, they succeeded in converting the proconsul of the province, Sergius Paulus.

Almost incidentally the account notes the shift from Saul to Paul (13:9), which is the name used for him in the rest of Acts. Luke does not call attention to it, but it is interesting to observe that the "Barnabas and Saul" designation at the beginning of the journey soon becomes "Paul and his company" (13:13) or "Paul and Barnabas" (13:43). It seems that Paul was the most aggressive member of the team, a kind of "take charge" personality, the one who confronted the opponents of the gospel and who made the speeches. It turns out that he was also the one who drew the wrath and abuse of the hostile crowds.

Map 9

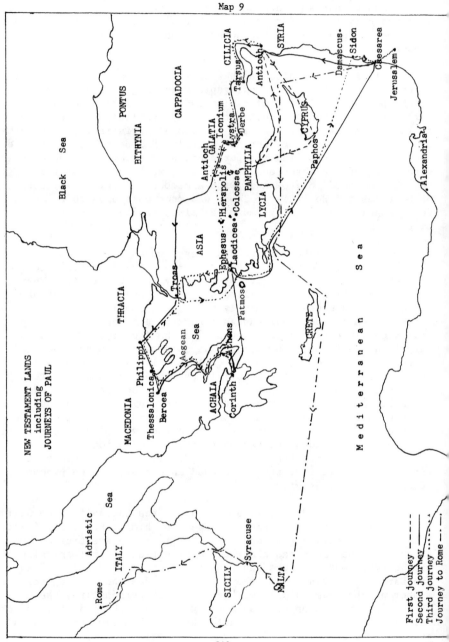

NEW TESTAMENT LANDS
including
JOURNEYS OF PAUL

First Journey -----
Second Journey ———
Third Journey ·······
Journey to Rome —·—·—

Having traversed Cyprus by foot from east to west, the team sailed to the small province of Pamphylia, located on the southern coast of present-day Turkey. At this point, John Mark left Paul and Barnabas and returned to his home in Jerusalem, a decision not explained. Probably because of the unfavorable climate in Pamphylia, Paul and Barnabas soon headed directly north to the higher elevation of the province of Galatia [Acts uses the local name, Pisidia] (13:13-14). Their first stop was a city with the same name as the one from which they had come: Antioch. We distinguish the two by referring to them as Antioch in Galatia and Antioch in Syria.

As they had done in Cyprus, they went first to the synagogue in Antioch. In what Luke understood as their typical approach to a Jewish audience, Paul proclaimed Jesus as the fulfillment of the Scriptures (13:16-41). Their initial success was spoiled by the opposition which "the Jews" had marshalled by the second sabbath they were in town. Whereupon Paul announced that, since they had rejected the gospel, he and Barnabas would take their appeal to the Gentiles (13:46). This fits into Luke's theme that the unbelieving Jews had forfeited their right to be called Israel.

The mounting opposition incited by the Jews forced Paul and Barnabas to leave the town. They visited three other cities of Galatia, founding Christian congregations in each: Iconium, Lystra, and Derbe (14:1-23). Despite continued opposition and being mistaken for deities (in Lystra), they persevered, appointed elders in the newly-organized congregations, retraced their steps to the coast, and set sail for Antioch in Syria. Their efforts had produced four new Christian churches, most probably those to whom Paul later addressed his Epistle to the Galatians. The members of their sponsoring congregation listened eagerly to their report of what had happened on the trip. The most significant part of their account turned out to be that in which they described how God "had opened a door of faith to the Gentiles" (14:27).

The Jerusalem Conference

The success which Paul and Barnabas reported they had had among the Gentiles aroused the strong disapproval of some of the more conservative Judean Christians who were visiting Antioch in Syria. They took the position that "Unless you are circumcised according to the custom of Moses, you cannot be saved" (15:1). Paul and Barnabas had not required circumcision of their male Gentile converts. This was a serious and fundamental issue, which sparked heated debate in Antioch. Acts says that, when it became clear that no resolution of the problem was possible there, the church appointed Paul, Barnabas, and some other members to take the question to Jerusalem for settlement. Evidently the original apostles were no longer in Jerusalem but were to be brought back to join the elders in deciding the issue (15:2).

The opposing positions are clearly stated. The conservative "party of the Pharisees" insisted that not only circumcision, but sumbission to the laws of the Torah, was necessary. In light of the earlier approval (11:18) of Peter's ministry to Cornelius, the reader may be somewhat perplexed by this new expression of hard-line conservatism. The liberal position at the Jerusalem Conference was stated by Peter! Referring apparently to his experience with Cornelius (15:7-9), Peter then asked, "Why do you make trial of God by putting a yoke upon the neck of the disciples which neither our fathers nor we have been able to bear?" (15:10) Then Paul and Barnabas were called upon to report on their work among the Gentiles (15:12).

After both sides had completed the presentation of their views, the presiding officer, James the brother of Jesus, quoting passages from several prophets, stated what he felt to be the consensus of the conference. As Luke records it, the decision was basically a victory for the "liberal" position (15:19) but contained a concession to the conservatives, based upon the rule which is first mentioned in relation to Noah (Gen. 9:4), as a basis for fellowship between Jews and non-Jews (15:20). A highly significant decision had been reached, one which would directly affect the missionary activities of the church: Gentiles are not required to submit to circumcision or to keep all the laws of Israel. The fact that such a question arose at all indicates that at this time, probably around 49 A.D., Christianity was not yet considered a religion separate from Judaism. The decisive split between church and synagogue was still several years in the future.

The Jerusalem Conference is another event of which we have a second account. Paul, in Galatians 2:1-10, refers to what must have been the same meeting we have just considered, as described in Acts 15. The site of the conference, the participants, the issue to be decided, and the main decision reached are virtually identical. However, some interesting differences emerge when the accounts are read carefully: (1) Acts says the church at Antioch sent Paul and Barnabas to Jerusalem; Paul says he went "by revelation." (2) Acts gives the impression that there was a rather large group of participants: members of the "party of the Pharisees," the apostles and the elders, and the delegation from Antioch. Paul says it was a somewhat private meeting, with only himself, Barnabas, Titus, some "false brethren," and those "who were reputed to be pillars," whom he specifically names—James and Cephas and John.

(3) In Acts it is Peter (Cephas) whom God had chosen to head the Gentile mission; Paul states quite decisively that he was the acknowledged leader of the mission to Gentiles, whereas Peter had been appointed missionary to Jews! (4) Acts says that, besides the decision not to require of the Gentiles circumcision and the keeping of the entire Torah, the Conference requested them to observe prohibitions against idolatry, unchastity, and blood (improperly slaughtered meat). Paul makes no mention of these "apostolic decrees" and, in fact, specifically states that nothing was added to his understanding of the content of the gospel.

As mentioned earlier, scholars have established the general rule that, when Paul and Acts differ on a given point of history, Paul's version is to be preferred. Surely we must follow that rule for our picture of the Jerusalem Conference. It is quite probable that the apostolic decrees (Acts 15:20,28-29) were not adopted at this meeting but were produced at a considerably later time for the specific purpose of establishing a basis for meal fellowship between Jewish Christians and Gentile Christians. Even Acts itself provides evidence that it was not part of the Conference's decision. When Paul, who was a participant in the Conference, later arrived in Jerusalem he was informed by the elders there of the existence and contents of those very decrees (Acts 21:25) as though he had never heard of them! Happily, on the main question at issue there is no discrepancy between Paul and Acts: Gentiles who want to become Christians do not have to become Jews first. The way was clear for the mission to Gentiles to proceed unhindered. Some of the story of how it did proceed in the decade following the Conference is told in the remainder of Acts.

The Second Missionary Journey

According to Acts, some time after the decision of the Jerusalem Conference was disseminated, Paul suggested to Barnabas that they visit the churches which they had organized on their first journey (15:36). However, the two veteran missionaries could not agree on the matter of taking John Mark along. Paul apparently felt rather strongly that the younger Mark's decision to return home in the midst of the earlier mission made it unwise to take him along this time. This disagreement resulted in the for-

243

mation of two teams, Barnabas and Mark heading for Cyprus, and Paul, with a new partner, Silas, setting out overland to visit the heretofore unmentioned churches in Syria and Cilicia (15:39-41), thence to the Galatian churches organized on the first journey (16:1-6).

This second journey occupies a position of great significance for Luke's picture of the spread of Christianity, for this presents Paul's crossing from Asia into Europe and planting the church in what today is Greece. Acts does not state that this was Christianity's first foray into a new continent, but it does seem to assume that. We know from Paul's Epistle to the Romans that there was a church in Rome quite early, but we do not know when or by whom it was begun.

In Lystra, Paul and Silas were joined by Timothy, who was half Jewish and who became a very dependable, valuable helper of Paul during his continuing travels. Under the guidance of the Spirit, this three-member team arrived at Troas, a city on the coast of the Roman province called Asia, a part of modern Turkey. There is a sudden, unexplained shift in the narrative from the third to the first person (16:10). In a nocturnal vision Paul received the historic "Macedonian call," which he interpreted as a directive from the Lord to cross the Aegean Sea and preach the gospel in Macedonia.

Acts describes in considerable detail some of the results of Paul's decision (16:11-17:15). At Philippi, they were assisted by a well-to-do woman named Lydia (16:14-15) but then found themselves arrested and jailed when the owners of a soothsaying slave girl brought charges against the missionaries for disturbing the peace (16:16-24). What they had disturbed was the complainants' source of income, for when the girl was exorcised of the demon, she could no longer make predictions. They spent only one night in jail, and by morning there had been an earthquake, the saving of the jailor from suicide, and the baptizing of his entire household (16:25-34).

When they left Philippi later that day, after apology from the city officials, they left behind a church that was to bring Paul a great deal of satisfaction and joy over the years, as we learn from his Epistle to the Philippians. Two other cities in Macedonia became sites of Christian congregations: Thessalonica and Beroea, in both of which Paul and companions found eager response to their preaching from the Gentiles and strong opposition from some Jews (17:1-14). In fact, Acts reports that Paul, the main target of the wrath of the Jews from Thessalonica who had come all the way to Beroea to oppose the missionaries, was forced

to leave the area before he had planned. Leaving Silas and Timothy in Macedonia with orders to rejoin him when possible, Paul
left for Athens, located in the southern part of the province of
Achaia, part of modern Greece.

The Acts account leaves the impression that Paul's visit
to Athens was as a tourist who was just biding his time until his
associates could join him and they could get back to their work
(17:16). Indeed, ancient Athens would have made an excellent
tourist attraction, although a very small city when compared to
modern Athens. The great Greek philosophers--Socrates, Plato, and
Aristotle--had lived, worked, and made their marks there centuries
before Paul arrived. Famous masterpieces of art and architecture,
many of them monuments to the old Olympian deities, adorned the
city and obviously caught Paul's attention. By his time the philosophical schools, including the Stoics, the Cynics, and the Epicureans, were in operation. Athens was a city of culture, learning,
and sophistication.

When Paul was invited to speak to the sophisticated Athen-
ian men who met regularly at the Areopagus, a rocky hill just
northwest of the famed Acropolis, he could not resist the opportunity to witness to Jesus Christ and the resurrection (17:22-34).
His approach to the Athenians was totally different from that to
the synagogue (ch. 13). His audience neither became angry, as had
many of the Jewish ones, nor responded with eager belief, as had
many Gentiles. With a few exceptions, the members of his audience
either mocked his message or dismissed it as unlearned or illogi-
cal. Apparently Paul left no permanent Christian community in
Athens when he moved on to Corinth, for we hear of no church there
in New Testament times. His presence in Athens is substantiated
by a reference in one of Paul's own writings, I Thessalonians 3:1,
written not very long after he had left that splendid city.

The next city to which Paul carried the gospel was Corinth
(18:1-18), physically not far from Athens but culturally, intel-
lectually, and religiously, vastly distant. This bustling political and commercial center was located on the narrow isthmus that
connected the Peloponnesus with the mainland. Each side of the
city had a seaport, which facilitated sea transportation from the
Adriatic to the Aegean Sea. Cargo destined to go farther than
Corinth was often transported overland from one seaport to the
other, where it was reloaded on waiting ships. The city was a
meeting-place and depository for nationalities, customs, religions,
and immoral behavior from both East and West. There was at least
one synagogue there, but the majority of the Corinthians were pagans. One of the most popular deities was Aphrodite, Greek goddess of love and beauty, whose worship often included sexual ex-

pression. For the most part, the population of Corinth was untouched by the philosophy of the culture associated with Athens.

Paul found a ready response to the Christian message in Corinth, and he remained there longer than at any place reported in Acts to this point in his missionary travels (18:11). It was there that he met a Jewish couple who had recently left Rome as a result of the expulsion of all Jews from the city on orders of the Emperor Claudius. Aquila and his wife Priscilla were tentmakers, as was Paul (18:2-3), who found it convenient to work and live with them. When he left Corinth, so did they, taking up residence in Ephesus, the city in Asia where Paul would spend two years on his third journey (18:18-19). Paul mentions them (with Priscilla shortened to "Prisca") in I Cor. 16:19 and Rom. 16:3-4, where he gives them high praise for their devoted service. In his letters, Paul never says his trade was tentmaking, but he does frequently state that he had supported himself by his work, a custom among rabbis, rather than depend upon the local people for his upkeep.

The church in Corinth grew rapidly and probably consisted mostly of Gentiles although the family of a prominent Jewish leader, Crispus, is reported to have become believers (18:8). Not everything went smoothly in Corinth, however. The usual trouble with some of the Jews (18:5-6) occurred there also, and they even brought charges against him before Gallio, the Roman proconsul of Achaia.

It is this mention of Gallio which allows us to fix a date for Paul's work in Corinth. An inscription found at Delphi indicates that Gallio assumed office in Corinth in either 51 or 52 A.D. This is the only verifiable date for Paul's life and work that we have, but it is very helpful in establishing probable dates for some of the other events referred to in Acts or his letters. The proconsul, says Acts, refused to deal with the charges of Paul's opponents on the grounds that they were a purely religious matter. It is likely that Luke included this account because it fits so well with his theme that the empire had no reason to be suspicious or fearful of Christianity. On his voyage back to Antioch in Syria at the close of his second missionary journey, Paul stopped off briefly in Ephesus and promised to return after he had reported to his home base (18:19-21).

Paul as Letter Writer

Paul did not invent the epistle as a literary type, but he did make effective use of it in dealing with problems and issuing directives from afar. Formally, his letters resemble those of others written at this time, sometimes reading like formal epistles and sometimes like more personal notes. Every one of them was written for a specific purpose, or purposes. When a problem arose in a church some distance away from where Paul happened to be and it was not feasible for him to travel to that church, or he was in prison, he would handle it by correspondence. Letter writing had become a common practice since the recent discovery that the papyrus plant supplied a good, relatively inexpensive writing material and since the far-flung provinces of the Roman Empire had been connected by good roads. It is almost certain that, except for brief closing greetings, Paul did not do the actual penmanship on his letters but dictated them to an amanuensis, or secretary. Apparently he did little, if any, editing or re-writing, for there are frequent interruptions in thought.

Not all the letters which bear Paul's name were actually his. There is general agreement among scholars that Romans, I and II Corinthians, Galatians, Philippians, I Thessalonians, and Philemon are by Paul, and that I and II Timothy and Titus are not his, excepting possibly a few passages. Scholars are not in agreement about the authenticity of Ephesians, Colossians, and II Thessalonians. All thirteen named above are arranged in a group following the Acts of the Apostles in our New Testament in the order, not of their writing, but of their length, beginning with the longest. We shall deal with them in what seems to be most probably their order of writing.

Letters to the Thessalonians

I Thessalonians fits so well into the story of Paul's second missionary journey as described in Acts that we may assert with confidence that it was written from Corinth shortly after Paul had been rejoined by Silas and Timothy, whom he had left behind in Macedonia when he escaped his enemies there and went to Athens (I Thess. 3:1-2). Timothy had gone back from Beroea to Thessalonica to provide any necessary help and leadership. Now Timothy had found Paul in Corinth and reported to him about the work in Thessalonica. The report was so glowing that Paul used almost half the letter to express his thanks and his love for them and to assure them that he had very often wished to return to them but had been prevented (chs. 1-3). This letter may be dated around 51 or 52 A.D. It is probably the earliest of Paul's letters and may be the earliest surviving piece of Christian literature.

In 4:1-12, Paul exhorts the Thessalonians to continue

their God-pleasing behavior, avoid immorality, love one another, support themselves with their own labor, and, in general, to lead the kind of life which would "command the respect of outsiders" (4:12). Then, in 4:13-18, Paul deals with a specific concern of the Christians in Thessalonica which Timothy had reported to him. During his abbreviated stay in their city Paul had undoubtedly included in his preaching the expectation of the early return of Christ, or the parousia. As we noted earlier, this was one of the themes of the early Christian preaching, and Paul speaks of it in most of his letters. In the period since Paul had left them, some of the members of the church had died, and their relatives and friends were concerned over the fate of the departed. They did not recall any statement of Paul that would cover this eventuality Apparently they had simply assumed that the parousia would occur so soon that there would be no deaths among them beforehand.

Paul assures the Thessalonians that there is no cause for worry. Those who will have died before the parousia will not miss out on eternal life but will "rise first" (vs. 16). Then the believers who are still alive when the Lord comes will be "caught up together with them in the clouds to meet the Lord in the air" (vs. 17). If they understand this two-phased concept of the resurrection, the Thessalonians need not be overcome with grief when a loved one dies ("falls asleep" is the euphemism used here). As for the time of the parousia, Paul warns in 5:1-11 that there is no way its arrival can be predicted because, like a thief, it will come when least expected. The appropriate stance, then, is for Christians to be alert, spiritually awake, filled with faith, love, and hope (5:8).

II Thessalonians is something of a problem for interpreters. Although it claims to have been written by Paul and begins in the same way as I Thessalonians, the treatment of the parousia in 2:1-12 is so different from that in the first letter that it is hard to accept Pauline authorship. Whether by Paul or by someone else, the epistle deals with two problems: (1) the claim by someone that the parousia has already arrived; and (2) the practice of some lazy believers of living off their neighbors.

The first problem is considered in chapter two. It was caused by the arrival in Thessalonica of a letter, which had Paul's name on it, asserting that "the day of the Lord has come" (vs. 2). The writer of II Thessalonians advises the believers to pay no attention to such a spurious letter, assuring them that the parousia has not occurred and, furthermore, will not occur until certain other things have happened: "the rebellion" and the revealing of "the man of lawlessness," which will be accompanied by "pretended signs and wonders" and the deception of many (2:3,9-10)

248

There has been much speculation about the identity of the man of lawlessness, but he is still a mystery. This whole section of chapter 2 (vss. 3-12) has the flavor and intensity of apocalyptic writing. At least it can be said that the point is firmly established: the parousia has not yet come and will not come until certain other things, cataclysmic and violent, will have occurred.

The second problem may have some relation to the first. In 3:6-13, it is commanded that idleness among the brethren not be condoned and that those guilty of it get busy and earn their own living. They are reminded of the rule "If any one will not work, let him not eat" (3:10). It is possible that the idleness referred to is that of persons who had been so sure of the early coming of the Lord that they relinquished their jobs in anticipation of the event. If the letter were written by Paul, the time of its composition would be a short time after I Thessalonians. If by an unknown writer using Paul's name to gain acceptance of his advice, the time of writing is some time after the death of the apostle.

Significant names, terms, and dates for this chapter

James, brother of Jesus	Macedonian call
Barnabas	Macedonia
Antioch in Syria	Philippi
John Mark	Lydia
Cyprus	Thessalonica
Sergius Paulus	man of lawlessness
Galatia	Beroea
Antioch in Galatia	Athens
Iconium	Achaia
Lystra	Corinth
Derbe	Aphrodite
Jerusalem Conference	Aquila
party of the Pharisees	Priscilla (Prisca)
Cephas	Gallio
apostolic decrees	I Thessalonians
Silas (Silvanus)	51-52 A.D.
Timothy	parousia
Troas	II Thessalonians
Asia	

CHAPTER XXIV

THE MISSIONARY BECOMES PASTOR

Biblical materials: Acts 18:23-19:41. Galatians.
                     I and II Corinthians

Essential reading: Acts 18:23-19:41
                    Galatians 3; 5
                    I Corinthians 1; 4-8; 11-15

Paul's return voyage from his ministry in the lands surrounding the Aegean Sea brought him to land at Caesarea in northern Palestine. Acts says his next step was to go up and greet the
church, without specifying whether it meant the congregation in
Caesarea or the mother church in Jerusalem. From there, he returned to his sponsoring church in Antioch in Syria (18:22).

The Third Missionary Journey

Luke knew of no important event to separate the second and
third tours of Paul, so he begins his account of the third journey
immediately upon concluding the second (18:23). Without mentioning
any traveling companions, Acts reports that Paul started out on
the same route as on the second journey, once again visiting the
churches in Galatia. Interrupting the account, Acts introduces
the Alexandrian Jew, Apollos, who had come to Ephesus while Paul
was in Syria or somewhere en route (18:24-28). Although Apollos
was an eloquent and learned preacher, his understanding of the
Christian faith was somewhat deficient when he arrived in Ephesus.
This was corrected by the couple who had lately moved there from
Corinth, Priscilla and Aquila. The Ephesian Christians encouraged
him in his plan to go to Corinth, and that is where he was when
Paul arrived in Ephesus (19:1).

If the Acts account is correct, Paul spent most of the
time on this third journey at the large Asian city of Ephesus, located near the Aegean Sea. He found there as eager an acceptance
of the gospel as he had known in Corinth and remained there for
more than two years (19:10,22). He encountered in Ephesus believers who had not heard of the Holy Spirit or received Christian
baptism (19:1-7). After basing his mission in the local synagogue
for three months, he moved to a rented hall, where not only resi-

dents of Ephesus but people from surrounding towns were converted under the influence of his preaching (19:8-10). This may help to explain the origin of the Lycus Valley churches of Colossae, Laodicea, and Hierapolis (Colossians 4:13), as well as of the rest of the seven churches for whom the book of Revelation was written (Rev. 1:11).

It is reported in Acts 19:21 that Paul was planning to leave Ephesus, visit the churches in Macedonia and Achaia which he had organized on his previous journey in those provinces, then return to Jerusalem before setting out for Rome. The first mention of helpers on this third journey occurs in the next verse; they are Timothy and Erastus. But Paul delayed his departure and found himself beset with trouble caused by the Ephesian silversmiths, who were upset over the sharp decline in the sales of one of their products, silver shrines of the goddess Artemis. They blamed this on Paul's preaching against idolatry and stirred up local worshipers of the goddess to protest the disrespect being shown her. The town clerk succeeded in quieting the mob and preventing harm to Paul and his Macedonian companions, Gaius and Aristarchus (Acts 19:23-41).

Paul's extended ministry in Ephesus, the longest of his career, provided him with opportunities to do more of what he calls (in I Cor. 3:6) "watering" the church in addition to planting it, which he felt he was especially called to do (Rom. 15:20). In other words, in addition to being a missionary/evangelist, he is now being called upon to be also a pastor, or shepherd, of Christian congregations. He did it through personal contacts and through correspondence. It is certain that he wrote several letters to Corinth from Ephesus. It is likely that Ephesus was the place of origin for Galatians. And, if those scholars who posit a period of imprisonment in Ephesus for him are correct, it is probable that Philippians, Colossians, and Philemon originated there. Paul himself says that he made a hasty visit to Corinth from Ephesus, of which Acts makes no mention (II Cor. 12:14a; 13:1-2), probably in an attempt to rescue a rapidly deteriorating relationship between himself and a group of the Corinthians.

The Epistle to the Galatians

Paul's letter to the churches of Galatia, although by no means the longest, is one of his most important. He does not say in the letter when or where he was writing it, but obviously it was sometime after the Jerusalem Conference because, as we have noted earlier, he talks about it in Gal. 2:1-10. It is possible that it was written from Corinth, where, according to Acts, Paul stayed more than a year and a half on his second journey. It is more likely, however, that it was written during his much longer stay in Ephesus, which would place it in the midst of the third journey, or around 54-56 A.D. Some scholars maintain that the churches to whom this epistle was addressed were located in northern Galatia. But since there is no mention in Acts of any missionary activity in that area, it is best to assume the recipients are the four churches in southern Galatia visited by Paul on all his missionary journeys, according to Acts: Antioch, Iconium, Lystra, and Derbe.

With regard to the situation which impelled Paul to write the letter, there is no doubt. Some time after Paul had established the congregations in Galatia, unidentified Christian preachers appeared, probably from the outside, proclaiming "a different gospel" (1:6) from that which Paul had given them and discrediting Paul's apostolic status (see 1:1). After the customary greeting (1:1-5), Paul comes directly to the point (1:6): this "different gospel" has been accepted by many of the Galatians, a fact which caused Paul shock and dismay. Somehow word of this disturbing situation had reached Paul and he was very upset over the news. Clearly he was in a "fighting mood" when he wrote.

Having asserted his divine call to be an apostle in the very first verse, Paul begins in 1:11 to defend the divine origin of his gospel. It was not passed on to him by other men; it came to him through a revelation (1:12). In the sections to which we have alluded above (chs. XXII and XXIII), Paul reviews briefly his life from his days as persecutor of Christians through the Jerusalem Conference (1:13-2:10), simply to show that he could not have received his gospel from the apostles in Jerusalem. He had been there only twice since his conversion (1:18 and 2:1)! The first time was very short; on the second occasion, those "reputed to be pillars" gave total approval to his gospel.

This almost irreverent attitude toward the Jerusalem apostles is even more strongly expressed in Paul's account of an incident in Antioch in Syria (2:11-14), where he publicly denounced Peter (Cephas) for his insincere behavior. Paul was not beholden to the human ecclesiastical leadership; his gospel came from a higher source.

Not until Gal. 2:15 do we begin to learn what there was about the "different gospel" that upset Paul so much. Evidently Paul's opponents in Galatia were saying that faith in Christ is not enough for salvation; it is necessary also to keep the Jewish law. This is why we often refer to them as Judaizers; they wanted to make keeping the law a requirement. This Paul saw as a perver-

252

sion of his gospel, which says that "a man is not justified by
works of the law but through faith in Jesus Christ" (2:16). To
teach otherwise is to imply that "Christ died to no purpose"
(2:21b).

Since the Torah lay at the heart of the problem in Galatia,
Paul felt that he had to deal with the nature and purpose of it,
and explain its status with respect to Christian believers. This
he does in Gal. 3-4. In the third chapter, Paul employs rabbinic
style exegesis of scripture, which at times seems complex and tor-
tuous, to establish the place of the Torah for the Christian. The
law, he says, was given long after the promise God made to Abraham
and in no way invalidated the promise. Implying that God had not
originally intended to deal with men on the basis of law, he as-
serts that the law "was added because of transgressions"(3:19) but,
even so, it was to be a temporary measure whose usefulness would
be over when the prior promise had been fulfilled. Besides its
temporary nature, the law had been delivered indirectly to men,
not directly, as was the case with the promise.

The promise which God made to Abraham, according to Paul's
argument, was that an "offspring" (3:16,19) would come, and the
coming of that offspring would mean the demise of the law. Now,
with the coming of Christ, the promise had been fulfilled. Hence,
the basis of God's dealing with men is not a law which has to be
obeyed but a promise to be taken by faith (3:21-22).

The law had been useful and had served its purpose. It
was like a "custodian" (3:24), usually a slave whose responsibility was to protect the child on its way to and from school. When
the child reaches maturity, it no longer needs the custodian:
"But now that faith has come, we are no longer under a custodian;
for in Christ Jesus you are all sons of God, through faith" (Gal.
3:25-26). Since Christians are saved through faith and free from
the law, it makes no sense to insist that Gentiles must submit to
circumcision and the other requirements of the Torah. It is the
same issue that the Jerusalem Conference had dealt with and sup-
posedly taken care of.

The main purpose and theme of Galatians are stated succinctly in the admonition, "For freedom Christ has set us free;
stand fast therefore, and do not submit again to a yoke of slavery" (5:1). It must have been very difficult for Paul, the zealous student of the Torah for so much of his life, to think of it
as "a yoke of slavery." Yet he had to establish in strongest
terms that salvation can not be earned by keeping the law; it can
not be earned at all. It comes only as God's gift, accepted by
faith in Christ.

Paul knew that such a strong emphasis on freedom from the law could easily be misinterpreted and abused. There would be those who would interpret Paul's teaching to mean license to do anything they felt like doing in the name of Christian freedom. To forestall such a perversion of freedom, Paul admonishes, "Do not use your freedom as an opportunity for the flesh, but through love be servants of one another" (5:13).

Paul developed his central doctrine of salvation by grace through faith in his later Epistle to the Romans, which will be considered in a later chapter. We hear no more of this threat from the Judaizers in the Galatian churches. It is probable that Paul's angry and forceful letter, supported by their fond memories of his early ministry among them (see Gal. 4:12-20), led them to reject the different gospel and renew their devotion to what they had learned from Paul.

The Corinthian Correspondence

Paul's relationship with the church in Corinth is the most stormy and challenging known to us. He visited them three times, wrote them at least four letters, and agonized about them to the point of being unable to work. Putting together information from Paul's own writings and the book of Acts, we can outline the relationship as follows:

1. Second missionary journey: Paul founds the church (Acts 18:1-18)

2. Paul writes Letter A (I Cor. 5:9), now lost or only a remnant preserved in II Cor. 6:14-7:1

3. Paul is visited by some members of the church (I Cor. 1:11; 16:17)

4. Paul receives a letter from the church (I Cor. 7:1)

5. Paul writes Letter B: I Corinthians

6. Paul makes a short, "painful" visit to Corinth (II Cor. 2:1; 12:14; 13:1)

7. Paul writes Letter C, a sharp letter, partly preserved in II Cor. 10-13, then worries about its effect (II Cor. 2:3-4; 7:8)

8. Having heard from Titus the reaction to Letter C, Paul writes Letter D, a letter of thanks: II Cor. 1-9

9. Paul visits Corinth a final time at end of third journey (Acts 20:2-3)

Of quite a different nature from Galatians, I Corinthians is of equal importance, but for different reasons. Instead of having to defend his gospel in polemical fashion, Paul in I Corinthians attacks a series of problems in the church at Corinth and answers several questions raised in a letter he had recived from the church. This letter gives us a better picture of Paul the pastor than we get from his other writings. We can hear him wrestling with practical problems which have beset this rapidly growing congregation, composed mostly of former pagans and set in the midst of a pagan city with an established reputation for low moral standards. Paul does not have to be concerned about Judaizers in Corinth. In a real sense, the problems in Corinth stem from the opposite danger: too much emphasis on freedom from the law!

Paul was in Ephesus, in the middle of his third missionary tour, when he wrote I Corinthians. He had already written the Corinthians one letter (no. 2 in above outline), as he says in 5:9-11, in which he had directed them to dissociate themselves from grossly immoral members of the church. It is quite possible that II Cor. 6:14-7:1 is a fragment of that letter, since it deals precisely with that subject.

In Ephesus Paul was visited by Chloe's people (1:11) and a trio named in 16:17, presumably all Corinthians. From them he learned of situations in the church which disturbed him, and he deals with these in chs. 1-6 and perhaps 11:17-34. He had also received a letter from them (7:1), in which they had raised several questions. These he answers in 7:1-16:4. The remainder contains greetings and statements of his personal plans, including the fact that he is in Ephesus and that Aquila and Prisca, ex-Corinthians now living in Ephesus, send greetings (16:5-24).

Disunity. Following the customary greeting (1:1-3) and thanksgiving (1:4-9), Paul discusses the existence of rival groups within the congregation (1:10-4:21). Apparently some have formed clusters on the basis of loyalty to a well-known apostle or preacher (1:12). Such division, says Paul, is unbecoming to believers and destructive of the unity which all have in Christ, who alone is the foundation of the church (1:13; 2:11). He implies that the Corinthians are following the wisdom of the world rather than the wisdom of God, and reminds them that most of them could not boast of impressive backgrounds according to worldly standards. They are important only because God chose the foolish, the weak, and the lowly for redemption in Christ Jesus (1:17-31). Leaders such as himself and Apollos are only servants who plant and water; it is God who gives the growth (3:5-9). So there is no room for snobbish cliques in the church.

Tolerance of immorality. In chapter 5, Paul is obviously upset with the church for failing to discipline one of its members for a flagrant and continuing violation of decency: a man is living with his father's wife (probably his step-mother), and the church has done nothing about it, even though Paul had already written them about it.

Legal disputes. Grievances against fellow-Christians are being taken to civil courts for settlement (6:1-8), presenting to the community an image of a group of squabbling persons who can not even live peaceably with one another. They should either submit such disagreements to a respected member of the congregation for arbitration or simply suffer injustice. The fact that the lawsuits are being brought in itself amounts to an admission that love does not control the church.

Extra-marital sex. Some of the men in the church have used Paul's own doctrine of freedom from the law to justify having sexual relations with prostitutes (6:12-20). These persons may have been influenced by a Gnostic notion that body and spirit are separate parts of the person, hence gratification of bodily lusts have no bearing upon one's spiritual condition. Paul rejects that idea and reminds them that their bodies also are "members of Christ" (6:15). Christians are already united with Christ; it is wrong to be united with a prostitute. Paul's answer is grounded in his conviction that the body is "a temple of the Holy Spirit" (6:19).

Questions about marriage. For the most part, from chapter seven onward, Paul is treating questions the Corinthians themselve had raised in their letter to him. We have to try to determine what the questions were by carefully reading the answers. In the case of chapter 7 that is not easy, for there seem to be several questions, all having to do with marriage: (1) Should Christians remain celibate? This question reflects the opposite attitude to the one in chapter 6; that is, the ascetic view which connects sexual activity with evil. Paul's answer is a clear "No" with the provision that temporary periods of abstinence for concentrating on spiritual activities are acceptable (7:5).

(2) Should we who are single remain so? Paul begins his answer in vss. 8-9, in which he advises remaining single (his own status) unless the sexual urge is too strong to be contained. He shifts to another question in vs. 10 and does not return to this one until vs. 25, where he begins to explain his advice about get-

ting married. It is significant that Paul makes a clear distinction between the answers he gives which are based upon a "command of the Lord" (vss. 6 and 25) and those which are his own opinion. It is the latter he is stating in vss. 25-35.

In this section Paul shows that his advice (7:25-35) to remain unmarried is based upon a very practical concern: he expects the early parousia and, in view of that expectation, he thinks it wiser to refrain from taking on new responsibilities (such as a wife) so that one can devote his attention to "the affairs of the Lord" (vs. 32). It is important to understand the reason for Paul's advice on marriage; otherwise, we may accuse him of being against it, which is certainly not the case (see 7:38).

(3) What about divorce? Paul's answer (7:12-24) indicates that this question arose in the context of the mixed marriage, that is, where one partner was a believer and the other was not. Standing on a command of the Lord (the teaching of Jesus as Paul knew it from the tradition), he says they should not divorce. But then, venturing his own opinion, he permits divorce if the unbelieving spouse desires it (7:15). (4) May a widow remarry? In his brief answer (7:39-40), Paul says a widow may remarry, but only another Christian; however, he thinks she will be happier if she remains unmarried!

The idolmeats issue. Pagan temples abounded in Corinth and, at many of them, deities were worshiped by sacrifice of animals. Some of the meat so slaughtered was eaten on the premises and the rest sold to local meat markets for re-sale to their customers. Very likely it was difficult to find meat in Corinth which had not come from a pagan temple. The question addressed to Paul was, May we as Christians eat this meat which has been sacrificed to idols (idolmeats)? Paul's answer is contained in chapters 8-10.

Some of the Corinthians, claiming the knowledge (Greek: gnosis) that pagan deities are not real, find no problem in eating idolmeats. Paul agrees with their position but issues a strong warning against ignoring the consciences of those Christians who do not understand it that way (8:7-13). A mature Christian will voluntarily limit his freedom if the exercise of it causes his brother to fall (8:13).

Chapter 9 appears to be Paul's extended illustration of that principle. As an apostle, he had the right to be supported by the people to whom he ministered, but he surrendered that right in the interest of furthering the gospel. Paul seems to be qualifying in chapter 10 what he had said in 8:4-6. Warning against idolatry (10:6-22), he makes a distinction between eating at home the idolmeats which were bought in the market and eating them in the temple of the pagan god. The former is acceptable; the latter is not.

Women preachers. In what is certainly the least convincing of his answers, Paul, in 11:2-16, handles the question, Must a woman who is preaching or praying in a public worship service wear a covering on her head? After a series of appeals to scripture, custom, common sense, and nature, Paul uses his apostolic authority to say simply, Yes! But the reader should not overlook the fact that there is no question about the propriety of the woman's praying and prophesying (preaching); the question is only about her attire.

The Lord's Supper. It is not clear whether this subject came up as a question from the Corinthians or as something Paul had heard about. He knows in detail the manner in which they have been observing the sacrament (11:20-22), and he is shocked by it. Those who come to the supper early consume all the bread and wine, with the result that they overindulge, while the poor, who arrive later, have nothing left for them. In order to correct these abuses, Paul passes on the complete account of the original Lord's Supper (11:23-26), followed by a warning that those who do not realize the seriousness of the sacrament "will be guilty of profaning the body and blood of the Lord" (11:27).

Spiritual gifts. The question which brought forth Paul's lengthy treatment in chs. 12-14 probably was, What should we do about those church members who have the gift of speaking in tongue and insist on showing it off at every church service? Paul acknowledges that there are many kinds of gifts (Greek: charismata), including that of glossolalia (speaking in tongues). All of them come from the same Spirit (12:4) and are given to different members of the church for "the common good" (12:7). As each member of the human body has its particular function to perform for the health of the whole body, so it is with the abilities bestowed upon believers.

There is one gift available to all, love (agape), which should govern the use of all the others (ch. 13). If they are not controlled by the love described in 13:4-8a, they are useless. In ch. 14, Paul deals more directly with glossolalia. He has that gift but rarely uses it (14:18-19) because it is of no value in instructing others. There is one guiding principle which should be followed when planning a service of worship: "Let all things be done for edification" (14:26c). This means that speaking in unknown tongues must be limited and provision made for their interpretation (14:27-33a).

258

The flow of Paul's treatment of spiritual gifts is interrupted by the puzzling paragraph, 14:33b-36, which prohibits women from speaking in church. This is so contradictory to 11:2-16 and out of keeping with such statements as Gal. 3:28, as well as with Paul's many references to female helpers in his various congregations, that we may properly question its authenticity. It is probable that this paragraph was inserted after Paul's death by a church leader who simply did not agree with Paul on the subject. We note the same attitude in the non-Pauline I Timothy (2:11-15).

The resurrection of the dead. In one of the most remarkable and valuable chapters in all of Paul's letters (ch. 15) is found the only New Testament attempt to explain the resurrection of the dead. Having established the fact of Jesus' resurrection (15:1-11), Paul replies to the assertion by some of the Corinthians that there is no resurrection for the believer (vs. 12). He insists that the resurrection of Christ and that of the believer are so closely tied together that there can not be one without the other (vss. 13-20).

Anticipating the natural questions, "'How are the dead raised? With what kind of body do they come?'" (15:35), Paul uses the analogy of a seed planted in the ground to point out that the resurrected body is not the same one which has been interred, but a new creation, "a spiritual body" (15:44). In true Hebrew fashion, Paul does not think of an immortal soul being separated from a mortal body at death (as did the Greeks), but he speaks of an act of God by which we are given a new image (vs. 49), in which our former mortal nature is replaced with immortality (vs. 53). The resurrection is clearly a vital part of Paul's gospel.

The contribution for the saints. A question had likely been asked regarding the offering which Paul had already requested for the relief of the believers in Jerusalem. In 16:1-4, he gives directions for the regular, systematic, and proportionate gathering of moneys in the period prior to his planned visit. Fulfilling his promise to Cephas, John, and James (Gal. 2:10), Paul is mounting a serious effort to help the poverty-stricken mother church, which apparently had abandoned the common treasury system described in Acts 2-6. He mentions it again in his later Epistle to the Romans (15:25-27).

II Corinthians

As noted in the outline of the Corinthian correspondence above, the book of II Corinthians, as we have it, contains parts of at least three letters; more than that, according to some scholars. Why, when, or by whom this material was put together is unknown, but there is no reason to suspect that it was not written by Paul. The short section 6:14-7:1, obviously out of place, may be a fragment of Letter A (no. 2 in outline), otherwise lost.

Letter C. Clearly of a different spirit from the first part of the book, II Cor. 10-13 is part of a severe letter written by Paul after he had returned to Ephesus from an unpleasant visit to Corinth. Outsiders, referred to by Paul sarcastically as "these superlative apostles" (11:5), had preached "a different gospel" (11:4), and the Corinthians had accepted it without question. These same people, probably not the Judaizers who upset the Galatians, had also belittled Paul's authority and planted doubts about his being a true apostle.

In what he calls "a little foolishness" (11:1), Paul reviews the history of his work among them, admits that he used restraint in his exercise of apostolic authority (11:19-21), and uncharacteristically boasts of his credentials (11:21-22) and his record as Christ's servant (11:23-12:13). He feels that the Corinthians' failure to uphold his apostleship has forced him into this listing of his accomplishments, travels, hardships, and divine revelations.

He also mentions his "thorn . . . in the flesh" (12:7), which he never identifies but which must have been some infirmity or chronic health problem. It may have been poor eyesight, as suggested by Gal. 6:11. After the Lord had refused his third request that it be removed, Paul concludes that its purpose is to keep him from undue pride in his own strength (12:7-10). Paul is planning another visit to Corinth (12:14; 13:1), and in the interim he hopes they will have seen the error of their ways so that he will not have to be too harsh in disciplining them (13:10-11).

Letter D. In the first part of II Corinthians, a relieved Paul gives expression to his joy and gratitude for the excellent report which Titus had just given him of the Corinthians' change of heart and their love for him. He speaks of the "painful visit" (2:1) made earlier and of the letter he had written "out of much affliction and anguish of heart and with many tears" (2:4). This seems to be a reference to Letter C, discussed above. Much of this letter, which extends from 1:1 through 9:15 (except for 6:14-7:1), is very personal in nature.

Paul admits that, after he had sent Titus away bearing the severe letter, he regretted having written so harsh a message and worried that it might cause a complete break in his relationship with the Corinthians. Unable to continue his work in Ephesus,

Paul had gone to Troas in hopes of meeting the returning Titus. Still distraught, he crossed over into Macedonia (2:12-13), where he met Titus, who brought him the great news that Paul's letter had produced the desired effect and that all was well with the church in Corinth (7:5-16).

II Corinthians 8 and 9 are concerned with the collection being taken in the churches around the Aegean Sea for the relief of the Jerusalem poor. Paul commends highly the churches in Macedonia as examples the Corinthians might well follow (8:1-7). Some scholars believe that chs 8-9 were not part of this "thankful letter" but belong to another letter or letters Paul wrote to encourage a good offering for the saints. We are considering them, however, as part of Letter D, written shortly before Paul visited Corinth for the last time.

Significant names and terms for this chapter

Aegean Sea	Chloe's people
Adriatic Sea	idolmeats
Apollos	spiritual gifts
Ephesus	glossolalia
Artemis	agape
Galatians	resurrection of the body
Judaizers	immortality of the soul
custodian	II Corinthians
I Corinthians	Titus

CHAPTER XXV

THE LETTERS FROM PRISON

Biblical materials: Philippians. Colossians. Philemon

Essential reading: Philippians 1-2; 4:14-23
                    Colossians 1-2; 4:7-18
                    Philemon

Three of the surviving letters of Paul were written in
prison. Since Acts says Paul was imprisoned in Rome for two years
and since he alludes to "the whole praetorian guard" (Phil. 1:13)
and to "Caesar's household" (Phil. 4:22), it has been assumed over
the centuries that Philippians, Colossians, and Philemon were
written in Rome. In recent times, however, scholars have pointed
to certain evidence which suggests that Rome may not have been the
place of origin:

(1) The terms "praetorian guard" and "Caesar's household"
do not guarantee that Rome is being referred to, for they were
used of residences of Roman governors in many places, such as
Caesarea and Ephesus. (2) The great distance from Rome to the
destinations of the letters would make the amount of communication
presupposed in them extremely difficult. This is especially true
of Philippians (see Phil. 2:25-30). (3) The runaway slave Onesimus (see Philemon) is far more likely to have sought refuge in a
large city nearer home, such as Ephesus, than in Rome, which is
over a thousand miles farther. (4) In both Philippians and Philemon, Paul states his intention to visit the recipients when he is
freed. If he were in Rome, this would directly contradict his
firm plan, as stated in Romans, to proceed from there to Spain
(Rom. 15:23-28).

If Rome is not a likely place from which the prison correspondence originated, what other possibilities are there? Acts
says Paul was in prison in Philippi for one night, in Jerusalem a
very short time, and in Caesarea for two years before the final
imprisonment in Rome. Paul himself speaks of having a record of
"far more imprisonments" than the superlative apostles in Corinth
(II Cor. 11:23), which suggests that Acts does not record all of
them. Paul's cryptic reference in I Cor. 15:32 to having "fought
with beasts at Ephesus," combined with the Acts report that he was

262

in Ephesus more than two years, during which he got into trouble with the silversmiths' union, has pointed to a possible Ephesian imprisonment.

Certainly, to assume that Ephesus is the city of origin for the prison epistles would clear up the difficulties associated with those writings. As for the Caesarean imprisonment, although it would have provided Paul with plenty of time to do some writing, it is fraught with the same difficulties associated with Rome as the place of writing for these letters. Obviously, the question of place affects directly the matter of time of writing. If the letters were written at Ephesus, the time would be around 55-56 A.D. If at Rome, they would be his last works and placed around 60-64. Assuming an Ephesian origin to be more likely, we shall consider them at this point.

Epistle to the Philippians

This joy-filled letter was written primarily as a thank you note to the congregation at Philippi, with which Paul had had only the finest relationship from the very beginning. With the Philippians, Paul had made an exception to his rule never to accept a salary from those to whom he ministered (Phil. 4:15-16). They had helped him in the past and, when they heard he was in prison, they sent him a gift, probably money, by the hand of one of their members, Epaphroditus (4:18). Following their instructions, Epaphroditus had remained with Paul as a personal servant (2:25) but had become seriously ill while there. The Philippians had heard of his illness, and he had been informed of their concern for him. This considerable amount of contact seems to indicate Paul's place of imprisonment was not too far from Philippi. When Epaphroditus recovered, Paul felt that it was time for him to return home, and we may assume that he carried the letter with him (2:25-30).

The epistle begins on a grateful, warm, and positive note. Paul looks upon his imprisonment, not as a terrible calamity or gross injustice, but as a new opportunity to spread the gospel (1:12-18). He is confident that he will be released so that he can continue to work for the Lord, but his personal preference is "to depart and be with Christ" (1:19-26). Among the Philippians there seems to have been no problem with which Paul felt he had to deal, but he gives them general admonitions about living a life "worthy of the gospel" (1:27).

When he counsels them to be humble in their relations with each other, it occurs to him that there could be no better example

263

of humility than Christ Jesus (2:1-5). He is reminded of a creda
statement current in the church and quotes it in 2:6-11. It is a
beautiful expression of the Christology (doctrine of Christ) of
the early church: Though divine, Jesus voluntarily divested himself of his divine powers and prerogatives in order to become ful
ly human, even submitting to the humiliation of crucifixion. As
result, God has exalted him to a position higher than that which
he had occupied before his humiliation; every tongue is to confes
him as Lord.

There is an abrupt change in the mood of the letter begir
ning at 3:2. In rather sharp language, Paul warns against persor
who seem to be boasting of their Jewish heritage and their adherence to the Torah. In a statement reminiscent of II Cor. 11, Pau
challenges the Judaizers to outdo his own record for zealous keer
ing and study of the law. Although he was proud of his accomplis
ments in that area, they do not begin to compare with what he has
found in Christ (3:3-11). Making no claim to having achieved per
fection as a Christian, Paul vows that he will continue to strive
for it (3:12-16). He goes on to exhort the Philippians to aim fc
similar Christian maturity, which includes mutual helplfulness,
joyful confidence, prayerful trust, and aspiration to the nobler
things (3:17-4:9).

Epistle to the Colossians

Paul's statement in Colossians 2:1 seems to indicate that
he had never been to the tri-city area of the Lycus Valley in the
province of Asia (part of modern Turkey). There was a Christian
church in each of the neigboring towns of Colossae, Laodicea, and
Hierapolis (Col. 4:13), but Paul was not the organizer of any of
them. These congregations probably owed their existence to the
activity and zeal of a Colossian named Epaphras (Col. 1:7; 4:12)
and others from the area who had responded to Paul's ministry in
Ephesus. The bearer of the letter to the Colossians was carrying
two others, one for the church at Laodicea (4:16) and a personal
message for one of the stalwart members of the Colossian congrega
tion, Philemon. The latter is included in our New Testament; the
Epistle to the Laodiceans did not survive.

The purpose of the letter to the Colossians is to combat
heresy (false doctrine) which had arisen in the area and which
threatened to undermine the true gospel which had been proclaimed
to them by Epaphras. Indeed, it was likely Epaphras who had come
to Paul, imprisoned perhaps in Ephesus, with the request that Pau
help him deal with this complicated problem, which had surpassed

his own ability to handle. Epaphras was in prison with Paul, according to Philemon 23, so the letters were being carried by Tychicus (Col. 4:7), mentioned in Acts 20:4 as an Asian who was among the group waiting to accompany Paul in his final trip to Jerusalem.

We must form our picture of the "Colossian heresy" from the statements Paul makes in opposition to it. If he already has it in mind when dictating 1:15, Paul must have seen it as threatening the supreme position of Christ in God's plan for the salvation of the world. The highest Christological statement to be found in Scripture occurs in 1:15-20, where, without any mention of his name, Jesus Christ is described as the image of God, an agent of creation, the center of the universe, the head of the church, the first to rise from the dead, and the embodiment of "all the fulness of God." It was through him that God had provided for the reconciliation of the world to himself.

This paragraph is so beautifully constructed and majestic in expression that some scholars suggest it may have been an early hymn which Paul appropriately quotes. He returns to this theme in 2:8-15, where he cautions against human ideas and traditions which can be so deceptive that they lead one to forget the uniqueness and the centrality of Christ as the only savior. The "elemental spirits" (2:8) and the "principalities and powers" (2:15) probably refer to personified spirits of the elements from which man was created and considered by many pagans to be worthy of worship. Paul does not question the existence of such invisible powers but considers them to be the enemy whom Christ has defeated by his death and resurrection (2:15). Probably the heresy assigned to these spirits some role in salvation, and Paul emphatically proclaims that only Christ is the savior and needs no assistance from any other beings.

Other elements of the Colossian heresy must have been limitations on food and drink (2:16,21), observance of special days (2:16), self-denial, and worship of angels (2:18). All of these, proclaimed by persons claiming special revelation and knowledge (2:18), are purely human inventions which threaten to take away the freedom which believers have in Christ (2:20-23). Judging from the way in which Paul attacks the false teaching, we may conclude that it was composed of elements from Christian teaching, philosophy, Judaism, speculation about angels, and a growing movement known as Gnosticism.

Named for its claim to be based upon a higher, secret knowledge (Greek: gnosis), Gnosticism taught a sharp dualism which considered all physical things to be evil and spiritual things good. Over the years, it developed a complex mythology, which included the notion that within each human body an immortal spirit, or spark of light, languishes as a prisoner yearning for release. The only hope for deliverance from the evil body is the power of knowledge, by which the spark (or soul) realizes what he is, whe he came from, and how he can return to the realm of light. Between the true God (or the figure of Light) and the evil world a hosts of hostile, invisible powers which seek to prevent the sparks' return to their home. To assist them in finding their w through this difficult maze, a "redeemer" is sent to provide the necessary knowledge by preaching to the imprisoned sparks, arous ing them from their stupor, and to arrange for their deliverance from their "prisons."

The use of Christian concepts and terminology made Gnost cism an insidious threat to Christianity, for many Christians we incapable of discerning the difference. An early form of Gnosti cism seems to have been an important element in the Colossian he esy. We will have occasion to notice, in some of the New Testa ment books written after Paul's time, how a more developed form Gnosticism posed a serious threat to orthodox Christianity. We not meet this particular heresy, reflected in Colossians, in oth early Christian literature. It is likely that Paul's strong ve bal assault on its various features was sufficient to bring the Lycus Valley Christians to recognize it as a perversion or aberr tion of the true gospel.

It is not until 3:5 that Paul turns his attention from t heresy to a more general set of admonitions. In 3:5-17, he advi es the Colossians to "put off the old nature with its practices" and "put on" the virtues, attitudes, and acts which are appropri ate for those who have been forgiven by the Lord and in whom the word of Christ dwells. A table of household duties (3:18-4:1), perhaps patterned after general ethical teaching of the time and given specific Christian coloring, follows. It deals very prac tically with the everyday relationships between husbands and wiv children and parents, and slaves and masters. Similar tables oc cur in Ephesians, I Peter, and Titus.

Epistle to Philemon

The shortest of the surviving letters of Paul, and the o ly one which can be called "personal," is that written to a membe of the congregation in Colossae, named Philemon. It has only one purpose: to implore Philemon to accept back without recriminatior or punishment his runaway slave, who had become a Christian and close friend of Paul. Onesimus, mentioned also in Col. 4:9, had escaped from the household of Philemon, whose home provided a

meeting place for the congregation (vs. 2), and had lost himself
in the large city (probably Ephesus) where Paul was incarcerated.
Somehow he and Paul had met and the two had become such close
friends that Paul referred to him as "my child" (vs. 10). Paul
had convinced Onesimus that the right thing for him to do was to
give himself up to his owner, doubtless assuring Onesimus that he
would send a letter along to make the reunion easier. Like Epaphras, Philemon may have gotten to know Paul while he was preaching in Ephesus.

Making no effort to condemn the institution of slavery,
which was very widespread in the Roman Empire at the time, Paul
asks Philemon to receive Onesimus "as a beloved brother" (vs. 16)
and "as you would receive me" (vs. 17). It appears that Paul expected an early release from prison and, when that occurred, he
planned to pay a visit to Colossae.

Among those who were at the same place as Paul, and who
sent greetings, were Epaphras (see Col 1:7 and 4:12) and Mark.
According to Col. 4:10, this is the same Mark who had deserted
Paul and Barnabas halfway through Paul's first missionary journey,
and whom Paul had refused to take along on the second (Acts
15:36-40). The intervening years had produced a change of heart
in Paul and perhaps a stronger commitment in Mark, whom Paul now
lists among his fellow workers (vs. 24).

Significant names and terms for this chapter

Philippians, Epistle to	Tychicus
Epaphroditus	heresy
Christology	Colossian heresy
Colossians, Epistle to	Gnosticism
Epaphras	elemental spirits
Colossae	Philemon, Epistle to
Laodicea	Philemon
Hierapolis	Onesimus
Lycus Valley	

267

CHAPTER XXVI

THE MISSIONARY LOOKS TO NEW FIELDS

Biblical materials: Acts 20-28. Romans

Essential reading: Acts 21:17-22:29; 28
                     Romans 1-3; 5-6; 13; 15:14-33

According to Acts, when Paul left Ephesus, he went again to Corinth by way of Macedonia and remained there for three mont (20:1-3). This ties into the information Paul himself gives in II Corinthians 1-9, probably written from Macedonia as he was en route to Corinth. Paul was concluding his mission in those part and had been thinking about where he would be going next. Of course, he was already committed to accompany representatives of the churches in the area to Jerusalem to deliver in person the money collected for the poor in that congregation. When that wa done, he had decided that he would go to the capital city of the Empire, Rome, spend some time there, and from there go to Spain, which lay at the western end of the Roman Empire. Anticipating this trip to places he had never been, Paul wrote a letter to th church in Rome, in which he "introduced" himself and his gospel and told of his plans. We assume that the Epistle to the Romans was written from Corinth around 57 A.D.

The Epistle to the Romans

Unlike the earlier letters of Paul, Romans was addressed to a congregation unknown to him except by reputation. Hence it does not deal with problems in, or questions raised by, that church. The only discernible reason for writing Romans is to de scribe the content of the Christian faith as Paul understood it and preached it, presumably so that the Christians in Rome would know it directly from Paul himself rather than have a distorted incomplete picture from anything they may have heard.

We do not know how or when Christianity reached Rome, bu Paul's statements in the thanksgiving section (1:8-15) suggest i had been there for several years. His plans to visit Rome and t proceed from there to Spain are told in the same section, taken together with 15:24 and 28. He also tells (15:25-27) of his mor immediate plan, which calls for him to carry the contribution for the poor, alluded to in I Cor. 16:1-4 and II Cor. 8-9, to Jerusalem. This would correspond to the trip described in Acts 20:3-21:17, except that Acts does not mention, at this point, anything about the contribution for the poor.

In Romans 15, Paul also allows us to see how he thinks about his mission as "a minister of Christ Jesus to the Gentiles" (vs. 16). It was his particular task to plant the church rather than nurture it (vs. 20). Now that the church has been planted (vss. 18-19,23) in the eastern end of the Empire, he feels impelled to seek new fields of labor. Although he does not say so here, Paul very likely is still working under the sense of urgency caused by his belief that Christ would soon return. Of course, Rome is not a new field, but Spain is, and that is his ultimate destination.

One of the continuing mysteries surrounding Romans is: If Paul's only reason for writing it was to introduce himself and his gospel to the church of Rome, why does he go into such detail in expounding his doctrine? Salvation by grace is fully dealt with in 1:16-8:9; chapters 9-11 wrestle with the question, Why do the Jews not accept Christ in larger numbers? The section 12:1-15:13 describes the kind of life expected of those who are justified by God's grace.

It seems odd that the sixteenth chapter is filled with personal greetings if Paul was not acquainted with the Roman Christians. The most likely explanation for this phenomenon is that Paul decided to send a copy of this summary of his gospel to the church in Ephesus and added chapter 16 to that copy. Whatever the purpose or purposes in Paul's mind when he wrote this epistle, chapters 1-15 stand as his best theological and literary effort. It has been suggested that an appropriate title for them would be "the Gospel according to Paul."

Salvation by faith. The theme of Romans appears in the first chapter (vss. 16-17). The gospel is the good news that the righteousness of God makes salvation available to everyone who has faith. Paul uses "the righteousness of God" to mean God's activity in redeeming sinful man. All persons are sinners, whether pagans, who followed idolatrous ways for so long that they became guilty of all sorts of wickedness (1:18-32), or Jews, who, even though they were given the Torah, did not live by it (2:1-3:20). Gentile and Jew are both lost (2:12), apart from the righteousness of God. At 3:21, there is a sharp transition: "But now . . . " Although all have sinned, God has acted in Jesus Christ to make

salvation possible for Jew and Gentile in the same way: "They ar
justified by his grace as a gift, through the redemption which is
in Christ Jesus" (3:24). They accept this gift by faith (3:25,28

For Paul, faith means the total acceptance of God's gift
of salvation. It includes the admission that one can not earn hi
salvation by his own efforts and is therefore lost if he depends
upon his own works. The terms justification, redemption, and sal
vation are used by Paul to mean virtually the same thing: the res
toration of the relationship between God and man through the deat
and resurrection of Christ (4:24-25).

Grace. Equally significant to faith in Paul's thought is
the concept of grace. Romans 5 provides a good picture of grace,
which is closely related to the agape he characterized so beautifully in I Cor. 13. "But God shows his love for us in that while
we were yet sinners Christ died for us" (5:8). Grace may be de-
fined as the saving activity of God on behalf of undeserving man
or the unmerited favor of God toward sinful humanity. The essential character of grace is seen in Paul's use of the word "gift"
in connection with it (Rom. 3:24; 5:15-16; 6:23). That which dis
tinguishes a gift from wages is that the gift is not earned. Al
though God knew that man could never earn anything except his own
death, he loves man so much that he offers him salvation from tha
death as a free gift (6:23)! That is grace.

Sin. Just as Paul realized that his doctrine of freedom
from the law could be abused (Gal. 5:13), so he was aware that
salvation by grace apart from works of law could be misinterprete
(6:1). But one significant result of man's acceptance of salvation by faith, says Paul, is that he is freed from Sin. He is
talking, not about individual acts of disobedience we call "sins,
but about an almost personified power which holds man in its gras
and provokes him to commit sins. The believer is so united with
his Lord that he may be said to have "died with Christ" as far as
his "old self" is concerned (6:5-6). That dying with Christ has
freed him from the power of Sin and enabled him to become alive
again under the power of a new master: God, or Righteousness
(6:11,16). Living under the new master, man realizes that sinnin
is an inappropriate way of life (6:2,15).

Free from the Law. We have seen that in Galatians Paul
tries to show the proper status of the Torah for believers and in
the process leaves a rather negative picture of it. In Romans 7
he gives a more positive impression, referring to the law as "hol
and just and good" (vs. 12). Unfortunately, Sin is able to use
the holy law to accomplish its own aims (vs. 13). It leads man t
think he can accomplish salvation only by obeying the law (works)

270

but the universal experience of mankind is that he can not obey it, no matter how sincerely he wants to (vss. 15-20). The only way out of this dilemma, says Paul, is through Jesus Christ, who freed us from the law when he brought salvation by grace (vss. 24-25).

Life in the Spirit. Paul has asserted that the believer has been freed from God's wrath, which is the state of not being reconciled with God (ch. 5), freed from Sin (ch. 6), and freed from the law (ch. 7). In chapter 8, he says he is also freed from death, that is, spiritual death (vss. 4-17). Life in the Spirit replaces living "according to the flesh." By "flesh," Paul does not mean the physical or bodily things; he means the purely human, the non-godly, non-spiritual lifestyle. By contrast, those in whom the Spirit of God (or "Spirit of Christ," or simply "the Spirit") dwells are children of God whom the Spirit aids in times of weakness, in the struggles of prayer (vss. 26-27), and in the midst of all sorts of trouble (vss. 28-39).

The problem of Israel. Chapters 9-11 form a unit in which Paul deals with a problem which is obviously upsetting him. The fact is that only a small number of Jews have accepted Christ. Being a Jew himself, Paul is so saddened by this that he says he would forgo his own salvation if, by doing so, he could bring them into the church (9:2-5). Theologically, it raises the question, Has God's word failed in its promise to the descendants of Abraham (9:6-33)? After considerable "thinking aloud," Paul concludes that, far from rejecting Israel, God is simply using their hesitancy to allow multitudes of Gentiles to come into the church (ch. 11). After "the full number of the Gentiles" have become believers, then "all Israel will be saved" (11:25-26), which will mean that salvation will eventually come to all peoples (11:32). When the enormity of his discovery sinks into his mind, Paul explodes in a glorious doxology (11:33-36).

Indicative becomes imperative. After eleven chapters of theology, in which Paul has expounded the facts of salvation (the indicative), Paul states some of the implications thereof in terms of appropriate behavior (the imperative) [12:1-15:13]. It is as though he were saying, "You are sons of God--therefore, act like sons of God!" As members of "one body in Christ" (12:5), they should use their various gifts for the service and edification of the whole community (12:6-8), let love govern their relations with one another (12:9-13), and repay evil with kindness rather than vengeance (12:14-21). They should be responsible citizens (13:1-7), love their neighbors (13:8-10), and be ready for the parousia (13:11-14). Reminiscent of I Cor. 8-10, Paul counsels tolerance of the freedom of others to decide for themselves what

271

may be eaten, and urges responsibility toward the weaker brethren (14:1-15:6).

Jerusalem and Caesarea

Shortly after Paul dispatched his letter to the church in Rome, we may assume, he left Corinth for Jerusalem, accompanied b representatives of the churches in Achaia, Macedonia, and Asia. The money, which had been collected over a considerable period, was to be presented with appropriate ceremony to the elders of th Jerusalem congregation. Acts describes the journey and names the men traveling with him (20:3-21:18) but says nothing about the rea purpose of the trip, as Paul stated it in Romans 15:25-31. It ma be that Paul saw this offering from the predominantly Gentile churches as more than an expression of love for the brethren. He may have hoped that it would remove any feelings of resentment to ward the Gentile mission which remained among the more conservative Jewish Christians in Jerusalem.

Most of the Acts account of the trip to Jerusalem is writ ten in the first person ("we") and it may be that Luke is using a diary kept by one of the men traveling with Paul. It includes a reference to an excessively long sermon by Paul in Troas (20:7-12 the account of a tearful farewell to elders of the Ephesian congr gation who met Paul at Miletus (20:17-38), and notations that the closer the company got to Jerusalem, the more urgent became the a vice that Paul ought not to enter that city (21:4,12).

From Paul's statements in Romans, it seems probable that Paul expected his sojourn in Jerusalem to be brief and that withi a few weeks after arriving there, he would be on his way to Rome. The statement attributed to him in Acts 21:13, however, sounds a lot less optimistic about the future. Luke's report of Paul's meeting with James and the elders (21:17-26) indicates that they were happy to see him but very concerned for his safety because o a widespread feeling among the Jews in Jerusalem that Paul had been denigrating the Torah and customs of Judaism. Although Acts says those who were angry with Paul were Jewish Christians (Acts 21:20-21), it is more likely that most of them were non-believing Jews.

The elders had devised a plan to make Paul appear as a loyal, law-abiding Jew who was not guilty of the rumors circulating about him and thereby, they hoped, defuse the situation. Although Paul, it is reported, went along with their plan, it did not prevent trouble, and he soon found himself on the verge of being lynched (21:27-31). He was rescued by a contingent of Roman soldiers, led by a tribune who thought Paul was a wanted criminal and placed him under arrest (21:32-38).

In Acts 22-26, Paul is credited with making four major speeches in his own defense. In the first (22:1-21), he related the story of his conversion to the angry mob, who became so enraged that Paul had to use his Roman citizenship to avoid a severe beating (22:22-29). In the second (23:1-10), delivered to the Sanhedrin in Jerusalem, he precipitated a dissension between the Pharisees and Sadducees by talking about the resurrection of the dead. The report of a plot against Paul's life prompted the tribune, Claudius Lysias, to transfer Paul to Caesarea (23:11-35), where he remained in prison for two years.

A trial of sorts is reported in chapter 24, during which Paul made a third speech (vss. 1-21) before the procurator Felix. But Felix delayed making a decision, and two years later was replaced by Porcius Festus (24:22-27). When Festus tried to arrange a trial for Paul in Jerusalem, Paul again used his Roman citizenship and appealed to Caesar (25:1-12). When Herod Agrippa II, who governed Galilee and Perea, arrived in Caesarea with his sister (who was also his wife!) Bernice on a state visit (25:13), Festus asked him to assist him in formulating a letter to send along with Paul to Caesar. This gave Paul the opportunity to make his fourth speech (26:1-23). Paul reviewed his life-story, including another account of his conversion (the third one in Acts) and his commission to preach Christ to the Gentiles. Festus and Agrippa agreed that Paul was innocent of any capital crime and could have been set free if he had not appealed to Caesar (26:30-32).

Rome at Last

After a two-year delay, it appeared that Paul would get to Rome, but not in the way he had in mind when he wrote his introductory letter to the church there. The story of Paul's last journey, told in Acts 27:1-28:16, in the first person, sounds like an eyewitness account of the fateful sea voyage. Paul and other prisoners bound for Rome, under guard led by a Roman officer named Julius, set out from Caesarea and sailed along the Mediterranean coast to Myra, a seaport in the province of Lycia. There the party boarded another ship, headed for Italy, which brought them to Fair Havens on the south coast of Crete.

Ignoring Paul's advice to spend the winter there, the officer ordered the captain to head for Phoenix, considered a more suitable place to winter. A terrific storm changed their plans. After drifting, rudderless and sailless, westward for two weeks,

273

the ship wrecked on the island of Malta, where they spent three months waiting for another vessel to take them to their destination. An Alexandrian ship, probably carrying grain from Egypt to Rome, took them to the Italian port of Puteoli, from where they traveled on foot to Rome.

Welcomed by the Christians in the capital city of the Roman Empire, Paul was placed under house arrest, which allowed him to receive visitors and continue his proclamation of the gospel (28:17-31). His preaching to the local Jewish leaders produced but few converts and Paul, as he had done in other places, announced that he would henceforth limit his evangelizing to the Gentiles. The book of Acts closes with Paul still awaiting trial at the end of two years.

The question as to why Luke did not tell what happened to Paul has been debated for centuries. Traditions have arisen in the absence of facts. One says Paul's case was heard by Caesar Nero, who acquitted him, but later he was re-arrested, tried, and executed. A more likely tradition also says Nero tried Paul, but convicted him and had him executed during Nero's persecution of Christians around 64 A.D. In any case, it is highly probable that Paul never realized the ambition, expressed in Romans, to preach the gospel in Spain.

The fact that Luke does not record Paul's fate strongly suggests that it was execution by the Roman government. To have recorded that would have seriously damaged the case which Luke was apparently building, namely, that Rome had no reason to fear or suspect Christianity, which deserved the same status as a legal religion that Judaism had been enjoying for some time. Rather than subject the church to jeopardy by reporting that the chief proponent of the Christian movement had been found guilty of a crime deserving death, he simply stopped the history of the church somewhat abruptly. He had told how the movement, begun with 120 believers at the time of Jesus' ascension (Acts 1), had grown and expanded until it had reached the very heart of the Empire.

Since the time of writing of Paul's "prison epistles" is unknown (see previous chapter), it may be that we have no material by Paul later than the Epistle to the Romans. This means that we have no source except Acts for the events which transpired in Paul's life following his writing of that letter. In the absence of supplementary or contradictory information, we may assume the Acts accounts of Paul's Jerusalem and Caesarean imprisonments, as well as of his eventful voyage to Rome, are essentially correct.

Significant names, terms, and dates for this chapter

57 A.D.

Spain

Rome

Epistle to the Romans

righteousness of God

justification

faith

grace

Sin

Caesarea

Jerusalem

Claudius Lysias

Felix

Festus

Herod Agrippa II

Crete

Malta

Nero

64 A.D.

flesh

CHAPTER XXVII

PAUL'S INFLUENCE LIVES ON

Biblical materials: James.   Ephesians.   I & II Timothy.   Titus

Essential reading: James 1-3
                     Ephesians 2; 4:1-16
                     I Timothy 3-5

        It is highly probable that Paul's death occurred no later
than 64 A.D. Tradition says that Peter also was executed in Rome
around that time. Already James, the brother of Jesus who became
head of the church in Jerusalem, had been killed in 62 A.D. by the
priestly leadership. In 66 A.D., the party known as the Zealots
instigated a revolt against Roman authority, and a bloody war
raged for four years, culminating in the destruction of Jerusalem,
including the beautiful Temple whose rebuilding was begun by Herod
the Great. Thousands of Jews lost their lives in the bitter struggle, which ended in 70 A.D. When it was over, the priesthood was
virtually annihilated, the party of the Sadducees was non-existent,
and the Temple services and sacrifices were discontinued. Palestinian Judaism barely survived and owes its continuation to the
dedication and zeal of the few Pharisaic rabbis who escaped death.
The original Christian congregation survived but only because it
had left Jerusalem prior to its destruction in 70 (see above, p.
167).

        After 70 A.D., the Jewish component in the Christian
church became a progressively smaller proportion of its total membership as the gospel found a ready response among the Gentiles.
Sometime after the catastrophe in Jerusalem, a follower of Paul,
whose name we do not know, traveled to all the cities to which
Paul had written letters and made copies of those he could find.
Obviously he did not find them all, for we do not have all his
Corinthian correspondence or his letter to Laodicea. How many
more unrecovered letters he may have written it is impossible to
say.

        We do know that Paul's letters were put together and cir-
culated among a large number of congregations, who eventually
treated them as scripture and read from them as part of the worship service (II Peter 3:15-16). This suggests that Paul's influ-

ence continued to permeate the Christian church long after his death. However, not everyone who read or studied Paul's writings understood them correctly, as we may observe by reading the Letter of James.

James

There are seven writings in the New Testament which claim to be epistles but whose titles bear only the writers' names and not, as do Paul's, the names of the addressees. Hence they are called Catholic (general, universal) epistles: James; I and II Peter; I, II, and III John; and Jude.

James begins like a letter, but it sounds more like a tract or a sermon and has no greetings at the end, such as we have seen in Paul's letters. The author identifies himself only as "James, a servant of God and of the Lord Jesus Christ," but the statement in 3:1 suggests that he was a teacher. Since the two most prominent men bearing that name had met death by the time of Paul's execution and since James was a very common name in those days, it is best to assume that we simply can not identify him any more specifically than does his own statement. As for the time of writing, we can not be more precise than to say it was written long enough after Paul's Epistle to the Romans for "Paul's gospel" of salvation by faith apart from works of the law to have been disseminated.

James is concerned with practical Christian living rather than doctrine. His major concern embraces his first two chapters: Christians who claim to have faith but who do nothing to help out their needy neighbors. It is not enough , he insists, to be a hearer of the word; one must be also a <u>doer</u> (1:22-25). Pure religion is "to visit orphans and widows in their affliction, and to keep oneself unstained from the world" (1:27). The absence of works can not be made up by faith (2:14). His assertion in 2:24 that "a man is justified by works and not by faith alone" sounds as though it were a deliberate reversal of Romans 3:28: "A man is justified by faith apart from works of law."

Very likely what has happened is precisely what Paul had sought to avoid by writing Gal. 4:13-15 and Rom. 6. There were those Christians who were resting on the laurels of their faith and doing nothing to clothe a shivering neighbor or feed a starving brother (James 2:15-17), probably appealing to Paul's teaching to justify their inertia. But the Paul to whom they appealed would be appalled by their defense, for he fully expected anyone who had received God's gift of salvation by grace to bear the fruit of the Spirit (Gal. 5:22-23; Col. 1:10).

We can not escape the fact that Paul and James saw the process of salvation from different points of view. But some of the difference may be removed if we recognize that they are using the terms "faith" and "works" with different meanings. As we have seen, Paul understands faith as man's receptive response to God's offer of salvation which includes total trust in Christ rather than self and submission to his will. James understands faith as intellectual acceptance of a doctrine as being true (2:19). What James calls "works" Paul speaks of as the "fruit of the Spirit:" genuine deeds of kindness and helpfulness to one's fellows in need Paul's statement about salvation by faith alone includes a reference to "works of law" (Rom. 3:28), by which he means acts of obedience done in the expectation that they will earn him salvation. Paul emphasizes what God has done in Christ; James stresses what man must do.

Since we know nothing about the identity of James' "audience," we can only assume from the exhortations in the letter something of the type of problems he had in mind as he wrote. He has even stronger condemnation of the wealthy class than Jesus has in the Gospel of Luke. They should not be given special treatment in the church (2:1-7), their grandiose plans can be frustrated by the Lord (4:13-17), and they live in luxury at the expense of their underpaid employees (5:1-6). The sins of the tongue come in for special treatment (3:1-12; 4:11-12; 5:12). That small member can stir up great trouble but it can also be the channel of great blessing. Mutual concern for the well-being of the members of the church is enjoined (5:13-20). Prayer, anointing the sick with oil confession, and restoration of the erring brother are ways to make Christian fellowship real. An intensely practical writing, James is surely relevant for every generation of Christians.

Ephesians

Some early manuscripts of Ephesians included "at Ephesus" after the word "saints" in 1:1, but the older ones do not have it. It seems best to consider Ephesians a kind of circular letter which was intended for Christians in many places, since there are no personal greetings. Claiming to be by Paul, it was likely written by an ardent admirer and follower of Paul who lived a generation or two after the great apostle, for the purpose of dealing with a tendency in the church which disturbed him. He obviously was thoroughly acquainted with Paul's writings and felt that he could give the church directions which Paul would have given if he were still alive.

278

By attributing the letter to Paul, the writer hoped to gain for his work some attention it would not get and to give it an authority it likely would not possess if he had sent it out in his own name. He has caught quite accurately the spirit of Paul's gospel, but he tips his non-Pauline hand when he speaks of the "holy apostles and prophets" (3:5), when he uses "church" to refer to the world-wide institution instead of a local congregation, and when he alludes to the church's being "built upon the foundation of the apostles and prophets" (2:19-20).

The problem he perceives in the wider church is not one with which Paul had to deal. Now much larger and more widespread, the church is beset by the threat of disunity, not like the disunity Paul addressed in I Cor. 1-4, but a sense of separation between Jewish Christians and Gentile Christians. In a passage reminiscent of Colossians, the author of Ephesians pictures Christ as sitting at God's right hand in a position of majesty, power, and dominion over all things, especially the church, "which is his body" (1:20-23). It was the blood of this exalted Christ (2:13) which made possible the reconciliation of both Gentile and Jew to God and to each other (2:14-16). Hence Gentiles who are in Christ are no longer outside the pale of God's people, but are "fellow-citizens with the saints and members of the household of God" (2:19).

As chapter four begins, the author appears to move from the "doctrinal" to a more practical concern, but the first paragraph is a call to the actual practice of the unity which he has convincingly portrayed in chapters 1-3. It is difficult to imagine a stronger statement of unity than 4:4-6:

> There is one body and one Spirit, just as you were called to the one hope that belongs to your call, one Lord, one faith, one baptism, one God and Father of us all, who is above all and through all and in all.

This unity should prevail even though there are great differences among the individual members of the body (the church), including the variety of gifts provided for the edification of the whole church (4:11-12).

He describes his conception of what the new life in Christ is like in 4:17-5:20. Unlike the old nature, exemplified by Gentiles before they "learned Christ," believers should be truthful, honest, peaceable, soft-spoken, forgiving, serious-minded, grateful, sober, and joyful.

In 5:21-33, the writer of Ephesians depicts the ideal relationship between husband and wife, which appears to be an elaboration of the short directive by Paul in Col. 3:18-19. Using the relationship between Christ and the church as a model, he depicts marriage in a way which reflects a more positive concept than does Paul's treatment in I Cor. 7. The table of household duties, clearly dependent upon Col. 3:20-4:1, occupies 6:1-9. A well-constructed description of spiritual warfare, including the offensive and defensive weapons required to win the battle against the devil and wickedness, follows (6:10-20). The writer may have been familiar with the Wisdom of Solomon (5:17-20), a book in the Old Testament Apocrypha, for he appears to be drawing upon its imagery in this description. The mention of Tychicus (6:21-22), one of Paul's helpers, lends an air of authenticity to the epistle.

The Pastoral Epistles

The three writings, I Timothy, II Timothy, and Titus, are so similar in concerns, organization, and style of writing that we may be sure they were written by the same person. Like Ephesians, these letters claim that their writer was Paul, but we must conclude that they are pseudonymous, that is, written under a false name. The time of writing is even further removed from Paul's day than was that of Ephesians. Many scholars believe that they were written in the early part of the second century A.D. The church had grown rapidly since Paul, new problems had arisen, and a more complex organization had come into being to deal with them.

Since early in the eighteenth century, it has been customary to refer to all three of them as the "Pastoral Epistles" because they contain instructions and admonitions to pastors of local congregations, especially the younger pastors. The author is unknown but must have been an older, experienced church official who, acutely aware of the dangers posed by false teachers, used the reputation and authority of Paul to provide guidance for the church of his day. He selected two of Paul's younger helpers, Timothy and Titus, as the addressees but his writings are not private letters. They sound more like regulations designed to be used by the leaders of the church.

The problem with which the Pastorals are concerned is the spread of false teaching, or heresy. For this writer, "faith" is the approved body of correct doctrine which is to be passed down from one generation of Christians to another. It is usually preceded by the article, as "the faith" (e.g., I Tim. 3:9; 4:1; II Tim. 2:18; Titus 1:13). As we have seen, neither Paul nor James understood "faith" in this way. That which does not agree with "the faith" is false teaching.

There are a number of hints given in the Pastorals which suggest the nature of this heretical doctrine: "Myths and endless genealogies which promote speculations" are propounded by persons who "have wandered away into vain discussion, desiring to be teachers of the law, without understanding . . . what they are saying" (I Tim. 1:3-7). There were those who, departing from the faith, had sought to impose an ascetic lifestyle upon the Christians (I Tim. 4:1-5). Others had taught that the resurrection had already happened, which had upset some people (II Tim. 2:17-18). "The circumcision party" was passing on "Jewish myths" instead of truth (Titus 1:10-16). From such evidence it is probable that there was more than one heresy troubling the churches at this time, but certainly elements of Gnosticism and a tendency toward Judaizing are identifiable among them.

The answer to this increasingly troublesome problem of false teaching, according to the Pastorals, is a dedicated, informed, disciplined ministry which adheres to sound doctrine and refuses to be led astray by "godless and silly myths" (I Tim. 4:7). The matter of authority in the church is now of crucial importance. There must be recognized officials who can identify certain teachings as false, declare them to be heretical, and discipline those who promulgate them.

The most detailed prescription for selecting church leaders in the Pastorals is found in I Timothy 3. Qualifications for candidates to be considered for the office of bishop (3:1-7) are more numerous than those for other offices; hence, we conclude that the bishop was the highest official in the local congregation. The bishop as overseer of a group of churches had not yet evolved. Virtually the same list of qualifications for the office of bishop is found also in Titus 1:7-11. It is clear that one of the bishop's duties is to uphold sound doctrine and oppose false teaching. Submission to their authority is essential if the church is to deal successfully with those who try to lead astray the faithful (Titus 3:1).

Requiring only slightly less strenuous qualifications was the office of deacon (I Tim. 3:8-13). In I Timothy 5, two groups of widows are discussed. The first (5:3-8) consists of "real widows," those who must be financially assisted either by their own families or by the church. The second (5:9-16) must have been comprised of workers in the church, for they had to be at least sixty years old and fulfill other requirements. Elders are also mentioned (I Tim. 4:14; 5:17; Titus 1:5-6) but, as with the bishops, deacons, and widows, no description is provided, either of their duties or their authority.

In II Timothy 2:15 and 3:1-9, the "pastor" is exhorted to be a good example for his people, a teacher of sound doctrine, always alert for false teachers who are looking out only for their own gain. He is to use the Scripture for "teaching, for reproof, for correction, and for training in righteousness" (II Tim. 3:16). The pastor is to be a faithful preacher of the word, a ready defender of the true faith, and a dependable evangelist, even if it means suffering for him (II Tim. 4:1-5). Some scholars believe that II Timothy contains fragments of genuine letters of Paul (such as 1:16-18; 3:10-11; 4:6-22), but this is by no means certain.

Significant names, terms, and dates for this chapter

66 A.D.

70 A.D.

Letter of James

Catholic epistles

Ephesians, Epistle to

body of Christ

Pastoral epistles

I Timothy

II Timothy

Titus, Epistle to

widows

the faith

bishop

deacon

CHAPTER XXVIII

THE CHURCH FACES PERSECUTION

Biblical materials: I Peter. Hebrews. Revelation

Essential reading: I Peter 1; 4
               Hebrews 1; 3; 7; 10
               Revelation 1; 4-5; 7; 12:1-14:13; 21

As the church expanded and established itself as a new force throughout the Roman Empire, it aroused opposition from various quarters. As we have already noted, many Jewish leaders, as Paul himself had done in his early life, opposed the gospel of Christ. It appears that there was a considerable amount of unofficial opposition from pagans in some of the communities where the church was gaining converts. Very likely the church's condemnation of idolatry and immoral living and its proclamation of the concept of only one God who demanded a pure and chaste life of his devotees, coupled with the unique gospel of Christ as the incarnate Son whose death brought salvation to those who believe, aroused negative feelings toward it.

Christianity did not totally escape persecution by the state, either. The first persecution by the Roman government directed toward Christians, at least that we know of, was ordered by the emperor Nero, who reigned from 54 to 68 A.D. He found the Christians in Rome to be a convenient scapegoat upon whom he could place the blame for the burning of Rome, an event for which Nero himself was responsible, according to the Roman historian Tacitus. But this attack upon the Christians did not extend beyond the city of Rome.

Despite Luke's attempt in his two-volume work (Gospel of Luke and Acts) to show that Christianity posed no threat to the Empire, there were two later emperors who initiated wider attacks on the church. The first was Domitian, who ruled from 81 to 96 A. D. Assuming the status of divinity, he ordered that statues of himself be set up at various places, to be made only of silver and gold. Emperor worship was promoted throughout the Empire, and participation therein came to be considered a test of loyalty. This caused serious problems for such religions as Judaism and Christianity because to worship any human being as god was clearly idolatry, hence forbidden. Apparently Domitian tried to purge the empire of unpatriotic religions, and this attempt produced a period of intense persecution of Christians, especially in Asia Minor where a new temple to the emperor had been recently built in Ephesus.

The other emperor under whom persecution of Christians occurred was Trajan, who reigned from 98 to 117 A.D. Correspondence between him and Pliny the Younger, one of the governors in Asia Minor, indicates that persecution of Christians was not a vigorously pursued policy, but when Christians were accused and convicted, the punishment was to be execution. An accused person could avoid punishment by denying that he was a Christian. The crime was simply unwillingness to curse Christ publicly and worship the emperor.

Some New Testament literature clearly reflects a time of persecution of Christians just for being Christians. I Peter, Hebrews, and the book of Revelation manifest concern for the believers who are faced with the threat of suffering for their faith and provide guidance and encouragement to them.

I Peter

Of the three periods of persecution described above (under Nero, Domitian, and Trajan), it is that under Domitian which seems most likely as the background for I Peter. It is addressed to "the exiles of the dispersion in Pontus, Galatia, Cappadocia, Asia and Bithynia," all provinces in Asia Minor. Nero's persecution was localized and limited to Rome, whereas evidence is strong for an organized campaign in Asia Minor against "non-patriotic" citizens during Domitian's reign. The statement in 5:13 suggests that the letter was written from Rome, identified by the code name "Babylon." "She who is at Babylon" is almost certainly the church in Rome which, by the time of writing (probably 90-95 A.D.) of I Peter, had accrued a great amount of prestige among Christians across the empire. It seems to have replaced the Jerusalem congregation as the church to which others looked for guidance and support in difficult times. The Roman origin of the letter ties into the choice by the author of the apostle Peter as the purported writer, for tradition connected Peter with the church at Rome and even says that he was executed there in the days of Nero.

The actual writer is using the name of Peter in the same way, and for similar reasons, that the writer of the Pastorals used the name of Paul: to gain a respectful hearing for his message. Although some scholars try to preserve Petrine authorship by pointing to the name of Silvanus (5:12) as likely the actual composer of the letter on the basis of Peter's oral instruction, a careful reading of it indicates otherwise. Even if one credits Silvanus (the name of one of Paul's helpers, called Silas in Acts) with the excellent Greek in which the letter was written and with the clear influence of Paul's thought at several points, there are other considerations which lead to a label of pseudonymous:

(1) The letter gives no evidence of the author's personal knowledge of the earthly life, teaching, and death of Jesus; it alludes only generally to his suffering. (2) The persecution which is assumed points convincingly to the time of Domitian, which is much too late for Peter's lifetime. (3) The writer refers to himself as an "elder" (5:1) rather than as an "apostle," which would be the natural title for Peter to use.

We assume, then, that the author was one of the leaders of the church in Rome during the last decade of the first century A.D. who, having heard of the persecution of the Christians in Asia Minor and not sure just how well they were prepared to face it without buckling, wrote to encourage them to remain loyal to the faith, even if it meant great suffering. He reminds them of their baptism, which gives them a living hope of eternal life, in which they ought to rejoice even though suffering may be their lot for a time (1:3-6).

He suggests at this point (1:7) that suffering is something valuable for testing faith for its genuineness, and perhaps for refining it. He returns to the subject in 4:12-19, where he again alludes to the "proving" value of the coming ordeal. But he now adds a more positive feature to suffering: it should be considered as something natural and normal for a Christian; further, it is a privilege, for it means one is sharing Christ's sufferings. If his suffering is solely "as a Christian," it becomes a means of glorifying God. But he admonishes his readers to make sure their suffering is not deserved! Persecution for the faith, then, is not something to be avoided, but to be welcomed. They need not fear if they "entrust their souls to a faithful creator."

In addition to the urgings to steadfastness under trial, there are exhortations to a life of holiness (1:14-16), love (1:22), and spirituality (2:1-12). In a paragraph reminiscent of Rom. 13:1-7, the readers are admonished to be subject to the government and to honor the emperor as well as lesser officials, who are instruments sent by God to keep order (2:13-17). This is a remarkable passage, for there is little doubt that the ordeal for which they are being prepared was caused by the policies of the very emperor they were being urged to honor!

285

Another type of patient suffering is recommended in the second chapter (vss. 18-25), an expansion of one of the guidelines in the table of household duties (2:18-3:7). Christian slaves who are mistreated by their masters are instructed to bear the abuse patiently because this would not only receive God's approval but would be following the example of Christ. Still another reference to suffering (3:13-4:2) suggests that to suffer wrong without retaliation may put the opponent to shame, a sort of victory by passive resistance.

The author of I Peter maintains the expectation of the coming end of things (4:7) and admonishes his readers to remember that in their daily living. They should not forget to pray regularly, to continue their love for one another, to practice hospitality, and to use their God-given abilities to the glory of God (4:7-11). Even if written by a "no name" leader, this epistle matches some of Paul's writings (e.g., Philippians) in spirituality, theological insight, moral earnestness, and genuine concern for the faith and well-being of the readers.

Hebrews

Probably the most beautifully written and most carefully constructed book in the New Testament is that bearing the title "The Letter to the Hebrews." It is at the same time the most mysterious, for it not only fails to mention the name of the author but provides only faint hints as to when, where, why, or for whom it was written. Even its literary type is puzzling for, although it ends somewhat like a letter, it has no epistolary beginning. Its title, obviously given much later than its time of composition is of no help in trying to figure out either the nature or the destination of the work. A careful reading of Hebrews suggests that chapters 1-12 may have been originally a homily (sermon) or a treatise, to which chapter 13 was added by another person perhaps to give it the appearance of a letter. The greetings from "those who come from Italy" (13:24) can not be used to determine the place of the writing of the book.

The author of chapters 1-12 was certainly a learned, dedicated Christian who was thoroughly familiar with the method of interpreting Scripture which had been developed by the Jewish colony in Alexandria and who was skilled in the Greek tongue. Of all the persons who have been suggested for authorship, Apollos seems to be the most likely (see Acts 18:24-28). The fact is, of course, that we do not know who it was, but that can be said of many New Testament writings. Hebrews, then, is one book which must be approached and interpreted solely on the basis of its contents, since we do not know the circumstances which called it forth, the identity of the writer, or the specific purposes he had in mind.

What does seem clear, however, is the general purpose. The author sought to persuade the original hearers or readers to maintain their faith and not give up hope that the sacrificial death of Jesus was sufficient for their salvation. The method he chose to accomplish this purpose was the careful selection and interpretation of scripture passages, on the basis of which he warned, encouraged, and reassured them to the end that they should hold fast their faith. If they did so, they could be confident that they would succeed in reaching the promised "rest" which even the heroes of earlier times had failed to do.

The larger part of Hebrews is taken up with demonstrating the superiority of the Christian faith to any previous religion, specifically Judaism. Although God had revealed his message in former times through the prophetic spokesmen, he had lately spoken through his Son, who is immeasurably superior to any other messengers whom God has created, including the angels (chs. 1-2). As God's son, Jesus Christ is certainly superior to Moses, who, in all his faithful work as leader of God's people, was still only a servant (ch. 3). Those who left Egypt under Moses' leadership never made it into the promised land because of their lack of faith (3:16-19). As Christians, the author insists, we have the possibility of entering God's rest, but if we lack faith and obedience, the same thing which happened to the exodus generation will happen to us (4:1-13).

Beginning at 4:14, the author develops the concept of Christ as the great high priest, who is superior to the Aaronic priesthood in every way. Having been "one of us," he can sympathize with our weaknesses and understand our limitations, a fact which should encourage us to approach him in prayer (4:14-16). The author reaches far back into the Torah to find the model for Christ's priesthood, the mysterious Melchizedek, who preceded Moses and Aaron by several centuries (5:5-10; 6:13-7:28).

As minister of a new covenant, Christ is the holy, sinless, exalted high priest who, unlike the Aaronic priesthood, does not need to offer sacrifice to remove his own sin. Neither does he continually offer sacrifices for the sins of others, for he has already performed the sacrifice which carries total and eternal validity: "He offered up himself" (7:26-28). It does not bother the writer that the picture he draws of Christ in the role of priest presents a logical impossibility. He speaks of Christ as both the sacrificial victim and the officiating priest (9:11-14). As victim, his blood makes possible the forgiveness of sins. As judge and savior, his coming again completes the salvation of "those who are eagerly waiting for him" (9:27-28).

Having developed rather thoroughly his point about the superiority of Christ and his covenant to all facets of the covenant of Moses, the author offers a series of admonitions which follow logically from his interpretation of the Old Testament (10:19-39). His main point is the absolute necessity to "hold fast the confession of our hope without wavering" (10:23), the basis of which is the total trustworthiness of God. We should help one another to persevere and encourage one another in loving service. The best way to make sure this happens is to continue to participate in regular congregational worship and fellowship, something which not everyone is doing (10:24-25). The expectation of Christ's return is still alive ("the Day drawing near") and should be a reminder for those who tend to be slack in their Christian commitment. A rather severe warning, not found in other New Testament writings, appears to rule out the possibility of a second repentance (10:26-31; see also 6:4-6).

The reference to past sufferings (10:32-34) successfully borne as an encouragement to endure present hardships (10:35-39) suggests that Hebrews was written during a time of persecution, and some scholars have tried to fit it into the Domitian period (see above, pp. 283-284), making the past sufferings refer to the persecutions under Nero. This would mean that Roman Christians were the persons being exhorted to hold fast. But it should be remembered that there were several earlier persecutions of Christians, at least some of which were reported in Acts (8:1-3; 9:1-2; 12:1-4), and that Hebrews does not state the source of the suffering.

If it came from non-believing Jews, it could have taken place very early in the history of the church. To suppose this would also explain the theme of the book, the superiority of Christianity over Judaism. Further evidences that suggest an early date for it are: (1) The book was well-known and esteemed early enough for Clement of Rome to make use of it in one of his writings near the end of the first century. (2) Some passages seem to assume that priests are still functioning and sacrifices still being offered (9:6-10; 10:1-2), which could not be the case after the Temple's destruction in 70 A.D.

The final verse of chapter 10 urges faith as a desirable characteristic for Christians in that time. That was sufficient to evoke an entire chapter on faith, beginning with a definition of it (11:1) and continuing with illustrations from Israelite history of how faith enabled its heroes to withstand various crises.

The understanding of faith as "the assurance of things hoped for, the conviction of things not seen" does not coincide with the concepts of faith we have noted already in Paul, James, and the Pastorals. Even with their faith, concludes the chapter, these worthies of the past did not receive what God had promised, but God has better promises for the present generation (11:39-40). The hearers (or readers) are admonished (ch. 12) to endure, as Christ did, in order to receive "a kingdom that cannot be shaken" (12:28). Suffering, always unpleasant at the time, should be viewed as God's disciplining of his beloved children and as the prelude to righteousness (12:7-11).

Although unable to speak with certainty or precision, we assign the writing to the period between the death of Jesus and the Fall of Jerusalem (70 A.D.) and suggest Jerusalem or vicinity as the most likely place of origin.

The Book of Revelation

A first reading of the book of Revelation may lead the reader to conclude that it is mysterious, but the fact is that all of the questions we are unable to answer conclusively about Hebrews can be answered rather easily when put to Revelation. It was written by a Christian named John, who must have been a leader of the church in the western end of Asia Minor, while in exile on the tiny island of Patmos, a short distance off the coast of the Roman province called Asia. He wrote during the critical days of fierce persecution by the Roman emperor Domitian (see above, pp. 283-284) to seven churches in the area in order to inspire and encourage them to remain faithful to Christ, not giving in to the demand that they worship the emperor, even if they were threatened with death.

The type of literature is apocalyptic, with which we have already become familiar in Daniel 7-12 (above, ch. XIV). By writing in this style, he could convey a coded message to the Christians without running the risk of having the enemy learn of his call to resistance. Like Daniel, Revelation was written in a time of great crisis for the people of God and assured them that God was aware of their anguish and would soon intervene in world history to bring it to an end. Unlike Daniel, the name of the writer is stated, and we have no reason to think it was a pseudonym. It has been assumed by some that he is the same person who wrote the Gospel and three epistles bearing the name of John, but there are compelling reasons to reject this assumption.

Chapter one relates John's experience on Patmos in which

he was told on the Lord's day by the Lord God to write down what was about to be revealed to him in a series of visions. The finished book was to be sent to seven churches, beginning with the one in the largest city of the province, Ephesus (1:10-11). Of the other six, only Laodicea has been mentioned in the books we have examined (Col. 4:16), but the likelihood is that all of them had come into being as a result, directly or indirectly, of the preaching of Paul in Ephesus during his long residency there (see Acts 19). Chapters two and three contain letters to each of the seven churches, each tailored to the situation in that particular congregation, pointing out its strengths and weaknesses and promising heavenly reward for those who "conquer," that is, resist the demand that they commit idolatry through emperor worship.

Following the letters to the churches is the long series of visions (4:1-22:5) in which are revealed the things to come, in several series of sevens, depicted with vivid imagery and bizarre symbolism. A brief outline will help us to grasp the nature and structure of the apocalypse:

4:1-5:14	a preliminary vision of heaven
6:1-8:5	the vision of the seven seals
8:6-11:19	the vision of the seven trumpets
12:1-13:18	the vision of the dragon and the two beasts
14:1-20	the vision of those who worship the Lamb and those who worship the beast
15:1-16:21	the vision of the seven bowls of God's wrath
17:1-19:10	visions of the fall of Babylon
19:11-20:15	visions of the victory of Christ over the dragon
21:1-22:5	the vision of the New Jerusalem

The book closes with an epilogue (22:6-21), in which John is reassured of the trustworthiness of the visions and of the early happening of the things he has seen in the visions, and the expectation that Christ is coming soon is reiterated.

In the first vision (chs. 4-5) the exalted Christ, called "the Lion of the tribe of Judah, the Root of David" and "the Lamb who was slain," is depicted as the only one in heaven who is worthy to open the seven seals which sealed a mysterious scroll. As the seals are opened one by one, John is allowed to see the four horsemen (6:1-8), the souls of those who have died for their faith (6:9-11), and the earthquake which rocked the entire earth (6:12-17). Before the seventh seal is opened there is described a new vision of heaven (ch. 7), in which there are two multitudes: the first consists of 144,000 Israelites; the second is an innumerable gathering of people of all nationalities who have successfully endured "the great tribulation." The white robes they are

290

wearing and the palm branches they are carrying symbolize their victory, and they are rewarded with total bliss and happiness in the presence of God.

The opening of the seventh seal reveals seven angels prepared to blow their trumpets. Each of the first four trumpet blasts (8:6-12) initiates a frightful calamity on the earth. The fifth and sixth blowings of trumpets (9:1-19) bring demonic locusts and hordes of cavalrymen who cut down a third of mankind, but these events do not cause the rest of them to abandon their idolatrous ways (9:20-21).

Before the seventh trumpet is blown, John is allowed to see two more visions, in which it is revealed that there will be a period of forty-two months during which the nations will be allowed to trample upon the holy city (11:1-3). The blowing of the seventh trumpet (11:15-19) reveals a host in heaven singing praises to God and Christ, and the opening of God's heavenly Temple.

The series of sevens is interrupted for the next three chapters (12-14), in which a protracted confrontation between the saints and the forces of evil is portrayed. The offspring of the "woman clothed with the sun" represents the members of the church, often referred to as "the saints." The dragon, who is angered because he can not devour her child and who makes war on the rest of her offspring, is clearly identified as "the Devil and Satan," who was thrown out of heaven by the celestial army, led by Michael. Closely allied with the dragon are the two beasts in chapter 13, one of which is permitted to prevail over the saints for forty-two months and the second of which tries to deceive the saints.

It seems certain that the Roman Empire is represented by the first beast and the Imperial Cult, promoting worship of the emperor, by the second. The entire theme and purpose of the book of Revelation is stated succinctly at the end of 13:10: "Here is a call for the endurance and faith of the saints." The scene in chapter 14 contrasts the blissful existence of those who worship the Lamb with the terrible fate of those who choose to worship "the beast and its image."

The seven bowls of God's wrath are then poured out upon the earth (chs. 15-16), bringing more plagues and anguish, the worst of which is destined for "great Babylon," the code name for Rome. The judgment of God descends in full fury (ch. 17) upon "'Babylon the great, mother of harlots and of earth's abominations'" who is also described as a "woman, drunk with the blood of the saints and the blood of the martyrs of Jesus" (17:5-6). Without question, the point made here is that the terrible suffering

291

of the Christians is caused by the mad demands of the arrogant emperor of Rome. But Rome's domination will not last; God has already determined that "the Lamb will conquer them" (17:14). The final victory of Christ over the dragon, the beast, and the false prophet is described in 19:11-20:15.

The saints who shall have endured the ordeal in which they are now involved may look forward to a most splendid and glorious dwelling in a new city, which John's final vision depicts as coming down out of heaven (21:1-22:5). No tears, no death, no sorrow will be permitted there. Its beauty and splendor are described in terms of the most precious materials known to man: gold, crystal, pearl, and all kinds of valuable gems. The city has no temple, no sun, and no moon, for the presence of God obviates the need for them. "He who conquers shall have this heritage" (21:7).

Behind this detailed and complicated description of visionary events which purport to announce things soon to happen lies a rather simple, powerful message to John's contemporaries. Using symbols, images, and phrases from such Old Testament books as Daniel, Ezekiel, Jeremiah, Joel, and Zechariah, he seeks to encourage his fellow-Christians to hold on to their faith and not give in to the demands of the Imperial Cult. He is fully aware of the suffering and anguish this is bringing upon them, and he expects it to get worse. But he is also convinced that God will not allow the situation to continue much longer. What Christians must do, he says, is to endure until God brings to defeat those evil forces which are now in control. If enduring brings death to the believer, that is nothing to shrink from, for God has prepared a most glorious life for him in heaven.

It should be remembered that the author of Revelation is not devising a blueprint of world history for centuries into the future. Rather, he is promising God's intervention in world events in the near future (forty-two months) as a way of reassuring and strengthening his brother-saints in a most difficult time. Rome is the enemy, and she must be resisted. How different is this attitude toward the emperor from that we noted in I Peter (2:13-17)! Perhaps the persecution had not become so intense at the time I Peter was written.

Significant name, terms, and dates for this chapter

Nero

Domitian

81-96 A.D.

Trajan

I Peter

Babylon

Silvanus

Hebrews, Letter to

Melchizedek

faith

Book of Revelation

John

Patmos

Ephesus

Laodicea

emperor worship

Imperial Cult

the Lamb who was slain

the dragon

woman clothed with the sun

Michael

mother of harlots

New Jerusalem

first beast

second beast

saints

CHAPTER XXIX

THE CHURCH FACES HERESY AND OPPOSITION

Biblical materials: Gospel of John.   I, II, and III John.   Jude
                       II Peter

Essential reading: John 1-4; 9-11; 15
                      I John 1-2; 4
                      II Peter 3

Of the six New Testament books which remain to be considered, all except one (III John) deal with false teaching, opposition from the synagogue, or both. Four of them contain the name
John in their present titles, but the author is not identified in
any of the books. Tradition connected all four with the Apostle
John, brother of James and son of Zebedee, but this is highly
questionable for several reasons. The probable date of their
writing (90-110 A.D.) is too late for us to assume that John the
Apostle was still living. One tradition even says that he was
killed at the same time as his brother James, which Acts says was
during the reign of Herod Agrippa I (41-44 A.D.).

The sophisticated theology in the Fourth Gospel seems in-
compatible with the likely thought patterns of an uneducated fish-
erman from Galilee. Further, if the same person is the author of
all four (the Gospel and the three epistles), he identifies himself in II and III John as "the elder," which would not comport
with the apostolic status of John, son of Zebedee. Such observations, taken together with the fact that no claim of Johannine authorship is made in the books themselves, point to the wisdom of
considering them anonymous.

The Fourth Gospel

We have noted in an earlier chapter (see above, ch. XVII)
some of the obvious differences between the Synoptic Gospels and
John, often called "the Fourth Gospel." It is clear that its author approached the story of Jesus in his own unique way rather
than use earlier gospels as sources. He may have been familiar
with Mark and Luke but, if so, he did not use their material unal-
tered. He probably had access to oral and written sources unknown
to the other evangelists, but we have no way of identifying or

characterizing them. Scholars today believe that at some points John is more accurate than the Synoptics, although he appears to be more concerned to present his interpretation of Jesus than a factual account of his activity and sayings. His portrayal of Jesus' ministry is vastly different from that in the Synoptics but his Passion narrative (chs. 18-19) corresponds rather closely to theirs.

We perhaps can not identify all the purposes and concerns the author had in mind when he sat down to write, but some of them can be rather easily spotted. His overall purpose is stated clearly in 20:31, which was the very end of the original Gospel. Chapter 21 is a later addition by another person, who probably wanted to designate the unidentified "disciple whom Jesus loved" (John 21:20-24) as the author of the book and to record the reinstatement of Peter (who had been martyred before the time of writing) into full discipleship. If the primary purpose of writing was to establish and secure the faith of Christians, some secondary purposes may also be noted:

(1) To oppose Gnostic claims and ideas. The unique prologue (1:1-18), which seems to take the place of an infancy narrative, seems designed to refute the teaching of the Docetists, who say that Jesus was divine and never became human at all; he only seemed to have a physical body. This view was related to the Gnostic concept of dualism, which saw everything physical as evil; only the spiritual could be holy. To avoid ascribing anything evil to Jesus, they denied his humanity. The writer of the Fourth Gospel, reflecting the orthodox Christian belief, states emphatically that the Word, who was God from the beginning and shared in the act of creation (1:1-3), did become flesh, a truly human being (1:14), whose divine nature was not recognized by most people (1:10-12). John probably had Gnostic terminology in mind when he identified Jesus as the shepherd (10:11), the vine (15:1), and the one sent from God (5:36), for these were terms used of Gnostic figures of revelation. Only Jesus really deserved to be so described, the author implies.

(2) To correct the claims of the Baptist's followers. Some Jews had concluded that John the Baptist was the messiah, and this "sect" was still in existence in the second century A.D. Acts 19:1-7 says that Paul encountered such a group in Ephesus. Evidently the author of the Fourth Gospel knew such a group (Could it also have been in Ephesus?), which was probably quite vocal in its continuing conviction about John. This would be considered a direct challenge to the church's claims about Jesus.

Already in the prologue (1:6-8,15) the inferior status of John is being established. But the whole section beginning at 1:19 and continuing through 1:42 presents John as stating so convincingly that he is not the messiah and extolling Jesus as Lamb of God, Son of God, and "he who baptizes with the Holy Spirit" that some of John's own disciples concluded that Jesus was the messiah and began to follow him. Instead of the ignorance and cu riosity about Jesus' identity we see in the Synoptics, the full identity of Jesus is proclaimed in the very first chapter of the Fourth Gospel.

(3) To refute Jewish charges against Christianity. This, too, is foreshadowed in the prologue: "He came to his own home, and his own people received him not" (1:11). The only Son of God must be either believed in or rejected and those who do not believe are condemned already (3:17-18,36). Early in his ministry the Jews were planning to kill him (5:18) despite the witnesses which supported his claims: John the Baptist (5:31-35); Jesus' "works" (5:36); the Father himself, whom they were incapable of hearing (5:37-38); and the scriptures (5:39-40), in which they presumed to be experts. John rarely makes a distinction among Jewish parties, lumping them all together as "the Jews" who are plotting against Jesus (11:53), or who are beginning to stone him (10:31), or who are spiritually blind (9:39-41).

The Fourth Gospel was written at a time when animosity be tween church and synagogue was intense, as is clearly reflected i the story of the congenitally blind man to whom Jesus gave sight (ch. 9). Jews who believed on Jesus as the messiah, in the latte decades of the first century, were put out of the synagogues if they did not leave voluntarily. Thus it happened to this man whe he attributed Jesus' power to God (9:33-34). The discussions between Jesus and the Jews (e.g., 7:14-24; 8:12-59; 10:22-39) likel represent more the conflict between Christians and non-believing Jews around 100 A.D. than actual conversations of Jesus with his contemporaries. The Fourth Gospel combats the insinuations (see 7:27; 8:41,48; 9:24; 18:30) and charges brought by the Jews against the church and its Lord by depicting the opponents as obtuse, stubborn, spiritually blind, directed by the devil, and out of touch with God.

(4) To remove any doubt that Jesus, although fully human, was the messiah, the savior of the world, the Son of God, and the Lamb of God who willingly gave his physical life that others may have eternal life. Not only in the accolades of chapter one but throughout the Gospel, Jesus is credited with having divine knowledge, power, strength, and attributes. He performed "signs;" told the Samaritan woman about her past life; offered living wate

spoke of himself as the light of the world, the bread of life, "the way, the truth, and the life;" and claimed that he was one with the Father. There is no struggling with temptations, either in the wilderness or in the garden on the night of his arrest. Jesus is fully in charge of every situation.

The Book of Signs. John 2-12 is often called the Book of Signs, because it is constructed around seven "signs," or what the Synoptics call "mighty works." There are three nature miracles, three healings, and one raising of the dead, but no exorcisms. Some of them are used by the author as springboards for the exposition of some spiritual insight. The feeding of the five thousand becomes the occasion for a lengthy discourse by Jesus on the bread of life (6:1-59). The healing of the blind man gives Jesus opportunity to speak of himself as the light of the world (9:1-41). The raising of Lazarus allows Jesus to teach about his being "the resurrection and the life" (11:1-44).

Since John had positioned the cleansing of the Temple at the beginning of Jesus' ministry (2:13-22), he used the raising of Lazarus as the event which prompted Jesus' opponents in Jerusalem to plot his death (11:45-53) instead of the Temple happening, as in the Synoptics. One of the surprising features of John's gospel is the total absence of parables, a teaching method which figures so prominently in the Synoptics.

The Book of Glory. Chapters 13-20 are sometimes called the Book of Glory because they describe Jesus' glorification through the suffering, crucifixion, resurrection, and return to the Father. Whereas the Book of Signs is addressed to a wide audience, the Book of Glory is aimed at the believers only. It begins with the significant statement that "Jesus knew that his hour had come to depart out of this world to the Father" (13:1). Chapters 13-17 are set in the context of Jesus' last meal with his disciples in Jerusalem (see above, pp. 219-221). Chapters 18-20 constitute John's version of Jesus' arrest, hearing before the high priest, trial by Pilate, execution, burial, and post-resurrection appearances.

The most striking departure from the synoptic account of the last days of Jesus is the dating of the events. All gospels say that the Last Supper was on Thursday after sunset and that the execution was on Friday. The Synoptics state that the meal was a Passover celebration, which means that Jesus' death occurred on the day of Passover. The Fourth Gospel, however, specifically says that it was not a Passover meal, for the Passover that year fell on the sabbath (13:1; 18:28; 19:31). This would mean that Jesus' death occurred on the day of Preparation for the Passover and at that time in the afternoon when the traditional Passover lambs were being slaughtered for the meal that evening. It is im possible to determine which dating is correct, but many scholars favor John's scheme. Others suggest that he placed the death of Jesus on the day before Passover in order to have the Lamb of God who takes away the sin of the world (1:29) sacrificed at the time when the Passover lambs were being slain.

The First Letter of John

It is by no means certain that the author of the Fourth Gospel is also the writer of I John, but they do have similar cor cerns, and they are written in similar style and with comparable vocabulary. Even if we assume that they come from the same write or from a common school of thought, we still are unable to say with certainty which preceded the other. Therefore we shall simply assign I John to the same time range that we gave the Gospel, 90-110 A.D. Despite the title, I John has none of the character- istics of an epistle and was probably a homily or tract which was circulated widely among the churches.

False teaching is one of the major concerns of I John. I begins with a strong refutation of the Docetist position that Je- sus was not really human (1:1-3) and later (4:1-3) labels those who maintain such a belief "antichrists." Also deserving of that designation are those who deny that Jesus is the messiah (2:22-2. It is important that members of the church test those who claim t be Christian prophets (preachers), for there are many false pro- phets (4:1). Whoever follows them has failed to distinguish the spirit of truth from the spirit of error (4:6). The false teach- ers boast about their knowledge of God (2:4), their love of God (4:20), and their fellowship with him (1:6; 2:6). They even clai to have risen above sin (1:8,10). This combination of teachings and attitudes points to the Gnostic character of the false teach- ers.

Proper conduct is the other major concern of I John, and it is closely tied to correct belief. Christians should strive t avoid sinning but, if they can not, they have the assurance of forgiveness (1:7; 2:1-2). They should keep the commandments of the Lord (2:3-5), avoid love of the world (2:15-17), and love one another in deed rather than in speech (3:17-18; 4:7-21). If they do this, they are walking in light rather than darkness (1:5-7; 2:8-11), they are following truth rather than falsehood (2:4), they love God rather than the world (2:15-17), they are motivatec by love instead of hatred (4:20; 2:9-11), and they "have passed out of death into life" (3:14).

It is clear that the author connects faith with conduct
and assumes that those whose beliefs are wrong will also engage in
immorality. Just as James was upset with those who professed to
have faith, yet refrained from deeds of kindness to the neighbor,
I John is annoyed by those who claimed to love God but showed no
love to one another. His call for love of the brethren is firmly
based on the conviction that God initiated the love (agape) relationship when he gave his Son for the sins of mankind (4:7-11,19).
The true believer responds to God's love by loving his brother.

II and III John

It is highly probable that II and III John were written by
the author of I John, for the style and language are the same in
all three. The writer of II and III John calls himself "the elder," but we do not know just what authority or status accompanied
that title. The content of the two letters implies that he wields
some control over congregations other than his own, but we do not
know how many there were or where they were located.

II John. This epistle is addressed to a congregation
("the elect lady and her children") for the single purpose of warning the members about possible visits from false teachers, many of
whom have gone out into the world. The same test recommended in
I John should be applied to them: Do they acknowledge the coming
of Jesus Christ in the flesh (vs. 7)? The same prescription of
love for one another, noted in the previous epistle, is included
in this one (vss. 5-6). The letter closes with a greeting from
the members of a sister congregation (vs. 13).

III John. Addressed to an individual, Gaius, this letter
commends its recipient for his hospitality to traveling preachers
who have visited the congregation of which he was a member (vss.
5-8). Another member of the same church, Diotrephes, had been un-
kind to persons sent by the elder to the congregation. In fact,
he habitually ignored the elder's directives (vss. 9-10) and tried
to stir up resistance to him. The elder states his intention of
denouncing him publicly on his next visit to the church. We know
nothing more about these two men, or about Demetrius, mentioned in
vs. 12. Apparently there was friction in the congregation, and
Diotrephes was attempting to dominate it. The elder allied himself with Gaius, Demetrius, and "the friends" (vs. 15), who the
elder presumed would side with him in any showdown with Diotrephes.

The Letter of Jude

The author of this writing identifies himself as Jude, the brother of James (vs. 1). The James who was prominent in the early church was the brother of Jesus who headed the church in Jerusalem after the original apostles had left the city, and it is undoubtedly this James whom the author claims as brother. However it is best to assume that the writer is unknown and uses the name of Jude to gain some authority for his writing. Neither the place of writing nor the destination is stated and nothing in the letter gives any help in determining either. Since the concept of faith as something which was "once for all delivered to the saints" (vs. 3) is the same as that in the Pastoral epistles and since the apostles live only in present memories (vs. 17), we can assign the writing to the end of the first or the beginning of the second century A.D.

It is clear that the purpose of the letter is to denounce false teachers and warn Christians against them. These "ungodly persons" have denied Christ and used the doctrine of salvation by grace as an excuse for licentiousness (vs. 4). They reject authority (vs. 8), gain influence by flattery and boasting (vs. 16), and cause divisions in the church (vs. 19). Like Sodom and Gomorrah, Cain, and Korah in the Old Testament, they will be severely punished. The readers should remember that the apostles predicted the coming of such persons and should arm themselves against them with prayer, faith, hope, and love (vss. 17-21).

II Peter

Almost surely the last New Testament book to be written is II Peter. Its concern with the problem of the delay of the parousia and its reference to the letters of Paul as already part of scripture (3:15-16) place it well into the second century A.D. We know that it was written after Jude because it incorporated so much of that little writing. Perhaps the third decade of the second century is as close as we can come to a date for it. Although it credits the apostle Peter with authorship, almost certainly he did not write it. We can say only that the author was an unknown second-century Christian who was trying to combat false teaching and used Peter's name to attach authority to his effort.

The warning against false prophets (ch. 2) is strongly dependent upon Jude, and we may assume that the church in the author's day was still beset with false teachings similar to those decried in that epistle. However, in chapter 3, a new heresy is opposed. The belief in the second coming of Christ had been challenged on the basis of the long delay (3:1-4). Those who say that the believers are misguided when they expect it to happen after all the time which has elapsed since Christ's first coming are simply ignoring two facts: (1) Time does not have the same meaning for the Lord as it has for men (3:8). What seems like a long time for us is not so at all for the Lord. (2) The extended time before the parousia is not a delay, but a manifestation of the patience of the Lord. He is simply giving more persons an opportunity to repent before it happens (3:9).

The author then reiterates the certainty of the coming of the day of the Lord "like a thief," accompanied by a conflagration which will destroy everything. The appropriate behavior of persons in the time before it happens, he counsels, is to live expectantly in holiness and godliness, looking forward to "new heavens and a new earth" (3:11-13).

Significant names, terms, and dates for this chapter

     90-110 A.D.

     Fourth Gospel

     Book of Signs

     Gnostic dualism

     Lazarus

     Book of Glory

     Docetism

     I John

     antichrist

     II John

     III John

     Gaius

     Diotrephes

     Jude, Letter of

     II Peter

     parousia

FOR FURTHER READING

Abbreviations used in citations:

IOCB = The Interpreter's One-Volume Commentary on the Bible.
       Abingdon Press, 1971
IDB = The Interpreter's Dictionary of the Bible. Abingdon Press,
       1962

Chapter I

Bruce, F. F. History of the Bible in English, 3rd. ed. Oxford
       University Press, 1978

Efird, James M. These Things Are Written. John Knox Press, 1978

Grant, Robert M. The Formation of the New Testament. Harper &
       Row, 1965

Chapter II

Bright, John. A History of Israel, 2nd ed. Westminster Press,
       1972

Kenyon, Kathleen M. The Bible and Recent Archaeology. John Knox
       Press, 1978

Wright, G. Ernest and Filson, Floyd V. The Westminster Historical
       Atlas to the Bible, rev. ed. Westminster Press, 1956

Chapter III

Harrison, R. K. An Introduction to the Old Testament. Wm. B.
       Eerdmans, 1969 [written from a viewpoint somewhat differ-
       ent from that taken in this book]

Speiser, E. A. Genesis. Vol. 1 of The Anchor Bible. Doubleday &
       Company, 1964

Tullock, John H. The Old Testament Story. Prentice-Hall, 1981

Chapter IV

Childs, Brevard S. The Book of Exodus. Westminster Press, 1974

Gray, John. "The Book of Exodus," IOCB, pp. 33-67

Severy, Merle. Everyday Life in Bible Times. National Geographic
       Society, 1967

Chapter V

von Rad, Gerhard. "Deuteronomy," IDB, Vol. 1, pp. 831-8

Chapter VI

Smith, Robert H. "The Book of Joshua" and "The Book of Judges,"
 IOCB, pp. 122-149

Chapter VII

Hertzberg, Hans W. I & II Samuel. Westminster Press, 1964

Chapter VIII

Gray, John. I & II Kings, 2nd ed. Westminster Press, 1970

Chapter IX

Corbett, J. Elliott. The Prophets on Main Street, rev. ed.
 John Knox Press, 1978

Lindblom, J. Prophecy in Ancient Israel. Fortress Press, 1962

Wolfe, Rolland E. Meet Amos and Hosea. Harper & Brothers, 1945

Chapter X

Ackroyd, Peter R. "The Book of Isaiah," IOCB, pp. 329-55

Blank, Sheldon H. Prophetic Faith in Isaiah. Wayne State University Press, 1967

Bright, John. Jeremiah. Vol. 21 of The Anchor Bible. Doubleday
 & Company, 1965

Henshaw, T. The Latter Prophets. George Allen & Unwin, Ltd., 1958

Hyatt, J. Philip. "Jeremiah," in The Interpreter's Bible, Vol. V,
 pp. 777-1,142. Abingdon Press, 1956

Chapter XI

Birmingham, George A. Jeremiah the Prophet. Harper & Brothers,
 1956

Eichrodt, Walter. Ezekiel. translated by Cosslet Quin. Westminster Press, 1970

Smart, James D. History and Theology in Second Isaiah. Westminster Press, 1965

Wright, G. Ernest. The Book of Isaiah, pp. 95-159. Vol. 11 of
 The Layman's Bible Commentary. John Knox Press, 1964

Chapter XII

Fritsch, Charles T. "The First Book of the Chronicles," "The Secc Book of the Chronicles," "The Book of Ezra," and "The Boc of Nehemiah," IOCB, pp. 208-31

May, Herbert G. "The Book of Ruth," IOCB, pp. 150-4

Murphy, Roland E. "The Book of Jonah," IOCB, pp. 480-2

Myers, Jacob M. Ezra and Nehemiah. Vol 14 of The Anchor Bible. Doubleday & Company, 1965

Chapter XIII

Crook, Margaret. The Cruel God. Beacon Press, 1959

Hanson, Anthony and Miriam. The Book of Job, in Torch Bible Comme taries. SCM Press, 1953

Leslie, Elmer A. The Psalms, Translated and Interpreted in the Li of Hebrew Life and Worship. Abingdon Press, 1949

Rhodes, Arnold B. The Book of Psalms. Vol. 9 of The Layman's Bit Commentary. John Knox Press, 1960

Scott, R. B. Y. Proverbs and Ecclesiastes. Vol. 18 of The Ancl Bible. Doubleday & Company, 1965

Chapter XIV

Foerster, Werner. From the Exile to Christ, translated by Gordon Harris. Fortress Press, 1964

Frost, S. B. "Daniel," IDB, Vol. 1, pp. 761-8

Metzger, Bruce M. An Introduction to the Apocrypha. Oxford University Press, 1957

Chapter XV

May, Herbert G. "Greece and Rome in the Biblical World," IOCB, pp. 1032-6

Stanley, David. "The Greco-Roman Background of the New Testament, IOCB, pp. 1037-44

Chapter XVI

Barrett, C. K. The New Testament Background: Selected Documents. Harper & Row, 1961

Bultmann, Rudolf. Primitive Christianity in Its Contemporary Se ting. World Publishing Co., 1956

Foerster, Werner. From the Exile to Christ, translated by Gordon E.
    Harris. Fortress Press, 1964

Vermes, G. The Dead Sea Scrolls in English, 2nd ed. Penguin Books,
    1975

Chapter XVII

Connick, C. Milo. Jesus: the Man, the Mission, and the Message, 2nd
    ed. Prentice-Hall, 1974

Feine, Paul and Behm, Johannes. Introduction to the New Testament,
    reedited by Werner G. Kümmel, translated by A. J. Mattill, Jr.
    Abingdon Press, 1966

For a viewpoint somewhat different from that taken in this book, see

Guthrie, Donald. New Testament Introduction, rev. ed. Inter-Varsity
    Press, 1971

Keck, Leander E. A Future for the Historical Jesus. Abingdon Press,
    1971

Léon-Dufour, Xavier. The Gospels and the Jesus of History. trans-
    lated by John McHugh. Image Books, 1970

Chapter XVIII

Boslooper, Thomas. The Virgin Birth. Westminster Press, 1962

Stauffer, Ethelbert. Jesus and His Story. translated by R. Winston
    and C. Winston. Alfred A. Knopf, 1960

Taylor, Vincent. The Life and Ministry of Jesus. Abingdon Press,
    1955

Chapter XIX

Beck, Dwight M. Through the Gospels to Jesus. Harper & Brothers,
    1954

Blair, Edward P. Jesus in the Gospel of Matthew. Abingdon Press, 1960

Conzelmann, Hans. The Theology of St.Luke. translated by Geoffrey
    Buswell. Harper & Row, 1960

Jeremias, Joachim. The Parables of Jesus, rev. ed. translated by
    S. H. Hooke. Charles Scribner's Sons, 1963

McArthur, Harvey K. Understanding the Sermon on the Mount. Harper &
    Brothers, 1954

Reumann, John. Jesus in the Church's Gospels. Fortress Press, 1968

Slusser, Dorothy M. and Slusser, Gerald H. The Jesus of Mark's Gos-
    pel. Westminster Press, 1967

Chapter XX

Jeremias, Joachim. <u>Jerusalem in the Time of Jesus</u>. Fortress Pres 1969

Molina, Bruce J. <u>The New Testament World</u>. John Knox Press, 1981

Saunders, Ernest W. <u>Jesus in the Gospels</u>. Prentice-Hall, 1967

Chapter XXI

Bowman, John W. <u>Which Jesus?</u> Westminster Press, 1970

Clark, Neville. <u>Interpreting the Resurrection</u>. Westminster Press 1967

Mackey, James P. <u>Jesus: the Man and the Myth</u>. Paulist Press, 197

Chapter XXII

Keck, Leander E. <u>Mandate to Witness: Studies in the Book of Acts</u>. Judson Press, 1964

Weiss, Johannes. <u>Earliest Christianity</u>, 2 vols. Harper & Brother 1959

Chapter XXIII

Conzelmann, Hans. <u>History of Primitive Christianity</u>, translated b John E. Steely. Abingdon Press, 1973

Hunter, Archibald M. <u>Paul and His Predecessors</u>, rev. ed. Westmin ster Press, 1961

Richards, Herbert. <u>Reading Paul Today</u>. John Knox Press, 1980

Selby, Donald J. <u>Toward the Understanding of St. Paul</u>. Prentice-Hall, 1962

Chapter XXIV

Betz, Hans Dieter. <u>Galatians</u>. <u>Hermeneia</u> Commentaries. Fortress Press, 1979

Conzelmann, Hans. <u>I Corinthians</u>, translated by James W. Leitch. <u>Hermeneia</u> Commentaries. Fortress Press, 1975

Ruef, J. S. <u>Paul's First Letter to Corinth</u>. Pelican New Testament Commentaries. Penguin Books, 1971

Chapter XXV

Keck, Leander E. "The Letter of Paul to the Philippians," IOCB, pp. 845-55

Schweizer, Eduard. <u>The Letter to the Colossians</u>, translated by Andrew Chester. Augsburg Pub. House, 1982

Chapter XXVI

Käsemann, Ernst. <u>Commentary on Romans</u>, translated and edited by Geoffrey W. Bromiley. Wm. B. Eerdmans, 1980

O'Neill, J. C. <u>Paul's Letter to the Romans</u>. Penguin Books, 1975

Chapter XXVII

Dibelius, Martin. <u>James</u>, revised by H. Greeven, translated by Michael A. Williams. <u>Hermeneia</u> Commentaries. Fortress Press, 1976

Kelly, J. D. N. <u>The Pastoral Epistles</u>. Harper & Row, 1963

Sampley, J. Paul; Burgess, Joseph; Krodel, Gerhard; and Fuller, Reginald H. <u>Ephesians, Colossians, 2 Thessalonians, The Pastoral Epistles</u>. Proclamation Commentaries. Fortress Press, 1978

Chapter XXVIII

Buchanan, George W. <u>To the Hebrews</u>. Vol. 36 of The Anchor Bible. Doubleday & Company, 1972

Selwyn, E. G. <u>The First Epistle of Peter</u>, 2nd ed. St. Martins Press, 1958

Stoffel, Ernest Lee. <u>The Dragon Bound: the Revelation Speaks to Our Time</u>. John Knox Press, 1981

Chapter XXIX

Brown, Raymond E. <u>The Gospel according to John</u>. Vols. 29 and 29a of The Anchor Bible. Doubleday & Company, 1966 and 1970

Caird, G. B. "John, Letters of," IDB, Vol. 2, pp. 946-52

Dodd, C. H. <u>The Interpretation of the Fourth Gospel</u>. Cambridge University Press, 1963

Reicke, Bo. <u>The Epistles of James, Peter, and Jude</u>. Vol. 37 of The Anchor Bible. Doubleday & Company, 1964

Apocalyptic literature, 13, 134,
157-9, 177, 216, 289-92
Apocrypha: Old Testament, 8, 10,
14, 150-2, 177; New Testa-
ment, 14, 180, 193
Apollos, 250, 255, 286
Apostasy, 68
Apostles, 228, 231-3, 238,
242-3, 252, 279, 300
Apostolic Fathers, 14
Aqaba, Gulf of: map, 49
Aquila, 246, 250, 255
Arabia, 235; map, 16, 36
Arabian Desert, 15; map, 81
Arabs, 38, 145
Aramaic language, 5, 176, 193,
221, 232
Archelaus, 164, 192
Areopagus, 245
Aristarchus, 251
Aristobulus I, 160
Aristobulus II, 161-3
Aristotle, 154, 245
Ark of the Covenant, 28, 53,
72-3, 80-2, 86, 91
Artaxerxes, 136
Artemis, 251
Asa, 93
Ashdod, 80; map, 65, 90
Asher: map, 65
Asherah, 66
Ashkelon, 80; map, 65, 90
Asia, 244-6, 264, 272, 284,
289; map, 240
Asia Minor, 154-5, 172, 284-5,
289; map, 16
Assyrian Empire, 4, 15, 20-2,
95, 99-108, 111, 115-6, 132,
138, 154; map, 36
Astarte, 127
Athaliah, 93, 96-7
Athanasius, 12
Athens, 245-7; map, 240
Augustus, 164

Baalism, 61, 66-71, 94-101,
109, 169

Baasha, 92-3
Babel, Tower of, 34-5
Babylon, 119, 124, 127, 129,
133, 155; map, 36; Rome as,
284, 290-1
Babylonian Empire, 15, 20-2,
34-6, 105, 111-29, 133, 154,
157-8, 176; map, 36
Babylonian literature, 4, 30-1,
34, 87, 144
Balaam, 57
Baptism, 231, 234-5, 244, 250,
285
Bar Cochba, 21, 23, 167-8
Barabbas, 223
Barak, 69
Barnabas, 184, 232, 234, 236-44,
267
Barnabas, Epistle of, 14
Baruch, 111-14, 120
Baruch, 11
Bashan, 19
Batanea: map, 165
Bathsheba, 82-5
Beatitudes, 201
Beelzebul, 195, 205
Beersheba, 17, 39, 56; map, 18,
36, 49, 65, 81, 90
Bel and the Dragon, 11
Benjamin, 39-41
Benjamin (tribe), 73, 80, 85,
89, 91, 132; map, 65
Bernice, 272
Beroea, 244, 247; map, 240
Bethany, 211-4, 218, 226;
map, 165
Bethel, 39-40, 91-4, 97, 98,
110; map, 18, 49, 65, 81, 90
Bethlehem, 164, 191-2; map, 18,
65, 90, 165
Bethshan, 76; map, 90
Biblical criticism, 1, 5-9, 23
Bildad, 149
Bishops, 281
Bithynia, 179, 284; map, 240
Black Sea: map, 16, 36, 240
Booths, Feast of, 55

Ecclesiasticus, 11, 150
Ecstatic prophets, 84, 106,
   120-2
Edom, 63, 123, 160; map, 49,
   65, 81
Edomites, 35, 39, 80, 88, 123
Egypt, 15, 40-8, 63, 88-9, 92,
   95, 99-102, 111-4, 118-20,
   124, 154-5, 158, 192; map,
   16, 36, 49, 240
Egyptian bondage, 20, 22, 42-7,
   51, 54
Egyptian literature, 4, 87, 144-6
Ekron, 80; map, 90
El, 66
El Shaddai, 26, 37
El-Amarna, 37
Elah, 93
Elders, 281, 285
Eli, 72-3
Elihu, 149
Elijah, 84, 93-6, 100, 135, 206,
   208
Elim, 48
Eliphaz, 149
Elisha, 84, 93, 95-6
Elizabeth, 192
Elkanah, 72
Elohim, 27, 29, 31
Elohist source, 27-8, 35, 40,
   42, 45-6, 125-6, 131
Emmaus, 226; map, 165
English Revised Version, 8
English translataions of the
   Bible, 6-9
Enoch, 33
Enoch, city of, 33
Enthronement psalms, 143
Enuma Elish, 30-1
Epaphras, 264-5, 267
Epaphroditus, 263
Ephesians, 13, 247, 278-80
Ephesian church, 250-1, 269, 272,
   278, 290, 295
Ephesus, 181, 246, 250-2, 255,
   260-4, 267-8, 284; map, 240
Ephraim, 42, 64

Ephraim (tribe), 64-6, 72; map,
Epicureans, 245
Erastus, 251
Erotic poetry, 143-4
Esau, 38-9, 123
Esdras, I & II, 10
Essenes, 167, 174-5, 194
Esther, 153
Esther, 10-11, 55, 152-4
Esther, additions to, 10
Ethiopian official, 234
Etiology, 32
Eucharist, 220, 258
Euphrates River, 15, 35; map,
   36
Evangelists, 184
Eve, 33
Evil, origins of, 32-33
Exile, Babylonian, 20-2, 113-4
   118-33, 157, 171
Exilic literature, 28, 53, 62,
   105, 124-6
Exodus, 10, 20, 44-52, 58, 67
Exodus from Egypt, 20, 22,
   44-51, 54, 63, 129, 287;
   map, 49
Exorcism, 199-200, 206, 297
Expiation, 54
Ezekiel, 93, 120-2, 132, 135
Ezekiel, 11, 120-2, 208, 292
Ezion-geber, 80; map, 49, 81
Ezra, 21, 25, 28, 125, 131-2,
   136-8, 171-3
Ezra, 5, 10-11, 21, 131-7

Fair Havens, 273
Faith, 4, 37-8, 116, 252-4,
   268-71, 278, 287-9
Faith and works, 252-3, 270-1,
   277-8
Fall of Israel, 20, 22, 101-2,
   125
Fall of Judah, 20, 22, 114,
   118-9, 124-5
Fall of man, 28, 32-3
False prophets, 84, 114, 118-9
   292, 298, 300

False teaching, 265, 280-2, 294, 298-300
Felix, 273
Fertile Crescent, 15, 35, 80, 95, 102, 115-6; map, 16
Fertility cults, 66, 94, 169
Festivals, Jewish, 47, 54-5, 92, 125, 137, 153, 156
Festus, 273
Flood, 28, 33-4
Florus, 166
Former Prophets, 10, 12, 61, 84
Freedom, Christian, 253-7, 265, 270-1
Gad, 57; map, 65
Gadara: map, 165
Gaius (companion of Paul), 251
Gaius (in III John), 299
Galatia, 241, 244; map, 240
Galatian churches, 241, 244, 250-4, 284
Galatians, 13, 234-6, 241-3 247, 251-4, 270
Galilee, 21, 160-6, 175-7, 197, 204-6, 225-6, 273; map, 165
Galilee, Sea of, 17-19, 70, 163-4, 197, 206, 226; map, 18, 65, 165
Gallio, 246
Gamaliel, 233
Garden of Eden, 30-3
Gath, 80; map, 65, 90
Gaulanitis: map, 165
Gaza, 17, 80; map, 65, 90
Gedaliah, 124
Genesis, 10, 20, 25-42, 125
Geneva Bible, 7-8
Gentile Christians, 167, 185-6, 229, 234-46, 253, 271-6, 279
Gentiles, 136-8, 150, 166, 176, 189, 232, 269-70
Geography, Biblical, 4, 15-19, 23-4
Gerazim, Mt., 139, 166; map, 165
German translation of the Bible, 7
Gethsemane, 221-2
Gibeah, 74

Gideon, 69-70, 73-4
Gilead, 19
Gilgal, 64, 74; map, 65, 90
Gilgamesh Epic, 34
Glory of Yahweh, 121-2
Glossolalia, 231, 258
Gnosticism, 256, 265-6, 281, 295, 298
God: of Abraham, Isaac, and Jacob, 39, 42, 46-7; attributes of, 34, 106, 116, 188, 269, 299; as creator, 29-32, 46, 55, 148, 150, 265; of the exodus, 46-7, 50-1, 64; the father, 209, 221, 296-7; and the Hebrews, 25, 29, 32, 35, 38, 50-3, 67; in history, 19, 29, 99, 127, 159, 289; ideas of, 26-8, 31, 33; of nature, 29, 34, 116
Golden calf, in Exodus, 52
Golden calves, in Israel, 91-2, 94, 97
Golden Rule, 202
Golgotha, 224
Goliath, 77
Gomer, 100
Good News Bible, 8
Goshen, 41, 44, 47; map, 49
Gospel, 197, 236, 241, 243, 252, 260, 266, 269, 283
Gospels, 12-14, 135, 160, 167, 174, 178-89, 193-4
Grace, 253-4, 269-71, 277, 300
Graeco-Roman world, 162, 168-9
Great Rebellion: see Jewish Revolt
Great Synagogue, 167
Greece, 15, 154, 244-5; map, 16, 240
Greek canon, 9-10, 150, 167
Greek culture, 154, 156, 162, 168-9, 245
Greek Empire, 15, 21-2, 144, 153-5
Greek language, 5-9, 107, 154-5, 162, 168, 171, 176, 193, 207, 232, 285-6

315